O. J. Simpson Facts and Fictions
News Rituals in the Construction of Reality

Abundant popular discourses surround the O.J. Simpson double murder case. By contrast, Darnell Hunt scruntinizes these very discourses
in order to further our understanding of the interests underlying them.
Exploring the relationships between O.J.'s trial, the social location of
television viewers (their race, gender and class) and everyday consciousness of social issues, his textual and audience analyses consider
the incredible allure of the trial as "media event." Looking beyond the
obvious explanations of celebrity, scandal and voyeurism, Dr Hunt
asks: Why was America so obsessed by this case? Why were so many
people invested in particular outcomes? And what are we to make of
the apparent racial divide in attitudes about the case, as shown in the
opinion polls? *O.J. Simpson Facts and Fictions* incorporates insights
from sociology and cultural studies to examine the implications for
race relations in the United States at the dawn of the new millennium.

Darnell M. Hunt is Associate Professor of Sociology at the University
of Southern California where he has received the Thurgood Marshall
Distinguished Faculty Award and the Raubenheimer Award for out-
standing Junior Faculty. He has written extensively on race, and media
and his previous book *Screening the Los Angeles 'Riots': Race, Seeing, and
Resistance* was also published by Cambridge University Press. Dr Hunt
has worked within the media and as a media researcher and was on
the staff of The U.S. Commission on Civil Rights. Born in Washington D.C. in 1962, he has lived in Los Angeles for two decades.

O. J. Simpson Facts and Fictions

News Rituals in the Construction of Reality

Darnell M. Hunt

CAMBRIDGE
UNIVERSITY PRESS

PUBLISHED BY THE PRESS SYNDICATE OF THE UNIVERSITY OF CAMBRIDGE
The Pitt Building, Trumpington Street, Cambridge CB2 1RP, United Kingdom

CAMBRIDGE UNIVERSITY PRESS
The Edinburgh Building, Cambridge, CB2 2RU, United Kingdom
http://www.cup.cam.ac.uk
40 West 20th Street, New York, NY 10011–4211, USA   http://www.cup.org
10 Stamford Road, Oakleigh, Melbourne 3166, Australia

First published 1999

Printed in the United Kingdom at the University Press, Cambridge

Typeset in 10/12pt Plantin   [GC]

A catalogue record for this book is available from the British Library

ISBN 0 521 62456 8 hardback
ISBN 0 521 62468 1 paperback

For Chinua and Akili

Contents

Figures

Tables

Acknowledgments

The research that culminated in this book was supported by many of my colleagues, family members, and friends. First, I must acknowledge the contributions of my colleague and wife, Angela James. Without her continual availability as a sounding board over the past four years, without her tolerance of my immersion in "all things O.J.," this work could not have been completed. Other members of my family – especially my father, Maurice Hunt – also provided me with much food for thought concerning case-related developments. My friends, as always, were a source of inspiration.

Around the academy, a host of colleagues supplied me with insightful feedback on drafts, pointed me to important literature references, or arranged opportunities for me to present my developing ideas to interested audiences. In alphabetical order, I would like to thank the following individuals: Walter Allen; Timothy Biblarz; Todd Boyd; Diana Crane; Kathryn Edin; Barry Glassner; Herman Gray; Pierrette Hondagneu-Sotelo; Parker Johnson; Elihu Katz; Micah Kleit; Prema Kurien; Kelly Madison; Douglas Massey; Antonio McDaniel; Melvin Oliver; Edward Park; Jane Rhodes; Judith Stacey; Margaret Zamudio; and my anonymous reviewers for *The Sociological Quarterly* and Cambridge University Press.

On the data collection, organization, and manuscript production fronts, people on both sides of the Atlantic played critical roles in making this project a reality. I am indebted to them all. From Los Angeles: my informants for their frank interviews, and Haywood Galbreath and Gregory McNeal for the contribution of their considerable photographic talents. From the University of Southern California: the Southern California Studies Center for funding the latter stages of data collection and analysis. From USC's sociology department: Patricia Ann Adolph, Deidre Gannt, Philip Harris, Dora Lara, Arthur Mickle, Kristin Nies, Julie Pinyan, and Faye Wachs for their data collection and office support. From Cambridge University Press: Catherine Max for her editorial acumen, and the production staff for their creativity and hard work.

Several media and/or Simpson case "insiders" offered background briefings that helped me properly contextualize my analyses. I would like to single out the following supporters for special thanks: Black Journalist's Association of Southern California; Ron Brewington; Shawn Chapman; Tom Elias; Haywood Galbreath; Marshall Lowe; and Dennis Schatzman.

Finally, there are a few women and men who, for various reasons, I cannot name, but who provided me with important information and leads to others. I truly thank you for your assistance. You know who you are.

Introduction: Knowing O. J.

People are murdered every day in Los Angeles. Often, we do not know by whom. Indeed, the Los Angeles Police Department (LAPD) investigated 5,130 murders between 1990 and 1994, but filed charges in only 54 percent of the cases.[1] In this respect, it is rather unremarkable that the murderer(s) of O. J. Simpson's ex-wife and her friend has (have) yet to be convicted in a criminal court. On the other hand, little else about what would be called the "Trial of the Century" was in any way typical.

I do not know O. J. Simpson. And I had rarely given him or the Brentwood scene a thought prior to the murders. But soon after the bodies were discovered, I found myself slowly being pulled into the orbit of this imposing case. Note two of my own journal entries just days after the murders. From June 17, 1994:

What an exercise in contrasts. The last few days have been among the most exciting and depressing of my life. In exactly one week I will be getting married. But for the past five days we have watched evidence mount in the case against O. J. Simpson for the murder of his wife and her friend. This O. J. thing has really upset me. What a thin line between fame, glory, riches, and disaster. I can only hope and pray that O. J. didn't do it, that something good will come from this regarding relations between men and women.

From June 21, 1994:

The O. J. Simpson case is in full swing. But the case as described in the media thus far seems a little suspect. Why didn't anyone hear anything? Why did the dogs start barking at about 11:10 pm, after O. J. was already on his way to the airport? Why did one of the witnesses request immunity from prosecution? Were drugs involved?

Given the other things that were taking place in my life at the time, one might wonder why I should have cared about a murder case involving a celebrity whom I had never met. What exactly had motivated my early interest?

Upon reflection, I realized that it all started with the June 17 news that Simpson had failed to turn himself in to the LAPD. Then, later

that day, the infamous Bronco "chase." When Simpson and his friend
Al Cowlings embarked on their rather bizarre, slow-speed trek across
the city's freeways and streets, my wife and I were busy entertaining a
house full of relatives and friends who were in town for our impending
wedding. We all prepared for the ceremony with at least one eye glued
to the televised spectacle, wondering "would he or wouldn't he?" at
reports that Simpson was suicidal. Then, of course, there were the
inevitable flash backs to the hypermediated beating of Rodney King,
and concerns – both spoken and unspoken – about the fate that awaited
Simpson if he were indeed taken into custody alive. Alas, the Bronco
ride came to an end, Simpson was cuffed, and the drama ended. Or so
we had thought.

On a remote island off the coast of Venezuela, thousands of miles
from the United States and the goings on in Los Angeles, my wife and
I found our honeymoon repeatedly infiltrated by media images (via
CNN International) of the preliminary hearing in the Simpson case.
The strangeness of this scene, combined with the difficulty I had pulling myself away from it, first alerted me to my own obsession with the
case. I, like millions of other viewers in the United States and around
the globe, had become hooked on any news about developments in the
case, news that might provide me with knowledge about Simpson's
innocence or guilt.

But what exactly *is* "knowledge?"

In one sense, the term denotes the storehouse of information we all
rely upon to make sense of and participate in the world around us. An
obvious source of such knowledge is our sentient experiences – what we
have seen, heard, touched, smelled, and/or tasted. But when it comes
to the question of Simpson's innocence or guilt, most of what we
"know" comes from mediated accounts of the case. That is, most of us
have not had direct contact with the defendant, we did not see or hear
the Bundy murders being committed, nor have we had the opportunity
to touch any items of physical evidence. Even if we had, there is no
guarantee the experiences would have provided us with infallible "knowledge" about the case. Day-to-day experiences, after all, once led most
people to believe that the Earth was flat, that it was the center of the
universe, and that the heavens slowly revolved around it.

Of course, the argument could be made that we live in more en-
lightened times today. Most of us learned in grade school about the
scientific method, about how we rely upon the bedrock of empirical
data to refute or tentatively support our hypotheses. Indeed, most
of us have a special respect for science because we believe it leads to
progress in what we "know" of the world. But the philosophy of science

is fractured today by debates about the scientific method and its under-lying assumptions (Laudan 1996). While positivists generally embrace the method and its attendant faith in objective observations and empirical "facts" (Sarkar 1996), post-positivists argue that all data are subjectively shaped by the observation methods selected, as well as the theories that prompted the research agenda in the first place (cf. Quine 1992).[2]

On what basis, then, can we even agree on how to make sense of the "evidence" in the Simpson case?

Legal proceedings provide us with very detailed responses to such matters. Indeed, prior to handing the Simpson criminal case to the jury, Judge Lance A. Ito gave jurors several detailed instructions about how to proceed with their deliberations. One sentence, in particular, offered jurors a rather succinct definition of "evidence": "Evidence consists of the testimony of witnesses, writings, material objects, or anything pre-sented to the senses and offered to *prove the existence or non-existence of a fact* [emphasis added]."[3] Proof. Existence. Facts. These terms, to be sure, are heavily loaded with epistemological assumptions. For example, the notion that we can use evidence to *prove* the existence of a "fact" echoes a positivist understanding of reality, one in which we assume empirical data can be objectively observed and evaluated. But what about the role of our "senses?" Don't they ultimately mediate between the material world we refer to as "reality" and our interpretations of it? Indeed, the jury selection process itself is a testament to the inevitabil-ity of subjective interpretations – otherwise attorneys would not be so routinely concerned about the backgrounds and experiences of the jurors ultimately empaneled.

Important traditions in the social sciences have long embraced this latter point, that "reality" does not exist in any universal sense (Berger and Luckmann 1966; Garfinkel 1967; Geertz 1973; 1983; de Certeau 1984). Undoubtedly, a material world does exist, but the "reality" of this world – what "common sense" presents to us as self-evident – depends upon the particular mix of knowledge we have at our disposal. While no knowledge is a direct reflection of some universal truth, none randomly occurs either. Knowledge is patterned by the elements of culture, the values, norms, beliefs, expectations, understandings, sym-bols, and experiences that fit with and flow from our interactions with important others and our positioning within important social structures (e.g., race, gender, class, sexuality, and so on). In other words, how we come to "know" what we think we know is largely constrained by the cultural context(s) in which we find ourselves. At the same time, how-ever, these cultural contexts are continually (re)shaped by social action – by what each of us say and do from moment to moment *because* of

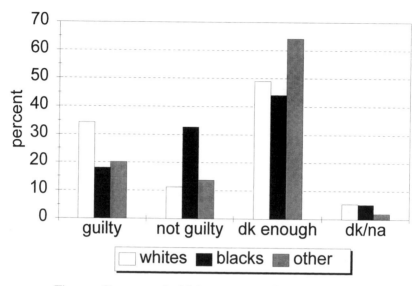

Figure 1. Simpson guilty? July 11–12, 1994, by race.

what we "know" about reality. Thus cultural contexts and knowledge mutually determine one another through endless circles of interdependence. To put it another way, we all participate in the construction of social realities as we *negotiate, share,* and *act* upon particular ways of seeing.

Ways of seeing, it seems, figured prominently in our national obsession with the Simpson case. Not long after the murders, opinion polls were heralding a major national divide concerning the question of Simpson's innocence or guilt. The dividing line? Race.

Figure 1 presents results of a nationwide survey conducted a month after the Bundy murders.[4] It was one of the first such surveys to explicitly ask respondents about their views on Simpson's innocence or guilt.[5] Despite the glaring observation that most people responded they did not yet know enough to comment on the question (i.e., 49 percent of whites, 44 percent of blacks, and 64 percent of other raced respondents), provocative racial differences among the remainder of respondents made the headlines. That is, whites were nearly twice as likely as blacks to consider Simpson "probably guilty" (34 percent versus 18 percent), while blacks were three times as likely as whites to conclude that the defendant was "probably not guilty" (33 percent versus 11 percent). Data on the views of "other-raced" respondents were typically either not reported in these popular accounts, or they were somehow lumped in with the data for either blacks or whites.

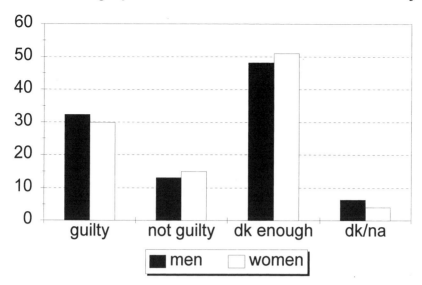

Figure 2. Simpson guilty? July 11–12, 1994, by gender.

If we continue exploring this data other interesting observations come to the fore. First, figure 2 suggests that gender in and of itself had little impact on how respondents negotiated the question of Simpson's guilt. That is, roughly equal percentages of men and women considered Simpson "probably guilty" (32 percent and 30 percent), while nearly equal percentages of men and women also responded that he was "probably not guilty" (13 percent and 15 percent).

In contrast, figure 3 suggests that education did have an impact of sorts – that those with at least a college degree were slightly less likely to consider Simpson "probably not guilty" than those with lower amounts of education. Only about 7 percent of respondents with at least a college degree and only about 11 percent of those with some college exposure considered Simpson "probably not guilty," compared to 17 percent of those with just a high school degree and 18 percent of those who dropped out of high school. But again, this "finding" was clearly overwhelmed by the large percentage of respondents in each education category who said they did not yet know enough to make up their minds.

What about sympathy for Simpson?[6] Figure 4 suggests that race played a major role in how people felt. That is, blacks were nearly four times as likely as whites to respond that they felt a "great deal" of sympathy for the celebrity defendant (39 percent versus 10 percent), while whites were three times as likely as blacks to respond that they felt "none at all" (24 percent versus 8 percent).

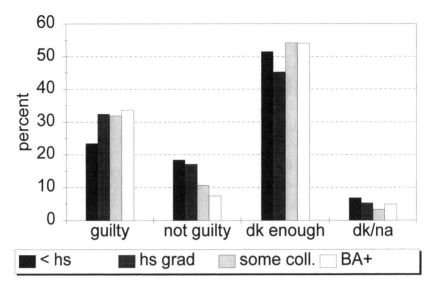

Figure 3. Simpson guilty? July 11–12, 1994, by education.

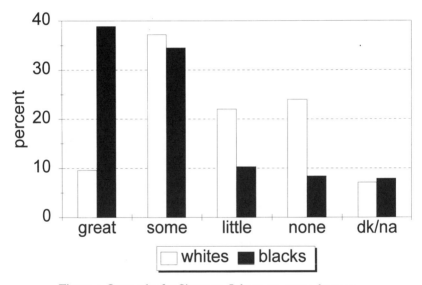

Figure 4. Sympathy for Simpson, July 11–12, 1994, by race.

Although not as pronounced as race, gender also appears to have affected how respondents answered this question – albeit not in the manner one might expect given the role domestic violence would play in case (see chapters 1 and 2). Figure 5 suggests that men were

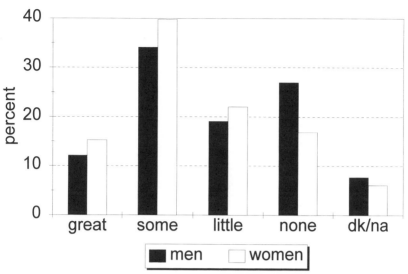

Figure 5. Sympathy for Simpson, July 11–12, 1994, by gender.

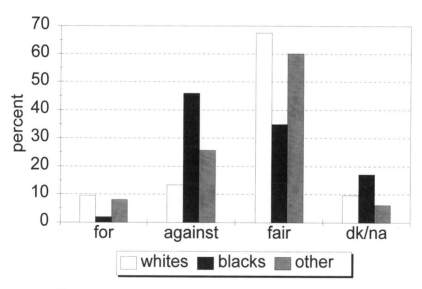

Figure 6. Media bias and blacks, July 11–12, 1994, by race.

considerably more likely than women to respond that they felt no sympathy for Simpson (27 percent versus 17 percent).

The survey also posed other questions to respondents ostensibly related to the case. For example, figure 6 presents the distribution of

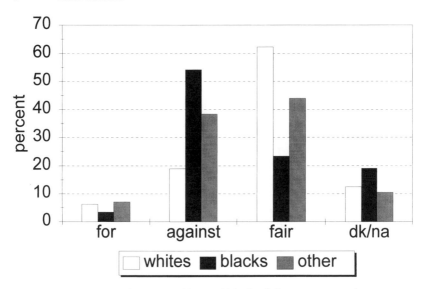

Figure 7. Justice system bias and blacks, July 11–12, 1994, by race.

responses to the following question: "In general, do you think the news media in the United States is biased in favor of blacks, or is it biased against blacks, or does it generally give blacks fair treatment?" While blacks were more than three times as likely as whites to respond that the media are biased against blacks (46 percent versus 13 percent), whites were nearly twice as likely as blacks to view the media as racially neutral (68 percent versus 35 percent). Note how "other-raced" respondents again occupied positions between what Hacker (1992, p. 16) has rather controversially identified as the "major races" in US society.

Finally, what about respondents' perceptions of the criminal justice system?[7] Figure 7 reveals that blacks were more than twice as likely as whites to believe that the criminal justice system is biased against blacks (54 percent versus 19 percent), while whites were nearly three times as likely as blacks to believe that the system is "fair" (62 percent versus 23 percent). Again, "other-raced" groups generally occupied positions between blacks and whites.[8]

So what are we to make of these survey findings? First, we might note that not long after the murders blacks and whites were already beginning to articulate opposing viewpoints on a number of issues related to the Simpson case – namely the question of Simpson's innocence or guilt, sympathy for the defendant, and the fairness of the media and criminal justice system. As we shall see, these opposing viewpoints would only harden as "evidence" was presented at trial. We might also note that the effects of gender and education on these viewpoints, in the few instances where these effects were present, were generally overwhelmed by racial effects. Of course, it would be inappropriate for us to settle on these conclusions without first exploring possible interactions between the various factors (i.e., between race, gender, and education). For example, were white males likely to respond differently than white females on any of the questions? What about college-educated black females versus black males with only a high school education? (I conduct such an analysis in chapter 9.)

Postmodern theory correctly prompts us to take heed of the fractured and multiple nature of subjectivity. We are all socially positioned according to numerous structures. In the United States, the structure of race co-exists with those of class, gender, and sexuality – not to mention generation, region, or religion. The resulting "subject," then, necessarily becomes the fluid intersection of often contradictory positions. In other words, it is never a "sutured" totality. This important insight has been cogently articulated in the work of scholars as diverse as Stuart Hall (1988), bell hooks (1990), Herman Gray (1995), and Ernesto Laclau and Chantal Mouffe (1985).

But to end our analysis here implies that subjectivities exist out there in social space like ideas in some mythical free market. They do not. The same structures that give birth to our multiple subjectivities also work to *pattern* them from moment to moment into hierarchies of salience. In the United States, race is a structure that plays a central role in this patterning process. When we ignore the resulting patterns we embrace what amounts to a form of radical individualism, one that misses the social forest for the individual trees.

For the moment, then, let us follow the lead of surveys like the one above and assume that raced ways of seeing did in fact play an important, *independent* role in patterning our understandings of the Simpson case. Moreover, let us assume that the case primarily symbolized an enduring conflict between blacks and whites. After all, as we shall see, this is precisely what popular accounts of the case repeatedly told us throughout the summer of 1994, the subsequent criminal trial, and beyond. The ever-present circulation of this knowledge had to have had some impact on how we approached the case. Right?

Probably. In the United States, race exerts its force as a powerful *representation* – as a common-sense, irresistible, and self-reproducing framework for explaining *and* justifying inequality in society (Prager 1982; Farr and Moscovici 1984; Omi and Winant 1986; 1994; Hunt 1997). The Simpson case, as I will demonstrate in later chapters, contained elements particularly potent in their ability to invoke our knowledge about race – especially our knowledge about blacks and whites. Socially determined yet fluid, this knowledge consists of tenets that continually adjust to the maneuvers of competing social groups. Race – and what we "know" about it – has everything to do with group status (Banton 1987).

"White," for example, first emerged as a pan-ethnic racial category in the United States following Reconstruction. Elites exploited this representation as an effective means to divide the working class (i.e., between whites and nonwhites) and limit the emergent class struggles of the late nineteenth century (Jordan 1968; Allen 1994; Omi and Winant 1994).[9] By the end of World War II, the category was expanded and "people from every corner of Europe were considered fully 'white'" (Hacker 1992, p. 9). "Whiteness" became a property of sorts, conferring upon its owner certain social privileges and comforts, if not "real" power (Harris 1995, p. 286). In contrast, the category "black" made its debut in the US context when Africans from various tribes were grouped together and defined on the basis of their "nonwhiteness." This representation, of course, functioned primarily as an ideology of exploitation supported by assumptions of black racial inferiority (Harris 1987; Omi and Winant 1986; 1994). Today, the labels "white" and "black" continue to define the top and bottom of the US racial-socio-economic order, thereby serving as important status anchors in an increasingly multiracial society (Hacker 1992).

Thus it is no accident that the Simpson case was popularly rendered in black and white. Individual actors in the United States helplessly rely upon this bipolar framework, despite its obvious shortcomings, to make sense of their own experiences and of their relationship to various social groups (i.e., their identity and relative group status). Actors also depend upon this framework for sizing up others, for interpreting their actions, and formulating responses to them. In this sense, actors and the others they endeavor to understand are "raced,"[10] and raced ways of seeing becomes "ritual."[11] While these rituals are sometimes aimed at contesting status hierarchies in society (e.g., calls for affirmative action or reparations for slavery), they are nonetheless premised on a representation that serves the ideological function of naturalizing group differences.[12] The media continually feed these rituals through the construction and circulation of common-sense, stereotypical images (Hall 1990). As we shall see, the so-called "Trial of the Century" invoked many such images – particularly of the people residing at the top and bottom of society.

Plan of the book

Much has been written about the Simpson case. Indeed, some might say, "too much." But while case-related books and articles abound, most of these narratives, especially the popular ones, focus on whether or not the famous defendant "did it," whether he brutally murdered his ex-wife and her friend. This book adopts a different focus.

What follows is *not* a book about Simpson's innocence or guilt. This is a book about knowledge – a book that applies insights from sociology and cultural studies in order to examine the *how* and *why* of what we "know" about Simpson's innocence or guilt. This knowledge, of course, drives the countless O. J. narratives constructed and circulated by the media, the ones we embrace and/or (re)negotiate with family members and friends. In the following chapters, I intentionally bracket the "truth" of these narratives, particularly the more popular ones, in order to more fully explore the ideological work they perform. That is, I problematize the easy acceptance of narratives supporting Simpson's innocence as well as those supporting his guilt. For Simpson's *actual* innocence or guilt has little bearing on the central concern of this book – tracing the *process* by which we all (re)affirm what we "know" about "reality." This process, as we shall see, is no trivial matter. It is a complicated one shaped not only by the types of information to which we have access (e.g., first-hand observations versus media accounts), but also by our group interests, and by our own personal negotiation of O. J. "facts" and "fictions."

I have conducted dozens of interviews for this book – with white journalists who "know" Simpson is guilty, with sources close to Simpson's defense who suspect that he is, with black journalists who "know" he was framed by police, with trial observers who believe in his innocence, with Simpson himself. All of these interviews underscore the significance of interests in shaping what we claim to "know" about the case. Indeed, my own social positioning as a sociologist and black male necessarily colors the analyses that compose this book. The reader will have to factor in this truth as s/he engages the following chapters.

We begin our study by considering a rather obvious question: What, exactly, are the underlying interests that drive the public's obsession with the Simpson case? That is, if this obsession is indeed more than the mere product of hypermediation and agenda setting (cf. McCombs and Gilbert 1986) – and if race, for example, matters – why? By excavating important interests (re)activated by the case, and tracing the construction and circulation of narratives about the case, this book attempts to explain the process by which the case inflamed public passions and became known as the "Trial of the Century."

In part I, "Theory," I supply the reader with the theoretical framework that undergirds this book. Chapter 1 explores elements central to the case that worked to guarantee its prime location on the national agenda, its status as "Trial of the Century." These elements include similarities between the Simpson case and other high-profile murder trials, the types of narratives in circulation about the case, and the comparative status of these narrative types. I conclude the chapter by proposing a theoretical model that conceptualizes the Simpson case as a hypermediated ritual in which case observers (re)affirmed their preferred versions of reality. Chapter 2 zooms in on a critical component of this theoretical model – "political projects" – and examines in detail how political interests and power influenced the relative status of the various narratives circulating about the case. Four political projects were central in this analysis: the Celebrity Defendant, Domestic Violence, Black "Other," and "Just-Us" system projects.

In part II, "News construction," I present a series of case studies that examine how newswork practices combined with political interests to shape the construction and circulation of case narratives at the macro level. Chapter 3 looks behind the scenes at "Camp O.J.," to critically examine the ideological biases of the Simpson newsworker corps. Despite journalistic affirmations of objectivity, the chapter reveals that newsworkers had various stakes in the case. Indeed, some of these stakes were associated with the four political projects outlined in part I. Chapter 4 analyzes a sample of case-related broadcasts by the only Los Angeles television station to cover the criminal trial gavel-to-gavel. It illustrates how ideological biases characteristic of the Simpson newsworker corps shaped the news narratives constructed and circulated within these broadcasts. Chapter 5 presents a case study of Los Angeles's (and the West's) largest daily newspaper, this time exploring how newsworker biases found their way into high-profile print narratives about the case. Finally, chapter 6 examines the totality of case-related news narratives constructed and circulated by Los Angeles's (and the West's) largest black newspaper. It demonstrates how the weekly newspaper's case-related narratives were explicitly constructed to counteract the mainstream narratives in circulation.

In part III, "Audience reception," I address enduring questions in the media literature about the relative power of media and audiences. That is, I empirically explore how real people negotiated the types of case-related narratives constructed and circulated by news media like those studied in part II. Chapter 7 presents a case study of two, small

Los Angeles-based groups – one black, one white – who were interviewed about the case during the prosecution's presentation of evidence in the criminal trial. Analysis of these interviews delves beneath the racial divide signified by opinion polls to the *whys* and *hows* of raced ways of seeing the case. Chapter 8 revisits the groups during the defense's presentation of evidence – to see if informant views have changed, and if so, why? The chapter concludes by summarizing the types of knowledge and interests informants brought to their respective encounters with media narratives about the case, and by considering the implications for the political projects outlined in part I.

In part IV, "Conclusions," I revisit the theoretical model proposed in part I in order to interpret the findings emerging from parts II and III. Chapter 9 presents some final observations about the ritualistic nature of the case and the underlying stakes that worked to place the case high atop the national agenda.

Part I

Theory

1   O. J. and ritual

> News reading, and writing, is a ritual act and moreover a dramatic
> one. What is arrayed before the reader is not pure information but a
> portrayal of contending forces in the world.
>
> (Carey 1975, p. 8)

During the early morning hours of June 13, 1994, two slashed and
mangled bodies – a white woman and man – were discovered lying in
pools of their own blood in Los Angeles' fashionable Brentwood district. Shortly thereafter, electronic networks around the world were
buzzing with news of the murders of Nicole Brown-Simpson and Ronald
Goldman, of evidence pointing toward the guilt of black football legend
Orenthal James Simpson. But Simpson's attorneys steadfastly proclaimed
his innocence.

Then, on June 17, a Los Angeles Police Department commander
made a shocking announcement to the media: the prime suspect had
failed to turn himself in to police as promised. An audible gasp filled the
press room. Hours later, Simpson was spotted south of Los Angeles,
on the Interstate 5, in the back of a white Ford Bronco. News of the
development quickly circulated throughout society. Ninety-five million viewers across the nation – one of the largest television audiences
in US history – watched helicopter video images of Simpson and friend
A. C. Cowlings slowly leading a growing contingent of law enforcement
vehicles back up the freeway. NBC postponed its coverage of the New
York Knicks championship basketball game. In Los Angeles, spectators
lined the freeway, hoping to get a glimpse of Simpson's vehicle, hoping
to witness history in the making. Many cheered the fugitive on. When
the caravan finally made its way to Simpson's Rockingham Avenue home,
the celebrity suspect was swiftly arrested. Simpson later pled "not-
guilty" in Los Angeles Superior Court and became the most famous
murder defendant in US history. So began the "Trial of the Century."

On October 3, 1995, nearly sixteen months after the murders, Los
Angeles and much of the nation came to a halt as time approached for
the reading of two verdicts. KTLA-TV had been the only local station

in Los Angeles to cover the Simpson trial gavel-to-gavel (see chapter 4). Against aerial shots of crowds and police on horseback, this is how a reporter for the station described the tense scene outside the downtown courthouse as the verdicts were being announced:

JENNIFER YORK: Well, Marta [KTLA anchor], while the verdict was being read we, ah, continued to see the layers of protection that the police were applying. As you can see, they still are applying that three-layer protection, the police on horseback, ah, forming a line on foot, as well as behind the men standing are the police in their ground units. Now we did watch, ah, the crowds absolutely cheer, jump up and down and, and clap. But noticing the streets and the activity away from the courthouse, it was amazing to see the surface streets throughout the downtown area, absolutely, ah, vacant. There were no cars on most of the surface streets except those that were parked in the parking lots around the criminal courts building. The freeways were absolutely a ghost town. There were no cars on the Harbor Freeway through downtown, nor the Hollywood freeway. Absolutely still. The entire city seemed to be still, just awaiting for the verdicts to be read. And again, after the verdicts of not-guilty were read, you could see the crowds were clap, clapping. And now, as a lot of the folks seem to be getting closer to the front of the building, via the corners, we see a lot of people walking through the streets, ah, and trying, it seems like the crowd is loosening up a little bit, ah, now the downtown slot is just filled with cars on the Harbor freeway. It seems as if the town itself is getting back to normal within just a few minutes of the verdict of not-guilty being read. We're flying over the downtown area. Back to you, Marta, in the studio.

Deliberating for less than four hours, a jury composed of nine blacks, two whites, and one Latino had found Simpson not guilty of murdering his ex-wife and her male friend. Some observers were obviously relieved by the verdicts. Indeed, as York reported for KTLA, many of those outside the courthouse cheered at the announcement, dancing jigs of victory in front of countless television and still cameras. For them, the prosecution had not proven Simpson's guilt beyond a reasonable doubt and the system had justly acquitted him. But other observers were shocked by the verdicts. Public reaction stories subsequently broadcast by KTLA and other news media graphically depicted the disappointment and frustration they felt. For them, the prosecution had amassed a "mountain of evidence" that proved Simpson's guilt beyond almost *any* doubt. The verdicts were a miscarriage of justice.

These conflicting reactions, as media commentators were quick to point out, seemed patterned along racial lines; they also contributed to escalating racial tensions in Los Angeles and across the nation. Note the strident tone of an editorial from the *Los Angeles Sentinel* (see chapter 6), the city's oldest and largest black weekly newspaper:

Table 1. *Racial differences in perceptions of Simpson's innocence or guilt, selected opinion polls, July 1994 to October 1995.*

Date[a]	Poll	Population	Findings[b]
7/1/94	CNN/USA/Gallup	US	"not guilty", B = 60%, W = 15%
7/7/94	Newsweek	US	should stand trial, B = 33%, W = 77%
7/12/94	Field Institute	CA	"guilty", B = 38%, All = 68%
9/17/94	LA Times	LA area	"not guilty", B = 28%, W = 5%
2/6/95	Harris	US	"not guilty", B = 68%, All = 26%
3/4/95	NBC/Wall St. Jour	US	"not guilty", B = 54%, W = 16%
3/17/95	CNN/USA/Gallup	US	"guilty", B = 25%, W = 67%
4/17/95	Newsweek	US	"not guilty", NW = 56%, W = 20%
5/16/95	Field Institute	CA	"guilty", B = 50%, W = 78%
5/17/95	ICR	US	4:1 = black:white doubt of guilt
7/20/95	ABC/Wash Post	US	"guilty", B = 22%, W = 78%
8/31/95	Harris	US	"not guilty", B = 67%, All = 24%
10/3/95	CBS News	US	innocent, B = 78%, guilty, W = 75%

[a] Indicates date the polling started. Note that 4/17/95 Newsweek poll indicates issue date, not polling date(s). Also, 7/20/95 ABC/Washington Post poll was conducted during that week.
[b] B = black, W = white, NW = non-white, All = all surveyed.
Source: ClariNet Electronic News Service.

The verdict is in. The trial is over. O. J. is not guilty. It is appalling to hear comments such as "Was the verdict fair? Was Justice served?" . . . THE EVIDENCE DID NOT CONVINCE THE JURY OF THE DEFENDANT'S GUILT BEYOND A REASONABLE DOUBT, AND THEY SAID SO. (Emphasis original)[1]

In contrast, Los Angeles' premiere, mainstream daily newspaper, the *Los Angeles Times* (see chapter 5), showcased a more resigned op-ed piece:

After a pre-verdict night of elation, with Americans seemingly hoping against hope that a largely black jury had weighed the evidence and decided against Simpson, the result struck like a blow – probably the point all along. For the black Simpson jurors, this apparently was payback time, time to stick it to white America as they feel white America has always stuck it to them.[2]

Opinion polls taken shortly after the murders and throughout the trial echoed this divide. Indeed, media reports had little to say about any possible gender or class differences in reactions to the case; they also found little to report on concerning the perceptions of Latinos, Asians, or Native Americans. Instead, media reports routinely underscored differences between the perceptions of white and black Americans (see table 1). For example, a poll conducted a few weeks after the murders had found that 60 percent of black respondents considered Simpson "not guilty," compared with only 15 percent of white respondents. A poll taken shortly after the verdicts were announced found the gap still there: this time 78 percent of black respondents considered Simpson innocent, while 75 percent of white respondents considered him guilty.

Sixteen months later, in a courtroom across town in Santa Monica, the nation again awaited the reading of verdicts in the Simpson case. This time, however, the legal venue was a civil court, and the verdicts would determine Simpson's *liability* for the deaths of his ex-wife and her male friend. Having been acquitted of criminal charges, Simpson now risked only his millions, not his liberty.

Nonetheless, public interest in the case was still intense. While President Clinton prepared to deliver his State of the Union Message to Congress that February evening, anxious media workers a continent away coordinated their efforts to inform the public about the verdicts the moment they were read. This was no easy feat as the judge in the trial had banned television cameras from the courtroom, justifying his decision with references to the "media circus"[3] that had afflicted the criminal trial. Word of the verdicts would now come via a radio feed provided for a few select media workers and the rather primitive flash-card system that they would then use to communicate the news to the public at large. Committed to reporting the verdicts live, KTLA pre-empted the President's message in order not to miss the flashing of the cards. Many stations across the nation followed suit.[4] This was the scene KTLA presented immediately after the verdicts were announced:

BLACK WOMAN, OFF-SCREEN: You know what, this is just ridiculous, it's disgusting... I knew this was going to happen.
LONNIE GARDNER: Hal [KTLA anchor], is that you? I'm sorry. It's really loud here, I apologize.
HAL FISHMAN: What's happening there, Lonnie?
LONNIE GARDNER: Okay, well, the crowds went nuts. Dan, I'm going to ask you to pan over for just a second, over to the crowds. You can see how packed it is over there. There was a loud cheer of support for this decision. Not only for the liability, but also for the 8.5 million and there were a couple of dissenting votes, a couple of ladies by my side say it's a travesty and it's going to split apart our community. But overall I would say the cheers were loud and supportive for this verdict.

After less than three days of deliberation, a white[5] jury decided that Simpson had probably committed the murders of his ex-wife and her male friend, that he was *liable* for their deaths.[6] The award: $8.5 million. Punitive damages of $25 million would soon follow. As in the criminal case, a cheering crowd outside the courthouse greeted news of the verdicts. But while the pre-verdict atmosphere outside the criminal court had been tense,[7] writer Joe Bosco told a KTLA reporter that the mostly white crowd outside the Santa Monica courthouse had seemed "festive" while awaiting the verdicts.

Electronic networks again started to buzz with contrasting images of elation and disappointment. As in the aftermath of the criminal verdicts, media workers quickly canvassed for public reactions to the verdicts, reactions that worked to underscore a racial divide in perceptions about the case. Again, opinion polls seemed to validate the notion that blacks and whites viewed the case differently. A *Time*/CNN poll, for example, suggested that only 18 percent of blacks agreed with the civil trial verdicts, compared to 68 percent of whites.[8] This difference in views, of course, was reflected in media coverage. Note the indignation exhibited in a *Los Angeles Sentinel* column by staff writer Dennis Schatzman: "The Simpson civil jurors claim that this charade was about 'justice' and not 'retribution.' That's what they said. I swear to God. But we all know better. Blacks are not the 'Bell Curve'[9] people the mainstream thinks they are."[10] In contrast, the editorial staff of the more mainstream *Los Angeles Times* seemed satisfied with these latest verdicts:

The prosecutors in the criminal trial, it's now clear, made many grievous judgment errors and were out-lawyered; in the civil case, the lawyers for the Goldmans and the Browns put on a stronger and more persuasive case, and they had a lighter burden of proof. The jury so responded. It could just be that the many pronouncements of a terminally ill US jury system were premature indeed.[11]

What are we to make of these divergent reactions to the Simpson case – first the criminal trial, then the civil trial? Why were the media *able* to exploit the case, to cultivate unprecedented levels of public attention for nearly three years? How, in a period of US history marked by pressing economic, foreign policy, and civil justice concerns, could a double murder case become such a national obsession?

It became quite fashionable among media critics over the course of the criminal trial to explain the obsession in terms of pleasure and profits. The proceedings, they proclaimed, had become a "media circus" that fed the public appetite for entertainment. In doing so, of course, they contributed mightily to media coffers. Hence, the engine that drove the process. Note how *Los Angeles Times* media critic Howard Rosenberg characterizes the case: "At last, something to overshadow that other obese spectacle, the Super Bowl. Inscribe it in stone: O.J. Simpson VII."[12] From the outset, however, I reject this rather common view. We cannot explain the fantastic allure of the Simpson case *solely* in terms of audience amusements and media profits. Although these factors obviously played a role, the Simpson case was clearly about much more.

Indeed, several provocative works argue for the centrality of race, class, and/or gender in both the unfolding of the case and the public's reaction to it (e.g., Fiske 1994, 1996; Abramson 1996; duCille 1996; Dyson 1996; Gibbs 1996; Gordon 1996; Hutchinson 1996; Cose 1997; Hunt 1997a; Lusane 1997; Morrison 1997). While I accept the centrality of these issues as a basic given, this chapter attempts to place their respective roles within a coherent theoretical context – one that helps us specify the *whys* and *hows* of the case's prime location on the national agenda, its status as "Trial of the Century." I begin this task by considering other high-profile murder cases from the past, by examining critical elements they share with the Simpson case.

The Simpson case as "popular" murder trial

Over the years, the nation has been exposed to countless murder trials. But only a relatively small number of these trials has piqued the curiosity, monopolized the attention, and inflamed the passions of the American public for any sustained period of time. That is, most murder trials do not become "popular" trials. The allure of these trials, it seems, is often rooted in a societal function they serve: they become high-profile forums for public debate about basic institutions like the criminal justice system. As Hariman (1990) notes:

Individuals and groups form their opinions, which are their means for making sense of the world and acting effectively to advance their interests, by interpreting . . . [popular] trials and reaching a verdict about the action under trial and about the relevant institutions represented in trial, including the institutions of law and government. Trials function in this way as forums for debate, as symbols of larger constellations of belief and action, and as social dramas used to manage emotional responses to troubling situations. (p. 5)

In other words, trials become "popular" to the degree that they help set the conditions of belief for pressing societal debates. Four earlier high-profile murder cases that achieved this "popular" status seem to parallel the Simpson case in interesting ways. By examining key elements of each case, we are provided with several insights about the intense public interest generated by the "Trial of the Century."

An earlier "trial of the century"

When the infant son of Charles and Anne Lindberg was reported missing from his bed on March 1, 1932, the ensuing search for the baby and kidnapper became a national obsession. Some two and a half months after the infant was reported missing, his body was found, not far from the Lindberg's posh New Jersey estate, buried in a shallow grave. The elder Lindberg, of course, had become an international hero after his historic New York to Paris flight in 1927. The immediate public outcry regarding the baby's disappearance reflected his celebrity. Thousands of letters, some purporting to have information about the crime, flowed into the Lindberg's home. Law enforcement authorities deviated from business as usual and quickly set up a make-shift command post in the family's garage.

When marked ransom money finally led authorities to suspect Bruno Richard Hauptmann, the public clamored for blood. Hauptmann was a recent German immigrant who, like Simpson, professed his innocence only to find the lion's share of his support within a relatively distinct social group. That is, whereas opinion polls suggested that blacks were more likely than others to sympathize with Simpson, it was German immigrants who seemed to support Hauptmann. Scores of these immigrants wrote Hauptmann letters affirming their belief in his innocence, many sending cash and checks to support his defense. Unlike Simpson, however, Hauptmann was convicted of first-degree murder in a criminal court. He was put to death by electric chair on April 3, 1936 amidst unresolved questions about the prosecution's case against him.[13]

Preceding the Simpson affair by some sixty-two years, the one-and-a half-month Hauptmann/Lindberg trial was billed at the time as both "The Trial of the Century" (Wallace 1994) and "the news media circus of the century." (Kane 1992, p. 69). Over a six-year period, for example, the *New York Times* published thousands of stories related to the Lindberg case.[14] Indeed, press coverage of the trial was so frenzied that rules were later adopted to ban still cameras in the courtroom (the trial, of course, was held before the widespread introduction of television).

Fact inspires fiction

The Sheppard murder case is another high-profile affair that parallels the Simpson case in interesting ways. On July 4, 1954, the wife of prominent physician Sam Sheppard was beaten to death sometime between three and four in the morning in the bedroom of their Bay Village, Ohio home. Sheppard, the only witness, claimed he was knocked unconscious by someone in the bedroom after he was awakened by his wife's scream or some other noise. He reported the crime at 5:50 am, after seeing what he described as a burly man with bushy hair on the premises. He claimed he had struggled with the man before again being knocked unconscious. When he awakened a second time, he stated, he was lying half in the water and half in the sand on the beach outside the Sheppard home. As in the Simpson case, the murder had taken place in a fashionable community, no murder weapon was ever found, there was no evidence of forced entry, and Sheppard – the husband – was the prime suspect from the beginning.

But in contrast to the Simpson case, the law enforcement investigation dragged on for weeks before Sheppard was finally charged. Indeed, the Cleveland press had written a scathing editorial entitled, "Getting Away with Murder" (July 20), charging that the police had failed to develop the case due to the high status of the prime suspect. These charges, of course, previewed those that would be made some forty years later by critics of the courtesies afforded Simpson by the LAPD. A week later, the paper wrote another critical editorial entitled, "Why Isn't Sam Sheppard in Jail" (July 30). Amidst public fervor, Sheppard was arrested that evening and arraigned in the presence of news reporters who apparently knew of the impending arrest.

Sheppard's two-month trial was extensively covered in newspapers throughout the nation,[15] and the courtroom was filled to capacity with news reporters. During this period, Sheppard – like Simpson – was described as a Jekyll and Hyde character by a female friend of his slain wife, and this description was trumpeted prominently in a newspaper headline. Moreover, the Sheppard prosecutors, as officials would do in the Simpson case, repeatedly leaked evidence to the press that they did not use at trial. Meanwhile, the press paid particular attention to evidence that incriminated Sheppard, often making "unwarranted inferences from testimony" (Kane 1994, p. 16).

Unlike Simpson, however, Sheppard was found guilty of second-degree murder. The verdict was rendered on December 21, 1954, after the jury in the case had deliberated for five days. But the case was overturned in 1966 due to publicity surrounding the trial, and again as in the Simpson case (i.e., the civil trial), a second high-profile trial was to follow. Coincidentally, perhaps, Simpson attorney F. Lee Bailey helped to acquit Sheppard in the retrial of a case that inspired the 1960s television series, *The Fugitive*, and the 1990s movie of the same name.

Murder sells

Yet another high-profile case seems to foreshadow the public's magnetic attraction to the Simpson case. On Saturday morning, August 9, 1969, the lifeless bodies of actress Sharon Tate (*Rosemary's Baby*) and four others were discovered at Tate's Hollywood Hills home by her maid. Tate and a friend were found hanging from a beam in the living room, both with multiple stab wounds. The friend's head was covered with a black hood, prompting an investigating officer to describe the murders as "ritualistic."[16] Two other victims, also dead from stab wounds, were found on the lawn. A fifth victim was found shot to death in a parked car in the driveway.

Like the Bundy Drive murders, the Hollywood Hills murders were gruesomely bloody. Moreover, Tate's husband – director Roman Polanski – was also out of town when told of the murders by LAPD officers (Simpson was in Chicago when officially notified of his ex-wife's death by the LAPD). The case quickly jumped to the top of the news agenda. "Each official act and comment, and any new discovery [in the Hollywood Hills case] received extensive news coverage" (Kane 1994, p. 24). Indeed, the *Los Angeles Times* – as it would do twenty-five years later in the Simpson case (see chapter 5) – followed the case each day with large front-page headlines, lengthy articles, and numerous side-bar stories distributed throughout the newspaper.[17]

Members of the Charles Manson family were eventually charged and convicted for the ritualistic crimes (as well as the LaBianca murders that were discovered a day later in the Silverlake area of Los Angeles). One of the defendants, Susan Atkins, was paid $80,000 for a tape-recorded interview with journalist Lawrence Schiller that presented her first-hand account of the crimes. Twenty-five years later, of course, Schiller would be a central figure in the Simpson case, both as the ghost-writer of Simpson's jail memoirs, *I Want To Tell You*, and as lead author of the bestseller, *American Tragedy: The Uncensored Story of the Simpson Defense*.

The chief prosecutor in the Tate–LaBianca murder trial, Vince Bugliosi, was also an accomplished writer. His 1974 bestseller about the Manson case eventually served as the basis for the popular film *Helter Skelter*. Bugliosi, like Schiller, would also be an important presence in the Simpson case. Throughout the Simpson trial and following the verdicts, Bugliosi travelled the news and talk show circuit proclaiming Simpson's guilt, the jury's ignorance, and the prosecution's ineptitude. These charges were cogently summed up in his own contribution to the Simpson-related literature, *Outrage: The Five Reasons Why O. J. Simpson Got Away With Murder*.

Cameras in the courtroom

A final case, the Claus von Bulow murder trial, set the stage for a critical aspect of the Simpson case's meteoric rise in the public arena: television cameras in the courtroom. On December 21, 1980, million-aire heiress Martha ("Sunny") Crawford (von Auersperg) von Bulow was found unconscious on the marble floor of her bathroom. She never regained consciousness. A year earlier, she had also been found unconscious, but lying in her bed. Her husband, Claus, had claimed that following an argument about his plans to marry another woman, Sunny had consumed several eggnogs and barbiturates. Meanwhile, Sunny's children charged that their mother's illness was the result of unnecessary insulin shots given to her by their stepfather, who stood to inherit $14 million, plus a $2 million trust fund upon his wife's death.

Von Bulow was formally charged with the murder and a six-week trial began in Newport, RI in 1982. During the trial, the von Bulows' maid testified that she had asked, "Insulin. What for insulin?" when she found a black bag in Sunny's room prior to her death (Kane 1994). This revelation led to a frenzy among the more than 200 newsworkers present to cover the trial. The judge had assigned 33 of the 135 seats in the courtroom to specific news organizations. Other newsworkers scrambled each day to claim the remaining seats. As in the Simpson criminal trial, less than 30 seats were usually left for members of the general public, who lined up for them as much as 90 minutes before courtroom doors opened.

When traces of insulin were finally identified in Sunny's blood samples, the jury found sufficient evidence to convict von Bulow and sentence him to thirty years in prison.

The case was later overturned, however, because prosecutors had withheld evidence from the defense, and the judge had allowed inadmissible evidence in. Harvard law professor Alan Dershowitz, who would become a member of Simpson's "Dream Team" ten years later, worked on the retrial. At the time, Rhode Island was one of the few states permitting live broadcasting of trials.[18] The fledgling Cable News Network (CNN) aired the retrial, prompting many viewers – as would also happen during the Simpson trial – to tune from their soap operas for live coverage of the proceedings. Energized by the case's notoriety, crowds surrounded the Providence, RI courthouse with "Free Claus" tee shirts. This scene, too, would later be repeated at the downtown Los Angeles courthouse hosting the Simpson trial.

On June 10, 1985, a jury found von Bulow not guilty in the retrial. The wealthy defendant had spent an estimated $1 million for his defense – an enormous amount, but nothing compared to the estimated $6 million that Simpson would spend. Later that evening, Ted Koppel hosted a debate about the case on *Nightline*. Three days later, von Bulow granted a live interview with Barbara Walters on ABC's *20/20*. Public investments in the case, including concerns about von Bulow's financial privilege and skepticism about his actual innocence, had transformed the case into a massive "media event" (Kane 1994, p. 69).

Narratives, Simpson, and the plausibility continuum

Several common threads connect these high-profile murder cases of the past. Each case involved victims and/or defendants who were famous or at least wealthy; the crimes were uniformly committed in posh environs; the media paid an extraordinary amount of attention to the investigation of the crimes and subsequent trials; the public seemed to be strongly invested in each case's outcome; and each case continued to provoke controversies of one sort or another long after the legal issues had been formally resolved. In short, "popular trials" like these have distinctive characteristics that set them apart from other cases (e.g., celebrity, media scrutiny, gore) and, moreover, they "usually lack the key element of symbolic closure provided by the trial's verdict" (Hariman 1990, p. 2). When we compare the Simpson case to these earlier cases, it quickly becomes obvious that the latest "Trial of the Century" had all of the necessary elements (with some to spare):

celebrity: a black football legend; his glamorous lifestyle and wealthy circle of friends; high-profile, and high-priced attorneys.

tragedy: two victims struck down in the prime of their lives; domestic violence out of control; a fallen American "hero."

violence: gruesome, bloody slayings; slit throats, multiple stab wounds.

conflict: a (black) defendant versus the champions of (white) victims' rights; a defense "Dream Team" versus the resources of a District Attorney who must win at all costs; expert witnesses for the defense versus expert witnesses for the prosecution.

"minority" lead players in criminal trial: a black defendant; a woman lead prosecutor; a black lead defense attorney; an Asian-American judge.

drama: poignant reflections on the victims; tearful families; devoted fans.

mystery: missing weapon(s); blood drops; footprints; fingerprints; gloves; socks; time-frames; demeanor; drug-hit theories.

scandal: secret sexual liaisons; evidence contamination; evidence planting; racially incendiary tapes; defense misconduct; prosecution misconduct; juror misconduct; a police officer testifying for the prosecution invokes the 5th.

spectacle: a low-speed Bronco chase, cheering fans and curious on-lookers; mafia informants take the stand for the defense.

controversy: the defense compares a policeman involved in the case to Hitler; the family of one of the victims, and members of the Jewish community are outraged.

suspense: will damning evidence against Simpson be revealed? Will Simpson take the stand? Will the jury be able to reach a verdict? Will enough jurors remain? Will Simpson spend the rest of his life in jail, or will he be set free? What will the public reaction be?

resolution: a criminal trial jury deliberates for less than four hours and finds Simpson not guilty of two counts of murder; a civil trial jury deliberates for less than three days and finds Simpson liable for the murders; trial post-mortems fill the airwaves and print media as participants and analysts put their own spin on what it all means.

Throughout the case, observers combined the above elements in interesting ways to set up several basic narratives about Simpson's innocence and guilt. These narratives were in actuality structured texts that depended upon convention and formulae (e.g., plotting and pacing) in order to tell their stories of motive, action, and causality (cf. Kozloff 1987; Berger 1997). More importantly, perhaps, they also grappled with core societal issues that were "personified in heroes, villains, and fools" (Brummett 1990, p. 188). This is significant because not only do we learn about the world and our place(s) in it through narratives, but narratives also provide us with a means for communicating what we have learned to others (Berger 1997). In the end, narratives are necessarily ideological because they invoke important societal norms and expectations. As van Dijk (1993) notes, "Narrative structures reveal not only the organization of mental models, that is, how an event is experienced, interpreted, and evaluated, but also, implicitly or explicitly, the norms, values, and expectations of the storyteller about social episodes" (p. 33).

The widespread availability of narratives surrounding the Simpson case accommodated a multiplicity of possible meanings and interpretations, thereby contributing to the case's popularity (Fiske 1994, 1996). But the various case readings, of course, were far from equal. Indeed, on the basis of how prominently the various narratives circulated throughout the mainstream media, they can be positioned along a continuum from the most "plausible" to the most "implausible." In other words, as popular trial, the Simpson case generated a range of narratives, each competing for dominance, but some gaining the upper hand in the struggle to set the conditions of belief (e.g., those hypermediated by mainstream news media).

Figure 8 presents the proposed "plausibility" continuum. It extends from dominant narratives that strongly affirm Simpson's guilt (i.e., "highly plausible"), to lower-profile narratives that assume a decidedly

Figure 8. The "plausibility" continuum.

neutral stance and, finally, to subordinate narratives that strongly affirm Simpson's innocence (i.e., "highly implausible"). Implicit in this arrangement is my acknowledgment of the socially constructed nature of "plausibility." That is, I do not mean to imply that a given narrative is more "plausible" than another in some *objective* sense; rather I mean that it is *subjectively* ordained to be so by those who have the power to define "reality" (e.g., mainstream newsworkers). Below I review five basic positions on the continuum, highlighting the spin the corresponding narratives placed on important case elements.

Incompetence. At the "highly-plausible" end of the continuum, we find dominant narratives that account for the (possible) acquittal of Simpson by underscoring the *incompetence* of police officers, prosecutors, the judge, and/or jurors. For example, in Vincent Bugliosi's best-selling *Outrage: The Five Reasons Why O. J. Simpson Got Away With Murder* (1996), all of the case principals are cast as incompetent. But Bugliosi reserves special criticism for the jury and prosecutors: "This book sets forth five reasons why the case was lost. But even these five can be distilled down to two: the jury could hardly have been any worse, and neither could the prosecution" (p. 18). In one critical respect, of course, incompetence narratives resonate with the one prosecutors carefully articulated in their opening statement: they all script Simpson as an enraged, obsessed, wife-batterer who committed the final act of control by murdering his ex-wife and her male friend. Prosecutors presented nearly sixty incidents in which Simpson had physically abused his ex-wife. Indeed, Brown-Simpson had left behind a diary describing her ex-husband's abuse, as well as a safety deposit box containing photos of her bruised face and apology letters from Simpson. Moreover, a counselor for a domestic abuse hotline said a woman – who, like Brown-Simpson, was named Nicole, had two young children, and lived on Los Angeles' West Side – phoned in days before the murders, fearful of her famous ex-husband who was stalking her. According to the prosecution's narrative, two developments caused Simpson's rage to explode on the day of the murders. First, Brown-Simpson rejected her ex-husband by denying him an invitation to join the family for dinner at a local restaurant after their daughter's (Sydney) dance recital. Second,

Paula Barbieri, a model who Simpson casually dated, left him a phone message effectively ending their relationship. The combination of these two blows drove an obsessive, humiliated Simpson to murder.

In addition to the motive outlined above, a "mountain of evidence" supported the dominant narratives about Simpson's guilt. For example, a "trail of blood" led from the Bundy murder scene, to Simpson's Bronco, up his Rockingham driveway, across the home's foyer, to socks on his bedroom floor. Sophisticated DNA tests linked this blood directly to Simpson and/or the two victims. Indeed, the odds that blood found on a sock at the base of Simpson's bed came from someone other than Simpson's ex-wife were about one in 9.7 billion. Similarly, a stain found at the Bundy crime scene could have been produced by only one in 170 million persons, and Simpson was one of them. Moreover, Simpson had cuts on his left hand when interviewed by police, the side of his body corresponding to the location of the Bundy blood drops. That is, the blood drops were found to the *left* of bloody footprints traversing the crime scene. If this was not incriminating enough, the bloody footprints were made by size-twelve, Bruno Magli shoes – Simpson's shoe size. Although Simpson denied owning the expensive, extremely rare shoes, photos introduced at the civil trial clearly showed him wearing a pair. Finally, Simpson could verify his whereabouts for most of the day of the murders, except a critical eighty-one-minute period that surrounded the execution of the crimes.

In order to reconcile this overwhelming evidence of Simpson's guilt with his (possible) acquittal in the criminal trial, dominant narratives about the case typically underscore the importance of police investigatory mistakes, prosecution tactical errors, faulty judicial rulings, and/or jury ignorance. First, police were enamored with the celebrity suspect from the earliest moments of the case. The lead detectives, for example, interrogated Simpson for only thirty-two minutes when he arrived from Chicago the day after the murders. Indeed, they allowed a number of apparent inconsistencies in his statement about the cuts on his hands to pass without deeper scrutiny, providing him with a respite from detection. A longer, more confrontational interrogation may even have produced a confession.[19] LAPD officials also accorded the famous suspect privileges not routinely given to murder suspects against whom so much evidence had been collected. They allowed him to remain free for several days after the murders, giving him time to amass a "Dream Team" of attorneys and consultants who quickly worked to neutralize the impact of important evidence against him. This preemptive activity was particularly damaging to the state's case because it went on for so long: LAPD officials accorded Simpson even more time when they agreed to allow him to turn himself in as opposed to going out and arresting him. The suspect's subsequent disappearance and the Bronco chase spectacle was an embarrassment to the LAPD that underscored the incompetence with which the department handled the case.

Similarly, dominant narratives often identify prosecution blunders as blunting the force of the case against Simpson.[20] District Attorney Gil Garcetti set the stage for these blunders by moving the trial from the seaside courthouse in Santa Monica, where the jury pool was overwhelming composed of whites, to downtown Los Angeles, where whites were a smaller percentage of the juror pool. This mistake would become a serious one when combined with rulings made by the presiding judge (see below). During the actual trial, prosecutors also failed to use important evidence, evidence that may have been the next best thing to a confession. For example, prosecutors failed to introduce into evidence Simpson's highly publicized run from police and the "suicide note" he left behind. These items clearly indicated a consciousness of guilt. Prosecutors also failed to introduce the statement Simpson made to police the day after the murders. While the interrogation had been too cordial and missed several opportunities, it nonetheless included a number of inconsistencies that prosecutors again could have used to expose the defendant's consciousness of guilt. Finally, prosecutor Christopher Darden violated an elementary tenet of trial strategy by asking Simpson to try on bloody gloves found at the crime scenes without first testing to make sure they would fit. Simpson, of course, struggled to pull the gloves on, mouthing to the jury that they did not fit. The explanations subsequently offered by prosecutors about shrinkage and the effect of wearing rubber gloves underneath, while reasonable, were feeble attempts to reverse a first impression that should never have been made.

Dominant narratives about the case also account for Simpson's (possible) acquittal by criticizing the rulings of the judge presiding over the case, Lance Ito. These rulings either limited the introduction of damaging evidence against Simpson or permitted the introduction of evidence that detracted attention away from relevant case "facts". For example, Judge Ito disallowed the introduction of Brown-Simpson's diary in which she wrote about beatings, stalkings, and other abuse she suffered at the hands of her ex-husband over the years. This evidence *would* later be allowed by the judge in the civil trial, Hiroshi Fujisaki. On the basis of a technicality, Judge Ito also disallowed evidence about the rarity of carpet fibers from Simpson's Bronco, fibers that were found at the Bundy crime scene. But most damaging, the judge ultimately allowed the defense to play the "race card" by permitting testimony about LAPD detective Mark Fuhrman's racial animus when absolutely no evidence existed that he had or could have planted evidence in the case. Jeffrey Toobin underscored the importance of this point in his 1996 bestseller, *The Run of His Life: The People v. O. J. Simpson*:

Almost from the day of Simpson's arrest, his lawyers sought to invent a separate narrative, an alternative reality, for the events of June 12, 1994. This fictional version was both elegant and dramatic. It posited that Simpson was the victim of a wide-ranging conspiracy of racist law enforcement officials who had fabricated and planted evidence in order to frame him for a crime he did not commit. It was also, of course, an obscene parody of an authentic civil rights struggle, for this one pitted a guilty "victim" against innocent "perpetrators." (p. 11)

In short, Judge Ito's admission of evidence about Fuhrman's possible racial animus set up F. Lee Bailey's infamous cross-examination of the detective about his use of the "n-word" (i.e., "nigger"). Fuhrman denied using the racial epithet in the last ten years to refer to blacks. When audiotapes surfaced near the end of the trial on which he was heard to repeatedly and casually use the epithet, the LAPD detective was subpoenaed by the defense and forced to plead his Fifth Amendment rights against self-incrimination for charges that ultimately had nothing to do with the murders.

Finally, dominant narratives about the case also identify jury incompetence as a major contributor to Simpson's acquittal. That is, the black jurors were so blinded by their obsession with race that they heeded lead defense attorney Johnnie Cochran's calls for jury nullification and delivered their not-guilty verdict after barely considering the evidence, if at all.[21] As Tom Elias put it in *The Simpson Trial in Black and White*, "The instant verdict demonstrated that there wasn't much consideration of the trial's voluminous evidence during whatever deliberations went on" (Elias and Schatzman 1996, p. 100). In *Another City, Not My Own*, Dominick Dunne (1997) is more blunt: "This jury could have watched a videotape of Simpson, knife in hand, slitting the throats of Nicole and Ron, and the verdict would have been the same" (p. 314).[22]

The "plausibility" of these dominant narratives about Simpson's guilt, I propose, can be inferred from the high profile they enjoyed in the public arena throughout the case. From mainstream media texts circulating shortly after the murders, to those circulating following the not-guilty verdicts in the criminal trial, and those circulating in the aftermath of the liable verdicts in the civil trial, Simpson's guilt was explicitly or implicitly defined as a matter of "common sense." Some examples:

> *Newsweek* magazine, June 27, 1994. "It will likely be months before a trial, but the *bizarre* swing of public sympathy toward Simpson worries officials [emphasis added]."

Vanity Fair magazine, June 1995. In his column on the trial, Dominick Dunne refers in passing to the defense claim of police conspiracy/cover-up as a "preposterous theory."

Los Angeles magazine, July 1995. The cover presents a darkened image of Simpson and previews a feature article labelled, "the Othello syndrome," referring to a psychological condition named for Shakespeare's black protagonist who is obsessed with and murders his white lover. Inside, the story's headline continues the comparison to this tragic character: "Don Juan in Hell. They stalk. They publicly humiliate. They murder. And afterward, they don't feel very bad. Welcome to the Othello Syndrome."

Time magazine, October 9, 1995. The introduction to the issue's cover story ("O. J. and Race: Will the Verdict Split America") implies, as the prosecution argued in closing, that the defense used race as a smoke screen to cloud overwhelming evidence against Simpson. The last two sentences sum up the article's position: "The defense's evocations of race in the trial *may have been only an inflaming diversion.* But on the subject of race, America is tinder dry this season [emphasis added]."

People Weekly, February 17, 1997. The headline of an article on the civil trial suggests that the liability verdicts are long overdue: "Thirty-two torturous months after the murders that became America's obsession, O. J. Simpson walks out of a Santa Monica courtroom carrying the burden of being found, *finally*, responsible [emphasis added]."

Overzealousness. Moving on to a somewhat "less plausible" position on the continuum, we find narratives about how police *overzealousness* backfired, about how officers' willingness to frame a guilty suspect created reasonable doubt. Like the dominant narratives reviewed above, these narratives generally affirm that an escalating obsession drove Simpson to murder his ex-wife. They also affirm that the evidence pointing to Simpson's guilt is ultimately overwhelming. At the same time, however, these narratives adopt the "less-believable" position that a number of police practices in the case were, at best, suspect.

For example, these narratives generally acknowledge that LAPD officers lied on the stand when they said Simpson was not considered a suspect in the early hours of the investigation, that the four detectives who left the Bundy murder scene that night did so to notify Simpson of his ex-wife's death. The narratives recognize this testimony to be just a cover story for activities that were initiated in the pre-dawn hours after the murders – the careful manipulation and transportation of evidence to ensure that a guilty suspect with ample financial resources did not evade being charged and convicted. Indeed, police evidence logs from the case revealed that detective Philip Vannatter, one of the lead detectives on the case, violated departmental policy by not immediately booking Simpson's blood reference vial at the LAPD's downtown headquarters. Instead, the detective carried the vial about fifteen miles across town to the Rockingham crime scene, where he said he delivered it directly to LAPD criminalist Dennis Fung. The presence of Simpson's DNA-rich blood sample at Rockingham provided Vannatter and/or other officers with an opportunity to plant blood on carefully chosen pieces of evidence, thereby strengthening the case against Simpson.

In *O. J.: The Last Word* (1997), famed criminal defense attorney Gerry Spence invoked similar observations to construct what is essentially an "overzealousness" O. J. narrative. That is, he suggests that questionable police practices,[23] combined with police lies to cover them up, ultimately backfired and set a murderer free:

When the police fabricate and fictionalize rather than tell the simple truth, as damaging as it may be, the credibility antennas of the jurors are raised. These were the same police whom the jury would be asked to believe when the prosecution claimed Fuhrman did not plant the glove. These were the same police who asked the jury to believe that the socks in the bedroom had not been fiddled with, even when the blood on the socks was discovered to contain EDTA, the blood preservative – a magical substance that must get soaked up into one's socks out of thin air [see below]. These were the same police who could provide no satisfactory explanation for how EDTA, as if by divine miracle, meandered into the blood on the Bundy gate. (pp. 180–1)

Mystery. At the neutral position we find lower-profile narratives about *mystery*, about important case-related questions that may never be answered. These narratives occupy a "plausibility" middle-ground on the continuum because they neither affirm dominant assumptions about Simpson's guilty nor subordinate ones about his innocence. Indeed, these narratives typically highlight a collection of questions that simultaneously point to innocence and guilt.

For example, given the intensive search of Simpson's home and the several square mile area around it and the Bundy crime scene, why was no murder weapon or bloody clothing (with the exception of the socks and gloves) ever found? Who was responsible for the seventeen unidentified fingerprints police recovered from the Bundy murder scene?[24] Why do the victims' autopsy reports suggest that at least two killers – one left-handed, one right-handed – were involved in the murders?[25] If Simpson had returned home and removed bloody socks after committing the murders, why didn't investigators find traces of blood on the light-colored carpeting leading to his second-story bedroom? How could Simpson possibly commit two murders, dispose of the murder weapon and bloody clothing, return to Rockingham, and take a shower in the brief period allocated by the prosecution time-line?

On the other hand, why didn't Simpson ask *how* his ex-wife had been killed when police notified him of her death? Did he already know? Why could Simpson account for his whereabouts for most of June 12, 1994 – except that crucial eighty-one-minute window covering the time that the murders were committed. And finally, why did Simpson lie about owning the rare Bruno Magli shoes he is clearly seen wearing in photographs introduced at the civil trial?

As Donald Freed and Raymond P. Briggs put it in *Killing Time: The First Full Investigation Into the Unsolved Murders of Nicole Brown Simpson and Ronald Goldman* (1996), a "credible confession" might be necessary to solve the "forensic puzzle" that remains in the case's aftermath:[26]

For now, the Bundy murders are still pieces of a scattered forensic puzzle. Only when physical time-lines and report evidence fit into a credible scenario with motive and opportunity, will we be able to say that the murders have been solved. To reach this point might require one additional element as well: a credible confession. (p. 232)

Rush to judgment. Moving to the "implausible" side of the continuum, we first find narratives about a police *rush to judgment*, about investigatory omissions and mistakes that worked to incriminate Simpson. These narratives strongly resemble the "overzealousness" narratives reviewed above but for one crucial element: these latter narratives affirm the defendant's innocence. In this sense, the narratives strongly resonated with the central defense claim that LAPD detectives assumed Simpson was the murderer shortly after discovering that the murdered woman was his ex-wife. Indeed, detectives were so sure of Simpson's guilt that they largely ignored other leads pointing to the real perpetrator or perpetrators. Instead, they selectively sought out evidence, coached witnesses, and shaded their own testimony to fashion a crime scenario consistent with their theory of Simpson's guilt.

Throughout the criminal trial, defense attorneys highlighted a number of case elements that worked to structure this narrative. First, four LAPD detectives left the all-important Bundy crime scene ostensibly to notify Simpson – who was *not* legally the next of kin – of his ex-wife's death. The detectives' subsequent warrantless search of Simpson's home signified the degree to which they were willing to violate the law in order to cement the conviction of a celebrity defendant who they believed to be guilty. Moreover, microbiologist John Gerdes's testimony that the LAPD crime lab was a "cesspool" of contamination, that Simpson's blood sample was improperly handled in the vicinity of crime scene evidence, and that blood swatches and other evidence may have been mislabelled suggested that the police's rush to build a case against Simpson resulted in careless evidence handling and analysis. And as all of the evidence collected in the case was first processed by the LAPD's crime lab, any findings by outside crime labs pointing to Simpson's guilt were necessarily suspect. As lead defense attorney Johnnie Cochran (1996) put it in his auto-biography, *Journey to Justice*:

> What we did believe – and what a competent, unbiased analysis of the evidence supported – was that a process far more complex and amorphously malevolent than a straightforward conspiracy had led the LAPD to charge him with the murders of Nicole Brown and Ron Goldman . . . What happened that night and over the succeeding days resulted from the unplanned interaction of sloth, carelessness, incompetence, dishonesty, bias, and ambition of the police and prosecutorial authorities involved. (pp. 273–4)

This, of course, was the same narrative that had framed large portions of Cochran's closing arguments to the jury.[27] In *Madam Foreman: A Rush to Judgment?* co-author Carrie Bess explained why she and other jurors found the narrative so compelling:

> "I think it was a rush to judgment, but the reason I say it was a rush to judgment is because in the first place the deputies left the bodies when they should have stayed on the scene," Carrie emphasizes. "That's rush. Second, you do all this work within a matter of three days, that's still a rush. Three to four days. And no matter what they say, he was a prime suspect. He was a suspect from jump street." (Cooley et al. 1995, p. 107)

Conspiracy. At the "highly-implausible" end of the continuum lies a collection of subordinate narratives about *conspiracy*, about illegal, secretive plots by police and/or third parties to manufacture evidence in the case. Unlike those narratives at the "most-plausible" end of the continuum, conspiracy narratives enjoyed little circulation (if any) in the mainstream news media. For these narratives worked to affirm the untenable thesis of Simpson's innocence. Simpson, of course, had always maintained his absolute innocence. As he put it in his jail-cell memoir, *I Want to Tell You*: "I want to state unequivocally that I did not commit those horrible crimes. I loved Nicole, I could never done such a thing. I don't think I even know anyone who's capable of doing such things. I can't think of anybody I've ever known who could have done something this terrible" (Simpson 1995, p. 15). Later, in his controversial post-verdict videotape, *O. J. The Interview*,[28] Simpson implies that police conspired to make him "look guilty": "I think obviously, the

LAPD – I don't know if they felt I was guilty or not – but obviously people in the LAPD went out of their way to make me look guilty."

Throughout the criminal trial, many of the charges central to conspiracy narratives were either explicitly or implicitly raised by Simpson's defense attorneys. For example, Detective Vannatter's transportation of Simpson's blood sample vial from LAPD headquarters to the Rockingham crime scene was characterized by defense attorneys as a sinister act, one that provided Vannatter with an opportunity to either plant Simpson's blood at the Bundy and Rockingham crime scenes or to contaminate evidence already collected from the scenes. Moreover, because Vannatter had clearly lied on the stand regarding his reasons for leaving the Bundy crime scene and searching Simpson's Rockingham home without a warrant, there was no reason to believe he had not lied about planting the blood. As Dennis Schatzman (see chapter 6) put it in *The Simpson Trial in Black and White*,

Remember what the jury instructions said: If it's found that a witness has lied on one issue, one can and must assume that the witness may be lying in other areas as well. So the blood found at the scene, and in the Bronco, and on the Simpson walkway, and testified to by detective Philip Vannatter, could be challenged because Vannatter had lied before. He lied about reasons why he sieged Simpson's estate without a search warrant. He committed perjury. That makes Vannatter a liar, doesn't it? You bet your sweet ass it does. Therefore, the blood and how it got where it was found is fair game for criticism, unless one believes that the LAPD detectives wouldn't lie. (Elias and Schatzman 1996, p. 223)

Another group of case elements that buttressed conspiracy narratives focused on crime scene evidence that was collected under suspicious circumstances. For example, blood on the back gate at Bundy apparently containing Simpson's DNA was not collected until three weeks after the murders. Interestingly, this blood had a higher concentration of DNA than blood collected from other areas of the crime scene the morning after the murders – despite presumably being exposed to the elements for far longer. Defense attorneys suggested, of course, that the higher concentration of DNA was a result of blood being planted from Simpson's DNA-rich reference vial.

Similarly, Simpson's white Ford Bronco, which prosecutors charged he drove to the Bundy murder scene, was the source of several pieces of blood evidence that were not collected until much later. An attendant working at a lot where the vehicle was impounded the day after the murders testified that he did not see any blood on the vehicle's console. Nonetheless, criminalists testified that they collected blood from this location weeks later, *after* records indicate someone had broken into the vehicle on the lot.[29] Moreover, traces of DNA different from Simpson's, his ex-wife's, and Goldman's were found on the vehicle's steering wheel (Freed and Briggs 1996).

Finally, a police video made at Rockingham to protect the city against property damage/theft lawsuits shows Simpson's bedroom and the rug where the socks were allegedly found. LAPD photographer Willie Ford testified he saw no socks when he shot the video, nor do they appear in the video. Since criminologist Dennis Fung testified he had not collected the socks until after 4:30 pm that day, defense attorneys argued they must have been planted by police. Indeed, a defense witness testified during the trial that blood stains on the socks linking them to Simpson and his ex-wife had soaked through both sides of the socks – an impossibility, the narrative suggested, if Simpson was wearing the socks and thus separating the sides when they were stained. The implication: someone had pressed (i.e., planted) the blood onto the socks when they were not being worn.

Most of the above charges of conspiracy on some level imply the planting of blood evidence from Simpson's and/or the victims' reference samples. To support this charge, defense attorneys used LAPD evidence reports to suggest that approximately 1.5 ccs of Simpson's reference sample blood was missing after taking into account portions of the sample that were used in prosecution tests. Prosecutors, of course, quickly mobilized to debunk this aspect of the conspiracy theory. First, they introduced a videotape in which the nurse who withdrew Simpson's blood, Thano Peratis, testified that his earlier testimony about the amount of blood he collected was only an estimate. The videotaping, however, occurred without defense attorneys present, and the tape featured a sizable gap that defense attorneys used to suggest that prosecutors had coached Peratis to change his testimony. Secondly, prosecutors suggested that repeated corking and uncorking of the blood vial could have contributed to the "missing" blood. Finally, and most significantly, prosecutors argued that any evidence stains containing planted blood would have to contain EDTA, a chemical preservative routinely added to blood samples to prevent them from coagulating. On July 24, 1995, defense witness Frederic Rieders indeed testified that EDTA was present in key evidence stains. The following day, a prosecution witness, FBI agent Roger Martz, admitted that what appeared to be EDTA had been present in the stains. But after meeting with prosecutors during the lunch break, he returned for the afternoon session and testified that the levels he discovered were insignificant. Critics of Martz's testimony noted that the FBI agent had little experience testing for the preservative and interpreting the results. Moreover, reports would later appear in the press questioning the veracity of the FBI's previously unassailable evidence laboratory, suggesting that FBI agents had shaded their testimony in the past to benefit prosecutors.[30]

The above charges of police conspiracy ultimately beg the questions of opportunity and motive. The answers to these questions were provided, of course, by LAPD detective Mark Fuhrman, the officer who allegedly found many of the key pieces of evidence in the case. Fuhrman was the officer who led three other LAPD officers away from the Bundy murder scene to allegedly notify Simpson of his ex-wife's death. Once at Simpson's home, it was Fuhrman who allegedly noticed a minute speck of blood near the handle of Simpson's white Bronco, which was parked outside on the street. It was Fuhrman who, minutes after officers were unsuccessful at contacting anyone inside via telephone, scaled the perimeter wall of Simpson's property without a search warrant. It was also Fuhrman who allegedly found the bloody match to the Bundy murder scene glove on a walkway behind Simpson's guest house, after being directed there by houseguest Kato Kaelin's account of loud thumps he had heard around 10:45 pm. Although prosecutors argued that several officers had arrived at the Bundy murder scene prior to Fuhrman, Fuhrman was the first *detective* on the scene, and as such, the first officer authorized to analyze and catalog evidence. Defense attorneys argued that this provided him with an *opportunity* to spot and retrieve a second glove from Bundy that he would later plant at Rockingham.

Defense attorneys also argued that Fuhrman had the *motive* to frame Simpson: racism. City records revealed that Fuhrman had filed for disability in 1981, claiming he hated policing areas heavily populated with "Mexicans" and "Niggers." Despite his trial testimony that he had not referred to blacks as "niggers" in the last ten years, several witnesses would testify that the officer commonly referred to blacks as "niggers" and that he particularly despised interracial couples like Simpson and his ex-wife. Indeed, in the audiotaped interviews made by screenwriter Laura McKinny that would later surface at trial, Fuhrman casually referred to blacks as "niggers" and even bragged about planting evidence against suspects in order to facilitate their convictions. But the climax of the conspiracy narrative would not occur until Fuhrman took the witness stand for a second time near the end of the trial and invoked his Fifth Amendment right not to answer a provocative question: "Detective Fuhrman, did you plant or manufacture any evidence in this case?"[31]

In a post-verdict interview on Black Entertainment Television (BET), Simpson provided his own answer to this central question. Not surprisingly, it echoed the conspiracy narrative:

For a long time, my lawyers will tell you, I wasn't buying any of that. I wasn't buying any of the Mark Fuhrman planted the glove. But at one point I looked at, when I saw him on the stand, and listened to him, I saw, I started seeing all these little inconsistencies in their testimony. I am totally 100 percent convinced that he did it.

Two books that surfaced surrounding the case extended the conspiracy narrative to include third parties. Stephen Singular's *Legacy of Deception* hit bookstores in late 1995. Singular, a Denver-based journalist, claims he was contacted by an informant inside the LAPD who led him to "facts" supporting the theory of a police conspiracy to frame Simpson. This informant also allegedly told the reporter that the officer or officers involved in the conspiracy had ties to a white supremacist organization. In August of 1995, Fuhrman would retire from the LAPD and move to Sandpoint, Idaho. Perhaps it is just coincidence, but this area is infamous for being home to a number of white supremacist organizations such as the Aryan Nations (Flynn and Gerhardt 1989). Singular reports that while he provided information about the alleged conspiracy to both the defense and the prosecution, only the defense was receptive, using some of it to develop their strategy for the criminal trial.

In the second book, *Blood Oath: The Conspiracy to Murder Nicole Simpson* (1996), Steven Worth and Carl Jaspers also report being contacted by an informant who had information about the case. But this informant actually claimed to belong to a highly trained group of assassins brought together by a white supremacist organization in order to incite a race war. Simpson and his ex-wife had been targeted for this nefarious plot because Brown-Simpson – a blonde, blue-eyed German native – was a race traitor who had married a high-profile "nigger" and given birth to two "mud children" (p. 65). By murdering Brown-Simpson and then framing the black football legend for the crime, the hate group hoped to exploit the conflict potentials of black distrust for a criminal justice system that whites generally affirm. Moreover, the informant claimed, Brown-Simpson was having an affair at the time with a Jew, Ronald Goldman. Thus outrage over the bloody murders might also work to inflame ever-present tensions between blacks and Jews – the two groups most despised by the organization. The informant also claimed that the organization kept both Simpson and his ex-wife under surveillance for months prior to the murders in order to collect the information necessary for engineering the elaborate conspiracy. These efforts included following Brown-Simpson in a white Bronco similar to Simpson's, and the use of phone taps and other sophisticated surveillance equipment. As in the Singular book, this book claimed that the racist culture of the LAPD facilitated the conspiracy, thus requiring the direct involvement of only a small number of department insiders:[32]

> It has always been our understanding from Skinner [their informant] that the frame masterminded by the "CAUSE"[33] did not require the involvement of large numbers of law enforcement officers or criminal support personal. Too often a party's guilt is predetermined by bias or misinformation . . . However, Skinner's incredibly detailed description of what took place presents a believable and likely explanation of what occurred. All of the necessary components existed in the "CAUSE" organization for the murders: motive, opportunity, and ability. (p. 214)

Incompetence. Overzealousness. Mystery. Rush to judgment. Conspiracy. In the end, a multitude of narratives about the case provided something for everyone. But mainstream news narratives about the case ultimately defined "plausibility," which set up some rather powerful collisions between O. J. "facts" and "fictions" for trial observers. As a consequence, the case's grip on the public's imagination was vise-like, many observers comparing daily developments to a tasty soap opera.[34] News "fact" actually *became* popular "fiction" on January 31, 1995 – one week after the start of opening statements in the criminal trial – when the Fox television network garnered sizable ratings for its airing of a hastily made movie about the case, *The O. J. Simpson Story*. Moreover, the case was the top story covered on US network news programs for most of 1995.[35] High levels of public interest continued throughout the trial, leading trial observers to change their television viewing routines, which decimated the ratings for syndicated programming unfortunate enough to be pitted against the live coverage.[36] Many local television stations in the Los Angeles area saw their ratings soar as a result of periodic trial coverage.[37] Internet users were also enamored by the case. Time-Life's Simpson website averaged about 325,000 hits per week during the criminal trial.[38] And not to be outdone, publishers of some of the case-related books cited above posted robust sales – especially when the books embraced dominant, "plausible" O. J. narratives.[39] Finally, when the criminal trial verdicts were read, 91 percent of all television sets in operation were tuned into the coverage. Only the first US moon landing and the funeral of John F. Kennedy attracted a larger *share* of the audience.[40] No other televised event in US history had attracted a larger audience in *absolute* terms (Fiske 1996).

Can we ultimately explain this amazing degree of public interest by identifying the Simpson case as a "popular trial?" True, the case clearly shared important narrative elements with earlier popular murder trials, and the more "plausible" case-related narratives may ultimately have an impact on the assumptions underlying key societal debates (e.g., the state of the US criminal justice system). Indeed, I explore this latter possibility in chapter 2. But the concept of "popular trial" as defined above seems somehow insufficient. It fails to adequately theorize the unprecedented level of public interest generated by the case, its ability to *monopolize* the public agenda like few popular trials before it. In the final analysis, it seems, the Simpson case is best understood by comparing it to a somewhat broader social phenomenon known as a "media event," and by considering the all-important role of ritual.

The Simpson case as "media event"

In *Media Events: The Live Broadcasting of History* (1992), Daniel Dayan and Elihu Katz posit a largely order-based[41] theory of "media events." This theory conceptualizes the phenomena as intricately connected with the smooth and orderly functioning of society. Drawing from anthropological work on ritual, the scholars maintain that members of society are motivated to participate in media events because these cultural "performances" (p. 78) help them (re)affirm the established order and their place in it. Indeed, much of the meaning of contemporary life is (re)negotiated and (re)enforced – "authenticated" – through these festive occasions:

We think of media events as holidays that spotlight some central value or some aspect of collective memory. Often such events portray an idealized version of society, reminding society of what it aspires to be rather than what it is. In any case, the portrait must be authenticated by the public, for the elementary reason that otherwise it will not work. (p. ix)

Dayan and Katz highlight several specific characteristics – each of which is necessary but not sufficient – that separate media events from more ordinary mediated phenomena. First, media events are broadcast with reverence and ceremony, a presentation that interrupts the routine and electrifies large audiences. Indeed, these events are so salient that they monopolize the media's agenda and the public's attention through norms of mandatory coverage and viewing. Although media events are always broadcast live by the media, they are preplanned, announced, and advertised in advance by other important societal institutions. Accordingly, the public perceives the coverage of these "high holidays" (p. 1) as the recording of a historical occurrence that is independent of media coverage. That is, media events are not generally understood to be a *creation* of the media. Nonetheless, the intense media coverage afforded these occasions necessarily transforms them into altogether different events. These new events convert the home into a public space where micro-level networks are disrupted, where members of society participate at the same time in macro-level integrative rituals. Even when media events address societal conflict, they ultimately celebrate "reconciliation" (p. 8).

Dayan and Katz identify three basic "scripts" or "narrative possibilities" for media events (p. 25): conquest, coronation, and contest. Each of these scripts corresponds to one of Weber's three ideal types of authority: charismatic (i.e., the power of personalities), traditional (i.e., the power of customs), legal-rational (i.e., the power of rules) (Weber 1958, pp. 294–96). Conquests, for example, are associated with charismatic authority. These media events consist of major human achievements like the Apollo moon landing, for example. Indeed, the conquest script is based on a conflict between the hero and norms, beliefs, or nature, and its central message is that the "rules can be changed" (p. 34). In contrast, coronations are pure ceremony, potent celebrations of tradition for tradition's sake (e.g., weddings, funerals, and homecomings). The coronation script corresponds to traditional authority and thus communicates that "rules are traditionbound" (p. 34). Finally, contests are "rule-governed battles of champions" (p. 26) that serve as a "training ground for the construction of social institutions based on rules" (p. 28). The contest script calls for nonpartisan television presenters and an audience that will judge the outcome. It is premised upon legal-rational authority, its central message being that "rules are supreme" (p. 34). As "popular trial" (Hariman 1990), of course, the Simpson case clearly follows this final script. Numerous examples of how the case celebrated the criminal justice system emerge in the following pages (e.g., see chapter 4).

But what about societal conflict, about the validity of Dayan and Katz's claim that media events ultimately celebrate reconciliation? In the end, I find their emphasis on order, and their model's corresponding submergence of conflict, somewhat problematic. The scholars seem to either subordinate the possible counter-hegemonic readings of these events to the events' integrative functions,[42] or they would define as something other than "media event" those phenomena that meet all of the other criteria but also foment ideological debate and conflict (i.e., the necessary but not sufficient rule). The Simpson case is most assuredly about more than just the murders and the trial outcomes. As we shall see in later chapters, ceremonial elements indeed pervaded the case and the public's reaction to it. But the case also tapped into enduring societal conflicts, into the struggle between counter-hegemonic projects for change and hegemonic projects for maintenance of the status quo. And much to the chagrin of authorities, "reconciliation" was not always the outcome celebrated.

In *Media Matters: Race and Gender in U.S. Politics* (1996), John Fiske conceptualizes "media event" in terms that center conflict theories of society. For Fiske, media events serve as public arenas wherein people engage in the political debates and political action that shape the world around us. Indeed, occurrences become media events only when they embody and (re)circulate the deeply conflicting currents of race, class, gender, and sexuality that flow through US society. In other words, discursive struggle – as opposed to reconciliation – is the motor that drives media events for Fiske. And this struggle always involves counter-hegemonic cultural currents, as well as mainstream, dominant ones. This is *why* media events electrify audiences.

While media events are necessarily triggered by "real" events, they are not simply discourses *about* the events. Fiske, like Dayan and Katz, argues that mediation creates a whole new type of event. In accord with postmodern theory, he further posits that this new type exists in its own right, with social consequences just as significant as the "real" event it represents:

> The term *media event* is an indication that in a postmodern world we can no longer rely on a stable relationship or clear distinction between a "real" event and its mediated representation. Consequently, we can no longer work with the idea that the "real" is more important, significant, or even "true" than the representation. (p. 2; emphasis original)

Fiske demonstrates this implosion between the "real" and the representational by exploring a number of recent "media events:" the Murphy Brown/Dan Quayle family values debate; the Anita Hill/Clarence Thomas Hearings; the 1992 Los Angeles "riots;" and, of course, the Simpson double murder case. For each of these occurrences, he identifies important discursive struggles that in many ways eclipsed the "real" events that (re)activated them.

In order to fully comprehend the magnitude of the Simpson case, I propose, we must combine Dayan and Katz's insights about the ritualistic elements of media events with Fiske's focus on the counter-hegemonic currents that also drive these events. That is, while media events often begin as ceremonies designed to celebrate and (re)affirm the status quo, conflicting cultural currents may mitigate against any final reconciliation and even incite movements for counter-hegemonic change. This view, of course, is consistent with Carey's (1975) classic "ritual model" of communication. On the one hand, this model conceptualizes communication as a symbolic process geared toward the "maintenance of society in time" and the "representation of shared beliefs" (p. 6). But on the other hand, the model acknowledges the counter-hegemonic potential of ritual: That is, "How do groups in society struggle over the definition of what is real?" Carey asks (p. 17).

Scholarship on secular rituals also underscore the hegemonic and counter-hegemonic potential of these ceremonies (e.g., see Turner 1969[43]). As Moore and Myerhoff (1977) put it, "Ritual may do much more than mirror existing social arrangements and existing modes of thought. It can act to reorganize them or even help to create them" (p. 5). In other words, while rituals generally work to bring legitimacy to "positions of particular persons, organizations, occasions, moral values, views of the world, and the like" (Moore and Myerhoff 1977, p. 4), these endless, ongoing cultural forms – "court trials," for example (p. 4) – may also serve as sites for cultural and political change. Ritual outcomes are far from pre-ordained. Indeed, in evaluating these outcomes, we might explore five distinct dimensions (Moore and Myerhoff 1977, pp. 15–17):

Explicit purpose. Rituals have an explicit, stated purpose. In the Simpson case, this purpose was to determine the defendant's innocence or guilt.

Explicit symbols and messages. Rituals work to make visible a valued ideology. In the Simpson case, the Great Seal of California, the prosecution's use of the moniker "The People," the mantra "innocent until proven guilty," and so on, were all symbols and messages meant to celebrate the virtues of our criminal justice system, and by extension, our system of government.

Implicit statements. Rituals covertly work to address important social and psychological issues. As we shall see in chapter 2, the Simpson case implicitly invoked a number of pressing political concerns.

Social relationships affected. Rituals affect our social roles, identities, and the attitudes we harbor toward others. In the Simpson case, "raced ways of seeing" were a major component of the ritual (e.g., see chapters 7, 8, and 9).

Culture versus chaos. Rituals attempt to portray the social world as "orderly and explicable and for the moment fixed." In the Simpson case, the media played a major role in this meaning-making process. Indeed, the Simpson media event was largely shaped by what Ettema (1997, p. 460) refers to as "press rites," media coverage that portrays *and* interacts with powerful individuals and/or institutions.

In the final analysis, the concept of ritual – particularly the indeterminacy of ritual outcomes – is consistent with Gramsci's (1971) model of hegemony. This model presents society as an unstable order shaped by the interaction of "organic consciousness" (i.e., level of consent) and a multitude of other historically contingent factors (i.e., level of coercion).

In other words, it acknowledges the potent effect of integrative, hege-monic forces like ritual without discounting the possible infiltration of counter-hegemonic ideas. This observation sets the stage for my con-ceptualization of the Simpson case:

Amidst anxieties inflamed by the millennium's end, the Simpson case became a society-wide ritual through which our most basic values, norms, and social structures could be scrutinized, celebrated, *and* chal-lenged. As we shall see in later chapters, this interpretive activity often worked to privilege a dominant take on reality, to facilitate consent for the hegemonic order. But at other times, this interpretive activity openly worked to reshape the status quo through counter-hegemonic affirma-tions of "fact" and "fiction." As a consequence, Simpson's criminal trial, for example, captured the imagination of viewers around the nation (and globe) as few events before or since. Gavel-to-gavel, live coverage on Los Angeles television and Court TV – as well as the preemption of regularly scheduled programming by network television, Cable News Network, and radio stations around the nation – signaled an important departure from the routine. Moreover, while the event was organized outside the media, namely by the state, ongoing media coverage was pre-planned, announced, and advertised in advance. It ultimately became a "high holiday" (Dayan and Katz 1992, p. 32), an unprecedented "con-test" where the media framed daily developments in terms of "winners" and "losers" (p. 33).[44] And as many media commentators (as well as the judge in the case) noted, the criminal justice system – with its notion of a "fair" trial, its litany of rules and procedures, its belief in the ability of jurors to ferret out truth beyond a "reasonable doubt" – was also on trial. In this larger trial, the media audience constituted the jurors, and a favorable outcome meant that they would (re)affirm the system and celebrate it.

But as per Fiske (1994, 1996) the case also necessarily tapped into enduring cleavages in US society – namely race, class, gender, and sexuality. This is why, for example, the media could so successfully exploit race in its stories about public reactions to the verdict. (The lower profile of other cleavages will be examined in later chapters.) Because each of these "cultural currents" is intricately bound up with campaigns to either change or (re)enforce the status quo, the public generally finds them "controversial," while media workers, by default, regard them as "newsworthy." Explicitly or implicitly, these political issues were invoked by narrative elements central to the Simpson case (see above), thereby ensuring the case's "popularity," its significance beyond just the murders or the immediate legal outcomes.

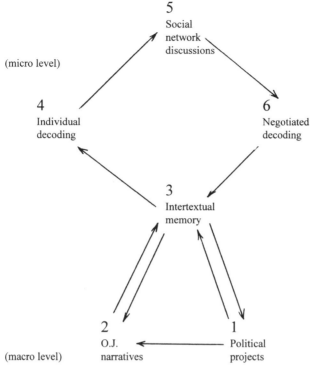

Figure 9. Theoretical model.

Figure 9 provides a simplified model of the rather complex process undergirding the Simpson "media event." The model is composed of six discrete factors: political projects, O.J. narratives, intertextual memory, individual decoding, social network discussions, and negotiated decoding. It describes a circular meaning-making process, one that links macro-level and micro-level phenomena through ritual.

At the macro-level, political projects (1) discursively work to either (re)enforce the status quo or to change it. Here, we find the influence of turbulent cultural currents like race, class, gender, and sexuality (cf. Fiske 1994, 1996). These political projects then shape the construction and circulation of O.J. narratives (2) (e.g., narratives of incompetence, overzealousness, mystery, rush to judgment, and conspiracy) through the comments of overt project proponents or by the representations of media workers who may be covert proponents themselves. That is, through the application of certain discursive and symbolic techniques, these narratives are packaged in hypermediated *texts*[45] that work to privilege certain encoded meanings about the case "facts," certain ideological understandings of the world (Hall 1973; Morley 1993).

Nonetheless, there is no guarantee that these intended meanings will be received by any given member of the audience (Morley 1974, 1980, 1992). For at the micro-level, a number of factors intervene between the meanings encoded into media texts and those ultimately produced by members of the audience (Fiske 1987). First, intertextual memories (3) act as a prism that refracts the content of media texts in ways that resonate with the "real" and mediated experiences of individuals (Gabriel 1988; Lipsitz 1990). These memories – a fluid reservoir of meaning – are directly shaped by the political projects (1) salient to individuals and by their prior experiences with media texts (2); they work through comparison and contrast to help individuals determine what a given text is and is not "about" (Hunt 1997). Individual decoding (4) refers to these initial acts of determination. But humans do not exist in a social vacuum; they are linked by various network ties to important others whose affection, approval, and/or respect they need and seek. Through social network discussions (5), individual audience members (re)negotiate their initial decodings of media texts in ways they consider socially acceptable (cf. Hunt 1997, 1997a). Often this acceptability depends upon the social location of network members, upon the imprints that race, class, gender, and sexuality have made on their life chances and subjectivities. The resulting negotiated decodings (6) work to celebrate and (re)affirm individuals' understandings of these locations; these ritual outcomes then feed back into the reservoir of intertextual memories (3) that individuals will invoke to make sense of subsequent media texts. The meaning-making process thus comes full circle.[46]

In short, the Simpson media event was (is) a phenomenon driven by a host of pressing political concerns, concerns that are likely to resonate differently with differently situated observers. While these concerns were initially invoked by particular narrative elements in the case (see above), they were amplified by proponents of important political projects whose comments rapidly circulated throughout the media. In the next chapter, I expand upon the notion of political project and trace the influence of four such projects heavily invested in particular case narratives and outcomes.

2 O.J. and politics

In the previous chapter, you will recall, I proposed a theoretical model for understanding the nature of media events like the "Trial of the Century." A diagram of the model (see figure 9, chapter 1) graphically depicted six discrete factors – political projects, O.J. narratives, intertextual memory, individual decoding, social network discussions, and negotiated decoding – that interact with one another in ways that periodically lead to galvanizing foci of public interest and investment. This chapter zeroes in on the first of these factors, political projects, and the role it played in the O.J. Simpson double murder case.

Politics, of course, literally refers to the gaining, using, and losing of power. And if we understand power as the ability – either through coercion or consent – to get people to act against their will, or as simply occupying a structural location that facilitates deriving benefit from the actions of others, then we get that much closer to comprehending the social significance of political projects. Inspired by Michael Omi and Howard Winant's (1986, 1994) work on "racial projects," I understand "political projects" to be discourses[1] that are (re)activated in order to simultaneously offer a common-sense explanation for political dynamics *and* to privilege certain political interests above others so that power might be redistributed (or its current distribution reinforced). In other words, any given political project necessarily resonates with certain interests; and these interests, often buried, invariably give birth to ideologies that profess to explain the nature of things, how a given way of seeing is superior to others, why a given allocation of power is more efficient, effective, or just than others.

Political projects, then, have everything to do with hegemony (cf. Gramsci 1971). Enduring social orders like the United States are ones that manage to continually fashion unstable equilibria out of the complementary forces of coercion and consent. Political projects, by definition, work to manufacture consent (e.g., privilege certain "common-sense" understandings) at the same time that they work to alter the possibilities for coercion (e.g., increase or decrease "inequality"). The ideas that constitute a given political project typically preexist its (re)activation, coming together only in decisive moments of "elective affinity" with articulated interests (cf. Weber 1958, p. 284). Thus the ideological goals of two distinct projects may actually overlap, while those of another pair may collide. Rarely is there the level of agreement between project goals, project tactics, and project proponents that would be necessary for maintaining a *stable* hegemonic order (cf. Hall 1986). Rather, there are always openings in this order through which potentially destabilizing projects (i.e., acts of "resistance") might advance. In other words, the hegemonic order is the product of a process, one that defies closure, one in which the interests and identities of project proponents are never fixed. Indeed, through the prism of dynamic and often conflicting discourses, this process actually works to overdetermine the world we experience. As Laclau and Mouffe (1985) note,

The fact that every object is constituted as an object of discourse has *nothing to do* with whether there is a world external to thought, or with the realism/ idealism opposition. An earthquake or the falling of a brick is an event that certainly exists, in the sense that it occurs here and now, independently of my will. But whether their specificity as objects is constructed in terms of "natural phenomena" or "expression of the wrath of God," depends upon the structuring of a discursive field. What is denied is not that such objects exist externally to thought, but the rather different assertion that they could constitute themselves as objects outside any discursive condition of emergence. (p. 8)

In this chapter, I advance a simple thesis: like the proverbial earthquake or falling brick, the O.J. Simpson murder case, too, cannot be understood "outside any discursive condition of emergence." That is, the case was not (and can never be) about *just* the physical act of murder, or Simpson's material status as innocent or guilty. The Simpson case ultimately became the media event it did because of the important narrative elements it possessed (see chapter 1). And these elements were particularly potent in their ability to (re)activate political projects centrally involved in shaping the world around us. In other words, underlying the unprecedented levels of public fascination with the case, underlying even the media's ability to exploit the tragedy for profits, rests an enduring ideological contest between competing social interests. These interests ultimately drive what I call the "Celebrity Defendant," "Domestic Violence," "Black 'Other,'" and "'Just-Us' system" projects. Throughout the case, these four projects continually jockeyed for position on the media's limited agenda (cf. Hilgartner and Bosk 1988). The agenda of the *mainstream* media, in particular, constitute the public sphere in a society characterized by a relatively large proportion of impersonal contacts (Iyengar and Kinder 1987; Schudson 1995). Accordingly, it is within this realm that project discourses vied for public attention and, ultimately, affirmation.

Below, I examine the nature of each of these four projects, its emergence in the case, and the process by which it worked to shape our understandings – and stakes – in the "Trial of the Century."

The Celebrity Defendant project

> The celebrities are The Names that need no further identification. Those who know them so far exceed those of whom they know as to require no exact computation. Wherever the celebrities go, they are recognized, and moreover, recognized with some excitement and awe.[2]

In his classic account of US politics, *The Power Elite*, C. Wright Mills (1956) identifies an intimate relationship between celebrity and wealth: celebrities are those prestigious "Names" who are literally celebrated by the masses, who accrue their prestige directly from the power and/or wealth they are thought to possess. Celebrities, to be sure, are necessarily media commodities, popular personalities guaranteed to attract audiences filled with awestruck fans. Moreover, as members of this rather exclusive power elite, they occupy a world from which they "look down upon, so to speak, and by their decisions mightily affect, the everyday worlds of ordinary men and women" (p. 3). It is this fundamental social divide that sets the stage for the Celebrity Defendant project.

On the eve of the Bundy murders, Orenthal James Simpson was, by most accounts, a wealthy celebrity. Football legend, occasional actor, and corporate pitchman, Simpson had amassed a wealth sufficient to live among the rich and famous in the posh Los Angeles neighborhood of Brentwood. He was also a welcomed figure at exclusive country clubs and resorts, frequently seen hobnobbing with the Who's Who of the golfing set.

But life was not always like this for Simpson. He would first have to escape life in a San Francisco ghetto, gang preoccupations, and flirtations with petty crime. As a 1978 celebration of his "most memorable [football] games" put it, "It was a ghetto life which O. J. experienced, but not the worst of ghettos. 'We always had money to eat,' O. J. is quick to point out. But he did live in a project and he did live a rough existence, so rough that had he not turned toward his natural gift in athletics, O. J. might have ended up in jail."[3]

Simpson's Horatio Alger, rags-to-riches saga would ultimately unfold over a thirty-year period, beginning with his storied career as a running back at the University of Southern California. In 1968, he was voted the best college football player in the nation and won the coveted

Heisman Trophy. After being selected by the Buffalo Bills in the first round of the 1969 National Football League draft, he soon became the first running back in NFL history to rush for more than 2,000 yards in a fourteen-game season. Other NFL records would follow, including achieving more 200-yard games than any other player at the time (Baker 1978).

But Simpson was more than just a great football player. He was also a "Name" – "O. J.," "The Juice." He was the charismatic man behind the "famed No. 32" that so many fans proudly wore on their T-shirts (Baker 1978, p. 12). Wherever he went he was instantly recognized. Excited fans routinely asked for his autograph. He always cordially obliged, a habit, of course, that would become an important matter of testimony during his criminal trial. Indeed, a 1985 retrospective on Heisman Trophy winners had this to say about Simpson: "He was the state-of-the-art halfback. He is a show business personality in much demand. But when all is said and done, Orenthal James Simpson remains in private as he comes across in public – a genuinely nice person."[4]

Whether or not Simpson was "a genuinely nice person," of course, would also become a salient issue in the criminal trial. But Simpson's possession of such an image was nonetheless an important factor in explaining his extraordinary success – on the field and off. In an era when other black athletes were militantly protesting US race relations from boxing rings, basketball courts, and the Olympic Village of Mexico City, Simpson diplomatically proclaimed his "disdain for 'politics'" (Johnson and Roediger 1997, pp. 203–04). His phenomenal accomplishments on the field, combined with the color of his skin, conveniently worked to divert attention away from these struggles, to affirm the status quo by default. For Simpson represented the visage of the non-threatening Negro, the former ghetto dweller who had made good, who could be invited into and celebrated in America's living rooms with minimal risk. In short, he was shrewdly able to translate his "nice guy" image into a valuable commodity, one that would guarantee his anointment as the first super-athlete pitchman, paving the way for Michael Jordan and the others who followed. Thus by 1977, *Advertising Age* had awarded Simpson its "Oscar" for being the top celebrity spokesperson. Simpson had by then also appeared in several popular motion pictures – e.g., *Capricorn One, Airport, The Towering Inferno* (*The Naked Gun*[5] series would soon follow) – and was widely recognized as the man running through airports in Hertz rental car commercials (Johnson and Roediger 1997). He had also been a recognized commentator on ABC's *Monday Night Football* and NBC's Sunday game coverage. Finally, unlike other prominent athletes known to have squandered fortunes, Simpson had wisely invested in a number of business ventures, including several fast-food franchises in the Southern California area. Indeed, *Business Marketing* in 1992 proclaimed him a "genius" for his ability to transcend sports and become a successful businessman (Johnson and Roediger 1997).

According to friends and lawyers, Simpson's net worth a year before the murders stood at about $11 million.[6] Combined with his magnetic appeal to the masses and intimate ties to the rich and powerful (he served on the board of directors of five corporations[7]), this wealth arguably admitted him to the ranks of what C. Wright Mills had described as the power elite. At the very least, his capital – financial, cultural, and social – seemed to place him in a world altogether different from the one inhabited by "ordinary men and women." This, of course, was precisely the concern that (re)activated the Celebrity Defendant project.

As William Ryan (1981) pointed out nearly twenty years ago, wealth in the United States is concentrated among the few. The bulk of the masses actually have a negative net worth, struggling from paycheck to paycheck to make ends meet. Thus the financial resources of the typical criminal defendant pales in comparison to Simpson's. For example, while about 80 percent of all defendants charged with felonies rely on public defenders,[8] overworked attorneys who are usually allocated only a few thousand dollars at most for out-of-court fees,[9] Simpson could use his millions to amass a "Dream Team" of attorneys, investigators, and experts. Moreover, while most murder defendants are coaxed to plea bargain in the face of seemingly insurmountable police/prosecution cases,[10] wealthy defendants like Simpson can afford to challenge every single piece of police/prosecution evidence – no matter how damning they may initially appear to be. Using Ryan's (1981, p. 8) lexicon, Simpson's wealth might be said to buy him more than his "fair share" of justice.

But Simpson was also a celebrity. As such, he was assumed to possess a measure of public goodwill – fueled by a combination of his legendary athletic accomplishments and "nice guy" image – that would also work to inoculate him against a jury conviction. Indeed, a CBS/ New York Times poll taken shortly after Simpson's arrest revealed that 44 percent of respondents had "personally" thought of Simpson as a "role model" prior to the murders.[11] Police and prosecutors evidently respected Simpson's atypical degree of public appeal because early in the case they waged an aggressive public relations campaign designed to shatter his celebrity persona. For example, "unnamed sources" leaked incriminating evidence to the press about Simpson's alleged involvement in the murders, the City Attorney provided the media with 911 tapes chronicling dramatic episodes of domestic violence involving Simpson and his murdered ex-wife, and lead prosecutors resorted to referring to Simpson in public only as "the defendant" – to deny him any social capital that might accrue from being known as "O. J." Meanwhile, others feared that Simpson's celebrity status might turn the trial into a "media circus" – that intense public interest in the fate of this celebrity, when exploited by profit-thirsty media, might somehow spill over into the courtroom and have an adverse affect on how attorneys actually tried the case.[12]

(Re)activating the project

When we examine mainstream news accounts of the case, we find that subtle precursors of the Celebrity Defendant project emerged very shortly after the murders. Three days after the bodies were discovered – June 15, 1994 – a front-page headline of the *Los Angeles Times* read as follows:

Police Sources Link Evidence to Simpson. Crime: Probe reportedly focuses on bloodstains at murder scene and the ex-football star's *home*. An arrest could come soon, the sources say. (Emphasis added)

This was the first article to report that police considered Simpson a suspect in the killings. The two articles that had appeared the previous day simply reported the discovery of the bodies and discussed how the Simpsons' friends had described them as a "vibrant couple." Interestingly, as reports of Simpson's possible culpability emerged in the paper, so too did terms selected to signify his wealth and celebrity. That is, the first day's articles uniformly refer to 360 N. Rockingham as Simpson's "home." But by the second day of stories, a transition of sorts had begun to take place in the *Los Angeles Times*. While the headline reprinted above refers to the N. Rockingham address as Simpson's "home," the second paragraph of the accompanying story suddenly recodes it as his "mansion": "Much of the investigation Tuesday focused on bloodstains that sources say were found in Simpson's car, at his Brentwood *mansion* and at his former wife's townhouse two miles way, where the crime was committed" (Emphasis added). Indeed, "mansion" was again used in the fifth paragraph of the same article. Other articles appearing in the *Times* during the first two weeks of the case would routinely draw attention to Simpson's wealth and celebrity, shifting frequently between "mansion" and "estate," only occasionally employing the more neutral "home" or "residence." For example, consider this front-page lead paragraph that appeared in the newspaper the day after Simpson was arrested:

A day after being captured outside his *5,700 square-foot Brentwood estate*, football legend O. J. Simpson spent Saturday under suicide watch in a 7-by–9 foot jail cell, where he is being held without bail as prosecutors prepare to seek murder indictments from the county grand jury. (Emphasis added)[13]

This stark juxtaposition of Simpson's "estate" and "jail cell" is clearly meant to underscore the life of luxury the defendant was accustomed to, and the degree to which prison symbolized his fall from grace. While *Times* newsworkers may or may not have considered themselves proponents of the Celebrity Defendant project, the discourses comprising the project were already in circulation. And as newsworkers went to work soliciting expert analyses and establishing the relevant case "facts," these discourses necessarily inflected the narratives they constructed.

Indeed, similar effects were evident throughout mainstream media coverage during the first few weeks of the case. On National Public Radio's *Weekend Edition Saturday*, Simpson was labelled a "fallen football hero."[14] On the same day, CNN's *Newsmaker Saturday* referred to his ordeal as "the fall of an icon."[15] Anticipating public concerns about Simpson's status as a wealthy celebrity, perhaps, LAPD Chief Willie Williams told reporters that Simpson would not be given special treatment after his arrest.[16] Finally, an avalanche of stories about the famous attorneys who would compose Simpson's "Dream Team" momentarily buried other items on the media agenda.[17]

As the case progressed, and, it seems, as observers increasingly credited Simpson's attorneys with achieving important tactical advantages, the central discourse of the Celebrity Defendant project began to take shape. The dismissal of the grand jury, for example, was apparently a pivotal point in the development of this discourse. In largely unprecedented fashion, a judge had dismissed the Simpson grand jury due to the proliferation of publicity surrounding the case (especially the City Attorney's release of the 911 tapes) and the possible prejudicial effect this may have had on grand jurors who admitted to hearing reports about the case. In a story entitled, "Why the O. J. Simpson Trial is Unusual," *Good Morning America* reporter Bill Ritter contrasted such "unusual" pre-trial procedures in the Simpson case to those typically found in Los Angeles trials. Simpson's wealth and celebrity, of course, were offered as important explanations. At this point, however, questions were still rampant as to whether Simpson's celebrity would on balance be an asset or a liability for his defense.[18] Accordingly, commentators openly speculated on CNN's *Capital Gang Saturday* whether or not Simpson could receive a fair trial in Los Angeles.[19] But when reports soon appeared of Simpson's million dollar reward for information about the killer of his ex-wife and friend,[20] his lead attorney was hailed as a "'master' of legal maneuvers,"[21] and the question appeared to be settled. The next day, a CNN *Prime News* story entitled, "Simpson's wealth means he enjoys more 'legal' firepower," explored the possible strategies that the wealthy defendant's attorneys might employ to his advantage. By August 1994 – roughly two months after the murders – *NBC Nightly News* was reporting that Simpson's defense team was too large to fit into his jail's waiting room,[22] and that the attorneys had hired the services of a high-powered jury consultant.[23]

The discourse about Simpson's legal privilege continued to crystalize in the months leading up to the trial. By the end of September 1994, *60 Minutes*' Andy Rooney had sarcastically reflected upon the issue of clever lawyers and their fees.[24] (Rooney, of course, would later be disgusted by the verdicts in the criminal trial and facetiously offer his own $1 million reward for the "killer" of Simpson's ex-wife and friend.[25]) Two days after the Rooney piece, NBC *Dateline* profiled the techniques trial consultants like Simpson's use to pick jurors.[26] Reports soon appeared throughout the media speculating about the advantages the black defendant might derive from the predominantly "African-American"[27] jury his defense attorneys had been able to seat.[28] Shortly thereafter, a poll of lawyers indicated that most felt the upcoming trial would result in either an acquittal or a hung jury.[29] The implication was that a clever playing of the "race card" by Simpson's high-powered attorneys would ultimately inflame the passions of the "African-American" jury.

The trial finally began in late January of 1995. CBS *Evening News* soon reported on prosecution charges that Simpson's defense attorneys were "sleazy."[30] Prosecutors argued that they had been "sandbagged" when defense attorney Johnnie Cochran introduced witnesses in his opening statement whose interview reports had not been turned over to the prosecution.

But it was not until three months into the trial that a *Newsweek* editorial would cogently articulate the central theme of the Celebrity Defendant project. The editorial appeared just as many trial analysts were crediting defense attorney Barry Scheck with skillfully neutralizing the credibility of LAPD criminalist Dennis Fung during cross-examination. Questioning the validity of racial discourses surrounding the case, the editorial vehemently argued that Simpson's wealth will be *the* determining factor in the trial's income:

Money is the defining element of our modern American criminal-justice system. If Simpson walks, as most lawyers think he will, what will have decided the outcome is not that O.J. is black, but that he is rich. He can afford to buy what F. Lee Bailey, Alan Dershowitz, Johnnie Cochran and others have to sell: the consultants on jury packing, the obliging experts who will contradict the

state's overpowering DNA and related evidence, and the defense lawyer's bag
of tricks for sowing doubts, casting aspersions and coaching witnesses.[31]

Important ideological assumptions are embedded in this quote, of
course. For example, the editorial essentially takes the state's DNA
evidence for granted, confidently declaring it "overpowering." It is telling to note that the editorial's author could make this proclamation
prior to the prosecution's actual presentation of DNA evidence at trial.[32]
It was as if Simpson had been damned by the author the moment he
was accused by the state and recognized to be wealthy. A trial-related
book entitled, *55 Things You'd Better Not Say Around O. J.* humorously
made the point:[33] "Just two more lawyers and you'll have enough for a
softball team." Indeed, Simpson had reportedly spent about $6 million
on his "Dream Team" of attorneys, including $100,000 for just one
expert witness (Coffey 1995). Like a witch surviving a burning at the
stake, an acquittal for the celebrity defendant could only be the sign of
his special powers (i.e., his wealth); it could *never* mean that a valid case
existed for reasonable doubt of his guilt. Faith in police and prosecution evidence had already been (re)affirmed. Thus another unstated
assumption of the editorial – and the Celebrity Defendant project – is
that Simpson is *obviously* guilty. Any doubt about this "fact" is attribut-
able to a broken system that produced profit-hungry attorneys who
sought victory over truth and, of course, a jury that could not distinguish
the evidentiary forest from the trees. As for this latter group, Marcia
Clark would note that society cannot afford to leave such important
decisions to a bunch of "moon rocks."[34]

Orenthal James Simpson, as many project proponents had predicted,
would be acquitted of the murders on October 3, 1995. The combination of his extraordinary legal resources, a closely followed trial, and
an unpopular outcome only worked to (re)affirm project proponents'
belief that the criminal justice system is broken and needs fixing. Some
proponents, for example, have argued for the establishment of professional juries composed of ex-judges and other legal experts – jurors,
they argue, who can see beyond the smoke screens crafty defense
attorneys might otherwise use to harvest doubt (Alexander and Cornell
1997). At the very least, they suggest, defendants should be required
to disclose to juries how much they paid for the testimony of their
experts (Trilling 1996). Meanwhile, some proponents have also suggested that the requirement of unanimous jury verdicts be abolished
(Willard 1997).

As we shall see in the next section, the assumption so central to these
proponents' arguments – that Simpson is obviously guilty – also worked
to strengthen support for the Domestic Violence project.

The Domestic Violence project

The O. J. Simpson story has nothing to do with the intellectual hand-wringing of complex Elizabethan tragedies and even less to do with the high-minded Greek heroes who, nobly and futilely, made reasoned choices in their struggle to resist fates they could not escape. Like it or not, Simpson is a 20th century Everyman.[35]

"Domestic violence," a phenomenon that is probably as old as "man" and "woman," only recently became defined as a "social problem" in this nation.[36] The above quote comes from a column that appeared in an East Coast newspaper two weeks after the Bundy murders. Its tone captures the frustration experienced by activists who have labored over the years to place domestic violence squarely at the center of the public agenda. The writer, Anne G. Sjoerdsma, notes how male commentators have failed to comprehend the Simpson case, how they have mystified the defendant's treatment of his murdered ex-wife as some great dramatic tragedy, instead of recognizing it for the common societal occurrence that it really was. As the column unfolds, she identifies other practices that work to marginalize public concerns about domestic violence, that unfortunately work to define it as a "women's issue." For example, she argues, the District Attorney in the Simpson case had erred by appointing a woman prosecutor instead of a black male, an important symbolic figure who might have sent "a message" that men of color "do not tolerate violence against women." While a black male would eventually join the prosecution team (i.e., Christopher Darden), concerns would persist about the degree to which the mainstream would connect with the issue of domestic violence, about the seriousness with which the media and legal system would address the abuse women routinely suffer at the hands of men. These and similar concerns, of course, worked to (re)activate the Domestic Violence project.

Although the precise incidence of "domestic violence" is unknown due to underreporting and definitional questions, the phenomenon is clearly widespread in the United States. Statistics show that domestic violence is the leading cause of injury to US women, claiming about four million victims each year.[37] Another important statistic to consider – especially given the circumstances surrounding the Simpson case – is that nearly a third of women homicide victims are killed by a husband or boyfriend,[38] men who likely abused them in the past. Despite these alarming statistics, as Sjoerdsma noted in her column, severe deficiencies exist in public, police, prosecution, and judicial responses to domestic violence. That is, the media often underestimate or minimize occurrences of domestic violence;[39] police frequently downplay these occurrences as private, family matters; prosecutors sometimes fail to press for tough sentences; and judges are known to give perpetrators meaningless "slaps on the wrist." In order to place these responses to the issue into proper perspective, a brief overview of theories about the phenomenon appears to be in order. These theories might be rather crudely divided into two categories: social-psychological and socio-cultural/structural.[40]

Theories in the first category locate the explanation for domestic violence primarily in the psychological processes and/or immediate experiences of individual perpetrators. Included in this category are four rather popular explanatory models. First, frustration–aggression theory portrays male offenders as individuals who face blocked goals, who first respond to these challenges with frustration, then with anger – an emotion which soon prompts them to exhibit the aggressive behavior so characteristic of domestic violence episodes (cf. Farrington 1980). A second model, social learning theory, posits that men "learn" about aggressive behaviors such as domestic violence, about when their use is likely to be tolerated or punished (cf. Walker 1986; Stets 1988). Thirdly, symbolic interactionism suggests that batterers "interpret the situations" surrounding their acts of violence so as to justify their actions (e.g., "Why did you make me hit you?").[41] Finally, social-exchange theory agues that family relationships involve rewards and costs, and that people naturally strive to maximize rewards and minimize costs (cf. Sonkin et al. 1985). When women concede control to batterers, the argument goes, batterers are rewarded with very little cost – especially when domestic violence cases are not vigorously prosecuted.

Each of these theories, of course, was implicit in prosecution accounts of the Simpsons' relationship. The prosecution, you will recall, had early on placed domestic violence at the center of its case against Simpson. Thus prosecutors began the murder trial not with physical evidence about the killings, but with evidence designed to establish the history of domestic violence afflicted upon Nicole Brown-Simpson by the celebrity defendant.[42] Echoing the logic of frustration–aggression theory, prosecutors explained Simpson's "final act" of violence against his ex-wife in terms of his frustration with and anger at being rejected by her in his attempts at reconciliation. This frustration and anger would grow, prosecutors later suggested, when Simpson's girlfriend at the time, Paula Barbieri, left him a telephone message just prior to the murders in which she broke off their relationship. Tenets of symbolic interactionism would be used to explain Simpson's state of mind during the infamous slow-speed Bronco "chase," his apparent belief that his own status as a "battered" husband somehow justified him abusing (and murdering) his ex-wife. Finally, social-learning theory and social exchange theory inspired prosecution arguments about the "slaps on the wrist" that Simpson had received for past abuse. Prosecutors presented nearly sixty episodes of domestic violence involving Simpson and his ex-wife. In several of the incidents, police were called to the scene, but they failed to arrest Simpson. With one exception – a 1989 incident for which he was sentenced only to probation, $470 in fines, and 120 hours of dubious community service[43] – Simpson never faced any legal charges. Moreover, the media and his employers largely minimized the significance of that one exception.[44] In short, the argument was that Simpson had "learned" he could abuse his wife with very minimal (if any) "cost." Indeed, when police arrived at the scene of the 1989 incident for which he would be charged, Simpson was reportedly confused about why officers wanted to arrest him when they had not done so during earlier incidents. "This is a family matter," he reasoned, "Why do you want to make a big deal out of it?"[45]

In contrast, the two major theories in the second category explain domestic violence in terms of broader socio-cultural and structural factors. First, noting that most domestic problems can be linked to finances,[46] stratification theory argues that men who experience low status and/or power carry their frustrations, disappointments, and stresses into the household (cf. Allen and Straus 1980). This angst, the argument goes, culminates in episodes of domestic violence when accompanied by particular triggers. It is important to underscore here how this argument differs from frustration–aggression theory. While the latter theory focuses primarily on managing the psychological states experienced by abusers, stratification theory suggests that domestic violence can only be meaningfully addressed by reducing the gross structural inequalities that give rise to it. Which brings us to the final explanatory theory, patriarchy (cf. Finn 1996). This theory argues that recent changes in male and female gender roles may be perceived by men as a threat to their "natural" position of societal dominance. It is worth noting that modern sports – the well-spring of Simpson's fame and fortune – had emerged to celebrate dominance (i.e. "male" athletes) and submission (i.e. "female" cheerleaders) just as women began to fight for their rights (cf. Messner 1992; Sabo and Jensen 1994).[47] Similarly, domestic violence became a practical tool that men could use to physically reassert control over "their" women. Indeed, over the last twenty years or so, other violent acts against women (i.e., rape, robbery, assault, homicide) have also been steadily increasing.[48] Once again, the explanation for violence against women is not found in the eccentricities of individual men as much as it is in the basic structural inequality between men and women. As Sjoerdsma put it in the column quoted above, "Simpson is a 20th century Everyman," and the sports culture that men celebrate taught him "either through silent condonation or 'manly' encouragement, to disrespect women."

(Re)activating the project

Not long after the bloody bodies were discovered on Bundy Drive, proponents of the Domestic Violence project began to make sense of the gruesome tragedy by synthesizing and applying key elements of the above theories. The impetus for these efforts would be found through-out the broadcast media on June 14, 1994 – the day after the murders were first made public – when a local social worker, Susan Forward, reported that Brown-Simpson had revealed in therapy sessions that her ex-husband battered and stalked her. The next day, newspaper stories would first identify Simpson as a suspect in the crimes. In the second paragraph of an article that appeared that day, the *Los Angeles Times* described the Simpsons as "strong-minded" and introduced the issue of domestic violence in this way:

Fit, attractive and accustomed to expensive cars and lavish lifestyles, they were strong-minded and witty people who seemed to command a room, *even during a stormy marriage and fitful attempts to reconcile*, friends said. (Emphasis added)[49]

Eleven paragraphs later, the article expanded on the issue by describing the 1989 incident:

Yet it was no secret that the relationship had been rocky at times. Three years before their divorce, Simpson pleaded no contest to a spousal battery charge after he allegedly kicked and hit his wife, yelling, "I'll kill you," at their estate on Rockingham Avenue. That incident occurred shortly after 3 a.m. on New Year's Day, 1989.

The next day, June 16, the newspaper would report on Susan For-ward's more incriminating revelations, as well as possible sanctions the social worker might face for violating Brown-Simpson's "privacy."[50] Then, a front-page *Times* story on June 17 would reveal details from a police report about the 1989 incident. Echoing key tenets of social learning and exchange theory, the story reported that Simpson had "severely" beaten his wife, and that he could not understand why police wanted to arrest him this time, given their failure to do so when they had responded to other incidents at his home:

O. J. Simpson beat his wife so severely in early 1989 that she required hospital treatment, and told police at his Brentwood mansion that he could not under-stand why they wanted to arrest him since it was their ninth response to a domestic disturbance report from the house, according to police reports released late Thursday.

But as quickly as domestic violence emerged as an important case issue, it would also slip to the background for a few days. Perhaps it was upstaged by Simpson's failure to surrender the next day, by the surreal, slow-speed "chase" that ended in his Rockingham Avenue driveway.[51] For it was not until two days after the 1989 police reports hit the newspapers that domestic violence would make its splash in the national media as *the* central issue in the case.

On June 19, stories first began to appear throughout the electronic media suggesting that the Bundy murders constituted a "domestic violence" case. For example, NBC *Nightly News* reported that the Simpson case had created a "fresh debate" on domestic violence.[52] On the same day, ABC's *This Week With David Brinkley* examined ways in which domestic violence can be solved. Meanwhile, as National Public Radio's *All Things Considered* explored the Simpsons' troubled marriage, guest Gil Garcetti, Los Angeles' District Attorney, said he would not be surprised if Simpson confessed to the murders. The next day, the radio program continued its focus on the issue by presenting an installment entitled, "Domestic Violence Haunts Millions of American Women." CNN's *Larry King Live* also tackled the issue with a June 20 episode devoted to how the death of Brown-Simpson might make the nation more aware of domestic violence. The CBS *Evening News* program for the day reported that the case had placed a spotlight on the problem of domestic violence in the United States. Indeed, a *Los Angeles Times* story the following morning reported that the California Assembly had passed a resolution requiring judges to "learn more about the importance of domestic violence cases."[53] Over the next week, television programs as diverse as ABC's *Nightline* (June 24), CNN's *Sonya Live* (June 21), NBC's *Dateline* (June 23, 28), and the CBS *Evening News* (June 22, 24, 26), would present dozens of in-depth profiles on domestic violence. Most of these programs featured interviews with prominent domestic violence activists and experts.

National print media followed suit. In its June 27, "Trail of Blood" cover story about the case, *Newsweek* allocated considerable space to the issue of domestic violence. Roughly a third of the lead article focused on the issue, while a sidebar story entitled, "When Did He Stop Beating His Wife?" quoted several researchers and activists devoted to the cause. Richard Gelles, head of the University of Rhode Island's Family Violence Research Program, underscored how important the Simpson case would be for raising public awareness about domestic violence:

You have to have tremendous compassion for Nicole Brown, for it took her death for people to realize that even the most wonderful public persona can still be a wife-beater. (p. 21)

In the same article, Mariah Burton Nelson – author of *The Stronger Women Get, The More Men Love Football: Sexism and the American Culture of Sports* – echoed key tenets of the patriarchy theory of domestic violence by linking Simpson's abuse of his ex-wife to sports. The football legend, she argued, "was raised in a sports culture that taught him to denigrate women . . . he learned the female role is to cheer for men and be sexually available to men. That's why he abused Nicole" (p. 21). In short, contrary to arguments that media coverage of the case worked to "exonerate" the sports "hero" (cf. McKay and Smith 1995), explicit links were being made early on between domestic violence, sports, and Simpson's apparent guilt.

But it was about two weeks after the murders, perhaps, that the most concrete signs began to appear of the success project proponents were having at moving domestic violence into the center of the political arena. On June 29, the following headline ran in the *Los Angeles Times*:

Domestic Abuse Shelters Will Get $6.1 Million. Violence: Spurred by Simpson case, L.A. and county officials address lack of space for those seeking refuge.

The next day, CNN's *Inside Politics* would report that the Simpson case had even prompted the US Congress to take a closer look at domestic violence. Several battered women, the program noted, had testified before a congressional committee about their experiences. About a month later, abusive spouses throughout the nation would complain that publicity surrounding the Simpson case had caused judges and prosecutors to slap them with tougher charges and sentences than would otherwise have been meted out[54] – precisely what project proponents had hoped for.

As the case was convincingly made for the link between domestic violence and the murders, project proponents took more than a casual interest in developments surrounding the upcoming trial. On August 2, for example, the lead paragraph of a *Los Angeles Times* article clearly alluded to the battle lines that were forming: "In another sign of the politicization of the O. J. Simpson murder case, feminist attorney Gloria Allred on Monday called on Dist. Atty. Gil Garcetti to ask for the death penalty against Simpson."[55] Allred and other project proponents had been outraged by Garcetti's decision to meet with local "civil rights leaders" on July 19. These activists, themselves motivated by another political project (see below), had sought to persuade Garcetti *not* to seek the death penalty against Simpson. Two months later, project proponents were again angered – this time by defense attempts to downplay the significance of domestic violence in the case. First, Simpson's attorneys had attempted to recode the incidents as "domestic discord." Secondly, they had even attempted to exclude evidence of these incidents from the trial, arguing that they did not constitute evidence of murder.[56] Throughout the media, of course, there was widespread discussion surrounding this issue. Judge Ito would ultimately squelch the debate by allowing into evidence only about a dozen of the nearly sixty incidents originally offered by the prosecution.[57] Midway through the prosecution's presentation of its case in chief, Joan Rivers would host an episode of *Larry King Live* that explored the trial "from a [white] woman's point of view."[58] Finally, to the chagrin of many project proponents, spousal abuse expert Lenore Walker would explain on ABC's *Good Morning America* why she planned to testify for the defense: Simpson, she felt, did not fit the typical profile of a batterer who then commits murder.[59]

That Walker ultimately never testified for the defense speaks to the fate awaiting project proponents at the trial's end. As allegations of police corruption and incompetence worked to refocus the legal proceedings, domestic violence again moved to the background. By the time the defense began its case in chief, the attorneys deemed Walker's testimony unnecessary – the verdicts would not turn on the question of domestic violence. Indeed, when jurors were asked to explain the not-guilty verdicts they delivered on October 3, one of the black women, Brenda Moran, told reporters that she had considered evidence of domestic violence to be "irrelevant" to the case (Abramson 1996, p. 19). This denunciation of project efforts obviously struck many proponents like a solid blow. Although Kim Gandy, executive vice president of the National Organization of Women, would say that "the media attention to the trial has brought domestic violence to the forefront,"[60] other proponents would have difficulty finding a silver lining in the verdicts' dark cloud. A group of battered women, for example, would tell CNN they all felt Simpson was guilty and that the verdicts had sent a dangerous message: batterers can literally get away with murder.[61]

Although the formal goals of the Domestic Violence project are distinct from those of the next – the Black "Other" project – proponents of the two projects, as we shall see below, had similar reactions to trial observers who might question Simpson's guilt.

The Black "Other" project

LARRY KING: So you had decided right there O. J. was not guilty?
JUROR BRENDA MORAN: Well, I did, but when Johnny Cochran [*sic*] started doing rhymes, you know, putting things in phrases that I could understand,

it was all over. There was no way I'd vote guilty. Had the prosecution done some sort of nursery rhyme or something, they may have had a chance.[62]

The above exchange between CNN's Larry King and black juror Brenda Moran never actually occurred. It was scripted by a comedian and then prominently displayed on an anti-Simpson website following the announcement of the verdicts. I chose to begin this section by quoting the exchange because it echoes an important ideological assumption underlying the Black "Other" project: "blacks" are less intelligent than "we" are. Throughout the Simpson case, project proponents would invoke "black otherness" – ignorance, tribalism, and savagery – in order to affirm their own superiority and, of course, their own understandings of case-related developments. More explicit invocations were frequently couched in jokes like the one quoted above,[63] while more implicit ones framed the mainstream news narratives constructed and circulated by newsworkers. Indeed, these socially located men and women may or may not have been conscious of their own ideological contributions to the project.

Nearly half a century ago, Frantz Fanon's (1967) *Black Skin, White Masks* posited a classic psychological interpretation of black–white relations: blacks and whites experience one another as "Others," as opposites essential for defining who one *is*, and by default, who one is *not*. Fanon roots this Manichean opposition in the dynamics set in motion by the fact of slavery, where "white" became associated with "master" and "black" with "servant:"

Out of slavery the Negro burst into the lists where his masters stood. Like those servants who are allowed once every year to dance in the drawing room, the Negro is looking for a prop. The Negro has not become a master. When there are no longer slaves, there are no longer masters. (p. 219)

Contemporary depictions of blacks as inferior stem from this primordial opposition, from white efforts to reinforce what amounts to a superiority complex (Bulhan 1985).

Over the years, other scholars picked up on this central dialectic in their own efforts to explain the intractability of racial oppression. Jordan's (1968) *White Over Black*, for example, exhaustively explored "American" attitudes about "the Negro" from 1550 until 1812. Echoing Fanon, he argued that the doubts the English faced about their own role as a civilized people prompted them to cast "the Negro" as a savage Other,[64] who by way of contrast, worked to affirm the civility of the English in their own minds: "From the first, Englishmen tended to set Negroes over against themselves, to stress what they conceived to be radically contrasting qualities of color, religion, and style of life, as well as animality and a peculiarly potent sexuality" (p. 43). Soon thereafter, of course, this distinction would prove particularly useful in justifying the role of Africans in US slavery.[65]

When mass media finally emerged on the scene, the transmission of these images of the "Other" would be greatly accelerated. D. W. Griffith's 1915 racist epic, *The Birth of a Nation*, for example, mass communicated the potent black stereotypes of "buck" (i.e., the brutal, hypersexual male), "mammy" (i.e., the stoic, earthy female), and "buffoon" (i.e., the comic, bumbling idiot). This cinematic spectacle powerfully dramatized the emergence of a new America, an America where the Ku Klux Klan rose to protect white womanhood from the sexual advances of black men,[66] where North and South healed their Civil War wounds and created a new union, a white union, to combat the growing political threat of black emancipation. Celebrated by President Woodrow Wilson, denounced by the National Association for the Advancement of Colored People (NAACP), and viewed by millions, the film exploited many of the same ideological assumptions that would (re)activate the Black "Other" project eighty years later.[67]

Over the years, Omi and Winant (1994) argue, racial projects have evolved in terms of the types of knowledge used to legitimate them. Early projects, such as the one Jordan (1968) describes and the one D. W. Griffith romanticizes, were primarily justified in terms of religion – that is, English = Christian = white = civilized, Negro = Heathen = black = savage. When science began to replace religion as *the* rational system of knowledge, studies of cranial capacity, IQ, and genetic predisposition were commissioned to (re)affirm the natural superiority of whites over blacks. Finally, confrontational struggles for group rights in the turbulent 1960s led to a more explicitly political encoding of race, one where inequality was more commonly understood in structural terms.

But as the policy recommendations in Herrnstein and Murray's (1994) bestseller, *The Bell Curve*, demonstrate,[68] the rationalizations of earlier periods are still very much alive. Indeed, many of today's social commentators cheerfully disregard decades of sociological findings about the structural causes of inequality and embrace, by default, what amounts to essentialist rationalizations. Note Dinesh D'Souza's (1995) reasoning concerning black intelligence:

Most people, myself included, do not want to live in a racial caste society. Yet *The Bell Curve* makes a strong case that cannot be ignored. Whatever the book's shortcomings, it remains an undisputed fact that the fifteen-point IQ difference between blacks and whites has remained roughly constant for more than three quarters of a century, even though the environmental conditions for African Americans has vastly improved during that period. (p. 475)

Large segments of the white public apparently shared D'Souza's convictions about this "undisputed fact." In a survey conducted immediately after the 1992 Los Angeles rebellion, Bobo et al. (1992) found that 44 percent of white respondents perceived blacks to be less intelligent than whites.

Nonetheless, in the current US racial order, overt expressions of racism are generally frowned upon or, at least, deemed "controversial." Although many may privately harbor rather racist ideas about "Other" groups, their public articulations about related issues are more acceptably framed through the use of "codewords" (Omi and Winant 1994). Stuart Hall (1990) refers to this practice as "inferential" racism:

> those apparently naturalised representations of events and situations relating to race, whether "factual" or "fictional," which have racist premises and propositions inscribed in them as a set of *unquestioned assumptions*. These enable racist statements to be formulated without ever bringing into awareness the racist predicates on which the statements are grounded. (p. 13; emphasis original)

Indeed, when we explore how the Black "Other" project was (re)activated by the Simpson case – how project proponents circulated age-old notions of black ignorance, tribalism, and savagery – we find the unmistakable traces of inferential racism at work.

(Re)activating the project

The Black "Other" project, unlike the Domestic Violence project, would stumble out of the starting blocks. Early traces of the project were rather sparse, building to a crescendo of circulation only as revelations began to appear about race's impending role in the trial. Although racial implications of the case had breached the media agenda almost immediately after the murders,[69] they seemed to explode onto the scene after July 17, 1994, when reports surfaced about defense plans to argue that racial prejudice prompted LAPD Detective Mark Fuhrman to plant evidence against Simpson.[70] These reports were based on an article that appeared in the July 25 issue of *The New Yorker* entitled, "An Incendiary Defense." In the article, reporter Jeffrey Toobin described the pending defense strategy as "surprising" and "dangerous" (p. 56), but noted that "the race card may be the only one in Simpson's hand" (p. 59). The suggestion, of course, was that Simpson's attorneys might somehow use this "race card" to overcome what seemed to be an overwhelming case against the defendant. Moreover, this "card" was "dangerous" because its use "threatens the tender peace of the city of Los Angeles" (p. 59). Translation: black trial observers (and jurors) – those who were most likely to have been incited to participate in the recent Los Angeles riots (see Hunt 1997) – are incapable of resisting this "card," its call to embrace emotion over rationality.

A lengthy succession of opinion polls soon followed, underscoring an apparent divide in black–white understandings of the case, one that seemed to (re)confirm white fears about the potency of the "race card" (for example, see table 1). Numerous articles and broadcast programs were devoted to understanding the apparent tribalism that prompted so many black observers to question Simpson's guilt, a guilt that most (rational) people accepted. A January 13 courtroom showdown between Johnnie Cochran and Christopher Darden over the use of the "n-word" (i.e., "nigger") – Darden's argument that its use would blind the jury to the "evidence," Cochran's response that the prosecutor's argument insulted black intelligence – captured the headlines. At issue, of course, was Detective Fuhrman's alleged use of the epithet and his possible racial animus. Several media analysts questioned the relevance of the issue, noting that the charges against Fuhrman seemed exaggerated.[71] To some observers, black support for a defendant who had little to do with "the black community" seemed puzzling.[72] Others found the answer for this tribalism in black suspicions about the criminal justice system.[73] Humor was also used to underscore the significance of black ignorance and, of course, its widespread prevalence (i.e., as per the polls). As the mock Larry King interview quoted above would later make fun of Juror Brenda Moran, a *Saturday Night Live* joke that aired during the prosecution's case in chief effectively questioned the intelligence of anyone who might question Simpson's guilt. To wild audience cheers, a white male delivered this line during the program's spoof of the news, *Weekend Update*: "Dismissed juror Jeanette Harris revealed this week that the jury is mired in dissension, divided into two groups: those who believe Simpson is guilty, and those who are just plain stupid."[74] The joke was premised on Harris' recent statement that she had not been very impressed with the prosecution's case. In short, what the black ex-juror had actually "revealed" to reporters was her own inclusion among the "just plain stupid" group. Those who "got" the joke were invited, by way of contrast, to celebrate their own superiority (cf. Berger 1993).

The ideological assumptions undergirding the Black "Other" project, of course, would be (re)energized by the not-guilty verdicts a majority black jury rendered on October 3, 1995. Throughout the media that day, a powerful juxtaposition was highlighted: in split screen after split screen, images of black trial observers (distastefully) celebrating the verdicts collided with images of white trial observers (more appropriately) expressing their disappointment (see chapter 1). Indeed, validating

Toobin's earlier warning about black irrationality, about the "race card's" threat to reason, Los Angeles District Attorney Gil Garcetti reacted to the verdicts with this statement:

We are all of us profoundly disappointed with the verdicts. We want to hear from the jurors before we make any other comments concerning their decision today. But it was clear, at least it is to me, and I think other members of the prosecution team, that this was an emotional trial, *apparently their decision was based on emotion that overcame the reason.* (Emphasis added)[75]

Garcetti's comments echoed a barrage of jury bashing that would home in on the jury's intelligence (i.e., the lack thereof). For example, former Los Angeles prosecutor Vincent Bugliosi, a fiery anti-Simpson trial analyst who appeared throughout the case on CNBC's *Rivera Live,* later described the jury as one that "did not have too much intellectual firepower."[76] And Marcia Clark, you will recall, had referred to the jury as a bunch of "moon rocks." My claim that perceptions like these were racially coded seems supported by common representations of the jury following the verdicts. That is, to project proponents, the jury became "a black jury," one that had nullified prosecution evidence in the name of emotionalism and/or racial solidarity. It was as if the non-black jurors had suddenly disappeared from the deliberation process. But they had not, of course, and the final verdicts were unanimous. Nonetheless, some analysts lamented the dismissal of juror Francine Florio-Bunten – a white female – as a juror who may have been able to comprehend the prosecution's complicated DNA evidence, whose vote for conviction would have at least produced a hung jury.

While black trial observers were scrutinized throughout the case for any evidence that might support key project assumptions, media depictions of Simpson offered him up as proof incarnate. For example, Toobin's (1996) post-verdict book, *The Run of His Life,* begins by firmly establishing Simpson's "ignorance." That is, before the book's prologue, before even its table of contents, Toobin presents without commentary the following letter from Simpson to his ex-wife:[77]

Well, it seems that the worst part is behind us. I want you to know that whatever you might think to the contrary *I'v* taken full *responcibility* for this. It *happen* and I'm doing everything possible to assure it *doe'nt* happen *again.* But sooner or later we must *starte* with our future. I *love* our time last weekend. I know to you it may not have been much but it showed we can get along.

I love you and losing you is the only thing that *madder* to me. So lets not forget the past. Let's work together (for the first time) to improve the *futurr live* together. *Know manner* what I love you. O. J. (Emphasis added)

That Toobin intended to set the stage for his readers by first establishing Simpson's "ignorance" is clear. For Toobin, it seems, the spelling errors were central to his rendering of "who" Simpson "is." Otherwise, he would not have displayed them so prominently at the front of the book. Indeed, forty-eight pages into the book Toobin finally describes Simpson as someone who "received virtually no education" in college, who can "barely write a grammatical sentence" (p. 48). So despite Simpson's movie and broadcasting career, despite *Business Marketing's* 1992 description of him as a business "genius," the wealthy celebrity is unmasked by Toobin as an illiterate hoax. This public "disrobing" of Simpson seemed to resonate nicely with other project assumptions the case invoked from the beginning.

For example, lurid details about Simpson's and his ex-wife's alleged sex life began circulating throughout the media soon after the murders (especially the tabloid press). Many of these accounts, like those originating in Faye Resnick's (1994) "tell-all" *Diary of a Private Life Interrupted* (released in mid October), invoked and seemed to fetishize images of the hypersexual black male. Indeed, Resnick claimed in her book that Brown-Simpson had told her few men could sexually satisfy her like Simpson. Similarly, Resnick's account of the alleged affair between Brown-Simpson and black football star and Simpson protégé, Marcus Allen, recalled stereotypes of the massive black phallus.[78] Without qualification, the *Star* reprinted Resnick's claim: "She recalls how Nicole was walking along the beach in Laguna, Calif., when she picked up a piece of driftwood that had been washed ashore. 'This is the size of Marcus Allen,' she grinned."[79] Interestingly, Resnick does not report that Brown-Simpson shared such information with her about other (white) male companions. For example, similar information was not circulated about Keith Zlomsowitch, the white male with whom Simpson observed his ex-wife having oral sex.

Beneath the project's (re)affirmation of these potent stereotypes about black male hypersexuality, it seems, were more foundational notions of the black male (e.g., Simpson) as animal, as savage beast. The grisly nature of the Bundy murders, of course, facilitated this comparison in the minds of project proponents. Vivid accounts of Simpson's physical abuse of his ex-wife only sharpened the image. Throughout the media, for example, reports of a 1993 911-incident depicted an enraged, out-of-control Simpson who could be heard ranting and raving for some unexplained reason in the background. Indeed, a March 29, 1995 episode of ABC's *Primetime Live* portrayed Simpson as something of a Dr. Jekyll and Mr. Hyde character who, although he may appear civilized in public, is "on occasion" transformed into a savage beast behind closed doors (see chapter 7). In the following excerpt, host Diane Sawyer is informed about this "other side" of Simpson that his ex-wife described to police as "like an animal":

SAWYER: What did you as a veteran of a number of these calls over the years think is the most important thing on that tape?

OFFICER: First of all, if you listen to the tape, um, ah, she, Nicole Brown describes this, ah, *other side* of Mr. Simpson – this rage that he gets into on occasion.

NICOLE: He gets a very *animalistic* look in him. All his veins pop out his eyes are *black*, just *black*, cold, *like an animal*. I mean, very, very weird. And at the end it just scared me. (Emphasis added)

While Brown-Simpson's depiction of Simpson may have been driven by a genuine fear, *Primetime*'s framing of the image worked to buttress central assumptions of the Black "Other" project.

Simpson's own physician, Robert Huizenga, inadvertently affirmed this image of Simpson's "other side" in his efforts to defuse it. With a rather telling analogy, Huizenga testified that Simpson was not as agile as he looked: although he "had the body of Tarzan," he "walked like Tarzan's grandfather." Indeed, Simpson's (black) body was put on display throughout the trial, most notably when photographs of him sitting only in his briefs were presented to the world by defense attorneys who sought to establish that he had none of the bruises or scratches that would result from a fierce struggle.

Simpson's "other side," of course, had also been implied by *Time*'s infamous darkening of the football star's LAPD mug shot taken shortly after his arrest.[80] On the cover, the magazine's name and the feature article's otherwise ambiguous title – "An American Tragedy" – were superimposed over Simpson's shaded body, confining it to a murky background. The effect, Seward Barry (1997) argues, was the creation of a visually "antagonistic" cover that worked to "emotionally" distance Simpson from the reader (p. 152). Moreover, by visually invoking stereotypes of the lurking threat of black violence (e.g., use of the retouched mug shot), the nature of the "tragedy" noted in the title was specified. As Seward Barry (1997) put it, "*Time*'s cover, in fact, lives up to its headline by suggesting a metaphor of the ambiguous 'American Tragedy,' but it seems to be a tragedy of stereotypically black versus white mired in bloody violence" (pp. 152–3). This "tragedy," of course, was all the more distressing because the alleged target of Simpson's rage, Nicole Brown-Simpson, symbolized the standard for white womanhood. Note how the *Los Angeles Times* reported the reaction of a woman friend shortly after she learned of Brown-Simpson's murder:[81] "She's blonde, she's tanned, she's absolutely beautiful," Goodfriend said. "I'm in shock."

While mainstream articulations of the Black "Other" project were generally presented through implication, insinuation, or code, more overt expressions of the project's tenets circulated freely on the margins of society. In *I Want to Tell You*, Simpson (1995) presents what he purports to be several racist letters he received while in prison. One letter (p. 116), for example, rather explicitly explained Simpson's "other side" in terms of his race:[82]

Filthy Murdering N---ER MOTHER F--KER S. O. B. COKE HEAD But you're not the only worthless n---er in this country. 98% of you are UNTERMENSCH S--T. The Ugliest species on the planet. UGLY HAIR, like wire, pig ears, primate noses, bulbous lips, and your ugly blackness. Unconscionable, irresponsible, dysfunctional, immoral, degenerate, perverted mother f--kers. The whole race is of the same kind. You deserve the gas chamber.

-- Anonymous
Postmark: Belleville, IL.

Similar sentiments were expressed on numerous internet websites over the course of the trial. The introduction to "Micetrap's O. J. Simpson Pages,"[83] for example, also had disparaging remarks for Jews and "race traitors:"

This page is a sarcastic tribute to a person that has done so many great things for our people in the past few years! O. J. not only murdered a race traitor – Nicole Simpson, but he is also accused of murdering a Jew – Ron Goldman! With these violent acts, this savage barbarian took the lives of two individuals that broke the greatest laws of nature and were no longer deserving of life! This animal single handedly slaughtered them and is worthy of at least a little admiration for his deeds. Now that there is one less nigger loving slag and money grabbing kike in this world we can sit back and watch the old Hertz Rental car commercials with "The Juice" as we giggle and snicker. We must congratulate this monkey for a job well done! Hooray for O. J. The Barbarian!

In short, proponents of the Black "Other" project used the Bundy murders to (re)affirm a timeless "truth" about blacks: "You can take the nigger out of the jungle, but you can't take the jungle out of the nigger." Or as duCille (1996) put it, "Illuminating Simpson's blackness, his 'dark side,' his hidden essential self became a way of explaining the crime, which at moments seemed less that he might have murdered two people than that he had fooled millions" (p. 137). Alas, it is this essentializing association that so concerned proponents of our final political project, the "Just-Us" system project.

The "Just-Us" system project

Racism, the promotion of white supremacy, is the primary reason why African Americans have served as the mudsills of American society. The need to respect constitutional government has been so twisted and perverted in the name of this objective that it is no wonder that many African-Americans long regarded law and order as an instrument for their repression.[84]

The above words were penned by no less a figure than Mary Frances Berry, the fiery Chairperson of the United States Commission on Civil Rights. In her book *Black Resistance, White Law*, the black legal scholar traces racism in the US legal system back to the arrival of the first twenty Africans at Jamestown in 1619. She then proceeds to lay out this system's history from the earliest days of the nation to the Los Angeles "rebellion" of 1992 (p. 232), a history replete with example after example of white manipulation of the law, of black repression by the police, and of the status quo's resiliency. The facts of this history, she argues, are what ultimately breed black distrust of the legal system.

In the early days of the Simpson case, of course, this black distrust was captured by a lengthy succession of opinion polls. A CBS/*New York Times* poll taken about a month after the murders,[85] you will recall, found that more than half of the black respondents – about 55 percent – felt the criminal justice system was biased against blacks; only about 20 percent thought it was fair. The findings for white respondents were almost the exact reverse: less than 20 percent of these respondents felt the system was biased against blacks, while about 60 percent considered it fair. This disparity in black/white perceptions might be (and frequently is) explained in terms of black paranoia. True, proponents of the paranoia thesis argue, racism in the legal system was once an unfortunate artifact of our nation's history, but in today's post-Civil Rights era these flaws have been corrected and the system is now more in tune with the spirit of the Constitution: justice is "colorblind." Black critics of the system are just holding on to out-dated answers in desperate attempts to make sense of the troubling trends that continue to afflict their community (cf. Collier and Horowitz 1997).

Of course, we can quickly resolve the question of whether the Constitution was originally intended to be "colorblind." It was not. It was written by wealthy white males who sought to create a state where they would be free from the tyranny of the English monarchy, where they would be free to practice a tyranny of their own at the expense of the nonwhite and the dispossessed. Indeed, as part of a compromise between the North and South, African slaves were to be counted as only three-fifths of a person (cf. Berry 1994). The Constitution was profoundly "color-sighted" from the beginning. But what of the claim that the legal system is nonetheless "colorblind" today?

Black legal scholar Derrick Bell (1992) provides us with a rather sardonic expression of the legal system's contemporary "color *sightedness.*" In his book *Faces at the Bottom of the Well*, he imagines the mass landing of extraterrestrials on January 1, 2000, along the East Coast of the United States. These beings are soon discovered to be "Space Traders" who have a startling proposition for the nation. In exchange for all sorts of precious resources and riches that the country sorely needs, they propose to take all of the African Americans living in the United States with them back to their star system. Black Americans immediately view the visitors as "distinctly unpleasant, even menacing in appearance," and their proposal as "bad news"(p. 161). In contrast, white Americans find the visitors non-threatening, "practical, no-nonsense folks like regular Americans" (p. 161). Moreover, "long conditioned to discounting any statements of blacks unconfirmed by other whites" (p. 161), most white Americans seem to rally around the proposal. A lengthy national debate thus ensues. At one point, media reports reveal that US officials had tried through secret negotiations to persuade the Space Traders to accept just those African Americans "currently under the jurisdiction of the criminal justice system."[86] The negotiators had then tried to convince the visitors of the offer's value, noting that it amounted to a sizable chunk of the black population – "almost half of the black males in the twenty- to twenty-nine year-old age bracket" (p. 190).

Although the Space Traders would ultimately reject this offer, Bell's tale nonetheless makes an important point about the US "criminal justice system:" it disproportionately incarcerates black males. Far from just a contemporary phenomenon, this tendency to target black males has deep roots in American history – roots extending to at least the informal "justice" system that flourished throughout the Jim Crow era. As Miller (1996) notes,

In the "informal" justice system in the United States, the most extreme punishments and unjust procedures for blacks were never beyond tacit support of a substantial proportion of the white population well into this century. Castration, lynching, and other vigilante-type actions were characteristically reserved for citizens of color and provided the backdrop and collective memory against which the formal criminal justice system functioned when it came to blacks. (p. 53)

Thus many black observers today refuse to use the term "criminal *justice* system," opting instead for the more neutral term "criminal *law* system" (Elias and Schatzman 1996, p. 51; emphasis added). Others, underscoring the system's propensity to process their black compatriots, sarcastically refer to it as the "Just-Us" system.

Important observations are worth noting about the "Just-Us" system. First, black Americans are overrepresented at every stage of system processing, from arrest to incarceration. For example, while black Americans make up only about 12 percent of the US population, they account for more than 30 percent of all arrests,[87] 44 percent of all prisoners, and

40 percent of prisoners on death row (Mauer 1994). Indeed, their life-time chance of being incarcerated, is 16.2 percent, compared to only 2.5 percent for their white counterparts.[88] Black males, in particular face an incredible 28 percent chance of entering state or Federal prison in their life times, compared to only a 4.4 percent chance for white males.[89] Accordingly, nearly a quarter of black males between the ages of twenty and twenty-nine are under the control of this system at any given time (i.e., prison, jail, probation, or parole). In short, this population is incarcerated in the United States at a rate almost five times that of its counterpart in South Africa just before the end of apartheid (Mauer 1994).

Much of this racial disparity, of course, can be attributed to police and prosecution practices. Spurred by national support for the "war on drugs," police departments tend to focus on "street" instead of "white-collar" crime (Miller 1996). This focus results in a targeting of inner-city areas where large portions of the black population reside. Moreover, at the prosecution stage, black defendants are often treated more harshly than white ones (Richey Mann 1987; Mauer 1994). Midway through the Simpson trial, a front-page *Los Angeles Times* article presented a classic example of how these factors combined to incarcerate a disproportion-ate share of Other-raced Americans.[90] Citing data from the National Institute on Drug Abuse, the article noted that white Americans make up about 68 percent of all those who had ever tried crack cocaine between 1991 and 1993, and about 54 percent of those who had used it in the previous year. But data from federal courts nationwide revealed that between 1992 and 1994 Other-raced defendants accounted for about 96 percent of the crack cases prosecuted. Similarly, only about 3 per-cent of the 8000 cases prosecuted by Los Angeles' District Attorney during the same period involved white defendants. The article also noted that a major racial disparity arises from *where* the case is prosecuted. In California, crack dealers convicted in state courts face a maximum five-year sentence, but often spend only about a year in jail. In Federal courts, however, convicted crack dealers face a mandatory ten-year sentence. No white defendant had been convicted of a crack offense in Los Angeles-area federal courts since Congress passed the stiffer man-datory sentence in 1986. That is, Other-raced defendants made up 100 percent of the cases prosecuted in the more punitive federal courts. "The Reality of a Racist Criminal Justice System," as Richey Mann's (1987) title asserts, is (re)affirmed with statistics like these.

But Orenthal James Simpson was clearly not the typical black defendant. When he was arrested, he was a wealthy celebrity who had seemingly enjoyed the goodwill of the Los Angeles Police Department in the past.[91] He even received what amounted to preferential treatment in the early stages of the case when, rather than arresting him once it was clear he was the prime suspect, officers actually negotiated with his attorney about when Simpson would turn himself in.[92] Despite this apparent incongruity between Simpson's experiences with the law and that of the typical black defendant, proponents of the "Just-Us" system project had ample reason to watch the case closely.

First, these observers knew all too well the abysmal record of prosecuting high-profile cases that Los Angeles' District Attorney had amassed in recent years. Project proponents were thus faced with the fear that this case, sure to be a high-profile one, might also become a win-at-all-costs, political vehicle for a District Attorney who would soon be seeking reelection. And although Simpson's image in the black community was somewhat ambiguous,[93] few welcomed an outcome that might add to the lingering bad taste of other recent, high-profile cases that had resulted in the downfall of prominent black men.[94] Although there would be debate about whether many of these defendants had actually deserved their fate, many observers were worried about the possible negative effects the cases might have on black youth in need of role models.

Secondly, and perhaps most importantly, the LAPD had a notorious history of policing the city's black community. Modelled after a paramilitary unit, infamous for its succession of racist police chiefs, and celebrated by America in the hit television series *Dragnet*, the LAPD had patrolled Los Angeles' inner-city over the years as if it were an occupied war zone (Davis 1990; Domanick 1994). Whether it was officers shooting a black woman in the back over a utility bill dispute,[95] Chief Daryl Gates' theory that black suspects were not like "normal" people because so many were dying from officer choke holds,[96] or the routine harassment of black motorists (including several celebrities),[97] black Angelenos had had more than enough experience with the LAPD to know what it was capable of. The fact that Chief Gates had finally been ousted in fallout over the Rodney King beating incident, and that a black chief from the outside had recently replaced him, did little to ameliorate black fears about a longstanding organizational culture that seemed firmly entrenched. This culture, which was vigorously supported by the Police Protective League, seemed to reflect the interests of a large contingent of white officers who, trained in the department's glory days, lived not in the city or in Los Angeles County, but in surrounding "white-flight" communities. The growing number of Other-raced officers within the department often found themselves at odds with this organizational culture, but with little power to do anything about it. In short, because this history was common knowledge among many (if not most) black residents of the city, it could not be ignored when it came time for them to confront the Simpson murder case. Indeed, it would prove to be an important component of the knowledge base used by proponents to (re)activate the "Just-Us" system project.

(Re)activating the project

Traces of key ideological assumptions underlying the "Just-Us" system project would begin to emerge shortly after the murders. Before the infamous Bronco chase, before Simpson was even officially identified as the prime suspect, *Los Angeles Sentinel* reporter Dennis Schatzman filed a scathing column on June 16, 1994 in which he accused the LAPD of reverting back to their "old habits" in the case (see chapter 6). Schatzman, like millions of others, had seen videotaped footage of police momentarily handcuffing Simpson upon his return from Chicago the day after the murders. The incident, Schatzman wrote, symbolized the racial double standard employed by law enforcement: "Think hard. How many times did you see convicted cannibal Jeffrey Dahmer[98] handcuffed during his well publicized arrest and subsequent trial? If you say 'none' then you get the prize."

Then, on June 17, the unthinkable happened. To an audible gasp, LAPD Commander David Gascon informed reporters that Simpson had not turned himself in as expected, that the football legend was now considered a fugitive from the law. Speculation that (black) gang members might be harboring Simpson eventually led Los Angeles' District Attorney to remind the public that aiding his escape was a crime. It also foreshadowed more explicit charges of black tribalism that would later follow in the case. But a few hours after the manhunt had begun, it was over. When a white couple told police they spotted Simpson and his friend A. C. Cowlings in a white Bronco, driving down a Southern California freeway, a surreal slow-speed pursuit ensued. Helicopters from a variety of local media provided aerial coverage of two black men fleeing from an ever-increasing cadre of Orange County Police, Los Angeles Sheriff's Department, California Highway Patrol, and LAPD squad cars. As such chases seemed to be an ever increasing staple of Los Angeles television news, city residents were quite familiar with them. Viewers knew, for example, that many of these chases had ended peacefully. But then they also knew that more than a few suspects had been wounded or killed in violent crashes – or by police bullets. And, of course, the brutal beating that had awaited Rodney King after his run from California Highway Patrol and LAPD officers was still a current topic of conversation. As the spectacle unfolded, television viewers heard many of Simpson's celebrity friends, several of them in tears, begging with the fugitive to turn himself in. It would have been impossible for project proponents to know – in the heat of the moment – whether the pursuit would end with Simpson being treated like the wealthy celebrity he was, or like so many other chases involving poor suspects, or worse yet, poor *and* black ones. That the chase ended peacefully in Simpson's Brentwood driveway might have momentarily allayed the concerns of project proponents. But subsequent events would prove to (re)activate these concerns with a passion.

In the weeks surrounding Simpson's preliminary hearing, a number of media programs began to explore the role race might play in the case. On June 27, for example, CNN's *World News* featured a call-in segment where viewers aired their views about the relevance of race in the case. On July 7, *Newsweek* writer Ellis Cose, himself a black male, told CNN's Charlie Rose that he did not feel race was an issue in the case, that it would be dangerous to read the case as symbolizing racial discrimination. And on July 11, CNN's *Larry King Live* explored whether the case would have garnered as much media attention if Simpson and his ex-wife had not been an interracial couple.

But it was not until after Toobin's July 17 revelation about the Fuhrman charges that a flurry of stories about race and the "Just-Us" system would blanket the media.[99] Community activist Mark Whitlock and retired Judge Ellen Morphonios, for example, disagreed on CNN's *Morning News* about whether the US judicial system is racist.[100] Meanwhile, opinion polls continued to show a major difference between the perceptions of white and black Americans about Simpson's guilt (see table 1, chapter 1). Many analysts tried to explain black doubt about Simpson's guilt by linking it to longstanding suspicions about the legal system.[101] On July 25, CNN's *Showbiz Today* aired a segment describing how "black leaders" are concerned that the Simpson case may result in the downfall of another black role model, an outcome that would prove detrimental to black youth. Finally, underscoring the political implications of the upcoming trial, reports appeared in the media concerning a July 19 meeting between local project proponents and District Attorney Gil Garcetti in which the activists had attempted to persuade Garcetti not to seek the death penalty against Simpson. Garcetti's later decision not to seek the death penalty, you will recall, was met with outrage by proponents of the Domestic Violence project.

As the case progressed toward trial, several developments would provide proponents of the "Just-Us" system project with fuel to power their cause. For example, lead LAPD Detective Philip Vannatter had testified during the preliminary hearing that he and three other detectives (including Mark Fuhrman) left the bloody Bundy crime scene to notify Simpson of his ex-wife's death. Upon arrival at Rockingham, the officers testified, Fuhrman spotted a speck of what appeared to be blood on Simpson's white Bronco, which was parked on the street. Fuhrman testified that this discovery alerted him to the possibility of additional victims inside the property. After unsuccessfully reaching anyone inside by telephone, Vannatter testified, he authorized Fuhrman to scale the walls. Only later did the lead detective receive a search warrant – after submitting a statement in which he told the judge that Simpson was out of town on an unplanned trip. However, because Vannatter knew at the time that the trip had been planned well in advance, Judge Lance Ito ruled on September 20 that the detective had acted with "at least reckless" disregard for the truth. Nonetheless, Ito allowed introduction of the Rockingham evidence, which included, of course, the bloody match to the crime-scene glove that Fuhrman testified he found behind the property. Ito's ruling and questions about police motives resulted in several media debates, including one between Simpson attorney Alan Dershowitz and former Attorney General Dick Thornburgh in which the Harvard law professor charged, to Thornburgh's obvious disdain, that police officers are trained at "testilying."[102] Then, as jury selection began in October of 1994, media reports examined the potential impact of defense claims that the prosecution was racially biased in their dismissal of potential black jurors.[103]

After the trial began in January of 1995, developments on the witness stand worked to (re)affirm the suspicions of project proponents. For example, media analysts awarded defense attorney Barry Scheck high marks for his dismantling of prosecution witness Dennis Fung in early April.[104] During cross-examination, Scheck had gotten the LAPD criminalist to admit to a number of questionable evidence collection, chain of custody, and storage practices that the defense attorney implied may have caused accidental or deliberate contamination. Issues such as Detective Vannatter's transportation of Simpson's reference blood vial to the crime scene, detectives' use of a blanket from the Bundy condominium to cover the bodies, and Fung's failure to change gloves between the collection of different blood stains, Scheck suggested, challenged the integrity of the physical evidence. Indeed, National Public Radio's *All Things Considered* for April 14 featured several black commentators who suggested that black trial observers may be reading these and similar developments as lending credibility to the defense's conspiracy theory.

Similarly, during the defense's case-in-chief the issue of EDTA would assume center stage. EDTA, an abbreviation for the chemical used to preserve blood reference samples, would be present in evidence stains if, as the defense alleged, police had planted or tampered with blood evidence in the case. On the morning of July 25, FBI agent Roger Martz corroborated the previous day's testimony of defense witness Frederic Rieders: he agreed that what appeared to be EDTA was found in evidence stains from the Bundy back gate and the socks collected from Simpson's bedroom. After a recess, however, the FBI agent qualified his earlier testimony and suggested that the amount of EDTA found was not significant.

Finally, project proponents were undoubtedly impressed with defense witness Herbert MacDonnell, a blood splatter expert who testified on August 1, 1995 that the patterning of blood stains on the socks collected from Simpson's bedroom indicating that blood had been pressed onto the socks instead of splattered. Moreover, the blood stains had seeped through one side of the socks to the other, suggesting that the blood was deposited on them when they were not being worn (i.e., a leg would have separated the two sides and prevented seepage). Defense attorneys, of course, combined this testimony with the EDTA findings to argue that blood was planted on the socks and that none of the other forensic evidence could thus be trusted.

But project proponents would not be provided with their "smoking gun" until the closing weeks of the case, when news reports began to appear about the existence of explosive audiotapes that might prove project proponents' claims about the "Just-Us" system. On August 14, 1995, for example, *Larry King Live* devoted an entire episode to newly revealed audio tapes – some of them recorded since the murders – on which Detective Fuhrman could be heard freely using the "n-word," as well as boasting about brutalizing and planting evidence against Other-raced suspects. Fuhrman, you will recall, had testified in mid-March that he had not used the word "nigger" in the past ten years. After a North Carolina judge was overruled by a state appellate court, Simpson's attorneys finally brought the tapes back to Los Angeles. On August 29, excerpts from the infamous tapes were played in court without the jury present. That evening, ABC's *World News Tonight*, reviewed the possible ramifications of the tapes, noting that Judge Ito would still have to rule on their admissibility. The following morning, the *Los Angeles Times* provided a transcript of the excerpts played in court. Many of the excerpts echoed key claims of "Just-Us" system project proponents. For example, Fuhrman reminisced about an LAPD that not only tolerated the brutalizing of black suspects but whose training officers set the example for how best to do so: "When I came on the job, all my training officers were big guys and knowledgeable. Some nigger'd get in their face, they just spin 'em around, choke 'em out until they dropped."[105] Judge Ito's ruling two days later permitted only two of the sixty-one excerpts to be played before the jury.[106] Outraged, Simpson's defense held a press conference to denounce the judge's decision; it was widely carried throughout the media.[107] A week later, September 6, Fuhrman returned to the courtroom to plead the Fifth Amendment to all of attorney Gerald Uelman's questions, including the one that undoubtedly rang most loudly in project proponents' ears: "Detective Fuhrman, did you plant or manufacture any evidence in this case?" However, still miffed by the severe restrictions Judge Ito had placed on the excerpts jurors might hear, the National Association for the Advancement of Colored People (NAACP) later that evening held a protest outside of the judge's courtroom.[108]

Conclusions

In many respects, we might most fruitfully understand the intense public interest in the Simpson case in terms of the opportunities and/or dangers it presented for proponents of the four political projects. As you will recall, I argued above that political projects are first and foremost about hegemony, that they are discourses aimed at either changing or reinforcing the existing balance of power in society. Each of the projects, with varying degrees of success, exploited the case to achieve proponents' desired political ends. In some instances, these ends were stated quite explicitly. In other instances, the ends remained implicit.

Proponents of the Celebrity Defendant project, for example, seized upon the Simpson case to expose what happens when criminal defendants have "too many" resources. Thus these proponents rallied for changes to the criminal justice system (e.g., the institution of non-unanimous verdicts, professional juries, pay disclosure for expert witnesses, etc.), changes that would work, in effect, to increase the conviction rate of "obviously guilty" defendants like Simpson. But when the District Attorney of a large urban area like Los Angeles can boast of a conviction rate well above 90 percent, we must ask ourselves what political interests are really being supported by such proposals.

Proposals to somehow neutralize the resources of criminal defendants conveniently overlook a simple fact: the state can (and typically does) outspend any defendant. Indeed, the prosecution in the Simpson case is estimated to have spent $9 million compared to about $6 million spent by Simpson (Coffey 1995). While Simpson was indeed privileged to benefit from the services of eleven attorneys, several investigators, and experts, the prosecution team had far superior resources: nine lawyers presented evidence in the case, dozens worked behind the scenes (Coffey 1995), and prosecutors could also enlist the investigative services of the LAPD, the Los Angeles Sheriff's Department, the FBI, the California Department of Justice, and Interpol. Moreover, some of these investigative services – as well as other consultant services[109] – were provided gratis and probably do not appear in the total figure spent by the prosecution.

In the final analysis, it seems, these proposals and omissions resonate with larger political interests.[110] While proponents of the Celebrity Defendant project were clearly preoccupied with exposing and neutralizing the extraordinary legal resources Simpson had at his disposal, they seemed less concerned with increasing the meager resources afforded the typical defendant. Revealing stories had appeared, of course, like a June 19, 1995 *Time* piece on the differences between Simpson's resources and those of most criminal defendants. But it would be a gross overstatement to say that the average defendant's financial hardships enjoyed anywhere near the amount of media attention that Simpson's privilege enjoyed throughout the case.[111] Nor did the case spearhead a movement aimed at increasing the resources of the average criminal defendant. Instead, the Simpson case – atypical by most accounts – had conveniently become *the* example for what happens when criminal defendants have too many resources. Ideologically, the project proposals were just a stone's throw away from other proposals that would limit the *rights* of criminal defendants in the name of "the war on crime," "the war on drugs," or "victim's rights." Proponents of these related projects avidly trade Constitutional protections against state persecution for a decrease in the (small) number of guilty defendants who actually go free.[112] Here, of course, is where the Celebrity Defendant and Black "Other" projects intersect.

In recent years, political projects like "the war on crime," "the war on drugs," and "victim's rights" have sparked a financially profitable[113] explosion in US prison incarcerations – especially among the poor and people of color. Because the Simpson case supported the illusion of a broken criminal justice system that routinely allows the guilty to go free, it worked to (re)affirm the resolve of those who benefit most from the coercive imposition of law and order: white Americans, especially white elites (cf. Berry 1994; Hacker 1992; Harris 1995; Miller 1996). Indeed, as Toni Morrison (1997) later put it in her case-related anthology, *Birth of a Nation'hood*, Simpson became a stand-in for an entire race of Others that requires constant "correction, incarceration, censoring, silencing" (p. xxviii). In this sense, the Celebrity Defendant and Black "Other" projects are hegemonic discourses aimed at reinforcing the status quo (i.e., the skyrocketing incarceration of Other-raced criminal defendants/the "othering" of black Americans) and, by default, the position of those groups already in power (i.e., white elites).

In contrast, we can identify both the Domestic Violence and "Just-Us" system projects as counter-hegemonic discourses aimed at disrupting the status-quo treatment of women and black Americans, respectively. While the hegemonic projects generally complemented one another throughout the case (i.e., guilty celebrity buys acquittal/ignorant blacks support guilty savage), the counter-hegemonic projects openly competed with one another for affirmation. That is, the visibility and legitimacy of domestic violence as a first-order social problem was largely (re)fueled by the belief that Simpson was a batterer whose abuse had escalated to murder. Conversely, the validity of claims about bias in the criminal justice system was (re)energized by developments pointing toward Simpson's innocence. Theoretically, of course, Simpson *could* be a wife-abuser who did not go on to murder his ex-wife. Alternatively, he *could* be a double murderer who was framed by the LAPD. But neither of these possibilities resonated as neatly with the aims of the two projects. Thus proponents of the Domestic Violence project were motivated to believe in Simpson's guilt, while proponents of the "Just-Us" system project wanted to believe in his innocence. In this sense, a positive development for one project was necessarily a negative one for the other. Indeed, following the not-guilty verdicts, the head of NOW's Los Angeles branch, Tammy Bruce, would blanket the media with her denunciations of both the verdicts and the largely black and female jury that had rendered them.[114] Said Bruce: "This jury decided to not do what it was impaneled to do. They decided these two lives were expendable, and they decided to move through the hatred and bigotry that Johnnie Cochran asked them to. And they are . . . an embarrassment to this city."[115] Although NOW would censure Bruce for comments that ultimately questioned the intelligence of the jurors, an unfortunate wound had been reopened.[116] Project proponents had once again driven an "unproductive" wedge between "feminists" and "women of color," as legal scholar Kimberle Crenshaw (1997) put it, by dismissing the jury as "simplistically and unjustifiably race-conscious" (p. 145). In the final analysis, the ideological underpinnings of this easy dismissal uncomfortably resonated with assumptions invoked by the Black "Other" project.

Although not every follower of the case may have considered her/himself a proponent of one of the four projects, the possibilities the case presented for each project nonetheless guaranteed a high degree of public interest. This was because the media that covered the case could tap into a glut of project spokespersons ready and willing to offer provocative (i.e., profitable) commentary. In other words, just by engaging in the day-to-day activities of newswork – the soliciting of expert analyses, the identification of salient case "facts" – newsworkers routinely constructed and circulated O. J. narratives that resonated with one or more of the projects. The result? There was a saturation of news coverage surrounding project-related issues, coverage that was driven both by project interests *and* the logic of media businesses. Simply put, the interaction of these forces set a public agenda where the Simpson case occupied the very top (see chapter 1).

In this chapter, I have focussed primarily on the political projects that worked to catapult the Simpson case to the top of the public agenda. Our understanding of this ascension would be incomplete, however, if we did not also explore the contributions of those women and men who covered the case for the news media, who constructed and circulated many of the O. J. narratives we regard as "truth," but who *may have been* project proponents themselves. How did the day-to-day activities of these newsworkers combine with the political interests saturating the case? This is the question that drives the next chapter.

Part II

News construction

3 Press rites and O. J. wrongs: behind the scenes at "Camp O. J."

> Few of us in the press corps were ever rational about it. The case devoured our waking hours and invaded our dreams. After the not-guilty verdict, many trial reporters were physically sick for weeks – earaches, flu, back pain. Was it just exhaustion – or something else? Many left the newspaper business altogether. (I am one of them.)[1]

I was present at the downtown Los Angeles courthouse on the morning the not-guilty verdicts were read, observing the hurried activities of newsworkers. The Simpson case was clearly the news story to end all news stories. Two-hundred and fifty phone lines[2] had been installed in the court's twelfth-floor pressroom to accommodate the day-to-day communications needs of the 1,159 credentialed newsworkers who covered the case (Coffey 1995). In addition to the suffocating presence of US media, news operations from more than a dozen foreign nations had also sent newsworkers to cover the latest developments.[3] Of the fifty-eight highly coveted seats in Judge Ito's courtroom, twenty-four had been set aside for this corps of newsworkers (Elias and Schatzman 1996). Seven of these seats had been permanently assigned to the *Los Angeles Times* (see chapter 5), two book authors, and four other mainstream news operations. The remaining seventeen seats were rotated between two other book authors and thirty-nine other news operations.[4] One of these less-favored news operations was the largest black-owned newspaper in the West, the *Los Angeles Sentinel* (see chapter 6). Interested members of the public regularly lined up during the predawn hours to enter a lottery for a chance at the few remaining seats that were not given to family members of the victims and defendant or members of the legal teams. This was "Camp O. J." – the $1 million dollar media complex of cable, scaffolding, and newsworkers[5] – minutes before the "Trial of the Century"'s climax.

As I scanned the scene, the telescoping transmitters of satellite trucks, which were poised to instantly feed video and audio narratives about the verdicts to any point on the globe, obscured my view of the skyline.

Some eighty miles of cable had been run throughout the encampment connecting these transmission facilities and television crews.[6] Media-owned helicopters circled directly overhead. Newsworkers not lucky (or privileged) enough to be inside the courtroom on this particular day huddled around the outside of the courthouse and just inside its doors. Camera operators scurried to position themselves for the best shots of the trial principals who risked entering through the front of the court-house. Television newsworkers struggled to block out the din of the grow-ing crowd – in which black spectators were clearly overrepresented – so they could hear control room directions in their tiny ear pieces. Print newsworkers, less pressed for time, casually canvassed the crowds for (literally) anyone willing to offer their reactions to the historic moment that was about to unfold. In small coalescing circles of interviewers and interviewees, thoughts about the impending verdicts were elicited, sup-plied, and recorded for insertion into the news narratives that would soon dominate the airwaves and printed press for days to come.

Then Judge Ito uttered the words all were waiting hear: "Okay, um, back on the record in the Simpson matter." Interviews came to a halt. An eerie silence replaced the rumble of the crowd. The anxiety visible on faces in the crowd was also evident on the faces of many newsworkers. This was an important moment for all. It had come after a lengthy trial in which the presiding judge had twice decided to ban and then rein-state live television coverage of the courtroom proceedings.[7] When the words, "not-guilty" finally blared from the monitors set up outside the courthouse and the portable receivers carried by people in the crowds, a loud cheer erupted. I watched as several newsworkers momentarily dropped their heads before frantically resuming their newsgathering activities. Apparently, the reaction in the twelfth-floor press room was similar: "Stunned silence reigned for a few minutes, before the mass of reporters recovered their equilibrium and quickly began filing urgent stories."[8]

The thesis of this chapter, while perhaps somewhat banal, has inter-esting implications for later chapters. Like the public at-large, I propose, the newsworkers who covered the Simpson media event had a heavy investment in its outcome. That is, as people who are (and have been) positioned at particular intersections of gender, class, race, and sexuality, most newsworkers had a stake in one or more of the political projects (re)activated by the Simpson case (see chapter 2). In some instances, this stake was likely an unconsciousness one, one that nonetheless re-fracted how newsworkers understood the case and, consequently, framed the narratives they constructed and circulated about it. But in other instances, the stakes were more obvious as newsworkers unabashedly became project proponents themselves, explicitly (re)affirming these projects in their news narratives. This chapter critically examines the ideological stances of newsworkers who covered the Simpson media event for traces of the four political projects outlined in part I. What do newsworker accounts of their own practices during the trial tell us about the relative influence of the various projects?

On the basis of several interviews with newsworkers who covered the case, broadcast interviews with newsworkers, and memoirs about the case, I explore this question in some detail. In this sense, the present chapter zeroes in on a critical determinant of the "O. J. narratives" box depicted in the theoretical model proposed in chapter 1 (see figure 9) – the producers of the narratives that have been privileged by mass-circulation. The remainder of part II (chapters 4, 5, and 6) consists of case studies that examine the manner in which newsworker biases shaped the narratives they constructed and circulated.

As former *Chicago Tribune* reporter Jessica Seigel notes in the quote that begins this chapter, covering the Simpson case undoubtedly meant long hours, few breaks, and physical exhaustion for the day-to-day trial reporters. But many of the newsworkers who "left the newspaper business altogether" after the verdicts may have done so, as she put it, because of "something else." This "something else," it seems, points to the various investments that people – newsworkers included – had in the trial outcome, and in the political projects (re)activated by the case. To understand how these investments might have been managed by newsworkers covering the Simpson media event, we must first come to terms with the nature of the case as "newswork."

O. J. as newswork

Newswork is a peculiar endeavor. Located at the intersection of Fourth Estate ideals about maintaining an informed citizenry, hegemonic concerns with surveillance, and industrial preoccupations with profitability, the day-to-day activities of journalists are necessarily shaped by a conflicting array of interests and expectations. While it is essentially true that the "ideas of the ruling class in every epoch are the ruling ideas" (Marx 1972), it is a gross oversimplification to say that what we observe in the news is directly transmitted to us from these ruling elites. In other words, conspiracy theories of news construction – while they may seem to aptly account for the hegemonic bias of news texts – overlook the tangle of often conflicting inputs that drive the process (see Hall et al. 1978). Indeed, the production of news texts is a complex process shaped by five critical factors: (1) the identification of "newsworthy" events; (2) the objectivity ideal; (3) journalistic routines; (4) the socio-political climate, and (5) business constraints.

"Newsworthy" events

Media scholars have long argued that "news" is not the result of events that simply assert themselves. "News" must first be recognized and defined as such by someone (i.e., newsworkers) on the basis of certain values (Lippman 1922; Epstein 1973). These values, often unwritten, are nonetheless generally agreed upon and basic to the journalistic trade. They include qualities such as timeliness (e.g., "breaking" news events), unexpectedness (e.g., accidents or disasters), and impact (e.g., economics, politics or national security). Taken together, these values help define what newsworkers mean by "newsworthiness," a rather subjective meta-quality that separates "news" from other more mundane events.

The Bundy murders and subsequent Simpson case were clearly "newsworthy" events. Apart from the various news values satisfied by the events (e.g., timeliness and unexpectedness), they represented a class of events that invariably qualifies as "news:" crime. As Emile Durkheim argued many years ago, crime serves an important function in society: it defines the boundaries of normative behavior (Durkheim 1964), while punishment of transgressors works to reinforce our belief in the rules (Vogt 1993). Crime is recognized as "news" to the degree that it challenges these rules and is perceived as a threat to the established order. Subsequent coverage of crime stories typically takes the form of morality plays about the "transgression of normative boundaries, followed by investigation, arrest, and social retribution in terms of the sentencing of the offender" (Hall et al., 1978, p. 67). This ritualistic cycle of threat, uncertainty, and retribution seems to motivate newsworkers to privilege crime above all other events and viewers to pay an inordinate amount of attention to crime narratives. As Osborne (1995) notes, "There is something obsessive in the media's, and the viewers', love of such narratives, an hysterical replaying of the possibility of being a victim and staving it off" (p. 29). In terms of newsworthiness, the more violent the crime the better. For violence represents a complete break with the rules, an anything-goes use of force that necessarily challenges the established order. Only officers of this order (e.g., police, military) may legitimately employ violence as a tactic. Accordingly, those who use violence in the commission of crimes are dealt with much more severely than other criminals. They are routinely described in the media as "thugs," "savages," and/or "hoodlums," labels that simultaneously express their lack of civility and (re)affirm the civility of society. As Hall et al. (1978, p. 68) put it, "The use of violence marks the distinction between those who are fundamentally *of* society and those who are *outside* it. It is coterminous with the boundary of 'society' itself" (Emphasis original). The near-decapitation of Brown-Simpson and the dozens of stab wounds found on her body and that of her male friend were obviously inflicted by some person or persons from "outside" the normative boundaries of "society." As such, the bloody crimes signified a transgression of these boundaries, a threat to the established order. Other narrative elements notwithstanding (e.g., celebrity and race), newsworkers quickly recognized the crimes and subsequent case as a newsworthy event of the highest magnitude.

The objectivity ideal

"Objectivity" denotes a transcendent, knowable, and verifiable "truth" that can be accurately communicated. It stands in opposition to "subjectivity," the idea that an observer's social location shapes the "truths" s/he sees, "truths" that may differ from those accepted by other observers. Journalism is a profession composed of newsworkers who are paid to observe events and construct narratives about truth. In the early days of journalism, the American press was unabashedly partisan in its news coverage of important events and issues. Indeed, most US newspapers were owned by political organizations and operated as their official propaganda organs (Schudson 1978). But coinciding with science's demonstration that all human inquiries about truth are necessarily subjective, newsworkers fervently rejected subjectivity in favor of the objectivity ideal (Schudson 1978; 1995). In one important respect, this move worked to increase the circulation (and profitability) of mainstream newspapers as readership was no longer strictly delimited along political lines. Neutral newspapers, in theory, could appeal to all readers. With the concurrent rise of the mass consumer culture, circulation became increasingly important as the measure by which advertisers – now the primary source of newspaper revenues – would be billed (Schudson 1978).

But more importantly for our purposes, the institutionalization of the objectivity ideal also worked to legitimate journalism as a profession, to accord newsworkers a status akin to that of doctors or lawyers, where respect would accrue from special training and skills that were socially visible. In other words, objectivity as a newswork ideal had become a professional cornerstone that could be identified, taught, and (re)affirmed – "facts" exist and newsworkers are uniquely qualified to uncover, verify, and report on them. Moreover, on the basis of this ideal, we can trust journalists to report *just the facts* in accurate, balanced, and fair news narratives. For opinion has no place in "straight" news; it belongs on the editorial page or in clearly marked columns. In short, affirmation of the objectivity ideal worked to promote a body of knowledge about truth that was arguably superior to the clearly biased truths associated with advocates of political causes. And because this new body of knowledge was supposedly based on detached observations, it could provide the citizenry with the unbiased "public knowledge" necessary for making informed decisions about current affairs (cf. Schudson 1995) – a basic requirement for a properly functioning democracy (McLuhan 1964). This institutional role, of course, was central to understandings of journalism as the "Fourth Estate";[9] it was also paramount in newsworkers' conceptualizations of themselves as "journalists."[10] Thus the spirit of the objectivity ideal lives on in the ethics statements of today's important professional journalism organizations:

Members of the Society of Professional Journalists believe that public enlightenment is the forerunner of justice and the foundation of democracy. The duty of the journalist is to further those ends by seeking *truth* and providing a *fair* and *comprehensive* account of events and issues. (Emphasis added)[11]

The National Press Photographers Association, a professional society dedicated to the advancement of photojournalism, acknowledges concern and respect for the public's natural-law right to freedom in searching for the *truth* and the right to be informed *truthfully* and *completely* about public events and the world in which we live. (Emphasis added)[12]

The responsibility of radio and television journalists is to gather and report information of importance and interest to the public *accurately*, honestly and *impartially*. (Emphasis added)[13]

But who determines "fairness" or "accuracy?" Can anyone "completely" or "comprehensively" report with "impartiality" the "truth" about *any* event or issue? As the effects of subjectivity are ultimately unavoidable, the objectivity ideal amounts to little more than a "strategic ritual" for professional newsworkers (Tuchman 1978). Indeed, newsworkers routinely manipulate time, space, and other elements in their narratives to fashion a "web of facticity," a presentational format that gives their interpretations the appearance of "fact" (Tuchman 1987, p. 332). That is, while newsworkers work to position their narratives as objective reflections of inherently newsworthy events, these narratives are in actuality the product of newsworkers' participation in elaborate professional rituals. Often this newswork documents events of major social importance, wherein newsworkers interact with the major players and provide the public with the sensation of participation. These "press rites," as Etemma

(1997) calls them, chronicle the cycles of breach, crisis, redress, and reintegration/separation that ultimately work to (re)affirm particular ideological understandings of the world. It is against this backdrop that we must examine the ideological stances of newsworkers who covered the Simpson case. To what degree did "press rites" reflect newsworker support of one or more of the political projects?

Journalistic routines

Above, you will recall, I argued that events must first be *recognized* by someone before they can attain the status of "news." In an otherwise overcrowded event-space, journalistic routines consist of the conventional practices that help newsworkers accomplish this all-important task, practices that ultimately define the domain of news that is circulated throughout society. One such routine is the assignment of news "beats." Because organizations cannot afford to assign reporters everywhere significant events are likely to occur, they tend to rely on centralized information outlets for the announcement of news (Epstein 1973; Gans 1979; Altheide and Snow 1979; Herman and Chomsky 1988; McManus 1994). These regular beats, of course, include key sites in the governmental bureaucracy, such as the courts, the police, City Hall, and so on. The officials who represent these sites thus become the primary sources of information for newsworkers. Crime news narratives, for example, are monopolized by police and court accounts (Hall et al. 1978). Newsworkers are motivated to regard these institutional accounts as "facts" and the officials who provide them as "legitimate" sources. Otherwise, the foundation on which the "objective" knowledge base described above is built begins to crumble (Altheide and Snow 1979). As we shall see in later chapters, the narratives produced and circulated by newsworkers covering the Simpson case depended heavily on "legitimate" sources for information. Below, what newsworkers said (and did not say) about these sources may shed some light on the influence the four political projects had on case-related newswork.

Another important journalistic routine involves monitoring the competition (cf. Ehrlich 1997). It is not uncommon to walk into a television newsroom and find several monitors continually tuned to the news broadcasts of the competition. Similarly, in both broadcast and print "story conferences,"[14] newsworkers routinely review the headlines of the newspapers considered to be important arbiters of the news agenda. By closely watching how these other media cover a given event – where they place coverage of the event relative to that of other events, which issues they explore in detail, which they deal with more summarily – newsworkers continually gauge the significance of the event, evaluate their own coverage, and make ongoing adjustments. A long-run consequence of this particular routine is what media scholars have described as "pack journalism" (Parenti 1986, p. 36) or the "momentum of news" (Altheide and Snow 1979, p. 170): that is, there is a tendency for news media to select from an infinity of potential news items those events that have already been selected – deemed "newsworthy" – by other news media. Over time, this practice tends to produce a jump-on-the-bandwagon effect in news selection that culminates in a rather standard news agenda from news medium to news medium (Ehrlich 1997). News coverage of the Simpson case clearly followed this pattern.[15] Indeed, newsworkers themselves were the primary sources for many of the news narratives circulated throughout the press and airwaves.[16] The result: a rather monolithic news agenda and a dominant analysis of the case that suffered few mainstream challenges.

A final journalistic routine establishes conventions for the packaging and placement of news narratives. In print journalism, for example, straight news narratives are expected to conform to the inverted pyramid format (Hall et al. 1978; Schudson 1995). That is, the most important "facts" comprising a narrative are understood to reside in the lead paragraph, with information decreasing in significance as it is located deeper and deeper in the article. The headline serves to summarize the general thrust of the overall narrative, while signifying with its size and placement the significance of a given narrative relative to others on the page. Page-one narratives, of course, are the most "newsworthy."

In television journalism, straight news narratives must be "written to video." That is, as a visual medium, television demands that pictures be an integral part of the narratives newsworkers construct and circulate. Accordingly, newsworkers generally privilege events that feature arresting images over those that do not. The more "newsworthy" narratives are typically featured at the front of the broadcast; they also tend to be lengthier than other pieces and feature a more complex structure of visuals and interviews (i.e., sound bites).

From the discovery of the Bundy murders, to the verdicts in the criminal trial, and beyond, packaging and placement routines established the Simpson case as a "newsworthy" event of the first order. Indeed, print narratives about developments in the case were regularly treated as page-one items[17] and television news broadcasts devoted more time to the case than any other issue.[18] As we shall see in chapters 4, 5, and 6, these packaging and placement routines also provide us with important findings about which case-related "facts" newsworkers considered to be the most important. My interpretation of these findings, of course, will be largely dependent upon the ideological stances examined below.

Socio-political climate

The socio-political climate is important to news construction because it affects the mix of information given to newsworkers by "legitimate" sources. These "primary definers" of news (Hall et al. 1978) typically provide newsworkers with information carefully screened to promote their own political and institutional agendas. In the long run, newsworker dependence on this information produces rather standard, hegemonic news narratives about the events in question. From time to time, however, the newsworker-official-source interaction produces coverage of conflicting views about socio-political issues. That is, when elite consensus on policy and tactics dissolves as it does periodically, this debate is reflected in the information provided to newsworkers by their sources (Schudson 1978; Alexander 1981; Hallin 1984; Parenti 1986; Iyengar and Kinder 1987; Herman and Chomsky 1988; Kellner 1990). Moreover, newsworkers sometimes examine these debates in "analysis" pieces and, with less frequency, "investigative" ones. But the objectivity ideal generally restrains newsworkers from venturing beyond the boundaries of "official" debates and asking questions that fundamentally challenge status quo visions of reality (Gans 1979). That is, one of the most damaging accusations that can be made against newswork is that it is biased. By remaining within the confines of dominant debates surrounding the issue, mainstream news organizations minimize their risk of offending large sectors of the public and maximize their chances for retaining the audience's attention.[19] For this reason, we would expect mainstream news narratives about the Simpson case to reside exclusively at the "most-plausible" end of the plausibility continuum proposed in chapter 1 (see figure 9). "Implausible" narratives – that is, those not affirmed by "legitimate" sources or at least highlighted in the debates between them – are rarely (if ever) circulated by mainstream newsworkers.

In the end, of course, what gets defined as "legitimate," "official," or "plausible" is also a function of who does the defining. That is, how journalists select their sources and organize the content of their news narratives depends upon their *perceptions* of the socio-political climate surrounding the event in question. Despite the objectivity ideal that undergird's the profession, newsworkers *are* people, and an impressive body of scholarship describes the significant influence social location is likely to have on peoples' perceptions (e.g., see Gramsci 1971; Fiske 1989; Kinder and Sanders 1996; Hunt 1997).

Race and gender, given the political projects (re)activated by the Simpson case, would seem to be particularly salient dimensions of social location. When we look at the US news media as a whole, we find that most of the decision-making positions are dominated by persons occupying a particular intersection of these two dimensions: white and male. Indeed, in 1995, roughly half of the nation's newspapers contained no newsworkers of color, while blacks constituted less than 5 percent of all newsworkers at daily newspapers (Campbell 1995).[20] Nonwhites are also woefully underrepresented in television newsrooms (Campbell 1995). The statistics for gender are no better. In 1989, men made up 94 percent of top management positions in news media (Solomon and Lee 1990). As recently as 1988, only 18 percent of television news directors were women (Solomon and Lee 1990). Moreover, when people of color and women manage to breach the boundaries of mainstream news organizations, they are generally forced to conform to the norms of the existing culture (Campbell 1995). This disciplinary action is ongoing and often quite subtle. It is accomplished through news planning conferences (i.e., acceptable topics), editing by superiors (i.e., acceptable narratives), informal conversations with coworkers (i.e., acceptable performance), and formal sanctions for policy violations (i.e., acceptable behavior) (Wilson and Gutierrez 1995). As media scholars have long noted, these cultural criteria generally work to (re)affirm status-quo versions of reality, understandings consonant with a society dominated by white males (cf. Gans 1979). The corps of newsworkers covering the Simpson media event reflected these realities. As noted above, only one black-owned media organization, the *Los Angeles Sentinel* (see chapter 6), received a regular seat in the courtroom. Virtually all of the nonwhite and female newsworkers permitted firsthand access to the trial worked for mainstream media organizations. In chapters 4, 5, and 6, I also examine the ideological bias of news narratives in light of these socio-political factors.

Business constraints

Newswork is a business dependent not only on the timely coverage of "newsworthy" events, but also on the *attraction* of audiences and advertisers (Altheide and Snow 1979; Gans 1979; Gitlin 1980; McQuail 1987). Journalistic values aside, the news business – like other media businesses – ultimately positions the audience as a commodity that can be sold to advertisers for profit (Golding and Murdoch 1991). In recent years, this business activity has been concentrated in the hands of an ever-shrinking group of multinational corporations that have obvious stakes in the product of newswork (Bagdikian 1992). First, the product of newswork must be entertaining. That is, it must attract and sustain audience interest long enough to satisfy the persuasion needs of advertisers. Secondly, the product of newswork must not create an environment hostile to the survival of the corporation (or major advertisers). Thus, certain taken-for-granted assumptions about the efficacy of corporate capitalism and related societal institutions are defined as beyond the scope of legitimate inquiry (Parenti 1986). These corporate interests become one of the primary factors that shape the cultures newsworkers face as they go about their day-to-day work of covering the news. While these interests do not *directly* dictate the content of news narratives, they nonetheless introduce *bias* by way of institutionalized norms about the types of newswork that superiors reward and punish. Meanwhile, the increasing concentration of ownership noted above diminishes the profile of narratives circulated by alternative news organizations. We are thus left with a rather homogenous supply of news narratives, despite the seeming proliferation of media outlets. As we shall see in later chapters, the news narratives that circulated throughout the Simpson media event were not only entertaining, they also exhibited a striking degree of homogeneity *vis-à-vis* the "plausibility" continuum outlined in part I. Much of this homogeneity was undoubtedly due to the corporate cultures that governed the various news organizations. But significant portions, as we shall see in the next section, can also be attributed to the ideological stances of the newsworkers who covered the case.

O. J. and newsworkers

Two days after the verdicts were announced, I was invited by staffers at ABC's *Nightline* to participate in a postmortem regarding the media's performance in the Simpson case. ABC's *Viewpoint: the Media and the Trial*, featured a town-hall meeting format, and involved 200 or so newsworkers, media experts, and community representatives. The host, Ted Koppel, invited a select group of guests to join him on the stage: members of the Goldman family, dismissed jurors Francine Florio-Bunten and Tracy Kennedy, and prosecutor Rockne Harmon. Defense attorney Barry Scheck joined the discussion from New York via satellite, as did the managing editor of *Newsweek* magazine, Maynard Parker. Surrounding the stage was a stepped seating area that rose toward the ceiling of the massive sound stage. The occupants of the rows closest to the stage were newsworkers who in one form or another had been instrumental in coverage of the case. These guests, like those joining Koppel on the stage, wore microphones. The remaining 200 or so people in attendance – myself included – sat in the higher rows. Four open microphones were provided for our participation in the discussion.

Koppel began the program with the following words: "The media circus. It's become the metaphor of choice for coverage of the Simpson trial . . . Lines between tabloid and traditional media blurred further." After offering these obligatory self-critical remarks about media exploitation of the case, the host identified the central question that would drive the evening's discussion: "How should journalists strike the balance between serving the public interest and feeding the public appetite?"

Thus began the media's post-verdict search of its soul. The setting, and what would follow in the remaining 103 minutes or so, struck me as a near perfect microcosm of how the newsworker corps generally approached the Simpson case. That is, despite a trial that featured nine black jurors, a black defendant, and news narratives about a "racial divide" in perceptions of the case, the guests invited to join Koppel on the stage were uniformly white and all had reason to favor prosecution narratives about the case. Moreover, of the fourteen microphoned newsworkers "nominated" by Koppel to speak during the program, eleven were white males.[21] Koppel did not ask any nonwhite and/or female newsworker to speak until the final 24 minutes of the 103-minute program.[22] As the work of Brunsdon and Morley (1978) suggests, Koppel's choices are telling in that nomination practices signify who a program host feels is qualified to speak on the issue at hand. Nomination also works to limit the domain of issues these speakers may talk about. Thus the last three speakers nominated by Koppel, two black men and a black women, were all acknowledged by him only at the end of the program, after the discussion had *explicitly* turned to race. Presumably, nonwhite newsworkers could only speak to matters of race, and race had nothing to do with the issues discussed in the preceding 79 minutes or so.

My interviews with newsworkers who covered the case reveal that the newsworker corps at Camp O. J., like the *Viewpoint* participants, was a highly segregated group: all were not created equal. As noted above, the seven permanent courtroom seats were all assigned to mainstream media – that is, media dominated by decision makers who are white and male. Only a "relative handful" of black newsworkers, for example, consistently covered the case for these media.[23] Alternative and minority media were not accorded the privilege of permanent seats in the courtroom. Indeed, the only black-owned news operation to receive *any* seat assignment in the courtroom, you will recall, had access to it only on a rotating basis. In short, representatives of the mainstream (i.e., white) media sat high atop the pecking order in the Simpson newsworker corps. Ron Brewington, a reporter covering the criminal trial for black-owned KJLH-FM in Los Angeles, described his experiences with this pecking order. Noting that he only "got to the courtroom once," Brewington said he and his black colleagues in the Simpson press corps regularly discussed their feelings of marginality. Black newsworkers, he added, largely "kept to themselves."[24] Haywood Galbreath, a photographer who covered the trial for the black press, concurred.[25] Moreover, Galbreath charged that the white newsworkers who represented mainstream news organizations actively tried to keep him and other black photojournalists out of the newspaper photo pool.[26] Below I discuss some important ideological implications of this hierarchical structure by reviewing newsworker positions on three important, case-related themes: Simpson's innocence or guilt; objectivity and race; and O. J. and newsworthiness.

Innocence or guilt

> I'll go to my grave believing he is guilty – no matter what the next jury decides.[27]

Although no representative poll data exists, evidence strongly suggests that the vast majority of newsworkers – reporters, writers, editors, news directors, and so on – were convinced before the trial began of Simpson's guilt. Two prominent media critics, for example, arrived at the same conclusion after interviewing many newsworkers over the course of the trial. In a sound bite airing on the *Viewpoint* program, Jon Katz noted that "most journalists covering the trial that I've talked to believe very strongly that O. J. Simpson is guilty." David Shaw, a staff writer for the *Los Angeles Times*, interviewed more than eighty newsworkers for a twelve-page pull-out section about media coverage of the trial that appeared in the newspaper shortly after the verdicts. Shaw also acknowledged that early on in the case the belief in Simpson's guilt dominated the newsworker corps, but he explicitly connected this observation to race. While the black newsworkers he interviewed had "varying opinions" on Simpson's guilt, the "white predominance" of the newsworker corps had a powerful effect: "The white predominance of the Simpson press corps manifested itself in many ways, most notably in the near-unanimous assumption that reporters shared with their editors and news directors: Simpson was guilty."[28] Indeed, Tom Elias, a white reporter covering the case for Scripps-Howard newspapers, expressed amazement at the notion that anyone could reasonably doubt Simpson's guilt. "No one believes people could support that clown [Simpson]," he said. "It blows the white mind away."[29] Thus, as he puts it in the quote that introduces this section, he will "go to my grave" believing in Simpson's guilt. Dennis Schatzman, a black reporter covering the case for the *Los Angeles Sentinel* (see chapter 6), shared courtroom seat C-12 with Elias. As he put it, Simpson had enjoyed "no honeymoon" with the newsworker corps. "From day one," he said, "the press had it in for O.J." Schatzman said that as he rode courthouse elevators, stood in the halls, and sat in the press room working on his stories, "routinely reporters would blurt out, 'He's guilty. We know he's guilty.'"[30] David Margolick, a white reporter for the *New York Times*, was generally regarded by the newsworker corps "as the best, most stylish writer covering the case."[31] He acknowledged that he too shared the "profound skepticism of the defense" that permeated the press room.[32] Finally, a white reporter for a major national newspaper who spoke to me off the record said s/he was also convinced early on of Simpson's guilt. Be s/he was reluctant to attribute differences in perceptions about Simpson's innocence or guilt to race. Instead, s/he proposed, these differences were a function of socio-economic status, the background and amount of education trial observers had. That is, those from "rougher backgrounds" and who have lower amounts of education are the "types of people Cochran was trying to reach" with the defense's conspiracy theory.[33]

Given these insights into newsworkers' thinking about the case, it is not difficult to make sense of the newsworker reactions to the verdicts I described above. The "stunned silence" that engulfed the twelfth-floor press room and the dropping of heads I witnessed outside the courthouse were the emotional responses of people who had had a stake in the trial's outcome. As Jessica Seigel, formerly a reporter with the *Chicago Tribune*, put it, many newsworkers had "bonded with the Goldman family during the long criminal proceedings and still sympathize."[34] Fred Goldman himself acknowledged that "the media has been exceptionally wonderful to us."[35] Perhaps the "something else" that Seigel speculates led her and other Simpson newsworkers to leave the profession was the profound frustration of not being able to block what to them was clearly a miscarriage of justice – an impotence at odds with newsworkers' conceptions of themselves as "journalists," with journalism's cherished status as Fourth Estate.

Seigel briefly returned to the Simpson case during the civil trial, this time to report on her former colleagues for *Buzz* magazine. One of the things she noticed was that Simpson now seemed more "imposing:"

Now, when court is in recess, Simpson just stands up and walks out. He saunters confidently into the hallway where journalists gossip and cultivate sources during breaks in testimony. His polished skin glows. He is relaxed. Tall. Smiling. When he stands, his muscular body and ingratiating charisma dominate a surprisingly large amount of space.[36]

She also noticed something else. By the middle of the civil trial, the newsworker corps had been divided in two groups: those who refused to admit that Simpson "gives you the willies," who said they "talked" to him in order to get "both sides of the story"; and those who criticized these colleagues for "sucking up to O. J."[37] At issue, of course, was the question of objectivity. What happens when the objectivity ideal precludes newsworkers from reporting what they perceive to be the "truth?"

Objectivity and race

I think race is an issue that forces reporters, ah, more than anything else, to worry about not giving offense. I, ah, think we are paralyzed on the subject by and large. And, and it seems to me sometimes that we concentrate on balance to the exclusion of truth.[38]

The objectivity ideal aside, many of the white newsworkers covering the case echoed the above quote from the *New Yorker*'s Jeffrey Toobin: they felt newsworkers had "bent over backwards, perhaps too far backwards at times" to be fair in their news narratives precisely because they were so sure Simpson was guilty.[39] Toobin, a former federal prosecutor, added that he thought news coverage "suffered" because newsworkers often treated "absurd" arguments the same as more "plausible" ones, "as if they were balanced."[40] Presumably, "giving offense" is a concern that, like political correctness, hamstrings newsworkers from "speaking frankly about race," from telling the "truth."

Nonetheless, other prominent newsworkers continued to (re)affirm the objectivity ideal, despite their own obvious biases. For example, while the *New York Times*'s David Margolick admitted he shared newsworkers' "profound skepticism of the defense," he said he "had to guard against it as best I could in my stories." The result? "I don't think I always succeeded . . . We all sort of influence each other and . . . maybe lose a little bit of our independence."[41] This "influence" and loss of "independence" to which Margolick alludes is both a function of journalistic routines (i.e., monitoring the competition) and particulars of the Simpson case (i.e., the length of the trial, the relatively small confines of the trial venue, and the corresponding high density of newsworker interactions). Newsworkers covering the Simpson case routinely relied upon one another as sources for their news narratives, especially when other information was hard to come by.[42] Given that the prevailing sentiment among the newsworker corps early on was that Simpson was guilty, this newswork practice only worked to reinforce the belief in the minds of individual newsworkers.[43] Indeed, Andrea

Ford, a black reporter who covered the case for the *Los Angeles Times* (see chapter 5), was labelled "pro-defense" by some of her colleagues for criticizing and calling attention to this tendency among newsworkers. Invoking the objectivity ideal herself, Ford retorted that she was "pro-journalism."[44]

My own experiences with Simpson newsworkers suggest that the objectivity ideal often served as a convenient tool to divert attention away from their own biases (i.e., we were *too* fair, *too* balanced), while simultaneously underscoring the bias inherent in alternative interpretations of the case. Following the verdicts in the criminal trial, for example, newsworkers from several mainstream news media contacted me for interviews about the role race plays in our perceptions of events like the Simpson case. Newsworkers typically began by asking me to account for "black" perceptions of the case – as if "non-black" perceptions needed no explaining. After providing them with the standard line about the importance of cultural background and experiences, I would then move on to discuss how these same factors also tend to bias *dominant* understandings of the case. These latter comments, of course, did not make it into the news narratives that were later circulated by the mainstream news operations.[45] Instead, my words were typically used in these narratives to offer an explanation for "the view blacks have of the case" – one that, unlike the dominant view (i.e., "truth"), was framed as clearly "subjective."

O. J. and newsworthiness

[T]he worst sins of American journalism seem to be on display in the Simpson saga.[46]

Newsworkers involved in covering the Simpson case often faced a troubling dilemma: on the one hand, as suggested by the above quote from the *Washington Post*, coverage of the case had exploded to the point where members of the profession began to question the story's newsworthiness relative to other issues; on the other hand, the story was so firmly entrenched atop the nation's news agenda that newsworkers feared nothing more than being scooped.[47] Throughout the case, members of the "legitimate" (i.e., newsworthy, objective) press sought to avoid being stigmatized by association with the "tabloid" (i.e., sensational, subjective) press, while simultaneously working overtime on a story that many felt was really the tabloids' "turf." Indeed, Geraldo Rivera, whose *Rivera Live* was devoted throughout both trials to exposing Simpson's "obvious guilt," inflamed the ire of "legitimate" newsworkers concerning this issue. As Rivera put it, "This is the first time that journalism's hypocrisy has really been shaken out of the bushes. The difference between the *New York Times* and the *National Enquirer* has gone from this big to this big [uses hands to indicate a gap that has closed]."[48] Defending the credibility of the venerable *New York Times*, David Margolick dismissed Rivera's observation:

Well, I think that Geraldo knows that what he says is nonsense. Ah, you know, ah. I don't take that terribly seriously. That's just hype. The reason that people are linking my paper and the *National Enquirer* is because I wasn't so elitist as to pretend they didn't exist. As you know, I mean, they were an important player in this entire story. This is their turf. They put twenty people on this story, you know.[49]

Indeed, the *National Enquirer* beat the "legitimate" press on several Simpson stories, including the 1989 domestic violence incident involving Simpson and his ex-wife.[50] Margolick's defensiveness regarding his decision to write about the *National Enquirer's* role in the case (i.e., "I wasn't so elitist") underscores how important it is for "legitimate" newsworkers to distinguish themselves from those that work in the "tabloid" press.

Much of this distinction, of course, is justified in terms of the centrality of newsworthiness for the "legitimate" press *as Fourth Estate*. While the "tabloids" routinely circulated titillating front-page headlines that the public might *want* to read – e.g., "How sex-mad Nicole seduced Marcus Allen under O. J.'s nose,"[51] or "Cops fear . . . Goldman's Dad Will Kill O. J."[52] – the front page of the "legitimate" press is supposed to highlight stories that the public *needs* to make informed decisions about the world around them. A black reporter for a local Los Angeles television station echoed this basic distinction between the "legitimate" and "illegitimate" press. S/he expressed regret at the way the Simpson saga had diverted the attention of newsworkers away from other, potentially more important issues. "I thought journalism was a higher calling," s/he said.[53] Howard Rosenberg, media critic for the *Los Angeles Times*, concurred. Two days after the verdicts in the criminal trial, he made this observation on ABC's *Viewpoint* postmortem: "Ah, yesterday in Los Angeles, four television stations went live to cover a news conference of a, of a juror in this case. Five minutes after that, the President welcomed the Pope. Nowhere on television, except CNN."[54] CNN's Jim Moret was undoubtedly relieved to hear the last sentence of the above statement. Like Margolick, he had earlier on the program moved to distinguish his employer from the likes of *Hardcopy, Inside Edition,* or even "ABC:"

Now, at CNN, we clearly covered the story to exclusion of others for the portion that we covered the trial live. We are, however, a 24-hour, all-news network, unlike ABC, for example. And when we would cover the trial for eight hours on a given day, there's, you know, 16 other hours that we would devote to other coverage.[55]

In short, a dialogue that ran through the *Viewpoint* program, that was picked up in interviews I had with newsworkers, and that was echoed in the public statements of other newsworkers, pointed directly to "legitimate" newsworker doubts about the case's newsworthiness relative to the coverage it received. I suggest that these doubts are connected, at base, to newsworker beliefs about Simpson's guilt and their unwillingness to seriously entertain the possibility that he *could have been* framed by police. A wealthy celebrity who buys an acquittal (i.e., the dominant, "most-plausible" narratives that newsworkers generally (re)affirmed) is not nearly as "newsworthy" a story as is one about a racially motivated conspiracy involving officials of the state to frame a double-murder suspect (i.e., the subordinate, "most-implausible" narratives newsworkers routinely rejected).

Conclusions

About two months after the verdicts were announced in the civil trial, I attended the second annual "Festival of Books" held at the University of California, Los Angeles. I was particularly interested in a scheduled session entitled, "Overcoming the O.J. Obsession,"[56] which featured Associated Press (AP) reporter Linda Deutsch and author Lawrence Schiller. Deutsch, of course, had reported on the Simpson case for the AP and, because she had covered most of the high-profile trials of the past twenty-five years, she was generally considered by her colleagues as the grand dame of trial reporting. Schiller, you will recall, had co-authored *I Want to Tell You* with Simpson and his "uncensored story of the Simpson defense," *American Tragedy*, with James Willwerth.

I entered the lecture hall of 300 or so seats just as the session was to begin, surprised to find only about half of them filled, primarily with white spectators.

Deutsch and Schiller began the session by taking turns commending one another's work. Schiller's book was the "best book on the trial." Deutsch "reported the facts and stayed away from rumor." Deutsch also used the session as an opportunity to promote a book by her late mentor, Theo Wilson. The book, *Headline Justice: Inside the Courtroom – The Country's Most Controversial Trials*, presented a trial reporter's view of many of the popular trials discussed in chapter 1. Wilson, who watched the Simpson case from the sidelines, had covered these earlier high-profile trials for the New York *Daily News*. Her account is interesting because of the observations she makes regarding the "bias" that tainted the Simpson newsworker corps:

I was dismayed by what I called "the flash and trash" surrounding the case – the hype, the manipulation of unseasoned media, the bias shown by commentators even before they heard evidence from the courtroom, the publication of rumors and gossip and leaks that violated every principle of trial reporting my colleagues and I practiced. (Wilson 1996, p. 12)

Wilson's "number one" rule, one she had preached to protégés such as Deutsch, echoed the age-old objectivity ideal: "Stay in the courtroom. The only important news is what the jury hears from the witness chair, what the judge rules on, and what the lawyers say *inside the courtroom*" [emphasis original] (pp. 12–13). Moreover, like the jury, newsworkers covering a trial should not make up their minds about the case until all of the evidence has been presented in court. As Wilson lamented, and as we saw above, this clearly did not happen in the Simpson case: newsworkers were convinced of Simpson's guilt not long after the bodies were discovered on Bundy Drive. Indeed, in the days immediately following the murders newsworkers were quick to circulate a number of news narratives containing incriminating information that later turned out to be false. For example, KCOP (Channel 13 in Los Angeles) reported that a bloody ski mask had been found at the murder scene. The Los Angeles *Daily News* reported that a bloody murder weapon had been found. CNN reported that police had found bloody clothing in Simpson's washing machine. KCBS and NBC reported that Simpson had had his hand in a golf bag during his plane flight to Chicago the night of the murders. And several news organizations reported that police had found blood on the golf bag.[57] This information, of course, had typically come from unnamed sources – that is, the "official" police sources that newsworkers tend to privilege, but who in these instances spoke only off the record.

So the response Schiller got when he punctuated his own thoughts on the case, perhaps, should not be surprising. "Many, many questions are unanswered," he said, shrugging his shoulders. "He may be innocent."

Snickers and guffaws rippled from the largely white audience.

In the final analysis, this chapter has sought to establish that a particular "truth" about the Simpson case was (re)affirmed by newsworkers very early on. This "truth," which newsworkers sought to validate by selectively invoking the objectivity ideal, ultimately resonates with three of the political projects outlined in chapter 2; it challenges the fourth. That is, the "objective truth" of Simpson's guilt is consistent with key ideological assumptions undergirding the Celebrity Defendant, Domestic Violence, and Black "Other" projects. The first political project, you will recall, worked to support the victims' rights movement and the "war on crime," to expose the dangers inherent in allowing criminal defendants to have "too many" resources (and rights). The second project worked to lift the visibility of domestic violence to the top of the public agenda, while the third worked to reinforce the "othering" of nonwhite Americans, especially blacks. The "truth" of Simpson's guilt that most newsworkers (re)affirmed supports each of these projects: it establishes the criminal trial verdicts as the prototypical miscarriage of justice, demonstrates the dangers of domestic violence out of control, and validates age-old notions of black "Otherness" (i.e., the savagery of Simpson, the bias/ignorance of black jurors and trial observers). In contrast, this "truth" works against important assumptions underlying the "Just-Us" system project, especially the position that the criminal justice system *unjustly* targets black males.

But how did this "truth" shape the actual narratives newsworkers constructed and circulated throughout the Simpson media event? In the next three chapters, we explore this question in detail with case studies of how three significant news organizations represented the case "facts."

4   Celebrating the process: O. J. and KTLA-TV

Boom. With a deep jolt, a drum is struck. The television screen fades in from black to reveal a still image of Orenthal James Simpson from the chest up.

String and wind instruments suddenly rise into a slow, rather ominous melody, marked at regular intervals by repeated strikes of the drum. Simpson, clad in a conservative grey suit, white shirt, and multi-colored tie, fills the left half of the screen. His arms and hands cannot be seen. His shoulders are directed about one quarter turn to the right, his head cocked slightly to the side, his mouth pursed. His eyes stare up and out into space, away from the television spectator.

Next to Simpson's head, dominating the right side of the screen, is a graphic formed with simple black and white letters and underlined in red: "The Simpson Trial." Below this sits the KTLA news logo. These graphics and Simpson's image rest against a white background framed in blue. Closer inspection of the background reveals that it is really a muted image of the empty criminal trial courtroom. As the music continues, the graphics and Simpson's image dissolve into the first of three or four sound bites from the previous day's testimony. These sound bites are framed by boxes that pop up at various locations around the screen, expanding in size until about three-quarters of the screen is filled. The last sound bite is punctuated by a graphic that expands from a point to fill the right one-third of the screen: "The Simpson Trial, Testimony Continues." The music fades up and out to the words of KTLA anchor Marta Waller:

Good morning, I'm Marta Waller along with KTLA legal analyst Peter Arenella. You're watching KTLA's continuing coverage of the O. J. Simpson murder trial. Court is expected to begin shortly. Here now, the latest developments . . .

So began KTLA-TV's coverage of the Simpson trial each day:[1] thirty-seven weeks of testimony, hearings, and motions. Like the other news organizations covering the trial, KTLA received its courtroom video and audio from a camera operated by Court TV. But while its competitors covered the early days of the trial in earnest before dropping out during "lull" periods, KTLA was the only television station in Los Angeles to stay with the trial for gavel-to-gavel coverage. The station was amply rewarded for these efforts. KTLA's daily live coverage, said news director Craig Hume, "was the top-rated program in Los Angeles during the course of the trial."[2]

This chapter presents a case study of KTLA's live coverage of the Simpson criminal trial. Against the ideological backdrop we examined in the last chapter, the general tendency among newsworkers to (re)affirm Simpson's guilt, this chapter explores a central question: Which O.J. narrative or narratives were privileged by KTLA's coverage? That is, how did narratives positioned at different locations along the "plausibility" continuum outlined in part I fare relative to one another in the coverage? Moreover, *how* was this ideological work accomplished?

To address these questions, I selected and analyzed a random sample of KTLA's criminal trial coverage. First, I randomly selected a day from each of the thirty-seven weeks of the trial. Then, from each of these identified days, I randomly selected an half hour of KTLA coverage. Next, for the resulting eighteen hours of coverage, I transcribed the comments of newsworkers and legal analysts. Employing van Dijk's (1993) work on elite discourse as my primary analytical framework, I concentrated on recurring newsworker practices and important themes that might shed some light on the O.J. narratives privileged by KTLA. Consistent with other qualitative research designs (Creswell 1994), I analyzed this data while simultaneously interpreting it and constructing narratives about it. The resulting analysis of "text and talk," as van Dijk (1993, p. 13) notes in his own work, is highly informal in its multidisciplinarity.

We begin with a brief overview of KTLA News and the people who contributed most directly to its Simpson coverage.

KTLA News

This is KTLA television, Los Angeles. Owned and operated by Television Productions, Incorporated, a service of Paramount Pictures, with studios adjoining the Paramount lot in Hollywood, transmitting from atop Mount Wilson, California, on television channel number five, a frequency of seventy-six, two-eighty-two megacycles.[3]

On January 22, 1947, KTLA-TV – the first television station in the western United States – signed on with the above words. At the time, there were only about 350 television sets in all of Los Angeles.[4] Today, of course, Los Angeles is the second largest media market in the nation, home to 22 television stations,[5] 3.7 million residents,[6] and nearly as many television sets. KTLA is now owned by the Tribune media conglomerate, owner of nine other television stations, four radio stations, four major newspapers, and about twenty other media related businesses.[7] An affiliate of the Warner Brothers (WB) television network, KTLA broadcasts WB programs during primetime hours and a host of syndicated programming throughout the remainder of the day. Its 10 pm newscast has consistently dominated the time period in Los Angeles for the past twenty years.

From its birth to the present, KTLA's news operation would participate in a number of historic moments for television and Los Angeles. In 1947, for example, KTLA News previewed the arrival of electronic journalism and paved the way for the news wars surrounding the Simpson case. The fledgling news operation provided its viewers with live coverage of a major factory explosion in East Los Angeles and became the first television operation to beat the print media with its coverage. Indeed, the *Los Angeles Times*'s front-page coverage of the disaster did not appear until the following morning.

KTLA was also a pioneer in feeding the public's appetite for news about celebrities. In 1949, the operation produced the first television program devoted to Hollywood entertainment news, *Hollywood Reel*. The program's reports about the lives of Hollywood's rich and famous foreshadowed the type of scrutiny these celebrities would receive years later on tabloid programs like *Entertainment Tonight, Hardcopy,* and *Inside Edition* – all key players in broadcast coverage of the Simpson saga. The program also undoubtedly contributed to a peculiar Los Angeles news culture that routinely ranks entertainment events as more newsworthy than other world affairs.

In 1958, KTLA News participated in another television first. Hovering over the Los Angeles Memorial Coliseum – the landmark site where O. J. Simpson would dazzle college football fans less than ten years later – the KTLA "telecopter" broadcast the first live television pictures from a helicopter. "Helicopter journalism" was thus introduced to the world (Tice 1992). Seven years later, during the 1965 Watts riots, the symbiotic relationship between mainstream news operations and Los Angeles law enforcement would be underscored when KTLA and other local stations bragged about using the new technology to provide LAPD officers with tactical information (Horne 1995). "Helicopter journalism," of course, would also be essential to media coverage of Simpson's "Bronco chase" twenty-nine years later.

In 1966, KTLA provided its viewers with unprecedented news coverage that would again foreshadow newswork practices central to the

Simpson case. KTLA was the only Los Angeles television station to provide live coverage of a coroner's inquest into the death of a black motorist who, after a routine traffic stop, had been fatally shot by a white LAPD officer. Johnnie Cochran, who would later become Simpson's lead defense attorney, represented the family of the victim and made his first live television appearance on KTLA.

Finally, in 1991, KTLA reporter Stan Chambers broke the story about the infamous beating of Rodney King by LAPD officers. Chambers had been provided with a copy of witness George Holliday's homemade video tape, which captured police officers inflicting fifty-six brutal baton blows on the black motorist. "I wanted to be as objective as possible and not sensationalize something as devastating as the tape," Chambers noted. "I wanted people to see it and make up their own minds."[8] After first airing on KTLA, the King beating videotape was hypermediated through thousands of broadcasts around the nation and world. When this stark video evidence of the beating failed to convince an "all-white" jury of the officers' guilt, the costliest uprisings in US history were sparked in Los Angeles (cf. Fiske 1994; Hunt 1997).

KTLA Newsworkers and legal analysts

> When I first heard about the murders of Ron Goldman and Nicole Brown Simpson I didn't really think very much of it, except that this was a terrible tragedy. I never could have known what kind of impact it was going to have on my life and that it would literally occupy an entire year. We wound up doing this coverage and it kind of evolved.[9]

In one important respect, the newsworkers most responsible for providing what "kind of evolved" into KTLA's day-to-day coverage of the Simpson trial closely resembled the larger mainstream newsworker corps: almost all of them were white. Moreover, the management team that made news planning decisions at the station – like at virtually all of its local competitors – was headed by white males.[10] However, KTLA legal analysts were a more racially diverse group. KTLA hired these on-air commentators because of their legal expertise and ability to interpret trial proceedings for viewers. Below, I provide brief vignettes for several of the major players in KTLA's Simpson coverage.

Marta Waller. Waller began working at KTLA in 1984 as a news writer. Over the years, she would hold a variety of positions at the station, including producer of the weekend news program. The Simpson case, as she notes in the above quote, would have a dramatic "impact" on her "life" – particularly her career at KTLA. She was named anchor of the station's gavel-to-gavel criminal trial coverage shortly before the start of the proceedings. Shortly thereafter, she was named anchor of the *KTLA Noon News*, a program that devoted much of its space during the trial to summarizing the latest case-related developments. She was promoted to co-anchor of top-rated *KTLA News at Ten* following the verdicts, joining anchor Hal Fishman, then a twenty-nine-year veteran of the station.

As Simpson trial anchor in KTLA's Hollywood studio, Waller would periodically make observations about the day's trial proceedings, elicit comments from the featured legal analyst(s), and introduce reports from various KTLA newsworkers on location inside and in front of the criminal courts building. After earning "accolades" for this perform-ance, Waller – a white female – filed a discrimination lawsuit against KTLA in 1997. The lawsuit claimed that she had recently been de-moted from her anchor positions because of her age and gender.[11] KTLA's white-male management team had replaced the then forty-four-year old Waller with a younger Latina on the noon news program. Meanwhile, Fishman, whom the suit claimed was opposed to a female co-anchor, resumed as sole anchor of the 10 pm news program. Fishman was a white male in his sixties.

Ron Olsen. Olsen had been a reporter at KTLA since the mid 1980s. According to his KTLA biography, he was one of the first newsworkers to arrive at the Bundy murder scene on June 13, 1994. He was also KTLA's primary newsworker inside the criminal courts building through-out the trial. Underscoring the ties between KTLA and its parent com-pany, Olsen regularly interviewed Jessica Seigel, a newsworker covering the trial for the conglomerate-owned *Chicago Tribune* (see chapter 3), for his live reports from the hall outside Judge Ito's courtroom. He occasionally filled in for Waller at the Simpson anchor desk. Olsen was a white male.

Craig Hume. Hume was KTLA's news director throughout the crim-inal trial. Pleased by the commercial success of the station's gavel-to-gavel coverage, Hume noted shortly after the verdicts that KTLA might pursue live, gavel-to-gavel coverage of other high-profile trials. He jus-tified these plans in terms of public access to the legal system: "I think the camera provides the public with an eye into the courtroom. And, ah, without that camera, people who want to follow the legal system in a trial have a difficult time doing that."[12] Hume, a white male in his early forties, would resign from his position about a year after the verdicts due to "philosophical differences" with the station's management.[13]

Greg Nathanson. As KTLA's general manager, a position he held throughout the criminal trial, Nathanson was responsible for the hiring and firing of KTLA management and for setting the station's general direction. This direction included maintaining a strong news operation, one that reflected traditional journalistic ideals of objectivity and facticity. Note Nathanson's reflections on KTLA's upcoming live coverage of the Simpson trial: "In some ways, you hope to stop the rumor mill and show the actual *facts*. The camera won't lie, and for the first time the story won't be filtered through 50 reporters and writers" [emphasis added].[14] Nathanson was also a white male.

Peter Arenella. Arenella was a frequent legal analyst for KTLA throughout the criminal trial. The University of California, Los Angeles (UCLA) law professor also served as a trial analyst for ABC News, the *Los Angeles Times*, and other news operations. Many trial observers credited him with having offered "the most reasoned, insightful analyses of all the expert commentators."[15]

Al DeBlanc. DeBlanc, also a regular KTLA legal analyst, was a criminal defense attorney who had previously been a sergeant for the LAPD. Two years after the verdicts, he would be described in *Buzz* magazine as an "articulate, light-skinned African American who seemed to favor the prosecution and had little doubt about Simpson's guilt."[16]

Irene Ayala. Ayala was the final legal analyst regularly featured in KTLA's criminal trial coverage. Ayala, a Latina, was a prominent area criminal defense attorney.

Eric Spillman. Spillman was a *KTLA Morning News* assignment reporter during the criminal trial. A more recent addition to the KTLA newsworker team, he provided reports from outside the criminal courts building throughout the trial. Spillman was a white male.

Walter Richards. Richards periodically substituted for Olsen inside the courthouse. On the day the verdicts were announced in the criminal trial, he joined Olsen for live reports outside Judge Ito's courtroom. Richards was a black male.

Other newsworkers. A variety of other newsworkers, dispatched to several locations throughout Los Angeles, contributed to KTLA's coverage of the verdicts in both trials. These newsworkers included veteran anchor Hal Fishman, longtime reporters Stan Chambers and Warren Wilson, and helicopter reporter Jennifer York.

Findings and analysis

Imagine the following scenario. On the eve of opening statements in the Simpson criminal trial, before any evidence has been presented in court, ABC's Peter Jennings opens the network's evening newscast with this story:

The trial of O. J. Simpson, murderer of his ex-wife Nicole Brown-Simpson and her friend Ronald Goldman, begins tomorrow in a Los Angeles courtroom. Prosecutors will present irrefutable evidence proving beyond *all* doubt that Simpson committed the brutal slayings. Simpson's high-powered attorneys are expected to attack this evidence on several fronts, hoping they can confuse the jury as to the relevant facts in the case.

Although most readers might consider this a rather "plausible" narrative, a number of institutional constraints prevented its *explicit* circulation by "legitimate" news media like ABC. Formally, at least, determination of innocence or guilt in the United States is left to the criminal justice system. This system awards criminal defendants a presumption of innocence that can be erased only by a jury conviction or guilty plea. The "legitimate" news media, as Fourth Estate, celebrate this system and ideals, if not its practices (see chapter 3). Thus mainstream news media are generally expected to proclaim innocence or guilt as "fact" only when case *outcomes* warrant doing so. True, newsworkers, as we saw in the previous chapter, are real people with political interests and opinions. But they are expected to suspend these biases when engaging in professional newswork – or at least bracket them by performing highly stylized rituals of objectivity.

In many important respects, however, KTLA's criminal trial coverage was a direct reflection of the newsworker corps' general belief in Simpson's guilt. That is, despite diligent efforts by KTLA newsworkers to maintain the all-important facade of journalistic objectivity, their own pro-prosecution bias crept into the station's trial coverage at critical moments. Below I attempt to trace the overt and covert paths of this bias by reviewing (1) the narrative structure of the typical day's coverage, (2) the framing techniques and practices used by KTLA newsworkers to motivate and validate these narratives and, finally, (3) salient themes emerging from the narratives that go to the heart of ideological struggles surrounding the case.

Structure

As the introduction to this chapter describes, the typical day's coverage of the Simpson criminal trial on KTLA began with an ominous musical theme and image of the defendant, O. J. Simpson. Sound bites from the previous day's testimony, like those used in conventional news narratives, were then integrated into the open to highlight what KTLA newsworkers considered to be the most newsworthy testimony. Typically these 10- to 20-second excerpts were selected from hours of testimony footage in accordance with the "dialectical mode of reporting" (cf. Epstein 1973). That is, in the name of balance, the selected sound bites usually included a combination of what newsworkers deemed to be pro-prosecution *and* pro-defense excerpts.

Following the sound bite sequence, graphics identified the upcoming program as KTLA's continuing live coverage of the Simpson trial. Anchor Marta Waller then introduced herself and the KTLA legal analyst(s) of the day. Waller's introduction of the analyst(s), of course, was also a "nomination" that served to establish the competency/legitimacy of the analyst(s) to speak on legal and other matters surrounding the case (i.e., "Al DeBlanc, KTLA legal analyst and *criminal defense attorney*," or "Peter Arenella, KTLA legal analyst and *UCLA law professor*") (cf. Brunsdon and Morley 1978). By contrast, Waller positioned herself as a novice in legal matters, but nonetheless a legitimate participant in the upcoming coverage because of the well-established role she would play as anchor in weaving KTLA's news narrative into a coherent whole. Indeed, other television news programs routinely provided viewers with enactments of the prototypical anchor role Waller would play during trial coverage. Waller lived up to the expectations of this role by seeming[17] to smoothly steer KTLA's narrative (and viewers) between various trial-related locations. After the above introductions and nominations, for example, Waller would typically "check in" with Ron Olsen outside the courtroom to get the latest information about what might be expected in court that day, especially any information about when proceedings might actually resume. After providing the requisite information, Olsen would then "toss" it back to Waller, who then either filled the time before the start of the proceedings by posing questions to that day's KTLA legal analyst(s) or by introducing commercials (e.g., "We're going to take a short break. We'll be right back"). These commercials – which promoted products as diverse as vocational training programs, weight-loss programs, legal and insurance services, pet foods, and prime-time KTLA programming – seemed to target a relatively large range of consumer types.

As a general rule, however, commercials never preempted the actual legal proceedings. For these proceedings, in accordance with the ritualistic dimension of media events, were treated by KTLA as sacred. That is, the deference Waller *as anchor* paid to the proceedings and to Judge Ito as presider (see below) worked to establish the proceedings as an integral part of the criminal justice system, to celebrate the important role they play in American democracy. Indeed, Waller rarely spoke over the proceedings, often stopping analysts in mid-sentence to announce the proceedings' start. Similarly, she would solicit analyst commentary only during breaks in the proceedings (e.g., sidebar conferences, adjournments, etc.). Although beyond the direct control of KTLA newsworkers,[18] the beginning and ending of proceedings were routinely announced by a slow tilt down and zoom out from the Great Seal of the State California. This symbol, of course, certified the proceedings as a state-sanctioned event. Adopted by the state's 1849 Constitutional Convention, the Great Seal depicts Minerva, the Roman goddess of wisdom, and inscribes the state's motto, "Eureka" (I have found it), against a backdrop of the Sacramento river and the Sierra Nevada mountain peaks. Together these elements work to celebrate "the People" and the vast natural resources that distinguish the state. While it is true that movements to and from the seal served to ensure that the pool television camera did not capture jurors or off-the-record court business, other, less symbolic objects could have been chosen as a focus. That they were not is rather revealing regarding the implied status of the proceedings to follow.

After the camera's move from the seal, the start of proceedings would then be announced by Judge Ito (e.g., "Okay, back on the record in the Simpson matter"), who also controlled the audio feed KTLA and other electronic media received from the courtroom. A medium shot would present the judge in profile, at his bench, as he instructed counsel for both sides to prepare to continue. A variety of shots – medium, medium close-up, wide – would display witnesses on the stand, attorneys at the podium, the reactions of spectators in the courtroom, attorneys seated at their respective tables, and, of course, Simpson. The camera would frequently move back and forth between these subjects, using the visual within the frame to contextualize the words heard coming from witnesses on the stand or examining attorneys. For example, the camera frequently sought tight shots of Simpson during moments of testimony that were filled with drama (e.g., when the verdict envelope was passed from the jury foreperson to the judge), especially those that were potentially incriminating (e.g., Ron Shipp's claim that Simpson told him he dreamed of killing his ex-wife). Early in the trial, KTLA legal analyst Al DeBlanc actually offered viewers a framework for making sense of the cameras' focus on the defendant:

Now, here they're focusing on O. J. Simpson. The jury is present. His demeanor and attitude now appears to be good. He seems to be content with what's going on. That's the kind of poker face you should have when you're in trial. It's when you start smiling and moving around and tapping people that you have to be careful.[19]

According to DeBlanc's logic, when Simpson did not display his "poker face" during these visual incursions he risked sending damaging messages to the jury (and television audience).

Earlier I mentioned that as a *general rule*, KTLA newsworkers treated the proceedings as sacred, failing to make comments over them or cut away from them while they were in progress. There were, however, exceptions to this rule – all falling in my sample *after* the prosecution's presentation of its case-in-chief. That is, I found four examples (the first three from the defense's case-in-chief and the last from the prosecution's rebuttal case) of Waller interrupting trial testimony in order to go to commercial. The first example involved defense attorney F. Lee Bailey's direct examination of an American Airlines pilot who was in the process of testifying about Simpson's "relaxed" demeanor during the flight to Chicago on the night of the murders.[20] The second example occurred during prosecutor Brian Kelberg's cross-examination of Dr. Robert Huizenga, a witness who had previously described Simpson as severely hobbled by rheumatoid arthritis.[21] The third example involved defense attorney Robert Blasier's direct examination of FBI agent Roger Martz about the presence or absence of EDTA in blood evidence samples – a determination key to supporting or rejecting the defense's conspiracy theory.[22] The final example involved defense attorney Barry Scheck's cross-examination of FBI agent William Bodziak about the possibility of more than one pair of shoe prints at the Bundy murder scene.[23] One interpretation of these exceptions to the rule is that KTLA newsworkers did not consider the vacated proceedings to be as "newsworthy" as those that the station stayed with. Moreover, since the exceptions all fall *after* the prosecution's presentation of its case-in-chief, it seems as if KTLA newsworkers placed a lower value on the *latter* portions of the trial containing the exceptions (i.e., the defense case in chief and the prosecution's rebuttal). In other words, it was as if the proceedings were no longer as sacred. Newsworkers apparently decided that viewers no longer needed to hear every single word of testimony without interruption as was the case during the prosecution's presentation of its case-in-chief. The implication that KTLA newsworkers may have privileged the prosecution's case-in-chief over the defense's, of course, raises the question of bias. In the following section, I explore some of the framing practices and techniques KTLA newsworkers used to emphasize the objectivity of their coverage while simultaneously conveying their own evaluations of the case.

Framing practices and techniques

KTLA newsworkers used several framing practices and techniques designed to camouflage their own interpretations of the case with the trappings of objectivity. These practices and techniques included graphics, direct denial, terms of impartiality, and viewer questions/comments.

Graphics. Newsworkers periodically used superimposed graphics to relay information about witnesses or developments in the case. As these graphics were rarely qualified by words such as "allegedly," "claim(s)(ed)," or "reportedly," they were meant to be received as "facts" (van Dijk 1993). For example, early in the trial a superimposed graphic identified LAPD detective Mark Fuhrman as follows:

Detective Mark Fuhrman. LAPD. Found bloody glove at O. J. Simpson's estate.[24]

Note that the graphic did not read he "allegedly" or "reportedly" or "claims to have" found the glove at Simpson's estate. Instead, the graphic accepted Fuhrman's account of finding the glove as an established fact – despite (or because of?) the defense's well-publicized conspiracy theory.

Direct denial. Another practice used by KTLA newsworkers involved the direct denial of pro-prosecution or pro-defense bias,[25] the explicit claim that they are not invested in the outcome of the trial. For example, Waller went to great lengths early in the trial to explain to viewers that the comments of KTLA legal analysts represent "simply an opinion" about trial developments "on any given day":

You know, there are a lot of things that . . . we would also like to take this opportunity to point out that our legal analysts are not, have no stake in the outcome of the trial and that your opinions, your's [Al DeBlanc's] and Peter Arenella's here or Irene Ayala's . . . it is simply an opinion on how the trial appears to be going from your perspective on any given day.[26]

Al DeBlanc, the legal analyst for the day, concurred and added that even if it *appeared* he was presently biased in favor of the prosecution, this could be explained by the fact that the prosecution was currently controlling the presentation of evidence:

What happens when we analyze the case sometimes, ah, we're very strong for the prosecution because the evidence that day is very strong for the prosecution. The next day we may be strong for the defense because the evidence for the defense is strong. But we're more, we'll sound more prosecution now because at this time, at this stage in the case, the prosecution is putting on their case. They have the burden of proof at this time.

Underlying this explanation for the early "appearance" of pro-prosecution bias, it seems, was the assumption that prosecution evidence will indeed be "strong" and that any defense challenges (i.e., during cross-examination) are likely to be weak.

Toward the end of the trial, Waller again worked to underscore the objective nature of live television trial coverage, this time by contrasting it to newspaper coverage. Veteran newspaper reporter Theo Wilson (see chapter 3), a guest on KTLA's *Noon News*, had just lamented on what she considered unfortunate changes in trial news coverage over the years. When she covered high-profile trials, she noted, newsworkers did not rely as they do today on pictures and legal analysts to make sense of trial proceedings – newsworkers "had to go in and tell our readers what it looked like in there." Against these remarks, which could be construed as a rather blunt critique of KTLA's own coverage of the trial, Waller posed the following question:

Do you think in some ways having the camera there so we are not getting (pause) what, what happened in the courtroom filtered through, you know, experiences of a reporter, but in fact directly from the witness, or the attorney, or the judge, in some ways is maybe a, a, an improvement in some ways? I mean, if we've lost on one hand, have we maybe gained on the other?[27]

Note how Waller's question was essentially a rhetorical one that worked to affirm the objective quality of television trial coverage. That is, her question already presupposed that this coverage comes "directly" from the courtroom, that it is not "filtered" through the "experiences" of newsworkers. And as anyone who believed in the sacred journalistic ideal of objectivity would appreciate, "direct" coverage is obviously preferable to "filtered" coverage. Indeed, despite her earlier reservations about contemporary newswork practices, Wilson quickly reversed field and agreed that live television coverage represents, as Waller had put it, "an improvement in some ways."

Terms of impartiality. A third practice employed by KTLA newsworkers to buttress their objectivity claims involved a reliance upon non-committal terms when confronted by potentially revealing trial developments. As the structure of KTLA's trial coverage required newsworkers to fill dead air time and/or forge transitions between analysts' commentary, these terms served as safe (i.e., seemingly neutral) and stock (i.e., readily available) responses for newsworkers. They provided newsworkers with the option of acknowledging significant developments without really commenting (i.e., maintaining the facade, at least, of impartiality). One such term that seemed to occupy a prime position in newsworkers' tool kits was the adjective "interesting." Early in the trial, for example, defense attorney F. Lee Bailey read from the preliminary hearing transcript during his cross examination of Mark Fuhrman in order to point out what legal analyst Peter Arenella would later describe as "inconsistencies" and "contradictions" in Fuhrman's testimony. In one of these instances, Arenella noted, Fuhrman in his preliminary hearing testimony referred to "gloves in the plural" (i.e., "them") at the Bundy crime scene – an impossibility if the detective had indeed found one of the bloody gloves at Simpson's Rockingham home. Fuhrman's explanation for the apparent inconsistency was that "them" referred to one of the bloody gloves *and* a knit cap also found at Bundy. But as Arenella pointed out to Waller, there was no reference to the cap in the question that had prompted the detective's response. Instead of characterizing this testimony as "damaging," "problematic," or even "troubling" (for the prosecution), Waller described it as "interesting" – a strategy that allowed her to acknowledge the apparent contradictions *and* solicit Arenella's comments (i.e., his "opinion on how the trial appears to be going") without jeopardizing her presumed stance of (professional) impartiality: "Mr. Bailey has asked if they can approach the sidebar with Judge Ito in the midst of this cross-examination. He does seem to be eliciting some *interesting* testimony from Detective Fuhrman as he goes through the preliminary hearing [emphasis added]."[28] As we shall see below, however, KTLA newsworkers frequently vacated this position of neutrality when testimony emerged that seemed to incriminate Simpson.

Another example of newsworkers' reliance upon "interesting" to connote impartiality involved a discussion between Waller and legal analyst Al DeBlanc. The issue: Will Simpson take the stand in his own defense? Arguing against the possibility, DeBlanc enumerated a number of "inconsistencies" in the defense's account of Simpson's actions on the night of the murders (e.g., his house was dark when the limousine driver arrived but he was getting dressed; he was debilitated by arthritis but he was chipping golf balls). With a smirk on her face, this is how Waller responded to DeBlanc's analysis: "Should be very *interesting* to see if he does that. But then you're confronted with the second *story*, that he was taking a nap, that he overslept [emphasis added]".[29] Note how in contrast to the example concerning Fuhrman's "inconsistencies," Waller did not stop here by merely describing as "interesting" the possibility that Simpson might testify. Instead, she added an additional sentence that worked to question the veracity of the defense's account of the evening (i.e., its "story"). Accepting this invitation to comment, DeBlanc punctuated his analysis: "Cross examination will take him over the grill on these inconsistencies." In other words, it would be more than "interesting" if Simpson indeed took the stand – it would be devastating for the defense.

A final example of newsworker's reliance upon "interesting" as a term of impartiality emerged near the end of the prosecution's case-in-chief, after prosecutors decided to drop several domestic violence witnesses. This prosecution decision had followed closely on the heels of another important trial development: the glove demonstration, which most commentators considered a disaster for the prosecution. Prior to the start of court for the day, Waller and KTLA reporter Ron Olsen – who was located outside the courtroom – speculated about the prosecution's next moves. Olsen suggested that perhaps prosecutors will recall Richard Rubin, the former Aris Isotoner executive, to explain why the gloves did not appear to fit Simpson during the demonstration. He also noted that prosecutors have referred to incriminating hair and fiber evidence that had yet to be presented. Against this backdrop of recent trial developments, Olsen twice deployed "interesting" to neutral(ize) his obvious confusion (or disappointment?) regarding prosecution strategy: "In the meantime, we all continue to wonder . . . and I'm sure Professor Arenella will want to comment on this: What's going on with the strategy of the prosecution? Things are getting very, very *interesting* [emphasis added]."[30] Then, seconds later:

And as we were discussing yesterday, Marta, you have to wonder what the prosecution is doing. Ah, are they reacting to the bloody glove demonstration? as [defense attorney] Johnnie Cochran charged? They say, "No," that has nothing to do with their decision to drop the four witnesses on domestic abuse. You have to wonder what they're doing, what their strategy is, and whether they're going to bring in rebuttal witnesses that they aren't calling now. Whether they're trying to, ah, set the, the defense off balance. It's, it's getting very, very *interesting*. (Emphasis added)

Viewer questions/comments. The fourth practice used by KTLA newsworkers to reinforce their journalistic presumption of objectivity involved the invocation of viewer questions and comments. Newsworkers frequently resorted to viewer phone calls and faxes in order to prompt legal analysts to discuss issues or concerns that, if directly raised by the newsworkers, might threaten their aura of impartiality. Presumably, KTLA newsworkers received numerous phone calls and faxes throughout the trial from viewers who sought to ask questions or make comments. Accordingly, newsworkers had to sort through all of this correspondence in order to select the items that would be aired. The examples I found in the sample suggest that newsworkers primarily used viewer correspondence to explore trial developments, evidence, or issues that worked to support the prosection's case. For example, early in the defense's presentation of its case-in-chief, Waller referred to a viewer fax to consider a theory of the crime consistent with prosecution accounts. In the fax, the viewer presupposed that the bloody glove – as Fuhrman maintained and the defense challenged – was indeed first found behind Simpson's home. Waller read the fax on air:

"One thing keeps bothering me regarding the Simpson case. I can't envision what would cause the three thumps Kato Kaelin heard outside his room the night of the murders. It seems to me that there would have to be a reason for the loud noises and that merely bumping into the wall wouldn't cause that. Is it possible that the air conditioner outside had some type of opening in it? The noise is consistent with someone consciously hitting something pretty hard to cause the type of noise described. Could the knife have been shoved into the air conditioner in order to hide it? *It would also account for the loss of the glove outside the room.* Has anyone thoroughly checked to see if there's anything there?" I, I, have to assume the police have checked it. But it's an *interesting* observation. (Emphasis added)[31]

Note how Waller essentially validated the underlying presupposition about the glove by declaring the theory "an *interesting* observation" (see discussion above). That is, she could have more fully contextualized the question by *also* noting the controversy surrounding the glove – by at least acknowledging defense charges that the glove was planted and/or the "inconsistencies" underscored in Fuhrman's testimony during cross-examination. Instead, echoing the graphic described above (i.e., "Detective Mark Fuhrman. LAPD. Found bloody glove at O. J. Simpson's estate"), Waller treated the viewer's presupposition as undisputed "fact."

Another example of this practice comes from a discussion between Waller and DeBlanc toward the end of the defense's case-in-chief, as they awaited Judge Ito's decision about the admissibility of the Fuhrman tapes. At the time, you will recall, news reports were already in circulation about the tapes including numerous examples of the detective using the word "nigger" to refer to blacks – despite his testimony during the criminal trial that he had not used the word in the last ten years. Although the tapes had not yet been released to the public, most trial observers expected the defense to use the tapes – if admitted into evidence by the judge – to impeach Fuhrman, to damage his credibility as a witness. At stake, of course, was Fuhrman's account regarding numerous pieces of incriminating evidence he had testified to finding (e.g., the Rockingham glove). Against the backdrop of the explosive impact the tapes could conceivably have on other case "evidence," the question Waller read on the air focused on a technicality, one that might (hopefully?) render the tapes inadmissible:

But there was a question submitted about, ah, the tapes and I'd say it's *interesting*. It says, "Isn't it possible that Fuhrman will challenge these tapes saying he wasn't informed he was being recorded? If he didn't know he was being recorded, aren't the tapes illegal and therefore inadmissible?"[32]

Despite Waller's sponsorship of the question (i.e., it was selected from many others for reading on the air; she considered it "interesting"), DeBlanc argued that it raised a moot point *vis-à-vis* the issue of admissibility. That is, because the recordings were made by a private citizen and did not include government action, their use in a court of law could not be challenged by Fuhrman. Moreover, the screenwriter who made the tapes, Laura Hart McKinny, would soon testify that the detective knew he was being recorded.

A final example of this practice comes from an exchange between Ron Olsen – who was substituting for Waller at the anchor desk – and legal analyst Al DeBlanc. It took place not long after Mark Fuhrman assumed the witness stand for the second time in the trial, this time to assert his 5th Amendment right against self-incrimination. In the aftermath of what may arguably have been the apex of the trial for the defense, Olsen "focused" KTLA's discussion of the day's developments (cf. Brunsdon and Morley 1978) by reading the following viewer question:

Okay, I'm gonna hit you with one from out of left field. *And the only reason I bring this up* is because I got a call, ah, a lady called me from Houston, TX. It was her dime so . . . I'm going to pass the question along to you. She said, "Would you please ask your legal analyst what happened to Ronald Goldman and Nicole Brown-Simpson?" (Emphasis added)[33]

Note how Olsen went to great lengths to make it clear that the concern raised about the victims should be attributed to the caller, not to him (i.e., "And the only reason I bring this up . . ."). This direct denial is similar to other tactics employed by KTLA newsworkers to inoculate themselves from charges of bias when they choose to raise issues that might be construed as partisan (see above). Indeed, the entire Simpson trial is only relevant to concern *for the victims* if it is assumed that Simpson is guilty. If Simpson were actually innocent, the "rights" of the victims would not be served by avoiding issues like Fuhrman's racism. The real killer(s) would still be free.

Themes

In the previous section, I reviewed a number of practices and techniques employed by KTLA newsworkers to reinforce their presumed journalistic stance of objectivity. I now turn to exploring how KTLA newsworkers and legal analysts negotiated four major themes emerging from the station's coverage of the criminal trial. These themes included "celebrity," "credibility," "evidence," and "race." As we shall see below, the stances newsworkers adopted *vis-à-vis* these themes – despite their efforts to present themselves as impartial – reveal their acceptance of key ideological assumptions embedded in dominant understandings of the case (i.e., the "most plausible" narratives outlined in chapter 1). Accordingly, many of these assumptions also undergird the hegemonic political projects I discussed in chapter 2.

Celebrity. Numerous comments made by KTLA newsworkers and legal analysts positioned Simpson as a celebrity who enjoyed privileges not accorded the typical murder defendant. While these observations were undoubtedly correct, newsworkers often jumped from them to a rather dubious conclusion, one that worked to support the Celebrity Defendant project: Simpson's resources unduly handicapped prosecution efforts to secure a conviction (see chapter 2). For example, early in the defense's presentation of its case-in-chief, legal analyst Peter Arenella suggested that because of Simpson's celebrity the prosecution may face a greater burden of proof than they would if he were merely an ordinary murder defendant:

Defendants are convicted all the time even though there are powerfully important unanswered questions about specific, ah, specific issues about how the crime was committed as long as it was proved that the person did it and he had the requisite intent. The point here is simply the fear that *this jury given who O. J. Simpson is* might want all of these questions answered before they convict, even though that's not the prosecution's burden.[34] That's the fear the prosecution has. (Emphasis added)[35]

Other newsworker comments worked to remind viewers, in case they had forgotten, about the "Dream Team" of attorneys Simpson had at his disposal. Note, for example, how KTLA reporter Eric Spillman paraphrased Judge Ito's complaints about errors in a brief filed by the defense in their efforts to have the Fuhrman tapes admitted into evidence: "In fact, in his ruling, Judge Ito says, 'Look, *you guys have twelve lawyers working for you.* You should organize this in a more, ah, simplistic form so that I can get to this information quicker and be able to make my decision [emphasis added].'"[36]

In the immediate aftermath of the not-guilty verdicts, of course, echoes of these commentaries on the undue advantages Simpson reaped from his celebrity status could be heard in the anguished reactions of several trial observers interviewed by KTLA newsworkers. For example, a white law student at the University of Southern California, Simpson's alma mater, told KTLA reporter Warren Wilson that she believed the not-guilty verdicts were the result of Simpson being "such a public figure":

I think that because he's, ah, *such a public figure,* I hope that the jury actually thought about what they were doing. Umm, there was a lot of evidence that they should have considered, and, umm, I hope they did. It doesn't seem like they did, though. (Emphasis added)[37]

Minutes later, a white male interviewed by KTLA reporter Michelle Ruiz not far from the Brentwood murder scene said he was "shocked" by the verdicts and blamed them on the "power of [Simpson's] money":

I just don't understand how, ah, with so many, so much evidence and, ah, and other information for the past nine months, the system, you know, could come up with such a verdict. Ah, you know, we are all very, I'm very shocked. And, ah, I think the prosecution did a wonderful job. But it just goes to show you that, the *power of money*. And, ah, basically, that's it. (Emphasis added)[38]

Note how this statement implies that the criminal justice system is somehow broken. That is, prosecutors "did a wonderful job" (Simpson was proven guilty) but the "power of money" still prevailed in the end (Simpson was acquitted). This observation places us but a few steps away from the central tenet of the Celebrity Defendant project: the system makes it too easy for criminal defendants to evade conviction (see chapter 2).

Credibility. Throughout the sampled KTLA coverage of the trial, newsworkers and legal commentators made numerous comments that either worked to question the credibility of defense attorneys and witnesses or validate the credibility of prosecutors and their witnesses. Three examples nicely represent KTLA's assessment of credibility. First, late in the prosecution's case-in-chief, Waller effectively dismissed the credibility of defense attorneys with her choice of language: "In the beginning of this trial, the defense *floated* a number of theories before the jury [emphasis added]".[39] The choice of the verb "floated," of course, implied that Simpson's attorneys were less concerned with "truth" than with concocting theories that might work to acquit their client. Waller continued by enumerating the various theories, wondering if in the face of "overwhelming" (i.e., credible) prosecution evidence defense attorneys would eventually have to settle on one theory:

They talked about the conspiracy theory, a rogue cop theory, that being Mark Fuhrman. The rush to judgement with the police racing over to Mr. Simpson's home, in their, their picture of what happened, rushing over there having decided already that, that he had committed the murders, contamination of the evidence, umm, the drug theory and of course the alibi theory . . . and there have been a couple of alibis that we've seen. When it's all said and done and these statistics are put out, assuming the jury accepts the statistics and says, "Okay, this is *overwhelming*," what happens in the minds of the jury that all these other theories were put before them? Is the defense obligated to put, to do something to explain away some of the theories or expand on them? (Emphasis added)[40]

Prompted by this question, Al DeBlanc launched into a 565-word commentary underscoring the problems he had with the theories "floated" by the defense – particularly the more conspiratorial ones. DeBlanc emphasized several points: LAPD officers had no motive to frame Simpson; Fuhrman could not have framed Simpson without help from several other officers; a conspiracy of this proportion would necessarily have involved many LAPD officers and criminalists who did not know one another prior to the night of the murders; the penalty in California for a conspiracy of this type is death; conspirators could not have known whether Simpson had an iron-clad alibi. In short, although he ultimately hedged his bet (i.e., the defense, after all, had yet to call its first witness), DeBlanc concluded that the burden faced by the defense "would be extremely difficult" to meet:

There are so many, ah, problems with it that it would be extremely difficult for the defense to meet this burden. I'm not saying they don't have some evidence. We have to wait and see. But at this point there has been virtually no evidence in that regard. Accusation only. And they have to get beyond an accusation.[41]

While the comments of KTLA newsworkers frequently questioned the credibility of defense attorneys, they routinely accorded prosecution witnesses – particularly LAPD officers – the presumption of credibility. For example, a major plank of the defense conspiracy theory rested on police reports documenting that four LAPD detectives (including Fuhrman and the two lead detectives) left the Bundy murder scene shortly after examining some of the evidence and travelled to Simpson's Brentwood home. Contrary to one of the conspiracy theories "floated" by the defense, lead detective Philip Vannatter testified that Simpson was not a suspect at the time. The officers, he testified, had travelled to Rockingham only to notify him in person of his ex-wife's death. Defense attorneys, however, sought to prove the officers went to Rockingham because they had already identified Simpson as a suspect in the murders. During cross examination, defense attorney Robert Shapiro established a number of points that questioned Vannatter's explanation for the visit – a visit that would ultimately result in Fuhrman scaling Simpson's fence, the officers entering the property without a search warrant, and Fuhrman allegedly finding the glove. First, Shapiro noted that Simpson was not legally his ex-wife's next of kin. Second, Vannatter could not name any other cases in which the lead detectives had left a murder scene prior to it being secured in order to make a death notification. Later, of course, the defense would present a mafia informant, Tony Fiato, to impeach Vannatter's testimony. Fiato would testify that Vannatter told him that when a woman is killed "the husband is always the suspect." Prosecutors retaliated by calling LAPD commander Keith Bushey during its rebuttal case to testify he had ordered Vannatter and the detectives to travel to Simpson's home for a death notification. For DeBlanc, the ex-LAPD sergeant, Bushey's (credible) testimony immediately settled any questions about the Rockingham trip: "What, what Commander Bushey has done is he has pretty much, ah, given evidence to, that tends to neutralize the discussion regarding Vannatter."[42]

A final example of the credibility differential KTLA newsworkers perceived between the defense and prosecution comes from comments made by Waller shortly after the not-guilty verdicts were announced. Against the backdrop of defense attorneys who had "floated" numerous theories throughout the trial, Waller portrayed prosecutor Christopher Darden as a principled, "underrated" prosecutor (i.e., "his closing argument was *so* compelling") who may retire from law practice because of "what he saw happened to the legal system" in the Simpson case:

> Chris Darden, umm, in, in some ways, may be the most underrated of all the attorneys . . . I mean, he really – his closing argument was *so* compelling. And I think we saw the real Chris Darden. And he had, I got the feeling he had a very, very difficult time during, throughout the course of this trial. And even expressed a tremendous amount of, of reservation and sadness with what had, with what he saw happened to the legal system — ah, to the point where he, I think, went so far as to say he might not even practice law after this. (Emphasis original)[43]

"What he saw happened to the legal system," of course, is that Simpson's "Dream Team" of attorneys (cf. Celebrity Defendant project) had been allowed by the judge and jury to "float" ridiculous theories and exploit legal loopholes (i.e., Fuhrman's impeachment on a "collateral" issue) in order to neutralize the "overwhelming evidence" pointing to the defendant's guilt. To KTLA portrayals of this evidence we now turn.

Evidence. Consistent with KTLA newsworkers' *a priori* assumptions about the high credibility of prosecutors and prosecution witnesses, they treated DNA evidence as an infallible barometer of Simpson's guilt. Indeed, when prosecution witnesses testified as to how infinitesimal the chance was that blood at the murder scene could have come from anyone other than Simpson, these statistics were directly applied by KTLA newsworkers as a numerical index of the defendant's guilt. The same is true regarding blood found in Simpson's Bronco and on objects at his home that seemed consistent with the victims. This leap in logic could not have been made unless defense claims about *how* the blood had been deposited was dismissed out of hand (i.e., as (in)credible). For example, as KTLA legal analyst Al DeBlanc reasoned:

> They [defense attorneys] would probably like to, to, to break this flow that's been so successful at this point for the prosecution. Because certainly the *amount of numbers that have been testified to* and the manner in which O.J. Simpson has been identified at the Bundy crime scene, the Bronco, and his home, along with the blood trail of the two victims. *That has got to be very powerful and compelling evidence to this jury.* (Emphasis added)[44]

Prompted by Waller to consider what might happen if certain jurors are not persuaded by the DNA evidence, DeBlanc talked about the possibility that the other jurors might "teach" DNA doubters "what they know about it and will try to persuade and convince them that this is reliable evidence and should be given great weight."

Another example of KTLA newsworkers treating DNA statistics as a valid and reliable barometer of guilt comes from the period shortly after the prosecution's failed glove demonstration. Legal analyst Peter Arenella commented to Waller that the prosecution "has to end strongly" in order to secure a conviction. His suggestion, of course, is that prosecutors revisit the DNA statistics – "you can't get more evidence, more powerful evidence than that":

> Ah, the bottom line is the prosecution has to end strongly here. Ah, and they're not going to end strongly if they end with hair and fiber evidence. The hair and fiber evidence isn't as powerful and it isn't as incriminating as their DNA evidence. *When you have one in 57 million odds* – which is what Gary Sims, the crime, the DOJ [Department of Justice] expert testified to yesterday – *you can't get more evidence, more powerful evidence than that.* (Emphasis added)[45]

As the discussion of DNA evidence continued, Waller and Arenella essentially dismissed the defense conspiracy theory that blood may have been planted to incriminate Simpson. The key topic: EDTA, the chemical used to preserve blood samples. As both prosecutors and defense attorneys had stipulated, if any of the blood were planted from reference samples, it would show traces of this preservative. In the following exchange, Waller accepted at face value prosecution claims about the absence of EDTA in blood evidence. That is, "They're not going to tell the jury that there was no trace of the preservative EDTA in that analysis." Besides, she continued, if in the unlikely event that traces of the preservative were found, prosecutors have provided us with several innocent explanations (e.g., "It's also in laundry soap"). Arenella agreed, noting that the prosecution's strategy of not bringing up the EDTA issue is a "wise decision" because it forces the defense to "put up or shut up" – a phrase he attributes to prosecutor Christopher Darden. If indeed defense attorneys raise the issue, he continued, prosecutors can "come back with their witnesses and their [overwhelming] evidence" during rebuttal. I present the rather lengthy exchange in its entirety:

WALLER: You know, last night as I went home, I was thinking about their decision that, one of the decisions the prosecutors have made is that they will not tell the jury the DNA analysis on three blood drops, including one of Mr. Simpson's socks, a drop of blood found on the back gate at the Bundy condo. *They're not going to tell the jury that there was no trace of the preservative EDTA in that analysis.* And the defense has contended all along that blood was planted and that if EDTA was found in the samples, that would prove it was planted because EDTA is used in the vials that contain blood samples as a preservative. *It's also in laundry soap. It's in a number of things in, in life there's EDTA.* And I'm wondering if they're not doing it because it might confuse the issue, and then the defense won't ever bring it up. I mean, it's almost like they've narrowed it down. *I feel like they're narrowing the focus and instead of keeping on something they don't need to tell them because it's a non-issue.*

ARENELLA: Marta, I think you're on to something. The, the def – the prosecution in this case has been somewhat defensive. And what I mean by that is that they have anticipated what the defense is going to do and then they've tried to rebut it before the defense has even done it. The EDTA controversy is an excellent example. I think this is a wise decision by the prosecution. Essentially what they're saying here is, "If the defense wants to claim conspiracy, put up or shut up." *Those are Christopher Darden's words in his press conference yesterday.* "Put up or shut up." They're putting the burden, in a sense, the, the tactical burden on the defense to raise the EDTA controversy to prove their conspiracy point and then in rebuttal they'll come back with their experts and their evidence. (Emphasis added)[46]

One month later, however, defense attorneys *would* raise the issue of EDTA during their case-in-chief. Indeed, they called toxicologist Frederic Rieders, who testified that traces of EDTA were found in several blood samples. They also called FBI Agent Martz – the prosecution witness who conducted the tests – in order to explain his written interpretation of the findings. During direct examination by defense attorney Robert Blasier on the morning of July 25, you will recall, Martz seemed to concede that the test results were "consistent with the presence of EDTA." But after a recess in which he conferred with prosecutors, a more aggressive Martz testified he was able to "prove" the evidence bloodstains did not come from preserved blood.

Later that day, KTLA newsworkers resumed the station's trial coverage by juxtaposing two sound bites from this morning and afternoon testimony that neatly captured the change. From Martz's morning testimony:

BLASIER: Agent Martz, would you agree that the pattern that you got on sock, Q206, is consistent with the presence of EDTA?
MARTZ: Ah, it certainly warrants further testing, ah, it responded like EDTA responded. Yes.
BLASIER: Is it consistent with the presence of EDTA?
MARTZ: Yes.[47]

From Martz's afternoon testimony:

MARTZ: There are many possibilities for those ion counts that I got. One is, it could be from another compound that had similar results. That's why I performed the daughter ion experiment to determine whether or not EDTA was present. *I was convinced that EDTA was not present in those samples.*
BLASIER: So you had made up your mind as to what you were going to find before you did the test?

MARTZ: That is not correct. I was asked to determine whether or not those blood-stains came from preserved blood. And those bloodstains did not come from preserved blood. *I was able to prove that on the first day.* (Emphasis added)[48]

Despite the apparent contradiction in Martz's own testimony (i.e., "it certainly requires further testing/I was able to prove that on the first day"), Waller effectively resolved the conspiracy controversy with her summary of the day's events:

A defense witness [Martz] testified this morning blood on a sock found in Simpson's home and on a gate at the Bundy residence does not contain the preservative EDTA. The testimony by FBI special agent Roger Martz contradicts the testimony yesterday by toxicologist Frederic Rieders. Martz's testimony *rejects* the defense's *claim* Simpson was framed by police. (Emphasis added)[49]

Note how Waller folds Rieders' "testimony" into the defense's "claim" (cf. van Dijk 1993, p. 252) – one that Martz's "testimony," of course, "rejects." Waller went on to ask legal analyst Irene Ayala about her thoughts on how quickly the defense would wrap up their case. The question of EDTA is not revisited.

Race. A final theme, one that repeatedly surfaced throughout KTLA's coverage of the case, was race. For example, KTLA newsworkers routinely used graphics to keep viewers apprised of the jury's changing racial makeup and to underscore their own discussion of these developments:

New Juror: #2179, 28-year-old, African American Female, postal worker, Married, lives in Compton.[50]

Then, seconds later:

Juror Makeup: 10 women, 2 men, 9 African Americans, 2 Caucasians, 1 Hispanic, 2 alternates remain.[51]

A subtext of KTLA newsworker commentary throughout the trial, the predominance of black women on the jury would provide many who were "shocked" by the not-guilty verdicts with a "plausible" explanation: Simpson is black/his black lead attorney played the "race card"/ignorant black jurors closed ranks and set him free (i.e., the Black "Other" project; see chapter 2).

Undoubtedly, the "race card" critics accused the defense of so successfully "playing" was strengthened by the Fuhrman tapes. That is, what better way to divert attention away from the prosecution's "overwhelming" evidence than by introducing the racist statements of a detective who defense attorneys "claim" framed their black client? When Judge Ito allowed defense attorneys to play before the jury just two of the sixty-one tape excerpts they had selected to impeach Fuhrman – any more, he ruled, would have been "cumulative" – proponents of the "Just-Us" system project organized a protest outside the downtown courthouse (see chapter 2). KTLA legal analyst Al DeBlanc, however, invoked the legacy of the Civil Rights Era to commend the judge for not allowing "vigilante pressure" to sway him from seeking "justice":

> Ah, what you have with a trial judge . . . a trial judge has a responsibility not to be affected by the outside forces – I mean, let's just go back to the civil rights cases. If you, if the, if you had an African American who was being tried, part of the problem was that many people felt that vigilante pressure caused the jury and the judge, or what have you, to not give justice. And so when a judge takes the oath the judge is supposed to ensure that justice occurs.[52]

In this classic example of "reversal" (van Dijk 1993, p. 261), DeBlanc essentially accuses *victims* of the "Just-Us" system (see chapter 2) of attempting to disrupt "justice."

In the end, of course, KTLA's continual return to the issue of race in its trial coverage echoed the issue's centrality in the case and in American society. As opinion polls revealed shortly after the murders and well beyond the not-guilty verdicts, there existed a significant divide between blacks and whites – if not in their actual beliefs about Simpson's innocence or guilt – in what they felt compelled to tell pollsters. Images circulated by KTLA shortly after the verdicts illustrated the depth of these stances for many trial observers, the magnitude of the investments they had in the trial's income. A white woman interviewed by KTLA reporter Michelle Ruiz near the Bundy murder scene, for example, began to cry as she reflected on the not-guilty verdicts. For her, police "mistakes" (racism?) had "backfired," allowing defense attorneys to exploit race in order to secure an outcome that "really shouldn't have happened":

> RUIZ: What's your reaction?
> WOMAN: Umm, well, I guess I knew this was going to happen. But it just seems to hit a little harder . . . when it actually goes down (starts to cry).
> RUIZ: You seem . . . very affected by the not-guilty verdicts.
> WOMAN: (in tears) Yeah. (someone shouts "Guilty!" from off in distance) I don't think it's fair with two women (sic) who were killed everywhere. I mean, to have someone get off like this. I guess, I guess it's because of *mistakes made by the LAPD*. I mean, *my mom married an LAPD officer and I guess I grew up with racism my whole life, hearing it in the house . . . but . . . it just really backfired.* Their actions just really backfired and it was really irresponsible on the part of Mark Fuhrman and just all those officers. They really need to rethink, umm, the hiring and training and just the ethical standards that those officers have because this really shouldn't have happened. (Emphasis added)[53]

Conclusions

Moments before a jury would announce its decision to either set Simpson free or to send him to jail for the rest of his life, Waller sat at her anchor desk in the KTLA studios with a former prosecutor, a retired trial judge, and legal analyst Al DeBlanc. The group seemed to be the antithesis of the "intense" crowd mounting outside the courthouse. Amidst jokes about the $100,000 book advance awarded to a dismissed black juror, Michael Knox,[54] they discussed the news that the jury had requested not to speak with either prosecutors or defense attorneys after the verdicts were announced. The consensus: "a very bad sign for the defense" – especially in light of the "inspirational closing argument [as opposed to 'compelling'] and inspirational presence of Mr. Cochran," as one of the commentators described it. When the jury finally acquitted Simpson moments later, Waller summarized the verdicts as follows: "More than one year after the murders of Nicole Brown-Simpson and Ronald Lyle Goldman, O. J. Simpson acquitted of, the murders. *And with four hours of deliberations* [emphasis added]".[55] Of course, KTLA's viewers might have read Waller's final sentence any number of different ways. For example, viewers could have construed it to suggest the prosecution's case was so suspect that jurors were able to quickly dismiss it. Alternatively, viewers may have interpreted the sentence as an indictment of the jury – that jurors were either derelict in their duties or they purposefully chose to acquit Simpson in an improper act of jury nullification. When KTLA's coverage of the trial is considered in its entirety, however, the resulting narrative clearly privileges the latter interpretation.

As I have attempted to demonstrate in this chapter, KTLA's coverage of the Simpson criminal trial simultaneously worked to reproduce dominant narratives about the case *and* reinforce an important division of labor: newsworkers report "facts;" commentators offer "opinions" and "analysis." KTLA newsworkers, you will recall, labored to maintain this duality with framing techniques and practices – including direct denial, terms of impartiality, and reliance upon viewer questions and comments. This was especially true for the relatively few instances in which KTLA legal analysts offered opinions or analyses that questioned the prosecution's case. Newsworkers typically described these observations as "interesting" – thereby consigning the observation to the realm of conjecture, speculation, opinion. When legal analysts offered commentary that questioned the defense case, however, newsworkers were more likely to explicitly concur, thereby assigning the aura of facticity to the commentary (i.e., newsworkers report "facts"). Thus the several important themes emerging from KTLA's coverage of the trial – celebrity, credibility, evidence, and race – were all framed to fit neatly into dominant narratives about the case.

In the next chapter, I present a case study of the *Los Angeles Times*'s coverage of the criminal trial. *How* and *to what degree* did the ideological assumptions of the Simpson newsworker corps also find their way into the pages of this influential newspaper?

5 (Re)affirming official sources: O. J. and the *Los Angeles Times*

The words "Los Angeles Times," set in large, bold letters, extend across the four center columns of newsprint. In the far right hand column, a forty- to fifty-paragraph article reviews the previous day's developments in the Simpson double murder case. A full-color photograph and two-column headline typically complement this article. In one of the other six columns comprising the front page, a sidebar story about the case often appears. Inside the newspaper, perhaps, another story or two expands on issues related to the case. This is what confronted the reader of the *Los Angeles Times* on a typical morning during the "Trial of the Century."

Its main offices situated just a block from the building housing Judge Ito's courtroom, the *Times* was well-positioned to be the "paper of record" in the Simpson case. But the *Times*, owned by the multi-billion dollar Times Mirror Company,[1] also had a daily circulation of about 1 million, making it the largest newspaper in Los Angeles and the fourth-largest newspaper in the nation.[2] It was one of only five news organizations awarded a permanent seat in Ito's courtroom (see chapter 3). It also had ample newsworker resources to devote to every facet of the Simpson saga, from the murders, through the criminal trial verdicts, and beyond. Indeed, the newspaper devoted five newsworkers to the case full-time for more than a year.[3] The newspaper published nearly 1,000 case-related news narratives between discovery of the Bundy murders and the criminal trial verdicts,[4] and more front-page news narratives on the case over this sixteen-month period – 398 – than any other newspaper in the nation.[5] Its metropolitan newsworker staff won a National Headliner's first-place award for its coverage of the verdicts.[6]

This chapter presents a case study of the *Los Angeles Times*'s coverage of the Simpson criminal trial. As in the previous chapter, I examine this coverage in light of the ideological stances of the Simpson newsworker corps that were discussed in chapter 3. *How* and *to what degree* did membership in this corps affect the newsgathering and newswriting of *Times* newsworkers covering the case? That is, which O. J. narrative or narratives were privileged by the *Times*'s coverage? Moreover, *how* was this ideological work accomplished?

In order to explore these questions, I first examine the totality of *Times* coverage (i.e., ninety narratives) of the investigation and other case-related developments during the first two weeks following the murders. Next, I examine a random sample of *Times* criminal trial coverage. This sample was selected according to the techniques employed in the previous chapter for KTLA-TV. That is, for this case study, I first selected the day *after* each of the thirty-seven days identified in the previous chapter. The resulting days, while representing each of the thirty-seven weeks of the criminal trial, are also the earliest dates that a morning newspaper like the *Times* could possibly report on what the electronic media (e.g., KTLA-TV) had covered on the previous day. In other words, by shifting the sampled days one day later for this chapter, I hoped to facilitate a comparison of electronic (i.e., KTLA) and print (i.e. the *Times*) media coverage of comparable trial developments and themes. Finally, for each of the thirty-seven sampled days, I examine all of the case-related narratives appearing in the newspaper, but pay particular attention to fifty-three page-one narratives. I again employ van Dijk's (1993) work on elite discourse as my primary analytical framework (see chapter 4).

We begin by briefly reviewing the history of the *Times* and meeting the newsworkers who contributed most directly to the newspaper's Simpson coverage.

The *Times*

> In the early decades of *The Times*, the paper's colorful prose was striking. There was little objectivity in those pages. Stories led the reader to one specific conclusion without a balanced presentation of the facts. Reading these stories now is amusing because their style runs contrary to the present rules of journalism.[7]

The *Los Angeles Times* was founded in 1881, when Los Angeles was still just a dusty outpost for cattle ranchers and oil magnates. The city population was only about 11,000 then,[8] and Los Angeles was little more than a faint echo of the more cosmopolitan urban center to the North, San Francisco. But the city would grow, of course, eventually eclipsing San Francisco as the social and economic center of the West and, increasingly, of the Pacific Rim. Today, Los Angeles' 3.7 million residents make it the second largest city and media market in the nation.[9] Much of the city's growth can be traced back to the political activities of the family that founded the *Times* and built it into one of the most prominent newspapers in the nation.

Harrison Gray Otis became editor and chief of the *Los Angeles Daily Times*[10] in 1882, after the fledgling paper had struggled for some eight months (Geis 1990). Otis, a rabid anti-unionist, was distressed by the growing union movement in the United States and vowed to keep the *Times* a free shop. His pro-business editorials and elite ties[11] soon cemented Los Angeles's reputation as a supportive environment for business investment, as an anti-union town. Indeed, while San Francisco's high degree of unionization at the time worked to discourage black workers from migrating to that city, Los Angeles's anti-union reputation attracted thousands of black migrants to the city who felt that in the absence of discriminatory union practices they might find work (Broussard 1993).

The *Times* was so essential to Los Angeles's status as an anti-labor town that the newspaper and its leaders apparently became the target of pro-union saboteurs. In the early morning hours of October 4, 1910, an explosion demolished the *Times*'s downtown building, killing twenty employees and injuring twenty-one others. Otis was away in Mexico at the time, and his son-in-law and future *Times* publisher, Harry Chandler, was several blocks from the building. The newspaper's immediate response foreshadowed how its leaders would respond to subsequent threats to its interests. Within hours, Chandler supervised the printing of an editorial about the event from an auxiliary printing plant. "They can kill our men and wreck our buildings," the piece defiantly read, "but, by the God above! They cannot kill the *Times*" (Berges 1984, p. 22).

By 1950, the population of Los Angeles had grown to about 2 million.[12] Much of this growth was spurred by *Times* led development projects over the last four decades. While publisher of the newspaper, Chandler would successfully promote many of these projects. For example, he was a strong booster for (and investor in) San Fernando Valley real estate development (Geis 1990). This project depended upon the largest engineering feat of the day: construction of an aqueduct system that in 1913 began diverting water hundreds of miles from the Owens Valley to Los Angeles. Chandler also lured the first automotive-related industry to Los Angeles (Geis 1990). Later, this industry – which promoted the use of automobiles over public transportation – would play a major role in shaping the growing city's sprawling freeway system and geography (Davis 1990). Finally, Chandler underwrote one of the city's first aviation ventures (Geis 1990), an industry that would later attract thousands of migrants seeking defense-related jobs during World War II (Davis 1990).

In short, the *Times* and its leaders clearly had a stake in Los Angeles. Accordingly, the newspaper has strongly supported in its pages over the years those forces committed to preserving order in the city, to maintaining the status quo power structure. While the newspaper's resulting "law and order" bias might be narrowly traced back to Otis' early anti-unionism and the 1910 bombing, it can be more broadly attributed to the city's "history of class and race warfare" (Davis 1990, p. 229). Indeed, throughout most of the twentieth century, the *Times* has enjoyed a symbiotic relationship with the LAPD and the anti-labor, racially inflammatory police chiefs who have run it (Domanick 1995). This relationship has cast a heavy shadow on the tenor of *Times* coverage, especially that concerning race and crime. As Domanick (1995) put it:

The city's oligarchy, led by the *Los Angeles Times*, had always wanted to perpetuate the city's ethos – growth and land speculation. And they demanded of the press total support of the myth of L.A. as a white spot, and a deliberate closed-eye distortion of reality. Thus crime news and police news was either studiously ignored or sanitized and written about in such an oblique style that it took a great deal of knowledge along with a decoder key to decipher a story's meaning. (pp. 132–23)

But the quote that begins this section, of course, contradicts Domanick's characterization of *Times* news coverage. This opening quote – extracted from a 1990, Times Mirror Company retrospective – contrasts today's *Times* with the "early decades" of the *Times*, depicting the more recent newspaper as one that conforms to the "present rules of journalism," that adheres to the journalistic ideal of "objectivity," that provides its readers with a "balanced presentation of the facts." When Harry Chandler's grandson, Otis Chandler, became the *Times*'s fourth publisher in 1960, he heavily invested in the latest news production technologies and embarked on a massive hiring of newsworkers. Company literature celebrates this leadership as the turning point that resulted in the *Times* ascendance into the ranks of the world's great newspapers (cf. Geis 1990). Below, I explore the legacy of Chandler's innovations, by first introducing important newsworkers behind the *Times*'s coverage of the "Trial of the Century," and by then examining the newspaper's objectivity claims in light of the narratives it constructed and circulated about the Simpson case.

The *Times* newsworkers

If its investment of labor power is any indication, the *Times* was heavily committed to covering the Simpson case. In the two weeks following the murders, forty-nine different newsworkers were named as contributors to the *Times* coverage of the case, while thirty-eight names – a few of them new – emerged from the thirty-seven days worth of news narratives sampled for my analysis of criminal trial coverage (one day for each week of the trial). Most of these newsworkers – consistent with the overall Simpson newsworker corps – were white men or women. With one prominent exception (see below), this finding is particularly true of the newsworkers who contributed to the page-one, case-related narratives published during the trial. The *Times*'s larger staff of writers and editors also reflect this observation: as is the case with most mainstream newspapers, it has been dominated throughout most of the newspaper's history by whites, particularly white males. Although women and people of color have made employment inroads at the *Times* in recent years,[13] the newspaper's organizational culture has been known to make these newsworkers feel like they have to adjust their newswork practices in order to remain "promotable."[14] That is, alternative perspectives on newsworthiness, news framing, or the "plausibility" of competing narratives conflict with mainstream conceptions of journalistic professionalism and must thus be suppressed. Below, I briefly introduce some of the important names behind the news narratives the *Times* constructed and circulated about the Simpson case.

Shelby Coffey, III. Coffey was the *Times* editor in chief throughout the Simpson case. In this position, he was responsible for setting the general direction of the newspaper. This direction, as writer Catherine Seipp noted in an *LA Weekly* article, was "cautious." Indeed, Coffey instituted strict guidelines during his tenure which specified "politically correct word-usage." He was known to abhor "surprises" in the newspaper, and his index finger was referred to by some *Times* newsworkers as the "delete" finger.[15] Coffey, a white male, would resign as editor in chief two years, almost to the day, after the verdicts in the criminal trial.

Leo Wolinsky. Wolinsky, also a white male, was the newspaper's metropolitan editor during the Simpson case. He strongly felt the case was "our story," but that the *Times* should not "tabloidize this thing."[16] Underscoring the newspaper's enormous influence on how other mainstream news media approached the case (i.e., the "jump-on-the-bandwagon" effect described in chapter 3), Wolinsky noted that shortly after the murders, newsworkers from around the nation checked in with his staff because they "were afraid to do anything without seeing what we were doing first."[17] Wolinsky, a colleague noted, was quite ambitious and had viewed the Simpson case as "a way to advance."[18] Two years after the verdicts in the criminal trial he was indeed promoted to managing editor for news at the *Times*.[19]

Jim Newton. Newton was the lead news writer for the *Times*'s Simpson coverage. Despite my observations in chapter 3 about the early tendency among the Simpson newsworker corps to (re)affirm the defendant's guilt, Newton cautioned viewers of CNN News in the first few days after the murders not to come to premature conclusions about the case.[20] Newton, a white male, had covered the LAPD beat for a year prior to the murders and thus had cultivated sources within the organization. Indeed, he wrote nineteen front-page narratives in the month after the murders which effectively previewed much of the prosecution's case against Simpson.[21] A colleague who spoke off the record suggested that Newton's "incredible sources" within the LAPD were the result of his ideological affinities with the department, his "channels into the Protective League."[22] During the criminal trial, Newton generally remained in the *Times* newsroom, constructing his daily front-page narratives from the notes of his co-writers who sat in court and from live television coverage. He contributed to nearly 100 percent of the thirty-seven lead narratives from the criminal trial sample analyzed below, and about 19 percent of the total sample (37/193).

Andrea Ford. Ford was the prominent exception to the racial rule I mentioned above – a black female, she was the lone nonwhite newsworker assigned full-time to the *Times*'s Simpson team. Ford co-wrote with Newton many of the *Times*'s early page-one narratives on the Simpson criminal trial. Indeed, she contributed to about 12 percent of the total narratives in the criminal trial sample analyzed below (24/193). During the trial, however, Ford gave numerous media interviews in which she was highly critical of the Simpson newsworker corps, accusing them – and her colleagues at the *Times*, by default – of being biased in favor of the prosecution (see chapter 3). Several newsworkers who knew her believe a conflict between Ford and the editorial staff at the *Times* eventually led to her "demotion" from the lead trial story to other, less significant sidebar stories.[23] Indeed, in the sample of *Times* case-related narratives analyzed below, Ford contributed to nearly 100 percent of the lead narratives prior to June 3, 1995, but only about 21 percent thereafter. Moreover, she was not a contributor to the lead narrative announcing the verdicts. Instead, she was assigned to write a sidebar narrative (page A3) about the consequences the verdicts might have for the district attorney's political future in Los Angeles.

In the aftermath of the Simpson case, Ford would leave the *Times*. A colleague at the newspaper noted that Ford had struggled to establish her voice there, that she "had like two personas:" one black and one mainstream (i.e., "professional"). She did not feel comfortable expressing her black persona in her writing for the *Times*, the colleague added, because of several "antagonists" at the newspaper. Although the National Association of Black Journalists named her Journalist of the Year in 1995 for her work on the Simpson case (Cose 1997), colleagues at the *Times* considered her courtroom narratives subpar. Ford's eventual departure was based on a "mutual agreement" between the newsworker and her critics at the newspaper.[24]

Henry Weinstein. Weinstein wrote and co-wrote several page-one narratives that focused on legal issues in the case. Many of these narratives were "news analysis" pieces that deviated from the straight reporting format of the lead narratives. He contributed to about 11 percent of the criminal trial narratives in the sample analyzed below (21/193). Weinstein was a white male.

Bill Boyarsky. Boyarsky, also a white male, wrote a regular column called "The Spin" that chronicled behind-the-scenes developments during the criminal trial. His nineteen narratives in the sample analyzed below account for about 10 percent of the criminal trial total (19/193).

Tim Rutten. Rutten wrote and co-wrote several page-one narratives on the case during the criminal trial, contributing to about 6 percent of the criminal trial narratives in the sample analyzed below (12/193). Rutten also co-authored defense attorney Johnnie Cochran's (1996) autobiography and trial memoir, *Journey to Justice*. Rutten was a white male.

Stephanie Simon. Simon, described as one of the "hottest properties" at the *Times*,[25] contributed to about 4 percent of the total articles in the criminal trial sample analyzed below (7/193). In a few cases, the young newsworker replaced Ford as a contributor to the lead article. Simon would also become a significant contributor to the *Times*'s coverage of the civil trial, writing or co-writing many of the page-one articles. Simon was a white female.

Peter Arenella. Arenella was commissioned by the *Times* to head a daily scorecard on the criminal trial called "Arenella, Levenson & Co.: The Legal Pad." A law professor from UCLA and a former criminal defense attorney, Arenella also served as a legal analyst for KTLA-TV's and ABC's coverage of the case (e.g., see chapter 4).

Laurie Levenson. Levenson was commissioned by the *Times* to be the other lead analyst for "The Legal Pad." A law professor from Loyola University and former federal prosecutor, Levenson was also a frequent analyst for other news media covering the case. Levenson was a white female.

Findings and analysis

During the two weeks following the Bundy murders, the *Times* published ninety case-related news narratives, or about six per day. Much of this coverage – as we might expect, given our findings about the newsworker corps' general belief in Simpson's guilt – worked to privilege prosecution narratives about the case "facts." During the thirty-seven days of coverage I sampled for the criminal trial analysis (one day for each week of the trial), the *Times* published 193 narratives, or about five per day.[26] This criminal trial coverage, despite obligatory nods at objectivity, also worked to validate prosecution understandings of the case, albeit more subtly. Below I attempt to trace the overt and covert paths of this bias by reviewing (1) the narrative structure of the typical day's coverage, (2) the sources *Times* newsworkers relied on for information about the case, (3) the framing techniques and practices newsworkers employed to position *Times* news narratives and, finally, (4) significant themes emerging from these narratives that underscore the ideological interests surrounding the case.

Structure

Two major factors distinguish the *Times*'s coverage of the Simpson case from the coverage of KTLA-TV we examined in the last chapter. These factors are both rooted in the structural qualities of the respective news media and explain why the bias evident in the pages of the *Times* was more understated. The first factor, of course, has to do with medium. Whereas the nature of live television broadcasting frequently required KTLA newsworkers to make off-the-cuff remarks and to fill air time with hastily considered analyses, *Times* newsworkers had the benefit of more time for reflection. That is, their deadlines for filing stories were at least several hours after the close of proceedings each day, giving them time to address concerns for balance, to self-edit their narratives for obvious signs of bias. Moreover, after these news narratives were filed, an editorial staff routinely scoured them for objectionable passages, making sure they adhered to *Times* standards (e.g., Coffey's "guidelines") before being released to the public in the morning edition. As we saw in the previous chapter, this was not a luxury afforded KTLA newsworkers for most of the station's daily trial coverage.

Another factor that worked to distinguish the *Times*'s coverage from KTLA's involved the compartmentalization of coverage. While KTLA's coverage was generally divided into news (i.e., the "factual" statements of newsworkers) and commentary/analysis (i.e., the opinions of legal analysts), the *Times*'s coverage was divided into several different categories, each denoting a particular relationship to the central journalistic ideal of objectivity:

Straight news. Here I refer to the conventional, inverted pyramid type of narrative that places the most important "facts" about a timely event (who, what, when, where) in the lead paragraph, with information decreasing in significance as it emerges deeper in the article. The very use of this format by newsworkers is intended to signify an adherence to the highest standards of the journalistic objectivity ideal. The page-one narrative that chronicled each day's courtroom developments, for example, was a prototypical "straight news" narrative.

News analysis. Here I refer to other news narratives that focus more on the "how" and "why" of recent developments. In the *Times*, many "news analysis" narratives about the Simpson trial were also page-one items. But unlike the "straight news" narratives, they were clearly marked as "news analysis," thereby justifying and legitimating any obvious deviations from the objectivity ideal contained within. Accordingly, these narratives frequently employed the opinions of legal "experts" as support for a number of propositions advanced about the case. Newsworkers routinely employed the comments of these "experts" to advance analyses of case developments congruent with dominant O. J. narratives. For example, note how key tenets of the Celebrity Defendant (i.e., Simpson's "celebrity" and "all-star defense team") and Black "Other" Project (i.e., "Downtown, where the suspicion of police is considered higher") are invoked in a page-one, October 4 "news analysis" narrative explaining the not-guilty verdicts:

> From the beginning, *legal analysts say*, they [prosecutors] appeared to be on the defensive, fearful of O. J. *Simpson's celebrity* and intimidated by his *all-star defense team*. They also were dogged by bad luck and a series of tactical miscalculations, including the decision to try the case *Downtown, where suspicion of the police is considered higher* and the impact of testimony concerning domestic violence is generally thought to be less. (Emphasis added)

The Legal Pad. A daily complement to (or substitute for) "news analysis" narratives, "The Legal Pad" was essentially a daily scorecard instituted by the *Times* to offer various perspectives on how the prosecution and defense cases were progressing, on which side, for example, seemed to have won the most recent day in court. Designed to resemble a lawyer's yellow note pad, this feature segment clearly crossed the boundaries of objectivity as contributors offered not only their opinions about the most recent events, but also their speculations about what these events might mean for the balance of the case. Peter Arenella and Laurie Levenson were featured daily (see above), along with several other legal "experts" who rotated throughout the course of the trial. Of the twenty-nine "Legal Pads" in the sample, nearly half (14/29) were clearly pro-prosecution, while another 38 percent (11/29) were mixed in their support, and only about 14 percent were clearly pro-defense (4/29).

Feature stories. These narratives were "sidebar stories" (i.e., tangential to the lead narrative) that substituted a more literary format (i.e., a narrative with beginning, middle, and end) for the inverted pyramid formula characteristic of "straight news" narratives. Accordingly, these items stood in a somewhat ambiguous position *vis-à-vis* the objectivity ideal. While they often incorporated many of the "facts" expected of "straight news" narratives, they also tended to more overtly foreground the reflections of the writer(s). As a consequence, these narratives were rarely accorded the same degree of facticity or journalistic prestige assigned to lead narratives or other "straight news" narratives about the case. In the criminal trial sample, in-depth consideration of perspectives that challenged dominant O.J. narratives were typically relegated to these, lower-profile narratives (see examples below).

Columns, editorials, and letters. These narratives were also clearly marked deviations from the objectivity ideal as they overtly expressed the opinions, speculations, and values of the writers. Throughout the criminal trial, for example, Bill Boyarsky ("The Spin") and Howard Rosenberg, the *Times'* media critic, constructed a number of narratives that unabashedly proclaimed their own personal views on recent case-related developments. These narratives stood out from the rest of the newspaper's Simpson coverage because they were often rather critical of dominant O.J. narratives or of mainstream media. But then these narratives never appeared on the front page and were clearly intended to be less significant or newsworthy than the "factual," "straight news" narratives highlighted with front-page placement.

The *Times* also routinely published "op-ed" narratives that adopted a variety of stances on some of the more hotly debated issues surrounding the case. Indeed, many of these narratives overtly (re)affirmed key tenets of the Celebrity Defendant, Domestic Violence, and Black "Other" projects. A smaller number worked to (re)affirm the ideological assumptions undergirding the "Just-Us" system project.

Less frequently, the newspaper's editorial staff offered its own perspective on some of these issues in "Los Angeles Times Editorials." Four such pieces appeared in the criminal trial sample. As one might expect given the prominent role the *Times* has played over the years in establishment Los Angeles, these editorials cautiously (re)affirmed the legitimacy of the LAPD and dominant O.J. narratives. The morning after the Fuhrman tapes were publicly aired, for example, a *Times* editorial suggested that the "LAPD has made significant efforts to reform itself," even if this "good work" is now being threatened by the specter of the tapes.[27] Following the not-guilty verdicts, another *Times* editorial suggested that the prosecution's case against Simpson was based on "mountains of circumstantial evidence," which unfortunately had been undermined by police "sloppiness" and the "remnants of racism and intolerance" in the LAPD. The writers considered it "a sad commentary on American racial divisions" that "most whites" found the case "convincing beyond a reasonable doubt," while "most African Americans felt possible police misconduct raised that doubt."[28]

Finally, in the "Letters to the Times" section of the newspaper, newsworkers periodically highlighted a select group of letters from readers who were concerned about case-related issues. Twenty-eight such letters appeared in the criminal-trial sample. Eighteen of the letters were clearly pro-prosecution (64 percent),[29] while only two were clearly pro-defense (7 percent). Given the volume of mail received by the *Times*, it is hard to interpret the dominance of pro-prosecution letters on the editorial page as anything other than a conscious choice of newsworkers.[30] That is, newsworkers could have balanced pro-prosecution letters with additional pro-defense or, at least, neutral letters. Even if the underlying decision rule was just to publish a representative sample of letters received, the end result combined with other framing techniques and practices to establish Simpson's guilt as a matter of common sense.

Jokes. Another segment that clearly deviated from the journalistic ideal of objectivity was the newspaper's daily presentation of humorous observations about the case. The jokes reprinted in "Cirque du O. J." typically originated in the monologues of the *Tonight Show*'s Jay Leno and other high-profile comedians, or they were submitted by *Times* readers. Within the criminal-trial sample, none of these jokes disparaged the prosecution or offered punch-lines dependent upon an assumption of Simpson's innocence. Most jokes traded on the assumption that Simpson was obviously guilty, as in this example: "The O. J. condoms they're selling outside the courthouse come with a 100% no-guilt guarantee. Even if the condom breaks and the DNA points to you as the father, Cochran will blame it on the police."[31]

In short, while the luxury of self- and staff-editing permitted *Times* newsworkers to sanitize the newspaper's "straight news" narratives about the case for most signs of obvious bias, compartmentalization allowed them to circulate information overtly supportive of dominant O. J. narratives (e.g., news analyses, editorials, letters, jokes) without threatening their journalistic presumption of "objectivity." But as we shall see below, even the "straight news" coverage of the *Times* exhibited the low-key echoes of pro-prosecution bias. At base, of course, this tendency was a function of the sources *Times*' newsworkers relied upon for "facts" about the case.

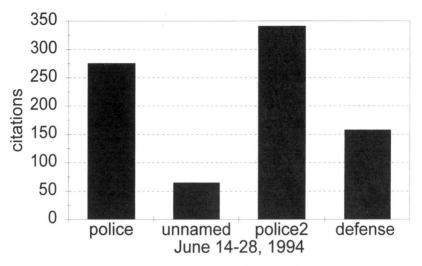

Figure 10. *Los Angeles Times* sources, June 14–28, 1994, by category.

Sources

Whereas the preceding examination of structures provided us with some insights about how *Times* newsworkers separated (and marked) what they considered to be "fact" from opinion, an analysis of the sources these newsworkers relied upon for information tells us much about the domain of "facts" newsworkers had at their disposal. I selected the totality of *Times* coverage for the first two weeks following the murders (June 14–28, 1994) – when important "facts" about the case were first established – in order to conduct such an analysis. Contained in these 90 news narratives were references to 1,427 sources, which I coded into roughly 40 different categories.[32] Figure 10 graphically presents the relative frequency of these sources by four key categories: "police," "unnamed," "police2," and "defense."

"Police" sources were those explicitly linked to the LAPD, other law enforcement agencies working on the case (e.g., the FBI), or the district attorney's office (e.g., the Simpson prosecutors). As it was widely reported by the third day after the murders that police considered Simpson the prime suspect, these sources provided newsworkers with information that generally worked to establish Simpson's guilt. "Police" sources combined to form the largest single category: 276 attributions (or about 20 percent of the total).

"Unnamed" sources were those *not* explicitly linked to the LAPD or district attorney's office, but who nonetheless provided "factual" information about the crimes, evidence, and/or investigation. These sources accounted for 65 attributions (or about 5 percent of the total). Due to the nature of the information provided by these sources (e.g., details about incriminating evidence emanating from the investigation), it is clear that most (if not all) of the sources were in actuality police sources who for one reason or another sought not to be identified. Indeed, some of the resulting "leaks" were undoubtedly part of an orchestrated police/prosecution effort to sully Simpson's image within the prospective juror pool, to increase the likelihood that a well-liked celebrity of his stature might be successfully prosecuted.[33] If we add these attributions to the "police" category (i.e., "police2"), we account for nearly a quarter of all source attributions (341 attributions).

In contrast to "police" sources, "defense" sources accounted for only 158 attributions (or about 11 percent of the total). These sources included Simpson's attorneys, expert witnesses hired by the defense, or others in an official position to offer newsworkers information about Simpson's version of the "facts." As figure 10 illustrates, early *Times* coverage of the case was about twice as likely to attribute information to "police" or "unnamed" sources (i.e., "police2") than "defense" sources. This discrepancy, of course, underscores the "near-monopoly" law enforcement sources enjoy when it comes to the discovery and circulation of "facts" about crime news (Hall et al. 1978, p. 68).

But the discrepancy appears even larger when we examine the *placement* of source attributions *within* the ninety news narratives. The inverted pyramid convention, you will recall, signifies that the most important "facts" are contained in the headline and lead paragraph, with "facts" decreasing in significance as one reads each successive paragraph. Figure 11 presents the distribution of law enforcement (i.e., "police2") and "defense" source attributions by paragraph (i.e., from the lead paragraph to paragraph ten). In addition to being a more frequent source of information for *Times* newsworkers early in the case, law enforcement sources also enjoyed a much higher placement than "defense" sources in the resulting news narratives. For example, seven *Times* narratives from the fifteen-day period contained law enforcement source attributions in the lead paragraph, compared to only one with a "defense" source attribution. Indeed, newsworkers more frequently attributed information to law enforcement sources than "defense" sources in every paragraph but the eighth paragraph – where law enforcement sources accounted for only eight attributions compared to eleven for "defense" sources. Of course, by the eighth paragraph, newsworkers had already established what they considered to be the most important "facts" in the news narrative.

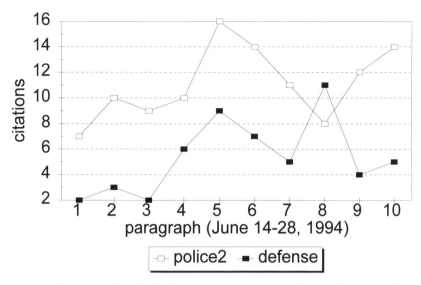

Figure 11. *Los Angeles Times* sources, June 14–28, 1994, by paragraph

In short, the above analysis suggests that shortly after the murders *Times* newsworkers designated law enforcement officials as the most important sources for "facts" about the case. This is, of course, is not surprising. As Hall et al. (1978, p. 68) note, "Crime stories are almost wholly produced from the definitions and perspectives of the institutional primary definers." Even though these defining institutions clearly had various interests that shaped the type and quantity of "facts" made available for circulation, newsworkers were compelled to trust the veracity of police and prosecution sources. Police sources, in particular, command this trust as a by-product of their participation in what might be termed "policework": "Many professional groups have contact with crime, but it is only the police who claim a *professional* expertise in the 'war against crime', based on daily, *personal* experience" (Hall et al. 1978, p. 68; emphasis original). Moreover, the overall "web of facticity" (Tuchman 1987, p. 332) that undergirds the journalistic ideal of objective news coverage routinely depends upon the presumed credibility of police officers and other official sources. If newsworkers begin to doubt this credibility, then the identification of source-generated information as newsworthy "facts" (i.e., as opposed to "opinion" or "propaganda") becomes a hopeless and unjustifiable exercise.

Below, I examine in more detail how this "symbiotic relationship" (cf. Fishman 1980, p. 154), combined with the ritualistic journalistic concern for objectivity, shaped the pro-prosecution bias inherent in *Times* coverage of the Simpson case. That is, I examine how newsworkers approached three important themes in their narratives about trial developments.

Themes

If we look within the trial narratives *Times* newsworkers positioned on the front page, a clear pro-prosecution bias begins to take shape in the newspaper's coverage. Appendix I presents the fifty-three page-one narratives in the sample, narratives that appeared to merely summarize the latest case-related developments. Upon closer inspection, however, three recurring themes stood out in these narratives, each central to the process by which *Times* newsworkers privileged prosecution understandings of the case. The themes were "credibility," "evidence," and "race."

Credibility. Perhaps the theme that most clearly exhibited the pro-prosecution bias of *Times* news narratives involved credibility – how newsworkers assigned it to witnesses and their testimony. For law enforcement officials testifying for the prosecution, their state-endorsed status automatically earned them a presumption of credibility. This presumption, of course, is consistent with my discussion above about the tendency of newsworkers to privilege law enforcement sources in the days following the murders. Indeed, in a stance that effectively turned the legal presumption of innocence on its head, newsworkers only questioned the prima facie credibility of law enforcement officials when the witnesses were caught in high-profile, "irrefutable" lies. Accordingly, the semantic practices employed by *Times* newsworkers throughout the trial revealed that they generally accepted the testimony and written reports of these officials as established "fact."

For example, despite longstanding defense accusations of a police conspiracy to frame Simpson – accusations repeatedly acknowledged in *Times* news narratives – several front-page narratives casually treated police accounts about the location, collection, and condition of key evidence as established "facts." Note the phrasing of a paragraph from a June 21, 1995 page-one story:

Those two stains [from the Bundy back gate and bloody socks] sit at opposite ends of the prosecution's so-called "trail of blood," which leads away from the two bodies and back to Simpson's house. The socks were *recovered* from Simpson's bedroom, and *also were stained with blood* that was genetically matched to his ex-wife. (Emphasis added)

To write that the socks were "recovered" from Simpson's bedroom, implies police did not *plant* them there as the defense contended. And to write that the socks "also were stained with blood" implies they were in this condition *when* "recovered" – a "fact" disputed by defense claims that the blood was later planted. Indeed, several police investigators and defense witness Michael Baden examined the socks shortly after the murders without noticing any blood stains. Discovery of the blood on the socks was not announced until several weeks later. If *Times* newsworkers did not have an ironclad faith in the credibility of law enforcement officials, in the facticity of their accounts about the location and condition of the socks, then they would have qualified the information presented in the above paragraph (e.g., "police say they recovered," "also reportedly stained with blood"). Similar semantic practices are found in a front-page item from June 29:

> The defense objections to the illustrative boards were wide-ranging and went beyond the timing of their introduction. The primary source of concern seemed to be photos of blue-black cotton fibers recovered from Goldman's bloody shirt, the socks *seized* from Simpson's bedroom and the glove *found* on the former football star's Rockingham Avenue estate. One of the fibers found on Goldman's shirt was wrapped around one of Nicole Simpson's bloody hairs. (Emphasis added)

Note how in addition to again implying that the socks were not planted (i.e., they were "seized" by police) the paragraph also implies that the infamous, bloody match to the Bundy glove was not – as the defense repeatedly argued – planted at Rockingham by Mark Fuhrman (i.e., it was "found" there). Indeed, newsworkers routinely used terms like "found" without qualification when referring to law enforcement accounts about the location and collection of the bloody glove.

   Consistent with the a priori credibility accorded to law enforcement officials and their testimony, newsworkers (selectively) suspended this semantic practice only when developments practically forced them to do so. For example, Mark Fuhrman's testimony about the glove was taken for granted as "fact" until the existence of the Fuhrman tapes was confirmed, when it became all but certain the LAPD detective had lied on the witness stand about his use of the word "nigger." This change in practice is clearly revealed in a front-page item from August 16, 1995 – the day after Judge Ito acknowledged that the tapes were so serious he faced a potential conflict of interest if he ruled on their admissibility.[34] Instead of continuing to treat the location and collection of the "Rockingham" glove as established "fact," newsworkers suddenly qualified this information by signalling that it was based on Fuhrman's *testimony*:

> Dist. Atty. Gil Garcetti has downplayed Fuhrman's importance in a case that involves hundreds of pieces of evidence and scores of witnesses. But Cochran said Fuhrman, who *testified* that he found a bloody glove behind Simpson's

house in the early hours of June 13, seemed to take a different view. (Emphasis added)

Moreover, note how the paragraph worked to cushion this change in semantic practice by raising the issue of Fuhrman's (un)importance to the case. Newsworkers attributed the idea that Fuhrman was central to the case to defense attorney Johnnie Cochran, who in turn based his argument on statements made by the detective himself – now an established liar. If Fuhrman was not an essential witness, as the district attorney contended (i.e., the case, after all, is "based on hundreds of pieces of evidence and scores of witnesses"), then the revelation that he lied on the witness stand should have little adverse impact on our overall faith in the prosecution's case. Of course, it would also minimize the potential cost of newsworker practices that earlier treated the detective's testimony as prima facie "fact."

While *Times* newsworkers routinely characterized the testimony and written reports of law enforcement officials as established "fact," they treated the testimony of defense witnesses who challenged these accounts as just that – "testimony." That is, the semantic practices used by newsworkers always qualified defense witnesses' statements, never bestowing upon them the aura of facticity. Terms like "said," "testified," or "stated" routinely preceded newsworker summaries of the information provided by these witnesses. For example, Rosa Lopez "testified" that Simpson's Bronco was parked outside Rockingham close to the time prosecutors said he was using the vehicle to commit the murders;[35] Robert Heidstra "testified" he heard voices and a gate slam outside Nicole Brown-Simpson's condominium nearly twenty-five minutes after prosecutors contend the murders occurred, thereby significantly diminishing Simpson's window of opportunity;[36] and Dr. Robert Huizenga "testified" Simpson's agility was severely limited by rheumatoid arthritis.[37] In short, *Times* newsworkers cautiously confined these sworn statements to the realm of "testimony" in their narratives – as they might also have done with many of the statements and written reports of law enforcement officials they accepted as "fact."

Evidence. Not surprisingly, newsworker appraisals of case-related "evidence" were a direct outgrowth of the credibility differential discussed above. That is, for newsworkers, the "evidence" (i.e., credible testimony) prosecutors presented in their case-in-chief overwhelmingly established the "fact" of Simpson's guilt, while "evidence" (i.e., incredible testimony) suggesting a police conspiracy or rush to judgment was discounted. In the sample of narratives I analyzed, the only instances of newsworkers acknowledging the "testimony" of defense witnesses as "evidence" emerged *after* irrefutable support for their statements had already surfaced. For example, following the public airing of the Fuhrman tapes, a front-page narrative from September 6, 1995 characterized the testimony of Kathleen Bell and Natalie Singer as "electrifying evidence":

Jurors in the murder trial of O. J. Simpson returned to work for the first time in a week Tuesday and were immediately confronted with *electrifying evidence* that Detective Mark Fuhrman disparaged interracial couples, bragged about making up charges and repeatedly used a vicious racial epithet. (Emphasis added)

In contrast, newsworkers routinely used phrases such as "wealth of evidence" or "mountains of evidence" to refer to law enforcement-generated information suggestive of Simpson's guilt. Moreover, newsworkers frequently announced this incriminating information in front-page headlines, while burying defense challenges to its validity or reliability deep in the article. For example, note the following page-one headlines. From February 16, 1995:

Simpson Defense Dealt Setbacks on Two Fronts: Courts: DNA tests tentatively link blood on ex-wife's gate to defendant. Key defense witness disappears.

From May 12:

Jury Told of Huge Odds Pointing to Simpson: Trial: Panel hears statistics about DNA matches. Defense questions methods used to derive the numbers.

Staring up from the front page of the *Times*, these two headlines worked to immediately establish the strength of the prosecution's case against Simpson and, by default, to question the strength of the defense's case. Moreover, consistent with newswork conventions, the headlines purported to summarize the most important information in the news narrative. So it is significant that the narrative corresponding to the first headline did not acknowledge defense suspicions about the blood on the gate until paragraph seven. That is, the blood had not been photographed or collected until July 3, 1994, more than two weeks after the murders. Defense attorneys argued that ample opportunity existed during this period for contamination or, as they would later argue, evidence planting. Similarly, the choice of words in the second headline is significant: the phrase "huge odds pointing to Simpson" essentially ratified the prosecution argument that DNA blood "matches" equal "guilt." Although "defense questions" about the tests were acknowledged in the subhead, the writers do not elaborate on the substance of these challenges until paragraph 34. In other words, the challenges must not be terribly significant. In short, if it were not for the tendency of newsworkers to accept the a priori validity of law enforcement-generated "evidence," the "newsworthiness" of the day's various events might have been reshuffled and the headlines worded differently to convey alternative appraisals of facticity.

Another example of how newsworkers privileged prosecution "evidence" comes from a July 26 front-page narrative covering the testimony of FBI agent Roger Martz. Martz, you will recall, altered his testimony about the presence or absence of EDTA in important evidence samples: in the morning he testified that he had obtained results consistent with the presence of EDTA and that the samples required further testing, while in the afternoon he claimed that he had proved on the first day EDTA was not present. The issue was significant, of course, because defense attorneys and prosecutors had previously agreed that the presence of the preservative would constitute "evidence" of the "fact" that blood had been planted from reference samples. This is how *Times* newsworkers summarized Martz's testimony in a page-one headline:

Stains Not From Preserved Blood, Simpson Jury Told

Note how no subheads were provided which might qualify the main headline, that might point out that the agent had actually altered his testimony from morning to afternoon. Moreover, the headline made no mention of the opposing testimony offered by defense witness Frederic Rieders the day before. While Rieders' testimony was mentioned in paragraph two of the accompanying article, and expanded upon in paragraph seven, newsworkers never characterized it as "evidence" on par with Martz's testimony. Instead, it was described in the latter paragraph as follows: "That was the strongest *testimony* to date of the defense's alleged conspiracy theory [emphasis added]". This choice of phrasing is rather telling. Instead of using the term "evidence" (e.g., "evidence consistent with the defense's alleged conspiracy theory"), newsworkers confined Rieders' statements to the realm of "testimony." In contrast, Martz's statements about the absence of EDTA ultimately attained the status of "evidence" for newsworkers. That is, subsequent articles repeatedly noted that the defense had offered no "evidence" to support their conspiracy theory – which, by default, endorsed Martz's testimony as "evidence" of the "fact" that no EDTA was present (i.e., prosecution witness testimony = "evidence" = "fact").

Race. Consistent with dominant narratives about case "evidence," *Times* news narratives presented race as a defense-initiated smoke screen that diverted attention away from the relevant "facts" of the two murders. News narratives privileged this position throughout the trial – from the earliest reports that the defense had labelled Mark Fuhrman a racist, rogue cop, to the revelation of the Fuhrman tapes, and to the not-guilty verdicts.

For example, when Fuhrman first took the stand early in the trial, a March 11, 1995 front-page narrative parroted, without attribution, the prosecution argument that even if Fuhrman were truly a racist, no "evidence" exists that he actually planted the "Rockingham" glove:

Fuhrman's alleged racism forms the most powerful *emotional* basis for the attack on his credibility and character, but even if the defense can *persuade the jury* that the detective is a racist – an allegation that he has vehemently denied through his attorney – that would not prove that he planted evidence. (Emphasis added)

Note how the paragraph reduced the specter of racism to an "emotional" appeal (as opposed to a "rational" one) that the defense may use to "persuade the [predominantly black] jury." Aside from echoing a key tenet of the Black "Other" project (i.e., black irrationality), the paragraph also nicely symbolizes the *Times*'s general stance toward "evidence" we explored above. Indeed, it is unclear what exactly would or could constitute for newsworkers "evidence" of the "fact" that the detective had planted the glove at Rockingham. Assuming that there were no eye-witnesses to the alleged act, and assuming that Fuhrman would not break down during cross examination in a Perry Mason moment and admit to planting the glove, we are left only with his "testimony" denying the act, and other "testimony" concerning Fuhrman's possible motives for planting the glove, his opportunity, and the condition and location of the glove. During cross-examination, of course, defense attorneys would point out a number of "inconsistencies" between Fuhrman's preliminary hearing and trial testimony concerning his actions at the Bundy crime scene and Rockingham (see chapter 4). Moreover, the defense would note a number of factors regarding the physical condition of the glove that seemed suspicious. For example, they would argue that the glove should not have appeared moist when it was "recovered" if it had indeed been dropped at around 10:45 pm the night of the murders (when Kato Kaelin said he heard three thumps behind his room). But as the testimony offered by Rieders four and a half months later about the presence of EDTA in blood stains would not constitute "evidence" supporting the "fact" of a police conspiracy for *Times* newsworkers (i.e., it was trumped by FBI agent Roger Martz's testimony = "evidence" = "facts"), neither did these early observations about Fuhrman and the glove.

In the waning months of the trial, amidst the furor surrounding the Fuhrman tapes, the issue of racism became more unavoidable for *Times* newsworkers. These tapes, you will recall, contained allegations of routine evidence tampering, references to a police "code of silence," and racist comments that the defense argued reflected Fuhrman's motive to frame Simpson. Nonetheless, *Times* newsworkers could still characterize the issue of racism as a smoke screen that diverted attention away from the relevant "facts" of the murders. A page-one narrative from August 9, 1995, for example, essentially endorsed the prosecution mantra (i.e., prosecutors "note") that the defense had offered no "direct evidence" to support its conspiracy theory:

Simpson has pleaded not guilty to the murders of Ronald Lyle Goldman and Nicole Brown Simpson. His attorneys have argued that a police conspiracy – including police officials who allegedly planted *evidence* and then leaked details of it to the media – is responsible for much of the *evidence* against their client. Prosecutors say that is ludicrous and *note* that the defense has not produced *direct evidence* of any such conspiracy. (Emphasis added)

Exactly one week later, a narrative about a lawsuit by a group of black police officers charging the LAPD's Police Protective League with "white supremacy" was buried deep inside the newspaper on page B3. Leonard Ross, president of the 500-member Oscar Joel Bryant Association, had earlier angered League officials by publicly declaring Fuhrman a racist. The *Times* published an excerpt from the lawsuit: "The league rushes to champion causes for white officers who prey on the black community . . . while brazenly refusing to provide even minimal assistance to deserving black officers."

Two weeks later – the morning after the Fuhrman tapes were aired in court – a front-page narrative noted that "rookie and veteran officers alike" felt that Fuhrman's racism did not "reflect" the LAPD. Tellingly, the newsworkers who wrote the item failed to include comments from members of the Oscar Joel Bryant Association.

After the not-guilty verdicts were announced, of course, race became the central (if subtly communicated) explanation for the outcome in several of the eight case-related narratives dominating the *Times*'s front page. Under a banner headline, for example, Jim Newton's lead narrative characterized the verdicts as something of an enigma: in "a mere three hours," a jury had dismissed the prosecution's "sophisticated DNA test" evidence and "powerful" circumstantial evidence. True, Simpson's "high-priced but often divided legal team" had attempted to challenge this evidence, but prosecutors had "responded to each point." In the end, as Newton put it, the verdicts "united jurors and Simpson in a strangely triumphant moment." They only made sense if viewed through the smoke screen of race:

Simpson smiled thinly and mouthed the words "thank you" as the not guilty verdicts were read. Two [black] jurors smiled back. Another, Lionel (Lon) Cryer, raised his left fist in a [Black Power] salute toward Simpson as the panel left the courtroom.[38]

Conclusions

In this chapter, I have attempted to illustrate some of the newswork practices by which the "paper of record" in the Simpson case, the *Los Angeles Times*, routinely constructed and circulated news narratives that privileged prosecution accounts of the "facts." That is, against the backdrop of journalistic claims about objective news coverage, I reviewed how structure, sources, framing practices, and themes worked to produce news copy about the case consistent with the dominant O. J. narratives generally embraced by the Simpson newsworker corps.

The print media constraints of the *Times*, in contrast to the live media constraints faced by KTLA-TV newsworkers, produced a compartmentalization of case-related narratives into various gradations of "objective truth." At the top of the objectivity hierarchy were "straight news" narratives about the case. These narratives, of course, included each morning's front-page summary of the previous day's proceedings. The less "objective" narratives about case developments – columns, editorials, letters – were typically positioned inside the paper. These narratives provided newsworkers with the opportunity to circulate unabashedly pro-prosecution perspectives on the case (and to a much lesser degree, pro-defense views), without threatening the legitimacy (i.e., "objectivity") of the insulated, "straight news" narratives. Indeed, juxtaposition with these clearly marked position pieces worked to highlight the presumed "objectivity" of the "straight" narratives.

But even the "straight news" narratives, as we observed, were biased in favor of the prosecution. Most fundamentally, newsworkers relied upon law enforcement officials as the preeminent sources of "facts" about the case. This was true not only in the early days of the murder investigation, but also throughout the presentation of the prosecution and defense cases in court. Indeed, newsworkers routinely employed subtle semantic practices to effectively accord an aura of facticity to the testimony and written reports of law enforcement officials. For newsworkers, law enforcement "testimony" automatically became "evidence" – culminating in the "mountains of evidence" pointing towards the "fact" of Simpson's guilt. Only when caught in irrefutable lies, would the credibility of these officials be questioned; only then might their testimony be denied the status of "evidence."

In contrast, newsworkers treated the testimony of witnesses who challenged dominant O. J. narratives as just that – "testimony." Information provided by these witnesses – particularly when it ostensibly supported defense allegations of conspiracy – was not accorded the status of "evidence," hence the often repeated mantra that the defense's conspiracy claims "have not been backed up with any evidence." In the absence of any "evidence" of police conspiracy, and in the shadows of the "mountains of evidence" presented by the prosecution, Simpson's guilt necessarily attained the status of established, if unspoken "fact" for *Times* newsworkers. Thus the "quick verdicts" acquitting Simpson were characterized as the direct outgrowth of the defense's clever use of race as a smoke screen, as an "emotional" abandonment of reason. In other words, the *Times* provided its readers with few options for understanding how a "rational" jury might find Simpson – even if he *is* a double murderer – "not guilty."

In the next chapter, I focus on the case-related narratives circulated by the *Los Angeles Sentinel,* a newspaper that adopted an altogether different stance on the "evidence" and "facts" of the Simpson murder case. Surprisingly, perhaps, concern for the journalistic ideal of objectivity also seems to have played a major role in the shaping of this newspaper's O. J. narratives.

6   (Il)legitimate transgressions:
O. J. and the *Los Angeles Sentinel*

Sandwiched between a thin red border, bright-blue bands extend across six columns of newsprint. The words "Los Angeles Sentinel" are centered inside the largest band, rendered in bold white letters.

Red, white, and blue.

The graphic design of the *Los Angeles Sentinel*'s nameplate resonates with the basic American values the newspaper celebrates. First, capitalism: the *Sentinel*, the nameplate proudly informs the reader, is "the largest black-*owned* newspaper in the West [emphasis added]." Education, another core value, is (re)affirmed on the nameplate by a simple slogan: "'Education will lead to the truth.'" Finally, truth, that basic object of American journalism's objectivity ideal, is also celebrated by the slogan.

Each week following the Bundy murders, the newsworkers behind the *Sentinel* negotiated these values and others as they constructed news narratives about the unfolding Simpson case. These narratives would be circulated on Thursdays, the day of the week that issues of the newspaper hit the streets. Underscoring the power differentials between the mainstream and alternative press, the *Sentinel* had a paid circulation of only about 25,000[1] – puny compared to the *Los Angeles Times*'s daily circulation of over 1 million (see chapter 5).

But the newspaper *did* have significant influence in the black community. As the only black-oriented news organization to share a regular seat in Judge Ito's courtroom, the *Sentinel* quickly became the eyes and ears of other black media in Los Angeles and beyond. Indeed, the newspaper's relationship with the National Newspaper Publishers Association (NNPA)[2] resulted in verbatim reprinting of its case-related narratives in black-owned newspapers across the nation.

This chapter presents a case study of the *Los Angeles Sentinel*'s coverage of the Simpson criminal trial. As in the previous two chapters, I examine this coverage against the backdrop of the pro-prosecution bias permeating the Simpson newsworker corps. How might this bias have affected the newsgathering and newswriting practices of *Sentinel* newsworkers covering the case? In other words, which O. J. narratives were privileged by the *Sentinel*'s coverage? And, finally, *how* was this ideological work accomplished?

In order to address these questions, I first examine the totality of *Sentinel* coverage of the investigation and other case-related developments during the first two weeks after the murders (i.e., twenty-eight narratives). Next, because the *Sentinel* is published only once per week, I also explore *all* of the newspaper's case-related narratives for each of the thirty-seven weeks of the criminal trial. This population of news narratives corresponds thematically to the samples selected in the previous two chapters, thus facilitating my comparison of findings across the three news organizations. As in the previous two chapters, I employ van Dijk's (1993) work on elite discourse as my primary analytical framework.

We begin by briefly reviewing the history of the *Sentinel* and meeting some of the newsworkers central to its coverage of the Simpson case.

The *Sentinel*

> Since the founding of the first black newspaper in this country in 1827, black publishers and editors . . . have been absolutely certain of their mission: to plead the cause of black people because the mainstream press either ignored them or maligned them.
>
> (Shipp 1994, p. 39)

Leon H. Washington, Jr. founded the *Los Angeles Sentinel* in 1932 as a moderate alternative to the progressive *California Eagle*, a competing black newspaper that would later fall victim to the Red Scare (Horne 1995). Over the years, the *Sentinel* has seen a succession of publishers come and go. Nonetheless, the newspaper has managed to earn the distinction of being the largest black-owned newspaper in Los Angeles and the West. Housed today in modest facilities along the city's major black thoroughfare, the *Sentinel* is produced weekly by a small editorial staff that includes just one full-time reporter.[3] The narratives of part-time newsworkers and syndicated black writers in Los Angeles and around the nation are hastily incorporated each week to fill out the balance of the newspaper's offerings. These editorial and production constraints usually result in more than a few typographical and/or grammatical errors in the copies circulated to readers.

Echoing the above quote, the *Sentinel*'s unpublished mission has always been to serve as an advocate for the black community in Los Angeles, to educate and inform its readers about important issues.[4] The newspaper thus overtly embraces an activist agenda, one that employs the mainstream values celebrated on its nameplate in order to expose what newsworkers perceive to be the injustice of mainstream social relations. Race and racism, to be sure, are the focal points of this agenda. Indeed, the typical edition of the newspaper contains numerous narratives about instances of racial discrimination not found in mainstream newspapers like the *Los Angeles Times* – particularly narratives about the treatment of blacks by employers, retailers and restauranteurs, or police. *Sentinel* newsworkers, unlike their mainstream counterparts, have much more latitude to champion causes of particular concern to the black community. From the perspective of mainstream journalists, it seems, this routine transgression of the objectivity ideal necessarily makes *Sentinel* news narratives less "plausible" than those constructed and circulated by "legitimate" news media. Note, for example, how the *Times*'s Bill Boyarsky described Dennis Schatzman, the newsworker responsible for most of the *Sentinel*'s Simpson coverage: "Schatzman is an advocate as well as a reporter, letting his personal beliefs and experiences, *as well as the facts*, shape his stories. This separates him from mainstream reporters, white as well as minority [emphasis added]".[5] The implication, of course, is that *only* "the facts" shape the news narratives constructed by mainstream newsworkers and circulated in mainstream news media. By contrast, advocacy journalism – because it is shaped by personal beliefs and experiences – is more likely to be "irresponsible."[6]

But the *Sentinel* also exhibits tendencies seemingly at odds with this activist role. Echoing Frazier's (1957) classic portrayal of the black press, *Sentinel* newsworkers devote a substantial amount of space to chronicling a separate black cultural world, one where the "achievements" of members of the black bourgeoisie are celebrated as "achievements" of the "race." These accomplishments are typically defined in terms of the middleclass values outlined above. Narratives about successful black businessmen, civic award recipients, and debutante weddings are thus legion in the pages of the *Sentinel* (particularly in the newspaper's "Family" section). While newsworkers behind mainstream newspapers like the *Los Angeles Times* often use the rhetoric of objective news coverage to justify "negative" portrayals of the black community (Wilson and Gutierrez 1995), those behind the *Sentinel* are devoted to circulating "positive" images of the community not typically seen in the mainstream news media. In the end, it seems, *Sentinel* newsworkers usually frame their distinctions between "positive" and "negative" in terms of the mainstream values embraced by black "society" (e.g., "ownership" and "education"), "fair play" values that elites often use to divert attention away from the root causes of social inequality in the United States (cf. Ryan 1981).

The *Sentinel* newsworkers

While the *Los Angeles Times* committed dozens of newsworkers to its coverage of the Simpson criminal trial, the *Sentinel*'s weekly coverage was shaped by just a handful of full-time newsworkers:

Kenneth Thomas. Thomas was the publisher of the *Sentinel* during the criminal trial. Although conflicting accounts exist, *Sentinel* newsworkers credit him with convincing Judge Ito to award the newspaper with a share of one of the highly coveted news media seats in the courtroom during the Simpson criminal trial. Larger mainstream media, this account goes, resented the possibility that the judge might award a portion of the seat to a newspaper with the *Sentinel*'s limited circulation and editorial focus (i.e., black community issues). But Thomas was able to successfully argue that the black community needed a representative in the courtroom and that the *Sentinel* – the largest black-owned newspaper in Los Angeles and the West – was the most worthy candidate.

Sentinel newsworkers also identified Thomas as the force behind the newspaper's decision to serve as an advocate for Simpson's defense. Shortly after the criminal trial verdicts, Thomas defended this editorial stance on the basis of what he perceived as the pro-prosecution bias of mainstream media. The *Sentinel*, he argued, had attempted to balance the biases of mainstream media by providing an alternative voice:

I believe that media coverage has been slanted, ah, from the get go. In the first place, there are two, not only two families that were involved in this tragedy, but three. (applause) All I heard up until the verdicts was two families. And I sympathize with them with all my heart and soul. And I'm very, very sympathetic toward the victims. And whoever the killers were, I hope that they are caught and done with as, as the justice system should do. But O. J. Simpson himself, given the circumstances that we're in today, is also, although he is not dead – I understand there is no comparison – he was a victim. (applause)[7]

This perspective, of course, had profoundly shaped the tenor of *Sentinel* coverage during the criminal trial. As one *Sentinel* newsworker who was skeptical of the defense's case put it: "The *Sentinel* was an O. J. advocate from day one. No amount of evidence could have changed this."

Thomas died of a heart ailment in December of 1997. At his funeral, Dorothy Leavell, president of the National Newspaper Publishers Association, attested to the pivotal role he and his newspaper had played in the Simpson media event: "If it had not been for Ken Thomas, the O. J. Simpson trial from a black perspective might not have happened."[8]

Marshall Lowe. Lowe was the managing editor of the *Sentinel* during the criminal trial. In this capacity, he had a direct hand in the narrative frames that shaped the newspaper's coverage, including the writing of headlines. He also acknowledged that the editorial slant of the *Sentinel* was "automatically pro-Simpson." Indeed, even though Los Angeles District Attorney Gil Garcetti met with the *Sentinel*'s management prior to the trial, and despite the numerous "hate calls" received by the newspaper in response to its trial-related narratives, the attempts at influence, he said, "had no effect on our coverage."[9]

Dennis Schatzman. Schatzman was possibly the most visible and outspoken pro-defense advocate to join the Simpson newsworker corps. He was the lead newsworker for the *Sentinel*'s coverage of the case, regularly occupying the seat the newspaper shared over the course of the trial with Scripps-Howard News Service and the *Pasadena Star News*. The twenty-one columns Schatzman wrote for the *Sentinel* about these courtroom experiences were reprinted throughout the trial in other black-owned newspapers around the nation. Schatzman was fired by the *Sentinel* for unspecified reasons one week before verdicts were rendered in the criminal trial. Following the verdicts, he co-authored with Tom Elias a case-related book, *The Simpson Trial in Black and White,* in which he tapped into his past experiences as a district court judge and civil rights activist to forcefully argue (against Elias) the case for Simpson's acquittal.

Nearly two years after Simpson was acquitted in the criminal trial, and six months after he was found liable for the murders in civil court, Schatzman died from a long-term illness.

Reflecting the importance of his columns for other black news media, perhaps, the wheel-chair-bound owner of New York's *Amsterdam News* travelled across the continent to Los Angeles to speak at Schatzman's memorial service – even though he knew Schatzman only from his Simpson columns and related telephone conversations. As a similar testament to Schatzman's vigorous support for Simpson's defense throughout both trials, several members of the Simpson camp – including Simpson himself – also spoke at the service.[10]

Emmanuel Parker. Parker is a *Sentinel* newsworker who periodically filled in for Schatzman throughout the trial. He replaced Schatzman as the lead newsworker for the criminal trial the week before the verdicts, when Schatzman was fired. Parker could not obtain a seat in the courtroom when the verdicts were read. Instead, he watched the reading on a small monitor on the first floor of the courthouse, noting the anguished responses of the law enforcement officers and other newsworkers present. In contrast to his publisher's pro-defense stance, Parker said he had doubts about whether Simpson was actually innocent. But he admitted that if he had been on the jury he too would have found enough reasonable doubt to vote for an acquittal.[11] Parker wrote eight case-related narratives for the *Sentinel* over the course of the criminal trial.

Fareed Muwwakkil. Muwwakkil was the *Sentinel*'s staff photographer during the criminal trial. Although he was not responsible for the courtroom photographs used by the newspaper (these were provided courtesy of the designated pool photographer), he provided shots of other case-related developments and of people he interviewed for a weekly public opinion feature, "The People's Pulse."

Findings and analysis

An article published in the *Columbia Journalism Review* three months before the start of the criminal trial cogently summarized what was at stake in the Simpson case for the newsworkers behind black-owned newspapers. In "O. J. and the Black Media," journalist and scholar E. R. Shipp (1994) identified five basic concerns that shaped the narrative frames used by these newsworkers to make sense of the media event:

> Is Simpson worthy of blacks' sympathy given his lack of involvement with anything black since his football playing days ended? Was he singled out for prosecution because of his preference for white women and because the murder victims were white? Have the mainstream media replaced the old lynch mob in destroying a black man perceived to have violated racial taboos? Is he the latest victim of a racist society's conspiracy to destroy black men? Can any black man, even one as wealthy as O. J., get a fair trial? (p. 39)

With the exception of the first question (it was quickly sidestepped), each of these concerns would figure prominently in the construction of O. J. narratives circulated by the *Los Angeles Sentinel.*

During the two weeks following the Bundy murders, the *Sentinel* published twenty-eight case-related narratives, or about ten in each of the three issues (June 16, 23, and 30). In contrast to the *Los Angeles Times* coverage we examined in the previous chapter, this coverage explicitly worked to counter the dominant O. J. narratives generally embraced by members of the Simpson newsworker corps (see chapter 3). Within the thirty-seven weekly issues I examined covering the period of the criminal trial, the *Sentinel* published 125 narratives, or about three per issue. These narratives – which newsworkers justified in the name of fairness and balance (i.e., given the pro-prosecution bias of mainstream media) – also openly challenged dominant beliefs about Simpson's guilt. That is, whereas the *Times*'s tendency to privilege pro-prosecution narratives was routinely camouflaged by the requisite trappings of objectivity, the *Sentinel*'s pro-defense bias was overt, strident, even self-righteous. Below,

I flesh out how *Sentinel* newsworkers articulated this stance by reviewing (1) the structure of the typical week's issue, (2) the sources *Sentinel* newsworkers relied on for information about the case, and (3) significant themes emerging from case-related narratives that highlight important ideological interests surrounding the case.

Structure

Three major factors differentiate the *Los Angeles Sentinel*'s coverage of the Simpson media event from that of its mainstream counterpart, the *Los Angeles Times*. First, and most obvious, the *Times* is ostensibly designed for a mass market, while the *Sentinel* is produced for and marketed to a specialized niche: the black residents of Los Angeles. Consequently, *Sentinel* newsworkers felt obligated to magnify aspects of the Simpson case they perceived as particularly relevant to members of the black community. These narrative frames, of course, were routinely motivated by the basic black concerns about the case Shipp (1994) outlines. And as *Sentinel* newsworkers quickly sidestepped the first concern – whether or not Simpson was worthy of black sympathy[12] – the newspaper became a strong advocate for his defense. If nothing else, Simpson appeared to be yet another prominent black male marked for destruction by a racist system. Thus, in the pages of the *Sentinel*, the criminal trial would and *could* became somewhat of a test-case, one that repeatedly invoked black suspicions and fears about the "Just-Us" system (see chapter 2).

A second important factor concerns the frequency of publication. The *Sentinel* is published only once per week and thus cannot compete with daily newspapers (or broadcast news, for that matter) when it comes to breaking news. Thus, *Sentinel* narratives were routinely written according to a "feature" format, one that eschewed the highly time-dependent, "straight news" conventions privileged by the *Times*. For example, the inverted pyramid convention so prominent on the front-page of the *Times* rarely structured the *Sentinel*'s narratives about the early murder investigation or about later trial developments. Instead, *Sentinel* narratives typically had beginnings, middles, and ends, and featured a more unrestrained use of rhetoric and commentary to contextualize not just the "who," "what," "when," and "where" of the previous week's trial developments, but also what newsworkers viewed as the "why" and "how." In this respect, nearly all of the front-page, trial summary narratives constructed and circulated by the *Sentinel* were similar in structure to the "news analysis" pieces periodically circulated by the *Times*.[13]

The third major distinction between *Times* and *Sentinel* coverage of the case concerns compartmentalization of narratives. While the *Sentinel* also classified narratives into functional categories, this compartmentalization was not designed to reinforce the facade of objectivity for its lead trial summary narratives, as was the case in the *Times*. That is, while the *Times*'s classification scheme championed a rather discrete, bipolar notion of trial coverage – "fact" versus opinion – the *Sentinel*'s scheme seemed to support a more continuous approach, where case-related narratives were grouped into categories defined by varying *mixtures* of "fact" and opinion. Six such categories stood out in the newspaper's coverage of the criminal trial: "O. J. vs. the People," columns, "The People's Pulse," editorials, letters, and advertisements.

O. J. vs. the People. In a telling reversal (i.e., the Simpson case was officially known as "The People vs. Orenthal James Simpson"), the words "O. J. vs. the People" were used by *Sentinel* newsworkers to label the newspaper's weekly narrative summaries of testimony and trial developments. This category of narratives constituted the *Sentinel*'s counterpart to the "straight news" narratives about case developments *Times* newsworkers typically presented on the front page throughout the criminal trial. Anything but "straight news," however, *Sentinel* trial-summary narratives were constructed by newsworkers who abandoned the inverted pyramid convention in favor of the "feature" format. As noted above, this involved the explicit use of rhetoric and argumentation to fashion narratives with beginnings, middles, and ends. Indeed, Schatzman's "O. J. vs. the People" narratives often began with quotes from famous American leaders, popular films, and even contemporary music in order to contextualize the previous week's courtroom developments in ways consistent with the *Sentinel*'s pro-defense stance. In the July 6 edition of the newspaper, for example, Schatzman quoted Abraham Lincoln and a black New York Supreme Court justice in order to set the stage for a narrative about why whites and blacks "view things differently." The issue: a *Los Angeles* magazine cover story entitled "The Othello Syndrome." The *Los Angeles* narrative described a psychological illness named after Shakespeare's famous black protagonist who murders his white wife out of jealousy; it discussed alleged defense plans to use the illness as an insanity defense. Aside from assuming that Simpson was guilty, Schatzman argued, the narrative also invoked a damaging stereotype about black men: their sexual obsession with white womanhood (e.g., the Black "Other" project). Schatzman, of course, had used the words of Lincoln to underscore the awesome power stereotypes possess to shape how whites – even legendary national heroes – rationalize their superiority over blacks:

[T]here is a physical difference between the black and white races which I believe will forever forbid the races living together on terms of social and political equality. And inasmuch as they cannot so live, while they do remain together there must be the position of superior and inferior, and I as much as any other man am in favor of having the superior position assigned to the white race.[14]

While Schatzman was the most frequently *identified* author of "O. J. vs. the People" narratives, the newspaper circulated twenty-two such narratives over the course of the criminal trial without a by-line.

Columns. The *Sentinel* circulated thirteen syndicated columns over the course of the criminal trial. With one exception, each of these columns was constructed by black males – either Jim Cleaver, A. S. Doc Young, or A. Asadullah Samad. By routinely challenging dominant O. J. narratives, the columns reflected and helped round out the newspaper's general stance toward the case. A Cleaver column from the June 15, 1995 issue, for example, invoked the infamous Tuskegee experiments and rumors of other conspiracies to support the notion that officials may have conspired to destroy Simpson. Similarly, a Samad column from September 9 of that year disputed Fuhrman's claim he was acting when he made the racist statements tape recorded by McKinny. Many LAPD officers, Samad argued, share Fuhrman's views.

The People's Pulse. This is a weekly *Sentinel* feature constructed by staff photographer Fareed Muwwakkil. It begins with a question regarding some current social issue and concludes with responses excerpted from Muwwakkil's conversations with four or five members of the black community. Each respondent is identified by name and a photograph. Over the course of the criminal trial, seven installments of "The People's Pulse" were devoted to questions about the case. In the September 14, 1995 edition of the newspaper, for example, Muwwakkil posed the following question: "In your opinion should Mark Fuhrman be prosecuted for perjury?" Each of the four people he selected responded "yes."

Editorials. Throughout the criminal trial, *Sentinel* newsworkers composed nine editorials that articulated the newspaper's stance on important trial-related issues – just in case it was not already clear to readers or could not be deduced from the newspaper's other narratives. For example, a March 23 editorial entitled "Oh, Please!" dismissed calls for the defense to "get on with the job of defending Simpson," for them to stop attacking the credibility of LAPD officers: "What would they have the defense do, join with the prosecution in making a stipulation that if the testimony comes from a police officer then, of course, it must be true?"[15] Similarly, a July 13 editorial entitled "Newsroom Bloodletting" explained Andrea Ford's apparent removal from the position of lead newsworker for the *Los Angeles Times*'s courtroom coverage, and her subsequent "reassignment" to "parameter" stories about the case (see chapter 5), in terms of the racist legacy that continues to shape Los Angeles's mainstream news media: "Blacks throughout the Southland are wondering why African Americans working for major media always appear to be going by way of the DODO bird. While at the same time, white men of equal caliber keep chugging along in this market."[16]

Letters. While the majority of case-related letters published by the *Los Angeles Times* over the course of the criminal trial were pro-prosecution, *all* of the thirty-two letters published by the *Sentinel* were pro-defense. That is, like their counterparts at the *Times*, *Sentinel* newsworkers favored letters that were consistent with stances their newspaper had either explicitly or implicitly adopted on case-related issues.[17] A letter published on April 13, 1995, for example, addressed questions about whether Simpson was worthy of black support, in a manner that worked to justify the *Sentinel*'s pro-defense stance:

O. J. Simpson may not be the most Afrocentric brother on earth, but he is doing more to enlighten the black community by accident than he could have ever done or could hope to do intentionally. After this trial is over even the most naive and uninformed blacks will know the racism and unfairness of the United States system of law.

Another letter, published on July 13, 1995 was mailed in from a reader in Grand Junction, CO. The author outlined seven "inconsistencies" in the case he felt supported his conclusion that LAPD officers had conspired to frame Simpson. In the end, he argued that "The only case against O. J. Simpson is the one concocted up by four enterprising detectives who took the law into their own hands."[18]

Advertisements. Throughout the criminal trial and beyond, mainstream media publicly declined to accept advertisements from those seeking to "profit off of the tragedy" – and this was particularly true in instances where profits might accrue to the Simpson camp. The *Sentinel,* however, had a different policy. Consistent with its stance that Simpson was innocent until proven guilty, and that the mainstream media had prematurely declared him guilty, the newspaper accepted advertisements throughout the trial for products depicting Simpson in a "positive" light. For example, an advertisement appearing on February 2, 1995 informed readers that "For the first time, you'll be able to hear a message from O. J.!" by purchasing a prepaid calling card from Juiceline Comm., Inc. Similarly, a September 7, 1995 advertisement placed by Collectibles, Rarities, Art and Special Holdings (CRASH) alerted readers to the availability of "This Century's Hottest Collectible" – a 21-inch bronze statue of "America's Greatest Running Back" entitled "The Juice."

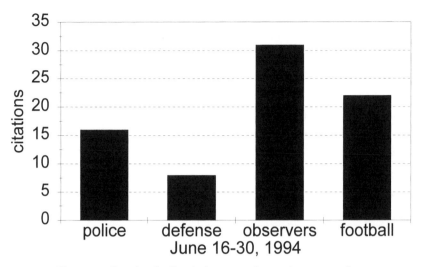

Figure 12. *Los Angeles Sentinel* sources, June 16–30, 1994, by category.

Sources

As we observed in the previous chapter, the sources newsworkers select for information dramatically color the narratives they construct. In the case of the *Los Angeles Times*, you will recall, we found that a heavy reliance upon police and prosecution sources culminated in narratives that generally privileged information pointing toward Simpson's guilt. *Sentinel* newsworkers, as we might expect from our above discussion, approached the selection of sources quite differently. Consistent with the newspaper's pro-defense bias, newsworkers relied heavily upon sources that might provide information challenging dominant understandings of the case. I examined the totality of *Sentinel* coverage for the first two weeks following the murders (the June 16, 23, and 30, 1994 issues) – when important "facts" about the case were first established – in order to analyze the newspaper's source-selection process. Contained in these twenty-eight news narratives were references to 134 sources, which I coded into roughly forty different categories.[19] Figure 12 graphically presents the relative frequency of these sources by four key categories: "police," "defense," "observers," and "football."

As in the previous chapter, I defined "police" sources as those explicitly linked to the LAPD, other law enforcement agencies working on the case (e.g., the FBI), or the district attorney's office (e.g., the Simpson prosecutors). Interestingly, *Sentinel* narratives did not attribute "facts" to "unnamed" (police) sources, as *Times* narratives routinely did. Perhaps this finding underscores the special relationship between police officials and *Times* newsworkers (see chapter 5), a closeness that was nonexistent in the case of *Sentinel* newsworkers. Furthermore, while "police" sources constituted the single largest category in early *Times* narratives about the case (341 attributions or about 25 percent of the total), it was far from the largest in the *Sentinel*'s coverage – only 16 attributions (or about 12 percent of the total).

Despite the *Sentinel*'s pro-defense bias, "defense" sources accounted for only eight attributions (or about 6 percent of the total). These sources included Simpson's attorneys, expert witnesses hired by the defense, or others in an official position to offer newsworker's information about Simpson's version of the "facts." As figure 12 illustrates, early *Sentinel* coverage of the case was about twice as likely to attribute information to "police" sources than "defense" sources – a ratio that exactly matched the relationship I found in the previous chapter for *Times* coverage. At first glance, these numbers appear to run counter to my claims about the *Sentinel*'s pro-defense bias. But when we examine the two largest categories of sources, it becomes clear why this disparity is largely irrelevant as far as the *Sentinel*'s stance is concerned.

By far, "observers" accounted for the largest category of sources in early *Sentinel* coverage – 31 attributions (or 23 percent of the total). These sources included trial observers, Simpson fans, and/or tipsters who offered newsworkers information about the case based on personal observations or information received from other sources. Often newsworkers identified these sources as "black" or "African American." They were never identified as "experts," and they were not famous. Nonetheless, newsworkers employed the observations of these sources to establish an alternative common-sense about the case, one that contested and overwhelmed the information provided by "police" sources in the pages of the *Sentinel*.

"Football" sources constituted the second-largest category – 22 attributions (or about 16 percent of the total). These sources included professional football players and other famous athletes acquainted with Simpson. Newsworkers employed information provided by these sympathetic sources to humanize Simpson, to inoculate his image in the pages of the *Sentinel* against coordinated prosecution efforts to neutralize it in the public at large (e.g., leaks about the Simpsons' history of domestic violence, grisly details about the crime, and so on).

In the previous chapter, we found that the *placement* of source attributions within *Times* news narratives further demonstrated the degree to which the newspaper privileged "police" sources. That is, the newspaper's

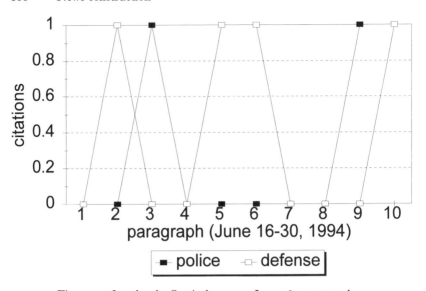

Figure 13. *Los Angeles Sentinel* sources, June 16–30, 1994, by paragraph.

lead narratives about the case all conformed to the inverted pyramid convention, which signified that the most important "facts" are contained in the headline and lead paragraph. Accordingly, "facts" decreased in significance as one read each successive paragraph. In *Times* narratives, you will recall, "police" sources were more likely than other sources to provide the "facts" reported in the lead paragraph and those directly beneath it. This pattern was nonexistent in *Sentinel* narratives. Because *Sentinel* newsworkers did not use the inverted pyramid format to construct their narratives, later paragraphs were just as significant as earlier ones in terms of establishing the important "facts." Indeed, figure 13 reveals no clear pattern in paragraph placement favoring either "police" or "defense" source attributions. While neither category accounted for any attributions in the lead paragraph, the most attributions either category accounted for in the second through tenth paragraphs was one.

In short, the above analysis suggests that shortly after the murders *Sentinel* newsworkers – in contrast to their counterparts at the *Times* – did not privilege "police" sources for "facts" about the case. Instead, they relied more heavily upon "observers" and "football" sources who provided information challenging dominant understandings of the case. This practice, of course, was consistent with the pro-defense stance advocated by the newspaper's publisher, a stance which, as we shall see below, also prompted newsworkers to diverge from their counterparts at the *Times* in how they treated important themes emerging from the case.

Themes

If we focus on the page-one O. J. narratives *Sentinel* newsworkers constructed and circulated throughout the course of the criminal trial,[20] we are provided with further insight into the process by which the newspaper's pro-defense stance was established. Appendix 2 presents the thirty-five narratives by edition. These narratives – like the "straight news" narratives on the front page of the *Times* – summarized a succession of case-related developments that *Sentinel* newsworkers deemed significant. As in the previous chapter, I examine three recurring themes that stood out in the narratives: "credibility," "evidence," and "race."

Credibility. In the previous two chapters, you will recall, KTLA-TV and *Los Angeles Times* newsworkers routinely accorded the presumption of credibility to police witnesses, their testimony, and their reports. Accordingly, certain "facts" about the case were established early on in their news narratives – such as the "fact" that LAPD detective Mark Fuhrman "found" the bloody match to the Bundy glove outside Simpson's Rockingham home, or the "fact" that the socks officers "found" on a rug in Simpson's bedroom had been stained with blood when "recovered." In contrast, KTLA and *Times* newsworkers treated the testimony of defense witnesses who challenged official accounts of the case as just that – as testimony. That is, semantic practices were routinely used to distinguish this testimony from the realm of established "fact" (e.g., a given witness "testified," "alleged," "said," "reported," and so on).

Sentinel newsworkers, in contrast, were much more reluctant to treat the testimony of *any* witness as established "fact." Indeed, newsworkers typically qualified their summaries of pro-prosecution *and* pro-defense testimony with terms like "testified," "alleged," "said," or "reported." Indeed, while *Times* newsworkers began the practice of qualifying Fuhrman's testimony only *after* the airing of the Fuhrman tapes, *Sentinel* newsworkers did so from the earliest moments of the trial. Note how Fuhrman's preliminary hearing testimony is qualified in a narrative from the January 25, 1995 edition of the newspaper, the first edition to circulate after opening statements:

Defense attorneys Johnnie Cochran, Robert Shapiro and F. Lee Bailey will be permitted to question Los Angeles Police Department Detective Mark Fuhrman – the man who *says* he found the "bloody glove" on O. J. Simpson's property – on his "racial animus." (Emphasis added)[21]

Another example of this semantic practice comes from a front-page, August 31, 1995 narrative on the Fuhrman tapes. This narrative informed readers that Fuhrman "said he found" the glove at Rockingham.[22] Throughout the trial, *Sentinel* newsworkers similarly qualified other witness testimony with this semantic practice.

In their efforts to challenge the credibility of pro-prosecution witnesses, *Sentinel* newsworkers also combined this semantic practice with more overt tactics. KTLA-TV and *Times* newsworkers, had depicted the domestic violence testimony of Nicole Brown-Simpson's older sister, Denise Brown, as "compelling"[23] or "unforgettable."[24] Mainstream newsworkers had responded similarly to the "dream testimony" of Ron Shipp – the black, former LAPD officer's claim that Simpson told him shortly before being arrested that he had dreamed of killing his murdered ex-wife. In contrast, *Sentinel* newsworkers explicitly discounted the testimony of both witnesses in a front-page narrative appearing in the February 9, 1995 edition. First, newsworkers did not accord the status of "fact" to Brown's testimony about an incident of domestic violence involving Simpson. Instead, they qualified her testimony about the incident by reporting that Simpson "allegedly" became enraged one night and threw Brown and his ex-wife out of the house. Second, if the incident had indeed occurred as Brown described it, newsworkers worked to minimize both its relevance to the case and the sincerity of Brown's tears by noting that the incident occurred in the distant past: "On Friday, and again on Monday, Brown choked up several times as she tried to recount what happened *several years ago* [emphasis added]."[25]

Sentinel newsworkers used similar strategies to question Ron Shipp's credibility. On the witness stand, for example, Shipp had described himself as Simpson's friend. While mainstream narratives routinely accepted this depiction of the relationship between Simpson and Shipp, the *Sentinel* narrative questioned it by placing the term "friend" in quotation marks. The narrative also described Shipp's responses to defense attorney questions about his "severe drinking problem" as a "series of half-truths." Indeed, capitalizing on admissions both Shipp and Brown made during cross-examination about their histories of alcoholism, the front-page headline introducing the narrative bluntly summarized the impression newsworkers worked to construct about the credibility of the two witnesses:

Two "Drunks" Join O. J.'s Cast of "Addicts, Liars": Ex-Police Officer Ron Shipp and Denise Brown Join Madcap Cast of Characters. (Appendix 2)

The reference to "addicts" and "liars" in the headline constituted a sarcastic appropriation of lead prosecutor Marcia Clark's words, a choice undoubtedly intended to further damage the credibility of Brown and Shipp. Clark had used the terms to impugn the credibility of defense witnesses Johnnie Cochran first mentioned during opening statements – witnesses who claimed to have seen several men rushing from the Bundy condominium at about the time of the murders (e.g., Mary Anne Gerchas) or who claimed to be able to provide Simpson with an alibi (e.g., Rosa Lopez). Consistent with its pro-defense bias, of course, the *Sentinel* had earlier heralded the revelation of these defense witnesses. Indeed, a front-page narrative from the February 2, 1995 edition had described them as "explosive missiles" targeting the core of the prosecution's case.

Earlier in this chapter, you will recall, I noted that trial "observers" accounted for the largest single category of sources for *Sentinel* newsworkers. Newsworkers often employed statements made by these sources to indirectly question not only the credibility of prosecution witnesses, but also the strength of the prosecution's case against Simpson. Again, the front-page, February 9, 1995 narrative provides us with a classic example of this practice. Note how newsworkers use an interview with a black activist to simultaneously ridicule the prosecution's strategy of beginning its case with motive witnesses *and* support the narrative's overall portrayal of Brown and Shipp: "The introduction of Shipp, Brown, as well as the two "911" tapes is a sharp departure from what prosecution attorneys normally do in a murder case – establish the crime scene, then set the defendant within it." Then, immediately following this paragraph: " 'That's because they don't have a case,' notes Morris 'Big Money' Griffin, a popular black activist seen in and around the Simpson trial courtroom almost every day. 'All they have is the testimony of a couple of drunks.' "[26]

Sentinel newsworkers also used analogy to underscore what they perceived to be major credibility problems for pro-prosecution witnesses. For example, well before news of the Fuhrman tapes surfaced, when mainstream news narratives still portrayed Fuhrman as a model witness, a *Sentinel* narrative began by comparing tobacco company claims that cigarette smoke poses no health risks to Fuhrman's testimony that he had not used the word "nigger" in the past ten years. Two words preceded the comparison: "Famous Lies?" And as if the point was not made here, it was reinforced in the third paragraph through the practice of using trial "observer" sources to comment on credibility: "In response to Fuhrman's testimony, Linda Williams, a local resident, called the *Sentinel* to say that the detective was 'a professional liar.' "[27]

Finally, *Sentinel* narratives also routinely challenged the credibility of mainstream news narratives about the case – particularly those that supported prosecution understandings of the case. In a March 30, 1995 narrative, for example, staff writer Dennis Schatzman castigated mainstream newsworkers for what he termed "journa-lying." That is, the narrative criticized mainstream newsworkers for minimizing questions about the veracity of police testimony by characterizing apparent lies as "mistakes." At issue was the public furor over recent statements made by defense attorney Alan Dershowitz, statements accusing the LAPD of training its officers in "testilying." The *Sentinel* narrative attempted to support Dershowitz's claims by calling attention to the "fabrications" Vannatter offered to justify entering Simpson's property without a warrant. This act, as the narrative put it, constituted "a wildly unapologetic violation of the Fourth Amendment."[28]

Evidence. In the previous two chapters, we found that the presumption of credibility KTLA-TV and *Los Angeles Times* newsworkers routinely bestowed upon police testimony and reports translated into an unshakable faith in prosecution "evidence" pointing toward Simpson's guilt. Conversely, the skepticism with which mainstream newsworkers received the testimony of defense witnesses who challenged police accounts worked to discount what might otherwise have been considered defense "evidence" of a conspiracy to frame Simpson. Not surprisingly, perhaps, *Sentinel* newsworkers articulated an alternative perspective on the case "evidence" throughout the criminal trial – one that affirmed the veracity of defense witnesses, that openly contested dominant O. J. narratives. From the earliest moments of the trial, for example, the *Sentinel* treated the defense's conspiracy theory as a plausible scenario for explaining the apparent presence of Simpson's blood at Bundy and Rockingham. Indeed, a narrative from the first edition of the newspaper issued after opening statements relied upon an "expert" source to identify a possible test of the conspiracy theory. In other words, months before the debate over the blood preservative EDTA would hit mainstream newspapers like the *Times*, a *Sentinel* narrative featured a black cardiologist who reported that the discovery of any traces of "heparin" (i.e., a form of EDTA) would effectively confirm the defense's conspiracy theory:

According to Dr. James Mays, a prominent Los Angeles cardiologist co-authoring a book on the Simpson saga, the vials that contain blood extracted from patients have a small amount of heparin at the bottom to keep the blood from clotting. "If any trace of heparin shows up on any of the evidence," Mays told the Sentinel, "then someone's got a major-league problem."[29]

Three weeks later, a front-page narrative returned to this "expert" source, who this time provided information *Sentinel* newsworkers used to cast doubt on the reliability of police evidence in the case. The

Bundy murder scene, according to Mays, had not been properly secured by police. This information, of course, echoed defense claims that the blood and fiber evidence incriminating Simpson was planted and/or the result of contamination.[30] The headline:

Police Security at Scene of Double Murder Termed "Lax" by Physician: Prominent Cardiologist Dr. James A. Mays reveals he was allowed by police to roam murder scene the day after the incident, "and I touched stuff."[31]

Unlike *Los Angeles Times* newsworkers, however, *Sentinel* newsworkers did not only rely upon "expert" sources to affirm or deny the existence of "evidence." As they did concerning the issue of credibility, *Sentinel* newsworkers also heavily relied upon ordinary trial "observer" sources to challenge prosecution "evidence." A narrative from the March 30, 1995 edition is a case in point. It was summarized with the following headline:

An Elusive Kaelin Highlights Holes In Prosecution's Case.

These "holes" pertained to the issue of Simpson's motive, which prosecutors sought to establish through the presentation of domestic violence testimony. The narrative quickly embarked on the task of illustrating these "holes." Its first paragraph introduced a trial "observer" source who minimized the significance of the domestic violence evidence thus far presented:

Gardner, a courtroom guest of his fraternity brother, defense attorney Johnnie Cochran this week, thinks that "the prosecution doesn't look like they're too secure in their position. I keep looking for them to drop the other foot and introduce more, stronger, damning evidence. So far, I have yet to see that strong evidence (that Simpson killed his ex-wife Nicole Brown Simpson and her friend Ronald Lyle Goldman)."[32]

Relying upon the same tactic, the narrative's fourth paragraph worked to reinforce Gardner's observations about weaknesses in the prosecution's case. This time, however, the issue was Simpson's fitness as a father, and the trial "observer" source was someone Schatzman interviewed in the snack shop of the courthouse:

All Monday morning, the deputy district attorney questioned Kaelin on whether or not he knew how many times Simpson failed to pickup or visit his two youngest children, Sydney and Justin. The exchange prompted one courtroom observer in the County Courthouse's 13th floor snack shop to query during a bomb-scare break: "Who gives a rat's a__?"

Despite their disagreements with the Simpson newsworker corps about the overall strength of the prosecution's case, *Sentinel* newsworkers seemed to concur with their mainstream counterparts on at least one important point: DNA tests effectively identified blood found at the murder scene as Simpson's. Where *Sentinel* newsworkers differed with their mainstream counterparts, however, was in the interpretation of this "evidence." That is, how did it get there? Thus a *Sentinel* narrative from May 18, 1995 acknowledged that the prosecution had introduced "its most damaging evidence" against Simpson with the testimony of Robin Cotton, the Cellmark scientist who described her laboratory's incriminating DNA findings to the jury in painstaking detail. But while KTLA-TV and *Los Angeles Times* newsworkers lauded Cotton's testimony as particularly compelling, the *Sentinel* narrative entertained the possibility, at least, that defense attorneys might neutralize it: "This week, their [defense attorneys'] work is cut out for them – how to convince the dwindling jury that the possibility exists that blood was planted to frame Simpson."

As the weeks progressed, and prosecutors presented increasingly discriminating statistics connecting Simpson to the murder scene, *Sentinel* newsworkers seemed to tire of the prosecution's focus on DNA "evidence." The question still remained: How did the blood get there? In a narrative from the June 29, 1995 edition – headlined "Attorneys: Forgetting Audience" – Parker sarcastically speculated about how the prosecution's "overly complicated" presentation of DNA evidence might be received by a juror:

"That cinches it! Yes, before this I doubted O. J.'s guilt, but after hearing this long, detailed, but nonetheless illuminating, statistical analysis of genetic markers, DNA frequency methods, alleles, databases, likelihood ratios, ranges, summing techniques, genotype and mixture frequencies and the probability of random error rearing its ugly head and significantly tilting the mathematical findings either for or against the defendant, everything suddenly came together and it dawned on me that the Juice did it!" NOT! (Emphasis original)[33]

In the end, the *Sentinel*'s evaluation of the case "evidence" was an inversion of that offered by *Los Angeles Times* newsworkers. So while *Times* newsworkers ultimately questioned the not-guilty verdicts by noting that prosecutors had "responded to each point" raised by defense attorneys in the case,[34] a front-page *Sentinel* narrative on the eve of the verdicts reviewed the prosecution's "three principal points" and offered defense witness testimony that appeared to challenge each of them. The headline:

Beyond a Reasonable Doubt – You Be the Judge[35]

And echoing the newspaper's suspicion of the prosecution's "evidence," the last paragraph of the narrative featured an infamous quote from the testimony of defense witness Henry Lee: "Something is wrong."

Race. While KTLA-TV and *Times* narratives throughout the trial portrayed race as a smoke screen, *Sentinel* narratives routinely identified race as *the* central issue in the case. *Sentinel* newsworkers took to heart the newspaper's unpublished mission statement about informing the black community and exploited the Simpson case as a high-profile forum for circulating important tenets of the "Just-Us" system project.

As debates raged about whether or not Simpson's defense amounted to "playing the race card," for example, trial observers who might otherwise count themselves as proponents of the "Just-Us" system project expressed concerns about the increasing profile of race in the case. Indeed, one civil rights group, the Congress On Racial Equality (CORE), publicly vowed to pursue civil rights violation charges against Simpson if he were acquitted by the predominantly black jury "and it looks like he did it." As the *Sentinel* had maintained the importance of race in the case from the moment Simpson was first handcuffed after returning from Chicago, newsworkers employed the practice of interviewing a trial "observer" source in order to discredit the threat. Celes King, who was also chairman of the California chapter of CORE, contrasted the Simpson case to the Rodney King beating case,[36] questioning how his organization could definitively establish Simpson's guilt solely on the basis of "circumstantial evidence":

"The question arises, however," King pondered, "is how does one decide if Simpson is guilty when a jury decides that he's not guilty?" In the Simi Valley case, King explained, a videotape showed the officers beating [Rodney] King to a bloody pulp in a Lakeview Terrace apartment complex parking lot. In the Simpson murder case, the civil rights leader added, "There are no witnesses, no weapon, just collateral issues and a lot of circumstantial evidence."

No doubt convinced by the so-called "racial divide" in public opinion, and what they perceived as the pro-prosecution bias of the mainstream, white-dominated media, *Sentinel* newsworkers seemed to equate "black" jurors with "pro-Simpson" jurors. A front-page headline from the May 4, 1995 edition summed up the newspaper's racial calculus:

Simpson Case Black Jurors: And Now There Are Only Seven: Although the defense appears to have suffered a loss of a potentially sympathetic black juror, with four of the five remaining alternates being African American, and the lone Latina left is married to a black man, the advantage still seems to lean toward Simpson.[37]

Indeed, this theme seemed to permeate *Sentinel* coverage throughout the trial. Two months later, in a front-page narrative entitled "O. J. Case: Often, Whites and Blacks View Things Differently,"[38] Schatzman noted that "Anglos" in the twelfth floor press room routinely questioned the credibility of defense witnesses while taking the credibility of prosecution witnesses for granted. The narrative went on from this observation to circulate a key tenet of the "Just-Us" system project, namely that the criminal justice system – dominated by whites and their pro-white biases – has traditionally meted out harsher punishment to blacks than whites.

This theme about racialized ways of viewing the case reached its zenith, of course, with the revelation of the Fuhrman tapes. In the previous two chapters, we observed that KTLA-TV and *Los Angeles Times* narratives, although they condemned the tapes, worked to establish them as tangential to other case "evidence" incriminating Simpson. Indeed, a front-page *Times* narrative from the morning following the verdicts, you will recall, selectively reported the views of LAPD officers who claimed that Fuhrman's racist views did not "reflect" the LAPD. In contrast, *Sentinel* newsworkers hailed the Fuhrman tapes as an expose on the LAPD's organizational culture, as a confirmation of key tenets of the "Just-Us" system project. Note the tenor of front-page headlines from three successive editions of the *Sentinel*. From August 24, 1995:

Fuhrman Tapes: Explosive Revelations for O. J. Defense And For Community

From August 31:

Fuhrman Tapes Validate Citizen Complaints

From September 7:

Massive Response to Ito's Two Excerpts Ruling

This final headline, of course, referred to angered proponents of the "Just-Us" system project – trial observers who felt that Judge Ito's decision to let the jury hear only two of the 61 tape excerpts presented by the defense amounted to a coverup of racist practices endemic to the LAPD. Indeed, the narrative quoted from a statement issued by outraged officials of the local NAACP: "'We feel that Judge Ito's ruling is an abuse of judicial discretion' and that his exclusion of that evidence 'will most certainly result in an even greater loss of faith and respect for our legal system.'" In short, contrary to their counterparts at KTLA and the *Los Angeles Times, Sentinel* newsworkers treated race as anything but a smoke screen.

Conclusions

Objectivity. KTLA-TV and *Los Angeles Times* newsworkers, as we saw in the previous two chapters, labored to maintain this all-important illusion throughout trial. And this was no simple task given the strong belief in Simpson's guilt that permeated the newsworker corps. Indeed, the subtle and not so subtle slips of the tongue and pen underscore the complexity of this journalistic ritual. The routine reliance on official sources confine it to the realm of fiction.

This chapter, of course, has illustrated that readers of the *Los Angeles Sentinel* were offered no such illusion of objectivity. When they picked up the small community newspaper each week during the trial, newsworker biases about the case were – to borrow a phrase the *Times* used to describe the *Sentinel*'s Schatzman – "in your face." *Sentinel* newsworkers followed the lead of their newspaper's publisher and established themselves as explicit advocates of Simpson's defense. Against what they perceived to be the anti-Simpson biases of white-dominated, mainstream news media, these newsworkers unabashedly worked to construct and circulate alternative narratives about the case. These alternative narratives, we found, employed semantic practices and other, more overt strategies to support a number of positions – that Simpson was innocent until proven guilty, that police and official sources had no special claim to credibility, that much of the prosecution's "evidence" had been convincingly challenged by the testimony of defense witnesses, and that the case represented a golden opportunity to expose the inner workings of the "Just-Us" system. In the end, the *Sentinel*'s transgressions of the cherished objectivity ideal were used by many within the newsworker corps to exclude the newspaper and its ("implausible") O. J. narratives from the ranks of the "legitimate" news media.

But how did people who followed the case from their homes make sense of these "legitimate" and "illegitimate" accounts of the case?

In part III, "Audience Reception," we empirically explore how real women and men reconciled the various O. J. narratives circulated by news media like KTLA-TV, the *Los Angeles Times*, or the *Los Angeles Sentinel*. A central concern of this exploration, of course, is the role "raced ways of seeing" may have played in the process.

Part III

Audience reception

7   Raced ways of seeing O. J.

> Reality is not given, not humanly existent, independent of language
> and towards which language stands as a pale refraction. Rather reality
> is brought into existence, is produced, by communication; that is, by
> the construction, apprehension, and utilization of symbolic forms.
>
> (Carey 1975, p. 12)

Despite an abundance of twists and turns, the road paved with literature on mass media continues to lead to one of two places: to a place
where media are assumed to be powerful relative to audience members,
or to a place where the opposite view is held to be true. At the former
place, scholars argue that media are successful at injecting hegemonic
ideas directly into the minds of rather passive audience members (cf.
Adorno 1991), or that any audience opposition to specific ideas is in the
long run overwhelmed by immersion in a world shaped by dominant
ideologies (cf. Althusser 1971). At the latter place, scholars counter that
audience members are active interpreters who often overlook or consciously subvert the meanings intended by the creators of media texts
(Klapper 1960; Blumler and Katz 1974; Fiske 1987). At stake in this
ongoing debate, of course, is our understanding of the degree to which
media actually construct "reality."

As Carey (1975) notes in the above quote, what we perceive as "reality" is shaped by an ongoing process of human communication. The
ritualistic nature of this process ultimately points to the precariousness
of "reality," the degree to which its coordinates must continually be
negotiated and (re)affirmed. As Laclau and Mouffe (1985) put it, what
we experience as the physical world is always "constituted as an object
of discourse" (p. 8). Media narratives – informed by important discourses, teeming with meanings, and circulated in texts – thus become
pivotal components of the process by which we all (re)affirm our preferred conceptions of "reality."

But this is not to say that message sent is necessarily message
received. Elsewhere I have explored what is best described as a *struggle*
between audience members and the ideologies inscribed in media texts,

noting that the outcome of the contest is always an open, empirical question (Hunt 1997). While the creators of media texts encode in them certain ideologies, thereby restricting the range of possible inter- pretations (Hall 1973), audience members are often quite resourceful in negotiating these texts in ways that comfortably resonate with their own experiences, concerns, and interests. This unstable, ongoing ideological contest is a major component of what Gramsci (1971) referred to as "hegemony."

In part II, you will recall, I presented case studies of three main- stream and alternative media whose newsworkers labored to construct and circulate O.J. narratives laden with ideological content. These newsworkers – shaped by their own social locations and constrained by institutional and professional imperatives – engaged in newswork prac- tices that produced varying accounts of the case "facts." In many in- stances, I was able to link these constructions of "fact" directly to one or more of the political projects outlined in part I. That is, far from self- evident, these case "facts" were direct reflections of the experiences, concerns, and interests of project proponents, some of whom were newsworkers themselves or, at the very least, had regular access to high-profile media forums. In this latter case, newsworkers unwittingly endorsed project assumptions simply by engaging in the day-to-day activities of newswork.

In part III, I turn to an examination of the other side of the meaning- negotiation process. This chapter and the next explore how two small Los Angeles-based groups negotiated the O.J. narratives constructed and circulated by media like those studied in part II. Given the central- ity of race in the political projects (re)activated by the case (see chapter 2), I deliberately foreground race in my analysis. That is, I attempt to trace the paths of raced ways of seeing in the ritualistic process by which study informants worked to (re)affirm their preferred understandings of "reality." My central question: What types of knowledge and interests shaped informant perceptions of the case "facts?"

The study groups

With the assistance of a local research firm, I selected two ten-member, Los Angeles-based groups – one black, one white[1] – that would enable me to simulate in the study environment meaning-negotiation pro- cesses that undoubtedly influenced most observers of the case (cf. Myers and Lamm 1975). Accordingly, the informants in each group were *not* selected independently of one another; instead, I deliberately sought friends and/or relatives who routinely interacted with one another in

Table 2. *Informant relationships with one another.*

White group

ELAINE and BILL (wife and husband, friends of MARY and BOB, and DONNA)

MARY and BOB (wife and husband, friends of ELAINE and BILL, and DONNA)

DONNA and VICKY (mother and daughter, friends of ELAINE and BILL, and MARY and BOB)

DAVID (MARY's stepson, BOB's son)

PAUL (MARY's son, BOB's stepson)

JIM (BOB's best man at his wedding)

TOM (BOB's good friend)

Black group

ELIZABETH, DENISE AND WILMA (sisters)

JAMES (friend of ELIZABETH and STEVE)

STEVE (friend of ELIZABETH, WILMA and CHERYL)

CHERYL (mother of JAMAL, friend of ELIZABETH, WILMA and STEVE)

JAMAL (son of CHERYL)

DARYL (stepson of ELIZABETH)

SKIP (WILMA's coworker)

BARBARA (ELIZABETH's friend)

Source: Screening questionnaire.

their daily lives prior to the interviews (cf. Hunt 1997). In this sense, the study groups were not traditional "focus groups" (Krueger 1994). Table 2 summarizes informant relationships with one another (I changed the names of informants in order to protect their anonymity). While all informants reported they had followed the trial closely,[2] most also reported they had regularly discussed developments with other group members since the Bundy murders.

While the study groups were clearly not representative of the black and white populations in the United States, I selected them in order to include a range of different statuses within each population. For example, men and women were represented nearly equally in both groups: six males and four females composed the white group; five males and five females composed the black group.

Members of both groups were also mixed in terms of socioeconomic status. Annual family income ranged from $14,000 to $100,000 in the white group (mean about $45,000) and from $14,000 to $50,000 in the black group (mean about $29,000). Roughly half of the white group members were college graduates, while only two of the black group members had obtained at least a college degree. All informants had obtained at least a high school degree.

Finally, informants ranged from 28 to 63 years of age in the white group (mean = 48.2) and from 28 to 59 in the black group (mean = 46.3).

The interviews

During the criminal trial, I tracked the two study groups over a six-month period. The first interviews occurred at the height of the prosecution's case-in-chief (March 30, 1995), at a focus group facility on Los Angeles's Westside. This location was only a few miles from the infamous Bundy Drive murder scene. The white group convened at 6:00 pm, the black group at 8:00 pm.

The second and third interviews occurred during the defense's presentation of evidence (August 1, 1995) and within hours after the reading of the verdicts (October 3, 1995), respectively. I scheduled the second interviews at the same focus group facility and conducted the post-verdict interviews via telephone.

Following works in the audience ethnography tradition (Morley 1974; 1980; 1992; Fiske 1989), same-raced facilitators (Bradburn 1983) began the first two interviews by showing each group a videotape designed to stimulate discussion. The first interview – the focus of this chapter – featured a seventeen-minute text from *Primetime Live*, an ABC news magazine that had originally aired the previous evening. This text focused on the release of the infamous 911 tapes on which Brown-Simpson asks for police protection from an enraged Simpson (see below). Following the screenings, facilitators prompted informants to discuss amongst themselves how they would explain "what they just saw." Facilitators then removed themselves from the discussions, allowing group members to set the discussion agendas. A standard set of questions was administered to each group only after discussion stalled.[3] Here again, the study groups differed from "focus groups" in the traditional sense (Krueger 1994). The entire interview process (screenings, questionnaire completion, and hour-long discussions) was videotaped and transcribed.

Other works have underscored the importance of oral culture, of "people's talk," as both the field and barometer of the meaning-negotiation process (Fiske 1989, p. 66). Accordingly, my goal was to analyze talk within each study group in order to trace the contours of the meaning-negotiation process *as it emerged* following members' reception of the selected text (cf. Hunt 1997) – that is, the *Primetime* text for the first interview. Indeed, I conceptualized this process as one involving ritual, where group members would likely *use* the interview process as an opportunity to (re)negotiate, (re)shape, and (re)affirm their views about case "facts" *and* their raced subjectivities (cf. Hunt 1997). Moreover, I assumed that each interview session represented but an iteration in an ongoing cycle of meaning-negotiation for informants.

In order to quantify the degree to which the immediate discussions influenced informants' views, facilitators administered pre- and post-discussion questionnaires that measured informant attitude changes on two scales: belief in Simpson's innocence or guilt and belief in the defense allegation that a white police officer framed Simpson.[4] I was particularly interested in any *attitude polarization* or *convergence* on these two scales, outcomes theorized to indicate group influences at work (Moscovici and Zavalloni 1969; Myers and Bishop 1971; Myers and Lamm 1975; Erickson 1988). Attitude polarization is defined as a phenomenon whereby "response tendencies generally favored by the subject population [e.g., each study group] tend to be strengthened by group interaction" (Myers and Lamm 1975, p. 299). In other words, if each group member's pre- and post-discussion positions on each case-related issue are measured on an interval scale (e.g., from 1 to 10), then the post-discussion group average, the theory predicts, should move farther along in the direction of the initially dominant point of view (i.e., the pre-discussion group average).[5] Attitude convergence refers to a similar process whereby the scale standard deviation decreases following group discussion – that is, when members' responses literally converge toward the group mean.[6]

I added two additional scales to the post-discussion questionnaires in order to gauge informants' feelings about the importance of "race" in the outcome of the trial and the fairness of trial news coverage.[7] This latter questionnaire also included other items (some open-ended) designed to identify informant interrelationships and trial viewing habits. I dispersed the attitudinal scales amongst these items in hopes of downplaying the prominence of the pre- and post-design. Finally, for the second interview only (August 1, 1995), I added a scale to the post-discussion questionnaire in order to gauge how informants felt about Simpson *prior* to the Bundy Drive murders.[8]

In short, by combining quantitative methods (i.e., attitudinal scales) with qualitative methods (i.e., audience ethnography), I sought to triangulate in on the *process* by which informants constructed meanings about the case. Indeed, others have argued that mixed-method approaches may in some cases provide the researcher with more robust findings than those obtained through purely quantitative *or* qualitative approaches (Cresswell 1994; Hunt 1997).

The interview context

By March 30, 1995 – when the study groups convened for the first interviews – 37 of 58 prosecution witnesses had already taken the stand

(Schmalleger 1996). Ron Shipp, a former police officer and Simpson acquaintance, had already testified that Simpson told him shortly after the murders about a "dream" he had had about killing Nicole Brown-Simpson (February 1–2, 1995). Denise Brown, sister of Brown-Simpson, had already shed tears on the stand as she described for the jury how, over the years, Simpson had physically and mentally abused her murdered sister (February 3–6, 1995). Pablo Fenjves had already testified about the "plaintive wail" of a dog that prosecutors used to fix the time of the murders at 10:15 pm – a time for which Simpson had no verifiable alibi (February 7, 1995). And Allan Park, Simpson's limousine driver on the night of the murders, had already described for the jury how he had started pressing Simpson's Rockingham buzzer at 10:40 pm, how Simpson had not answered until after a shadowy black figure about "six foot, two-hundred pounds" entered the front door at 10:55 pm (March 28–29, 1995). The implication: no one had seen Simpson at home until Park saw him entering the house about forty minutes after the murders; moreover, the prosecution pointed out, Rockingham was just a brief, five-minute drive from the Bundy Drive murder scene.

On the Thursday morning of the first interviews, a front-page headline in the *Los Angeles Times* summarized the previous day's trial testimony:

Limo Driver's Testimony Centers on Bronco, Luggage. Simpson trial: Park and another witness also offer confusing accounts involving piece of mystery baggage.

The murder weapon had yet to be found and prosecutors suggested that Simpson may have hidden the weapon, along with bloody clothing, in a piece of luggage Park had seen that was still unaccounted for.

Meanwhile, that day's edition of the *Los Angeles Sentinel* featured a front-page Dennis Schatzman narrative critical of whites for refusing to accept the possibility that police witnesses might lie. The headline:

It's True, But . . . Often, White Men Can't Think, Either

The narrative concluded by accusing mainstream media of what Schatzman called "journa-lying," of minimizing the obvious lies of police witnesses like Vannatter in order "to protect the image of the men in blue" (see chapter 6).

In court that day, Sue Silva from Westec Security testified about the Rockingham security system. In an attempt to explain why Simpson, after committing murder, would enter the front of his house instead of some more stealthy rear entrance, prosecutors homed in on the workings of the security system. A CNN/USA Today/Gallup poll released less than two weeks earlier (March 17, 1995) had indicated that 67 percent of white respondents thought Simpson was probably guilty, compared to only 25 percent of their black counterparts (see table 1. The *Primetime* text about a 911 incident involving Simpson and his wife in 1993 – which informants would screen during the interviews – had first aired on ABC the previous evening.

The primetime text

The media text screened for study informants was produced for *Primetime Live*, an ABC news magazine that aired at 10:00 pm on March 29, 1995. This program bills itself as a "blend of hard-hitting investigative reports, newsmaker interviews and compelling human interest and feature stories."[9] As a "news" program and a product of the ABC news operation, *Primetime* is beholden to a litany of journalistic values, ideals, and routines – not the least of which include the reliance upon "facticity" (Fishman 1980; Tuchman 1987), and the closely related "strategic ritual" known as "objectivity" (Schudson 1978; Fishman 1980; Tuchman 1987). A transcript of the text is presented in Appendix 5.

The text opens with a dramatic summary of events surrounding "the night she [Nicole Brown-Simpson] called for help." *Primetime* anchor Diane Sawyer (white female) hosts this seventeen-minute video and interviews three police officers who responded to Brown-Simpson's infamous 911 call in October of 1993. All of the officers – Officer Lerner (white male), Officer Lally (white male), and Officer Kent (white female) – describe their assessment of the situation and their conversations with Simpson and/or Brown-Simpson. The text presents these assessments both through on-camera interviews and voice-over narration. It intersperses these assessments with the voices of Simpson and Brown-Simpson, courtesy of a secret police tape-recording made that evening of the officers' conversations with the estranged couple.

The text begins with a brief sound bite from the 911 tape. This is followed by a sound bite from court testimony in which Officer Lerner testifies that Brown-Simpson was "visibly shaken" that evening. From here, the segment moves to Brown-Simpson's Gretna Green home, where Sergeant Lally describes the events of the evening to Sawyer and points out where on the property they occurred. The audiotape of Simpson explains that he and Brown-Simpson had gotten into an argument that evening. Sawyer reveals that the argument revolved around one of Brown-Simpson's ex-boyfriends, of whom Simpson was jealous. The text then introduces Officer Kent as the female officer who "stayed with Nicole Brown as the other officers calmed Simpson down."

Officer Kent describes Simpson as full of rage and says she could tell by "just the look in his face" that "she [Brown-Simpson] was in danger."

The text juxtaposes this depiction to sound bites from the tape in which Brown-Simpson explains her history of disputes with Simpson and how she had managed these conflicts in the past. But her methods, it seems, were not successful in this incident: Simpson arrives at her home and, according to Officer Lally, splinters her door in a rage. Sound bites from the tape feature Simpson denying responsibility for the broken door. But Officer Lally tells Sawyer that Simpson "had a problem with, ah, admitting mistakes."

The text continues with sound bites from Brown-Simpson who notes Simpson had not hit her that evening, or in the last four years, but that she had nonetheless been frightened by him. But Simpson sound bites claim the argument was caused by Brown-Simpson. Police officers comment on both perspectives, supporting Brown-Simpson's and discounting Simpson's. Indeed, Sawyer notes that Simpson, apparently conceding his culpability, agreed to pay for the splintered door. Officer Lally then explains to Sawyer that the officers did not arrest Simpson that evening because the incident constituted just "a trespass and a vandalism." The balance of the text focuses on the officers' warnings to Brown-Simpson about the dangers of escalating violence in domestic conflicts. The text concludes with a sound-bite preview of the next day of testimony in the murder trial. This sound bite features prosecutor Christopher Darden (black male) sparring with defense attorney Johnnie Cochran (black male) over upcoming evidence in the case.

Consistent with the logic of journalistic practice (e.g., see Altheide and Snow 1979), *Primetime* newsworkers *frame* and *package* the above text from the onset. That is, newsworkers use the preview of the piece like a headline or lead to privilege certain narrative elements over others, to establish a slant for the segment consistent with certain concerns (cf. Brunsdon and Morley 1978; van Dijk 1993). These concerns, as we shall see below, resonate with key tenets of the Domestic Violence, Celebrity Defendant, and Black "Other" projects (see chapter 2), and the ideological biases permeating the Simpson newsworker corps (see chapter 3).

Amidst dissolves between a photo of Simpson and Brown-Simpson smiling together at a reception, a police car with lights flashing, and the Gretna Green location of the incident, newsworkers preview the segment:

SAWYER: Tonight, a *Primetime* exclusive. A tape of Nicole Brown Simpson recorded in her home on the night she made that 911 call. For the first time, O. J. Simpson and Nicole in their voices telling what happened.

BROWN-SIMPSON: He gets a very animalistic look in his . . . all his veins pop out, his eyes are black . . . it's just black cold . . . And when I see him it just scares me.

SAWYER: Two of the police who were there that night tell the story – a minute by minute account that sheds new light on the troubled relationship the state says led to murder.

OFFICER: And I told her, just by looking at him, that she needs to get away from him, that he was going to end up killing her one of these days. (dissolve to preview of second segment)

Despite journalistic nods at objectivity (e.g., "the troubled relationship *the state says* lead to murder"), this opening establishes a particular tone for the piece, framing the remainder of the text in accordance with the dominant, most "plausible" O. J. narratives reviewed in chapter 1. This framing, of course, depends as much on what is *not* shown/said as what is (cf. Brunsdon and Morley 1978; Hunt 1997). For example, Sawyer announces that "for the first time" both Simpson and Brown-Simpson will tell "in their own voices" what happened that evening. But the preview then proceeds to present only the voices of Brown-Simpson, who describes Simpson's "animalistic look," and Officer Kent, who said she warned Brown-Simpson that Simpson "was going to end up killing her one of these days." The preview concludes on this note, *without* the voice of Simpson explaining his own behavior during the incident. The newsworkers who edited the *Primetime* preview obviously had access to Simpson's voice (i.e., it is heard later on in the segment) and could have used it in the preview. Their decision not to do so is indicative of the particular frame that organizes the entire text.

This frame, in short, identifies Brown-Simpson as an innocent victim of spousal abuse, and Simpson as a guilty, out-of-control, "animalistic" batterer. Indeed, throughout the text, Sawyer careful depicts Brown-Simpson as a sympathetic character (i.e., the vulnerable female), her demeanor and actions described in sexist and/or stereotypical ways that work to elicit compassion:

SAWYER: . . . In the aftermath of the troubled night the estranged couple each tells a separate story as a *frightened woman lets down her guard* to the policeman who answered her call. (Emphasis added)

SAWYER: In a tired voice, Nicole Brown, *wearing a tee-shirt, gym shorts and barefoot,* told police how she dealt with Simpson and how she felt about it. (Emphasis added)

SAWYER: She seemed *so tired, so deeply weary.* (Emphasis added)

SAWYER: Finally, it was time for Sergeant Lally to go. His last memory was of Nicole Brown *in her kitchen,* apologizing for the trouble she had caused the police. (Emphasis added)

Sawyer and the officers interviewed in the segment also work to construct a sympathetic image of Brown-Simpson with their references to her name. Sawyer and the officers routinely refer to Brown-Simpson as "Nicole" – someone we all know on a first-name basis – and/or

"Nicole Brown" – someone who, despite her legal adoption of Simpson's name, is somehow distant from him. This treatment worked to (re)affirm Brown-Simpson's status as a pure, innocent victim.

In contrast, the text's naming of Simpson portrays him rather unsympathetically. He is "O. J. Simpson" in first reference, and "Simpson" thereafter. Never is he just "O. J." Similarly, his defense attorneys are referred to twice as the "Dream Team" (once by Sawyer and once by prosecutor Darden), echoing Celebrity Defendant project arguments about Simpson's unfair ability to buy his way out of the murder charges (see chapter 2).

The text also works to counter Simpson's depiction of the incident. That is, when newsworkers opt to use his voice from the police tape, and his words offer an explanation for his behavior, interviewees' comments immediately follow to counter Simpson's explanation. As media scholars have noted, this technique allows newsworkers to make important narrative points without actually saying it themselves, without jeopardizing their veneer of objectivity (cf. Fishman 1980). In the following exchange, Officer Lerner confronts Simpson about damage to a door at the Gretna Green home of Brown-Simpson. Simpson denies responsibility for the damage, but the issue concludes with Sergeant Lally telling Sawyer that Simpson had a "problem" with "admitting mistakes":

LERNER: You did a hell of a job on that door, I got to tell ya.
SIMPSON: That door was already broke, you know. The bottom part was already broke.
LERNER: . . . Have you got any objection to paying for repair?
SIMPSON: I don't object to paying, but I can't believe that she can't tell them that this door was already broke! And the door – my kids broke the door!
SAWYER: The split is still there.
LALLY: Yeah, the split, the whole thing's still split. Apparently this is the same door.
SAWYER: So when they're talking about the bottom part being broken already, they're really talking about this sill?
LALLY: That's what the kids broke. Yeah.
SAWYER: Just this part.
LALLY: That's what Nicole told me. Yeah, just that little bottom part. And, ah, but this thing was split all the way up this side.
SAWYER: Because the door was locked –
LALLY: Right, exactly. He blamed the kids for breaking the door. That thing was split all the way up the top. *And, ah, I think he had a problem with, ah, admitting mistakes.* (Emphasis added)

Newsworkers also rely upon repetition to reinforce the dominant frame. For example, the description of Simpson's "animalistic look" and Brown-Simpson's fear of him is repeated throughout the text – once in the preview portion (see above) and throughout the remainder of the text – to support the notion that Simpson had an "other side."[10] Indeed, "animal(istic)" appears in the text three times to describe Simpson; "black" and "frighten(ed)(ing)" appear four and three times, respectively, as Brown-Simpson describes elements of his countenance. Moreover, Sawyer and the officers use "scare(s)(ed)" eight times in the text to describe Brown-Simpson's reaction to Simpson. As all of these depictions visibly come from the mouths of white speakers to describe a black subject (or Brown-Simpson's reaction to him), they combine in the text to activate potent racial stereotypes. These stereotypes, of course, have long been used in the West to establish the superiority and innocence of whites, the inferiority and guilt of blacks (see chapter 2). This broader binary opposition – the core of the Black "Other" project – nicely parallels the differing depictions of Brown-Simpson (i.e., "idealized blonde beauty") and Simpson (i.e., "essential black savage") found elsewhere in the text.

For example, newsworkers reinforce the notion of Simpson's "other side" by the use of juxtaposition in the text: a domesticated, smiling Simpson from the preview (i.e., one consistent with his celebrity image) sharply contrasts with a shouting Simpson on the police tape. Newsworkers punctuate this juxtaposition later in the text with Officer Kent's poignant memory of her warning to Brown-Simpson:

KENT: Well, I told, um, Nicole about these domestic situations – that they usually escalate to where somebody really gets hurt or even killed. And I told her *just by looking at him* that she really needs to get away from him because he was going to end up killing her one of these days. (Emphasis added)[11]

The techniques/devices described above all work together to present Simpson as a frightening figure, one who is obsessed with Brown-Simpson and violently jealous of her attraction to other men. That he had not hit Brown-Simpson that evening, or in the previous four years, is mentioned only in passing, buried between descriptions of his "other side" and Sergeant Lally's memory of Brown-Simpson's "prophetic" words:

SAWYER: It is important for the defense, though, sections of this tape. For instance, when she says, he hadn't hit her that night, right?
LALLY: That's correct, he didn't.
SAWYER: What did you as a veteran of a number of these calls over the years think is the most important thing on that tape?
LALLY: First of all, if you listen to the tape, um, ah, she Nicole Brown describes this, ah, *other side* of Mr. Simpson – this rage that he gets into on occasion.
NICOLE: He gets a very animalistic look in him. All his veins pop out . . . his eyes are black, just black, cold, like an animal. I mean, very, very, weird. And at the end it just scared me.

LALLY: At some point, ah, she said, "Well, I, I'm not afraid of him hitting me again because he hasn't hit me in the last four years. Ah, he had to do a lot of community service."

NICOLE: . . . he had to do a lot of community service and stuff like that for it. I just always believed that if it happened one more time that . . . I don't totally think I believe it would happen, but I was just scared. I think if it happened once more it would be the last time.

LALLY: I thought that was very *prophetic* when she said that to me. (Emphasis added)

In short, the *Primetime* text works to (re)produce a particular perspective on Simpson's innocence or guilt. Through its focus on domestic violence – the establishment of Brown-Simpson as an innocent victim and Simpson as a guilty batterer – the text produces a binary opposition that invokes powerful racial (and gendered) meanings, meanings that work to (re)affirm the validity of dominant, "plausible" O. J. narratives. "Just by looking at him," to borrow Officer Kent's words, we all know he is guilty.

Simpson Reads Primetime

Not surprisingly, the subject of the *Primetime* text – O. J. Simpson – was highly critical of it. First, Simpson argued that *Primetime* newsworkers incorporated "only parts" of the 911 tapes in the text, effectively taking his ex-wife's words out of context. Contrary to dominant O. J. narratives about his obsession with his ex-wife, Simpson said the incident had been sparked not by his jealousy about an ex-boyfriend, but by the presence of "Heidi Fleiss hookers[12] and drug addicts in the house with my kids." Brown-Simpson's call to the police that evening, Simpson argued, was "done out of anger, not fear. Her point was getting back at me." He emphasized that "nothing physical" had happened between them, adding that he had not kicked in the door because it was already splintered when he arrived at his ex-wife's house. But Brown-Simpson, he said, had talked to him and the police officers in "two different ways," creating the impression that she was afraid of him. He said she apologized to him the next day for calling the police.[13]

Which narrative about the 911 incident would study informants ultimately find more "plausible?" The one constructed by Simpson, where the incident constitutes just another relatively harmless round in the couple's ongoing game of revenge and reconciliation? Or the one constructed by *Primetime* newsworkers, where Simpson is cast as an obsessive, (black) brute who eventually commits the final act of control by murdering his ex-wife? In other words, which narrative is most consistent with what informants *know* to be the "facts" of the case?

Group affirmations

Given the findings of the March 17, 1995 opinion poll cited above (see table 1), one might expect to find significant differences in how white and black informants negotiated meanings about the case during the March 30 interview. Indeed, this is exactly what I found when I analyzed the first meetings of the two study groups. Informants in the white group generally agreed that Simpson was guilty of murder and that Mark Fuhrman, the white police officer who had testified he found a bloody glove at Simpson's home, was innocent of planting evidence in the case. The post-discussion mean for the white group was 3.2 on the Simpson scale (1 = "guilty," 10 = "innocent") and 8.9 on the Fuhrman scale (1 = "guilty," 10 = "innocent"). In contrast, informants in the black group were suspicious of the prosecution's case against Simpson and considered it likely that Fuhrman may have planted the glove and other evidence against him. The post-discussion group means on the scales for this group were the exact opposite of those for the white group: 9.1 on the Simpson scale (1 = "guilty," 10 = "innocent") and 3.3 on the Fuhrman scale (1 = "guilty," 10 = "innocent"). With one exception, pre- and post-discussion scale averages for each group suggest that discussion contributed very little to attitude polarization or convergence. That is, prior interactions likely caused members of both groups to arrive at the interviews in virtual agreement, already near the extremes of the scales. The exception, however, pertained to the black group's belief about the likelihood that Fuhrman may have planted evidence. Prior to discussion, black informants were somewhat ambivalent on this question, but following discussion they moved toward believing in the detective's guilt (see table 3).

Appendix 3 summarizes the emergence of discussion themes in both groups. While talk in the white group moved from a consideration of domestic violence, to the wealth of incriminating evidence against Simpson, to the improbability of conspiracy, in the black group it moved from questioning *Primetime*'s portrayal of Simpson's "rage," to holes in the prosecution's case, to the high likelihood of conspiracy. In order to look more closely at these rather divergent discussion trajectories, at the *process* by which informants in the two groups (re)affirmed important case "facts" and positioned themselves relative to these realities, I examine in detail how each group treated seven central themes emerging during the interviews: the strength of the prosecution and defense cases, science and DNA, domestic violence, wealth and celebrity, race, conspiracy, and the *Primetime* text. When informant exchanges were compared across these themes, important differences in experience, interests, and knowledge surfaced.

Table 3. *Perceptions of Simpson's innocence or guilt, and Fuhrman's innocence or guilt in framing Simpson, before and after discussion, by group.*[a]

Group	Before discussion	After discussion
	Simpson's innocence/guilt	
Black	9.3	9.1
White	2.9	3.2
	Fuhrman's innocence/guilt	
Black	4.5	3.3
White	8.7	8.9

[a] Scales from 1 to 10, 1 = "guilty," 10 = "innocent"
Source: Pre- and post-discussion questionaires, March 30, 1995.

Prosecution and defense cases

To put it bluntly, informants in the white group generally considered the defense case (although its case-in-chief had not yet begun) to be rather weak, its promises repeatedly "falling through the hole." On the basis of the defense's opening statements, its cross-examination of prosecution witnesses, and other public statements, informants in this group concluded that the defense case would amount to little more than a confusion of and a distraction from the prosecution's evidence. Indeed, informants derisively referred to Simpson's attorneys as the "Dream Team," describing them as "high-priced" lawyers skilled at digging up shaky witnesses and painting their obviously powerful client as an arthritic man physically incapable of murder:

VICKY: ... When I listen to the opening statements and the defense fanned their case out, and I think first off when a person is innocent, they would probably not need quite so many lawyers. High-priced lawyers.
MARY: The Dream Team!
BOB: Yeah.
VICKY: I think that is an indication, and then as Cochran began to lay out the case, they saw it and as we've seen the Rosa Lopez [defense witness] thing which I think it blew up in their face; Mary Anne Gerchas [another defense witness] blew up on their face ...
DONNA: Credible witnesses.
VICKY: ... the poor crippled, arthritic O.J. with a bod ... I mean, come on!
MALE: His arms are ...
VICKY: Wow! This guy looks pretty good.
DONNA: That's a 46-year-old man!

VICKY: I don't know if he's like crippled. I mean, they just . . . so many things they [the defense] threw out there. It's like, if the guy is innocent, stick with things that aren't going to keep falling through the hole.

Informants in the black group, however, had a strikingly different reaction to the prosecution and defense cases. Informants accounted for their doubt about Simpson's guilt with what they viewed as gaps and/or inconsistencies in the prosecution's explanation for why/how Simpson committed the murders:

CHERYL: But they're [the prosecution] saying it was premeditated, so he had to plan. He had to have a plan to do it.

DENISE: He had a plan to kill her [Nicole]. And he'd be a poor planner . . .

CHERYL: [If] he did, he did some really poor planning.

DENISE: . . . 'cause why would you bring all that trash [blood, bloody glove] back to your own home?

CHERYL: It don't make sense.

DENISE: It doesn't make sense. It's too many loose ends here. I mean, I'm gonna go and kill Nicole and then go track it all back to my own house, like "Come and get me?"

CHERYL: And then also . . . they [the prosecution] said at 10:05 or 10:06, to-day, he called Paula [Simpson's girlfriend] on the phone. That means he called her on his way to Nicole's [the murder scene] . . . or while he was there. Which really doesn't make sense . . .

DENISE: It doesn't make any.

Meanwhile, as the dominant perspective concerning Simpson's guilt was affirmed in the white group, members challenged David – one of two dissenters (Elaine, a fifty-seven-year-old retail salesperson, was the other) – to commit to his position, to say that Simpson would/should take the stand. But David, a thirty-six-year-old trade officer, refused to back down and responded that the defense "may shock people" and put Simpson on the stand. Other informants quickly dismissed this affront to the group common sense about the case. Indeed, Mary, a fifty-year-old secretary, believed "with every ounce" that if Simpson did testify, he would "crack" and incriminate himself during cross-examination:

BILL: I want to ask David, do you think O. J. is going to testify?

DAVID: No.

BILL: Why do you think he is not going to testify?

BOB: Because he is guilty!

DAVID: I don't know.

BILL: You know [about everything] all night. Now, you don't know?

DAVID: It's funny, you are . . .

BILL: Why don't you know, David?

DAVID: What's interesting is the fact that . . .

BILL: He doesn't have to [take the stand], you're right.

VICKY: He'll probably hang himself if he does.

DAVID: I don't know. I was thinking about that today, whether he should testify. I think they [the defense] may shock people and put him on the stand.

MARY: Personally, I think O.J. . . . I think there is going to be enough . . . Personally, really I just feel it with every ounce, but I could be totally wrong. I have a feeling that there is going to be some evidence that comes out that's gonna be so . . .

PAUL: Overwhelming.

MARY: . . . overwhelming, O.J. will crack.

In contrast, informants in the black group did not discuss the likelihood that Simpson might take the stand. Doubtful of his guilt, yet aware of his infamous flight from the police,[14] these informants believed Simpson knew more about the murders than he could/would ever publicly state. Indeed, informants generally believed Simpson had been framed and that he or his family would somehow be harmed if he revealed what he knew about the murders. Furthermore, informants believed both the prosecution and defense had exculpatory evidence that had not been made public:

JAMAL: So, so . . . are you saying that he's [Simpson] possibly been set up?

ELIZABETH: Yes.

DENISE: Very much so.

DARYL: I don't think he did it. I think he knows who did it though . . .

JAMAL: I think there is some involvement . . .

JAMES: He know who did . . . because his children would get killed if he tell it. It's the mafia. But he knows who did it. He knows who did it.

JAMAL: There's a lot of involvement that they're [the prosecution and defense] not bringing up.

Theoretically, of course, both the certainty of Simpson's guilt that defined common sense in the white group and the doubt affirmed by members of the black group might be explained in terms of what social psychologists refer to as "belief perseverance" (Anderson et al. 1980; Ross and Lepper 1980). That is, the more closely we analyze our theories and explain how they *might* be true, the more resistant we become to discrediting information. This analysis of favored theories is essentially what occurred in group discussions. On the one hand, white informants generally dismissed the gaps/inconsistencies in the prosecution case pointed out by the transgressions of David and Elaine, and did not consider many of those discussed by the black group (i.e., potentially discrediting information). Instead, informants tended to (re)affirm theories that supported Simpson's guilt or offer new theories that might complement those they already embraced when they arrived for the interview. On the other hand, black informants did not discuss

Simpson's flight from police, or his ability to support an alibi for nearly every hour of June 12, 1994, except that during which the murders allegedly occurred (i.e., potentially discrediting information). Instead, they privileged theories explaining why Simpson might flee and still be innocent, and why his behavior that evening was not consistent with the actions of someone about to commit premeditated murder. That is, these informants also concluded their discussion by either (re)affirming their prior theories (i.e., concerning Simpson's innocence) or advancing new complementary theories. Undergirding all of these competing theories, of course, were certain basic assumptions about the nature of "evidence" – about how you would know it if you saw it. It was in these subterranean regions that group orientations toward science and DNA shaped the discussions in important ways.

Science and DNA

Informants in the white group seemed to accept DNA technology as an infallible source of evidence. Nowhere in their discussion did they entertain the possibility or likelihood that DNA testing could produce false positives or that statistical estimates could be exaggerated. In the following exchange, informants debate the source of blood found in Simpson's Bronco. Implicit in this exchange is a reliance on DNA testing as the definitive arbiter of truth: was it just Simpson's blood? Or was it the victims' blood, too? Elaine – who was otherwise suspicious of the prosecution's case – seemed to represent the group mind-set when she noted it had not yet been "proven" that the victims' blood was found in the Bronco. Why? Because "DNA has not been done . . . yet."

VICKY: So there's little drops of the victims' blood in the car?
DAVID: No, not victim's blood. They never found any victims' blood.
DONNA: They never found any victims' blood. They found O. J.'s blood in his car.
(loud talking)
BILL: Most people blame . . .
VICKY: The opening statements, she said that they found the victims' blood.
DONNA: Yes! But it was proven that it was only O. J.'s!
ELAINE: It hasn't been proven yet. DNA has not been done . . . yet.

In contrast, informants in the black group generally discounted the utility of the prosecution's scientific evidence. It was not that these informants viewed science in general or DNA in particular as inherently flawed systems of knowledge, instead they seemed to embrace the defense argument that compromised inputs will necessarily lead to compromised outputs – no matter how sound the system. Thus the "unexplainable" evidence against Simpson could ultimately be explained for them in terms of compromised inputs, compromised through either negligence or intention.

DARYL: That was a bunch of bull. The whole DNA thing. From the beginning.
CHERYL: 'Course there are a lot of things that are unexplainable about O.J., too. You know about the blood. That blood trail, I mean, you have to explain . . .
DENISE: What, how things . . .
STEVE: Somebody put that trail there.

Meanwhile, as discussion progressed in the white group, informants took inventory of the "evidence" against Simpson, classifying it, categorizing it, weighing it. Mindful of the fact that results of the DNA analyses had not yet been introduced through testimony, the group wrestled with just how much "evidence" is enough to justify police entry into Simpson's Rockingham estate without a warrant. Bob – a sixty-one-year-old manager for California state unemployment – invoked intertextual memories of the infamous Nightstalker[15] case to suggest that sometimes cases hinge on single pieces of "evidence." But Vicky – a thirty-three-year-old housewife – reminded group members that police had collected "like three hundred pieces of evidence" incriminating Simpson that night.

BILL: If somebody had said "I saw O.J. do it," we wouldn't be in trial right now.
TOM: You know, there is one thing that is sort of bad is, there is only that one drop of blood on the door and on the Bronco . . .
JIM: I think they need more evidence to prove that . . . they've got circumstantial evidence . . . they've got circumstantial evidence.
(loud talking)
TOM: I think they were going inside.
JIM: I mean they've got a lot of evidence.
(Everybody talking at once)
JIM: At the end they were just gonna go . . .
BILL: They were gonna go in that house with or without a search warrant. There is no doubt in my mind.
VICKY: I would have!
(loud talking)
BOB: The guy who's a night stalker, the only evidence they had on him was that there was a beer can with his fingerprints next to the body and that is the only thing that placed him at the scene of the crime.
DAVID: They have a partial license number.
VICKY: They have like three hundred pieces of evidence on that night.

But these "pieces of evidence" are precisely what members of the black group could/would not take for granted. Daryl – a twenty-eight-year-old inventory worker – noted the flap surrounding a KNBC report about Brown-Simpson's blood being detected on socks police found in Simpson's bedroom the morning after the murders (see chapter 1). Defense members had suggested (and would argue when DNA tests finally confirmed the report) that since DNA testing had not yet been performed on the socks, the LAPD source of the leak could only have known this if the blood had been planted. Nonetheless, Cheryl – a fifty-nine-year-old in-home childcare practitioner – cautioned other members to be wary of news reports, to rely only on court testimony as to matters of "fact." While she continued to raise troubling questions about "unexplainable evidence" incriminating Simpson, other informants in the group found ways to "explain" it. Detective Vannatter's transport of Simpson's blood sample from LAPD headquarters (where it could have been booked into evidence) to Rockingham, for example, seemed to signify police efforts/willingness to frame Simpson:

DARYL: But wait a minute, with the socks . . . if you remember the socks? They hadn't taken even the socks out to be tested yet. And then the story came out in the newspapers that it was his blood and the socks hadn't even tested yet.

CHERYL: We should really talk about things that have been presented in court, not things that are in the newspapers. Cause half of those things weren't even true. But I mean as far as what's been presented in court . . .

ELIZABETH: They found . . .

CHERYL: . . . and the blood in the Bronco, and the blood up the walk . . .

DENISE: And in the foyer! Right?

CHERYL: . . . how you gonna explain that?

BARBARA: They found the . . . they brang [sic] the blood from downtown that they drawed from O. J.

In short, while members of the white group generally assumed that the "evidence" against Simpson was solid, objectively knowable, members of the black group repeatedly questioned the source of each piece of "evidence," not taking for granted its prosecution-imbued meaning for the overriding question of innocence or guilt. This basic difference in reasoning styles, of course, permeated most of the issues discussed in the groups. But nowhere was this difference more salient than in the discussion of domestic violence.

Domestic violence

For members of the white group, domestic violence was *the* explanatory narrative necessary for making sense of the heinous crimes. In legal terms, this "motive" rested on a depiction of Simpson as a man obsessed with his ex-wife, who would risk fame and fortune to prevent anyone else from "having her" if he couldn't. Indeed, summing up the general group sentiment, Paul – a twenty-seven-year-old college student – noted that Simpson had a "disease of jealousy:"

PAUL: I don't think that O.J. just had a bad temper, I think O.J. had a disease of jealousy. You know it's just like a person having a disease with alcoholism or a person having a disease with drugs. O.J. had a disease with jealousy. And you know, people can be cured, you know, there's a lot of people in prison that have killed their wives over jealousy and finding their wives with different lovers, stuff like that.

Thus, the white group generally accepted *Primetime*'s portrayals of Simpson with little cognitive dissonance. Despite Elaine's and David's continuing transgressions of the group common sense about Simpson's guilt – that is, their invoking of the domestic-violence-doesn't-necessarily-lead-to-murder argument – other informants held on to the Simpson-as-obsessed-killer narrative. Indeed, the same logic employed by the transgressors to question Simpson's motive was used by other informants to challenge defense claims that racism prompted Fuhrman to plant evidence against the defendant:

BILL: I think most of us have already heard the telephone [911 call tape] and, and his voice in the background swearing . . . to where he . . .
ELAINE: Domestic violence doesn't mean they're going to end up killing . . .
VICKY: Right . . .
(loud talking)
TOM: Fuhrman being a racist doesn't preclude him . . .
VICKY: That's right!
TOM: . . . putting evidence out . . .
DAVID: Does not make him guilty either . . .
JIM: With the camera on them . . .?
TOM: . . . him beating Nicole does not preclude him killing her.
MARY: Who do you think killed her then . . . if O.J. didn't? Who killed her?

In the black group, however, the specter of domestic violence assumed a different status in relation to the question of Simpson's innocence or guilt. Informants in this group began their discussion by challenging *Primetime*'s portrayals of an enraged Simpson (see Appendix 3). Ultimately acknowledging that the famous couple had a troubled relationship, informants felt both parties were to blame, and reasoned that Brown-Simpson would not have remained in such close contact with her ex-husband if – as the prosecution suggested – she was afraid he might kill her:

JAMAL: One thing I noticed about O.J. is that he wasn't as enraged as they may, as they have wanted you to think. And he pointed out that she wanted to get together, those are new things that I just heard, that she wanted to get back together. And I always . . . I never thought that she was a perfect angel, nobody is perfect. He said that he let her beat him. So, that shows another side to the coin. I mean, I was just always sure . . . I don't doubt that he hit her. But I'm pretty sure she did her dirt too.

ELIZABETH: Oh, she did. She did a lot, baby.

DENISE: Well, I felt like they were, like, two people that knew how to push each other's buttons, you know . . . whatever she sets you off, I mean, him off, she knew what to do, and he knew how to set her off. So they argued and carried on all the time. But I don't feel like Nicole Brown-Simpson was afraid of O. J. Simpson.

WILMA: I feel like if Nicole had gotten all these beatings and rapings that she claims she got from O. J. But he's a strong man and I know he could probably beat her real good. But why would she stay with O. J.? Why wouldn't she go and get a divorce? And get it over with?

DENISE: And move a way away.

CHERYL: She should've moved a little farther away!

DENISE: Why did she move within walking distance from O. J. Simpson?

As discussion of domestic violence continued in this group, a few informants conceded that Simpson indeed had a "sickness" of jealousy and that it might have something to do with the ego frustrations of an aging athlete. And although domestic violence never moved informants as a convincing motive in the case, the following exchange surrounding the experiences of Elizabeth – a forty-year-old nurse – reveals their appreciation of domestic violence's significance as a social problem:

ELIZABETH: Once you get hit, you get immune to it.

(Laughter)

CHERYL: I don't know, they say . . . I don't know if you get immune to it, but they say it is a syndrome . . . that are abused.

ELIZABETH: I went through it ten years, you know.

DENISE: Who?

ELIZABETH: Who you think?

DENISE: I don't know!

CHERYL: Let's not get personal.

(laughter)

CHERYL: They're sisters [Elizabeth and Denise].

ELIZABETH: I mean, you have to just make up your mind and leave, you know.

CHERYL: I don't know, from what I've seen on TV, it's not that easy sometimes for women to leave.

JAMAL: And it's not easy for men to let go either.

DENISE: You went through it for ten years, it couldn't have been easy for you either.

ELIZABETH: I said it wasn't easy. No way is it easy.

DENISE: I mean, all I can say is, one hit and I would've been out of there myself.

CHERYL: That's a lot of women, but see . . .

DARYL: It's easier said than done.

In the end, however, the Domestic Violence project (see chapter 2) resonated much more fully with the white group, providing most members with a credible narrative for the case. Black informants, while sensitive to domestic violence issues, found the links to the case to be much too tenuous. Not surprisingly, perhaps, similar differences characterized how the two groups positioned themselves relative to the Celebrity Defendant project.

Wealth and celebrity

Informants in the white group generally embraced key tenets of the Celebrity Defendant project, agreeing that prosecutors faced an uphill battle in the case due to Simpson's millions and his popularity with the public. Most of these informants, you will recall, derisively referred to Simpson's attorneys as the "Dream Team," a cadre of high-priced and high-powered problem-solvers particularly adept at exploiting legal loopholes, "tearing witnesses apart," and sullying the truth surrounding the case. Money, group common-sense affirmed, can buy almost anything – including (in)justice. Indeed, given Simpson's resources, the fact that his investigators had yet to identify the "real" killer(s) seemed to underscore the conclusion that no one else could possibly be involved:

BOB: Well, wait a minute. O.J.'s got money for investigators. Don't you think that if anybody else was involved, that those guys wouldn't be tracking them down to come and say "Hey, here's your killer." They say they can't find anything!

While informants in this group generally resented Simpson's use of financial resources, they seemed to consider his case a gross aberration in an otherwise effective, adversarial courtroom tradition. In the following exchange, for example, informants cast prosecutors as underpaid champions of justice (i.e., heroes) and defense attorneys as higher-paid pragmatists (i.e., villains); at the same time, however, informants conceded that if "wrongfully accused of murder" they would spend whatever was necessary to put on a vigorous defense. Mary's solution, it seems, effectively reconciled these potentially conflicting positions. Adamant in her disdain for the "Dream Team," she imagined Simpson prosecutors *as* defense attorneys and pledged never to hire the likes of Simpson's attorneys:

BILL: Our system does work better than that [the Simpson case]. And those who have been in court before know that that's not how the norm is.
MARY: But it is if you've got money! There is a difference if you've got money and if you . . . as far as whether you . . .

BOB: You don't have all this.

BILL: But you gotta remember, there's still guilt and there's still innocence . . .

MARY: Yeah, I know.

BILL: If you're guilty it shouldn't make any difference whether you got money or you don't have money.

BOB: Mary, if you were wrongfully accused of murder you'd run over to Cochran [Simpson's lead trial attorney] tomorrow . . .

MARY: No, I wouldn't!

BILL: She couldn't afford Cochran.

BOB: If you had the money, would you go over to Bailey [another Simpson attorney]?

MARY: No, I would not!

BOB: . . . or anybody that would get you off . . .

MARY: I would go to Tourtelo [Fuhrman's attorney], but I wouldn't go to Cochran.

DONNA: I'd go to Marcia Clark [lead prosecutor]! She is okay in my book.

VICKY: No, she is not a defense attorney.

BILL: She will be some day.

DONNA: Some day.

TOM: Where she'll make more money.

In contrast, informants in the black group failed to explicitly link Simpson's relatively abundant financial resources to possible case outcomes. As with the white group, however, these informants still managed to resent his wealth and celebrity – albeit for a different reason altogether. Black informants generally perceived wealthy celebrities like Simpson (particularly athletes) to be racial traitors who would typically prefer a white woman over a black one, thus squandering their resources on racial outsiders instead of keeping them within the community:

CHERYL: Most sports guys are supposed to get white women . . .

DENISE: They do . . .

JAMAL: Most guys with a certain income . . .

DENISE: I was just getting ready to say that . . .

ELIZABETH: Thank you. You're right . . .

JAMAL: You reach six figures and it's like, hey, I got six figures, I got to get a white woman . . .

ELIZABETH: Ohhh . . . that's the first thing they do . . . a white woman.

JAMAL: And it really hurts me cause there's so many black women who deserve to have those things . . .

ELIZABETH: Thank you.

JAMAL: . . . a fine home and a fine car. And that's what every black man out there is working for . . . that's what his goal should be, it's like, "Well, I'm gonna reach down and bring some woman up here and show her the good life."

DENISE: Thank you. Thank you. That's right . . .

ELIZABETH: But instead they going the other way.

Implicit in this understanding was that black entry into the "white world" – symbolized by the possession of white women like Brown-Simpson – could only be purchased with wealth and celebrity. Indeed, Simpson himself was denied entry into this world until "*after* he made it:"

BARBARA: Well they say O.J. was in the white world too much . . .
ELIZABETH: He . . . he was . . .
JAMAL: Well he was and he never looked back . . .
JAMES: He was around rich people all his life.
ELIZABETH: Not all his life . . .
CHERYL: What he means is, after he made it he was.

Thus, while informants in the black group found it difficult to separate issues of wealth and celebrity from issues of race, their white counterparts had no such problem. For these latter informants, wealth and celebrity represented a dominant, stand-alone force in the case – it dramatically shaped the trajectory of the trial and would have a major impact on any outcome, especially one in Simpson's favor. For their black counterparts, however, neither Simpson's wealth and celebrity nor the trajectory of the case could be understood without foregrounding race.

Race

The degree to which the black and white groups diverged in their explicit affirmations and denials about race was rather striking. While black informants saw race as a pivotal issue in the case, white informants generally predicted that race would be an insignificant factor in the trial's outcome. Following discussion, informants in both groups were administered a scale (1 = "very important," 10 = "not at all important") to gauge how significant a role they thought race would play in the trial's outcome. The mean for the white group was 7.5, suggesting that informants felt race would not be terribly important. In contrast, the mean for the black group was 3.8, indicating that race would likely play an important role.[16] Accordingly, perhaps, white informants rarely referred to themselves in racial terms when talking about the case, while black informants openly talked about themselves as raced subjects throughout their discussion.[17] That is, discussion of case-related issues in the black group seemed to position informants as black subjects; in the white group, however, discussion worked to position informants as subjects outside race.

For white informants, it seems, their general faith in police/prosecution "evidence" was dependent upon maintaining an image of the criminal justice system as a "colorblind" institution capable of ferreting out truth, capable of separating the guilty from the innocent irrespective of race. Consequently, there existed little incentive for these informants to consider the issue of race, to even speak of themselves as raced subjects. The Simpson case, as most in the group saw it, was about murder; the decision rules to be applied in the determination of innocence or guilt should be the same whether the defendant (or victim) was "black," "white," "green" or "yellow." Indeed, Mary condemned "black people" for repeatedly raising the issue of race, describing them as "more racist than *the* white people [emphasis added]:"[18] Accordingly, several informants sought to sanction David when he again transgressed the group common sense, this time by invoking race. In the following exchange, Bill, a forty-nine-year-old private investigator, labelled David "the biggest racist here" for suggesting that racism might exist in the LAPD, and that it might have something to do with the education levels of officers:

BILL: People are human.
DAVID: Right.
MARY: But you know, I think that black people are more racist than the white people.
DAVID: Whatever. The point I was trying to make is, along with that, racism goes along with education. I mean it's, it's . . .
BILL: What?
DAVID: . . . a lot of people . . .
BILL: Where do you get this information, David? I know the smartest people I know are very racist and some of the dumbest are very fair. My god!
DAVID: I am saying, Bill, generally speaking . . .
DONNA: That was a profound statement.
(Laughter)
TOM: Educated people are more racist?
DAVID: . . . I am saying . . .
BILL: You sound like the biggest racist here!

Ironically, perhaps, while informants in the white group criticized blacks for challenging the notion of a "colorblind" criminal justice system (i.e., raising the issue of racial bias), informants in the black group condemned whites for not abiding by the system that the white group stridently affirmed. That is, black informants' interactions with and observations of white trial observers led these informants to see whites as violators of a key tenet of US jurisprudence: assuming that Simpson was guilty before he was proven to be so in a court of law. Indeed, when Jamal raised the possibility that blacks might be similarly guilty of prejudging the case (but in reverse), Denise, a forty-four-year-old administrative assistant, countered that this position was reasonable: defendants in the United States are supposed to be assumed innocent until proven guilty. In the end, these informants agreed that whites, not blacks, had adopted the unreasonable stance on the case:

DENISE: The whites, though, they all feel like O.J. Simpson is guilty.

ELIZABETH: They all feel like that.

JAMAL: But that's all I've been trying to say . . . is if we were a group of white people, it'd be a different conversation here this evening . . .

JAMES: "He's guilty!"

DENISE: You can hear them in elevators, in restaurants . . . "He's guilty." I heard a man in an elevator say one morning . . . I mean he wasn't talking to me, of course. I said what I had to say, but he said, "Oh! I don't know why they're wasting so much time, why don't they just throw the book . . . he's guilty." And so his partner is, you know, kinda hot for him to shut up and he kept up . . . And I think, "Your mamma could have killed her too . . . or anybody could have killed her [Nicole] . . ."

ELIZABETH: They come all the way down here to say the man is guilty.

DENISE: They don't know . . . I asked people like, "Was you there?"

JAMAL: But, but black people, what I trip on is that black people stand up and say just as strongly and just as matter-of-factly, that he's not guilty . . . that he was set up.

DENISE: That's right, that's right.

JAMAL: But we don't know . . . we don't know.

ELIZABETH: But I know even . . .

CHERYL: He has no history.

DENISE: But basically I'm trying to say you're innocent . . . until proven guilty.

JAMAL: Exactly.

But from the perspective of most informants in the white group, Simpson *had* been "proven" guilty. These informants seemed so sure of police/prosecution "evidence," so sure the criminal justice system was essentially "colorblind," that they could/would easily dismiss defense "evidence" as nonsense – especially that concerning the possible role of race in the case. Indeed, even granting David's dissenting view that Fuhrman might be a racist, that he may have planted the glove, most informants felt the *remaining* "evidence" overwhelmingly pointed to Simpson's guilt. As Bill put it, "there is still a lot there." In other words, these informants generally understood any wrongdoing on the part of the police/prosecution as merely facilitating/expediting the conviction of an obviously guilty defendant, one with ample resources to hire crafty attorneys. And these attorneys, Simpson's "Dream Team," seemed to be the informants' worst nightmare. From their vantage point, defense attorneys had not only successfully confused the "evidence" that so clearly implicated Simpson, but as several informants put it, they had played the "race card," levelling an underhanded assault on the justice system itself:

BILL: I don't know what Fuhrman's background is. He seems pretty intelligent to me on the TV. I don't think he is smart enough to run a conspiracy against O.J. like you're seeing speculation on.

DAVID: I don't think he is. But is he a racist?

BILL: He may be.

DAVID: Probably.

TOM: What if he is, what does it mean?

MARY: It doesn't matter whether he is or not. The race card shouldn't have been brought up in this trial.

TOM: So what if he is a racist? What does that mean to you?

MARY: Cochran [the lead defense attorney] brought it [race] up.

DAVID: What I think they're trying to say is that if he is a racist, then . . .

MARY: It still doesn't prove anything, he didn't plant the glove!

DAVID: What it proves is that some of their [police] actions in light of that can be seen as . . . biased.

BILL: David might be right, he could have planted . . . this could have been slanted towards keying in on O. J. . . . you could be right, David. But there is still a lot [of evidence] there.

In contrast to white disdain for the "Dream Team" and its use of the "race card," informants in the black group spoke of the defense attorneys – Johnnie Cochran, in particular – as if they were heroes. The notion that the defense had played the "race card" was never an issue in the group. Here, the importance of race was taken for granted. Confronted with what they viewed as anything but a "colorblind" criminal justice system, and cognizant of what they understood as white investment in this system, informants in the black group grappled with their predicaments as black subjects in America. Elizabeth expressed utter frustration with the unfolding trial, how it seemed to reflect the dominant position of whites and their views, the subordinate position of blacks and their's. Indeed, exclaiming that "I hate to look at 'em" [white people], she toyed with the idea of quitting her job in order to avoid direct contact. But other members of the group chided her to reconsider this option, to "deal with it in a positive way":

ELIZABETH: I'm getting ready to quit my job . . . cause I just don't like them [whites] no more.

(Laughter.)

ELIZABETH: You hear what I'm saying?

CHERYL: But you know, don't quit your job.

ELIZABETH: I'm ready to quit my job . . .

(Loud talking)

ELIZABETH: It's the same . . . It's the case.

CHERYL: This case. It's the case!

JAMAL: Well, that's what you got to realize, that if we were a group of white people.

CHERYL: Don't do that, though.

ELIZABETH: I'm serious.

CHERYL: . . . but learn how to deal with it in a positive way . . .

JAMAL: But if we were a group of whites sitting here . . .

DENISE: . . . turn it into a positive thing . . .

ELIZABETH: You look at this court every day . . . you look at court every day. I look at court every day, almost . . . I get mad and the more I look at it, the crazier I get.

(laughter)

ELIZABETH: I'm serious, the more I look at it, the madder I get . . . I hate to look at em.

In short, race-*as-representation* permeated the trial through and through for black informants and spilled over into their own lives, their sense of powerlessness in society. As group discussion moved from one trial development/revelation to the next, these informants seemed to (re)-evaluate the practical and symbolic implications for the status of black people in the United States. In contrast, informants in the white group generally viewed race as a straw horse in the case, its significance also blown out of proportion in the broader society. Indeed, group common sense suggested that the "race card" amounted to little more than a clever defense ploy to divert attention away from the real "evidence" and, even worse, call the legitimacy of the criminal justice system into question. When this common sense was challenged by dissenters, other group members worked to mute the transgressions. In other words, while key tenets of the "Just-Us" system project were affirmed by black informants and David's transgressions, they were generally dismissed by the white group. For this latter group to affirm the project, members would ultimately have to accept the "implausible" possibility of conspiracy.

Conspiracy

In the Simpson media event, the notion of conspiracy surfaced repeatedly in the narratives constructed and circulated about the defendant's innocence or guilt (see chapter 1). It also emerged several times in both study groups' discussions (see Appendix 3). Defense charges that police officers knowingly and willfully sought to frame Simpson for the murders or that prosecutors sought to bury/distort exculpatory evidence were essentially charges of conspiracy. As we found with the issue of race, the two study groups had rather divergent reactions to these charges.

Informants in the white group generally believed Simpson had both the motive and opportunity to commit the murders, while Fuhrman (and by extension the police/prosecution) had little motive or opportunity to frame the celebrity defendant. As he had done before, however, David expressed a dissenting view on this issue. But when he invoked intertextual memories of the Rodney King beating as evidence of the

LAPD's propensity to perpetrate conspiracies (see chapter 2), he was rebuffed by two group members. These informants framed the King beating incident as either a justifiable use of police force or just an aberration in an otherwise noble police department record. As Mary put it, "There are probably some bad cops, but not the majority." Accordingly, the "evidence" (i.e., findings pertaining to the Simpson case *and* past LAPD performance), as informants in this group generally saw it, did not support defense claims of conspiracy. It did, however, support the charge of Simpson's guilt:

BILL: David, you look for a motive, which O. J. did have. You look for opportunity, O. J. had it. And then you look at the tremendous amount of circumstantial evidence that tends to lean towards her [Nicole's] ex-husband who does have a bad temper and everybody apparently knew it at the [police] station. To say that "Well, they [the police] were leaning towards him" is probably an understatement. I have no doubt they were; he was a suspect right from second one.

BOB: Right!

BILL: . . . and when they went over that gate [at Simpson's estate without a search warrant], they went in there [with Simpson in mind] as a suspect and not as a victim.

BOB: Sure.

WOMAN: They are not stupid enough to plant the evidence.

BILL: But to say this is a conspiracy because you know two policemen who are [bad cops] . . . I suppose that these are bad cops.

DAVID: Not at all. I am not saying that at all, I'm saying that . . .

MARY: There are probably some bad cops, but not the majority.

DAVID: People want to do whatever they want to do.

BILL: Police are human and they can lie, they can cheat, and they can go on drugs just like anybody else, that's true, but now . . .

DAVID: They can beat a black motorist [Rodney King] 19 times [sic] on videotape for the first time and still get off.

BILL: Don't get me started on King!

MARY: Yeah, don't start with that. There's too many against yah.

(loud talking)

Informants in the black group, however, stridently embraced the notion of conspiracy. Invoking intertextual memories of other recent, high-profile trials,[19] Jamal – a thirty-six-year-old painter – pointed to a white "conspiracy" to discredit and ultimately eliminate prominent black males. This "plan," it seems, explained for informants the prosecution's "mountain of evidence" against Simpson in a way that allowed them to keep open the possibility, at least, of his innocence. That is, black informants considered it quite likely that the most damning evidence was planted, while other exculpatory evidence was concealed by the police and/or prosecution. The holes and inconsistencies these informants saw in the prosecution's case, combined with the vigor with which Simpson was being prosecuted, only worked to support the theory:

JAMAL: You said something downstairs, and we haven't touched on it . . . all being people of color, but what about the fact that some people think there's a conspiracy to bring down prominent black men?
DENISE: They [whites] doing it . . . one by one.
CHERYL: They are doing it.
JAMAL: And if they're doing that, where are they going? You know what I mean? What are they planning?
CHERYL: Who knows . . . look at their history . . . who knows what they plan?

Indeed, several informants in this group viewed the Simpson trial as a "set-up for a race war," a conflict they felt would inevitably work to further disadvantage blacks relative to whites. Group common sense told black informants that the subordinate status of blacks in America was neither accidental nor solely the outgrowth of black capabilities or efforts. Whites were invested in doing whatever was necessary to keep blacks at the bottom of society. Of course, informants in the white group generally considered it "ludicrous" that anyone would believe such a conspiracy could exist, that such accusations could have anything at all to do with the "facts" of the Simpson case. In the final analysis, these divergent takes on the issue of conspiracy – on what is and/or can be – neatly paralleled each group's general orientation toward media portrayals of the case "facts." Accordingly, the two groups received and negotiated *Primetime*'s narrative about the 911 incident in strikingly different ways.

The Primetime *text*

In the questionnaire used to screen prospective group members, informants from both groups were asked to list the newspapers and magazines they regularly read. Half (5/10) of the informants in the white group reported they read the *Los Angeles Times*, while the remaining informants listed other media such as *Time* magazine, *Newsweek*, the *Torrance Daily Breeze* (a local newspaper), and *Playboy*. Nearly two-thirds (6/10) of informants in the black group reported they read the *Los Angeles Times*; the remainder listed publications such as the *Los Angeles Daily News* (another local newspaper), and the black-oriented magazines *Jet* and *Ebony*. Interestingly, none of the black informants reported reading Los Angeles' largest black-owned weekly, the *Los Angeles Sentinel*, a paper that undoubtedly had a major impact on black discourses about the case (see chapter 6).

Following the group discussions, a media fairness scale (1 = "fair," 10 = "unfair") was administered to informants. Findings indicated that white informants were somewhat ambivalent about the media's fairness (mean = 4.8), while their black counterparts felt coverage was more "unfair" than not (mean = 7.4). Given the high level of *Los Angeles Times* readership in both groups, it is noteworthy that the groups differed somewhat in their perceptions of how "fair" the media had been thus far in covering the case. That is, it appears that groups may have arrived at conflicting appraisals of essentially the *same* news narratives. In any event, this was certainly the case for the *Primetime* text.

Informants in the white group generally received the *Primetime* text in a *referential mode* (cf. Liebes and Katz 1993), discussing the most important news in the text in terms of the presented narrative or their own experiences, failing to consider the text *as construction*.[20] That is, their reflections on the *Primetime* text tended to echo and uncritically affirm key ideological positions embedded in it. Accordingly, most informants regarded Simpson's jealous rage, Brown-Simpson's fear, or the "good job" done by the police on the scene as the most significant news in the segment:

DAVID: Well I think Nicole thought she was gonna be killed by this guy. I think the rage that he had.
BILL: I think the whole idea of the video was to show that the police had done a good job . . .
MARY: Yeah, that's what I picked up.
BILL: I think everybody knew that O. J. had a bad temper, and everybody knew that Nicole had . . . I mean we heard the 911 a long time before this came out.
BOB: Yeah!
BILL: I thought the 911 was more informative.

Nonetheless, as discussion continued in this group, David again challenged the emerging consensus and described the *Primetime* text as "totally slanted," as "PR for the LAPD." The other transgressor, Elaine, quickly supported his view by noting that Simpson could be heard talking "like a regular person" on the secret tape recording, not the enraged and jealous lunatic the text portrayed him to be. But this comment – like others she offered throughout the interview – was essentially ignored by the rest of the group. Instead, attention remained focused on David, who was clearly seen as a threat to the dominant view in the group. Group members took turns dismissing and/or explaining away his observations, sanctioning him for transgressing the emerging group consensus. He was clearly just "down on the police":

MARY: We all knew it [the 911 incident] . . . we had heard it before.
DAVID: It [the *Primetime* text] was totally slanted.
ELAINE: I only heard O. J. on the background talking like a regular person.
BILL: How was it slanted?
(shouting/loud talking)

DAVID: The one woman cop saying, the one woman cop going like, "I told her, I told her, he is gonna kill you." You know?

BILL: But she didn't know the tape was going either, remember?

DAVID: She wasn't on the tape. She was being interviewed and said she had told her that.

MARY: Yeah, but they go through counseling. The police knew what they were talking about. They confront this situation every, almost every day.

DAVID: Sure!

DONNA: Every day!

MARY: They know what's gonna happen. And like Paul said there are thousands of people in prison.

BOB: The purpose of the tape was to show like Bill said that the police are doing a good job. They've been taking a bashing in the press and everything. So, this is their opportunity to go show that they do a good job.

DAVID: Of course, this is PR for the LAPD.

DONNA: You are really down on the police.

Instead of echoing ideological stances privileged by the text, informants in the black group read the text in a *metalinguistic mode* (cf. Liebes and Katz 1993), questioning the techniques, devices, and interests that undergird its construction.[21] Accordingly, these informants frequently homed in on points that were either buried in the text or mentioned only in passing. For example, Wilma – a fifty-four-year-old educator – described the report that Simpson had not physically hit Brown-Simpson in four years as "the most important news" in the segment. Other informants pointed to news of the officer's secret taping of the incident, questioning whether it marked the beginning of the LAPD "planning this whole thing" against Simpson (i.e., the "conspiracy"):

WILMA: The part that she said that . . . that he didn't hit her in four years.

CHERYL: In four years.

DENISE: Well, I hadn't heard that before.

JAMAL: What to me was most important . . . was that that officer was taping . . . that was . . .

STEVE: That's against the law.

JAMAL: Well they say it was legal.

DENISE: They said it was legal.

JAMAL: Well, for some reason he at that time chose to tape.

DARYL: But, wait a minute . . . I thought, when you tape somebody you have to let them know they're being taped.

ELIZABETH: Well, the FBI don't . . .

(laughter)

DENISE: The police could do whatever they want to do, I mean they go on your property, they rummage through your house . . . go through your things . . .

WILMA: Okay, why did he have a tape recorder in his pocket?

ELIZABETH: He went there to tape.

JAMES: Because based on the fact that . . . on how many times they had been there . . .
DENISE: So they went prepared for whatever.
JAMES: They went prepared.
DENISE: Well, he did make the point . . . that he said . . . Well, if you're going to nail O. J. Simpson, you needed to have your facts, you need to have everything together . . . so . . .
JAMES: Because now he's going . . .
CHERYL: That might have been the beginning of them planning this whole thing.

In many respects, black informants' identification of "the most important news" in the *Primetime* text was consistent with the *mode* in which they talked about the segment. While informants in the white group (with the exception of David and Elaine) strictly understood the text in a referential mode, their black counterparts generally discussed the text in metalinguistic terms. That is, black informants' openness to the possibility of conspiracy prompted them to discuss the text *as construction*, as the product of newsworkers who relied upon certain techniques to fashion a coherent narrative, a "one-sided" narrative:

CHERYL: You know what you have to remember about this whole program? (shouting/loud talking)
CHERYL: I don't know when they taped this program, but all this was done after the fact. So, the police woman could have been saying that just to make . . . to try to put on for points.
DENISE: Right.
CHERYL: It may not have been like that at all.
ELIZABETH: She might be . . . to cash in to.
CHERYL: Well, I think she would cash in but she's tried to make it look one way.
DENISE: One-sided.
CHERYL: The whole tape is one-sided.

In short, informants in the black group "worked very hard" to read the *Primetime* text and maintain their initial perspectives on the Simpson murder case (cf. Condit 1994, p. 432). These informants were suspicious of the prosecution's case against Simpson, and considered it likely that Mark Fuhrman – the white officer who allegedly found a bloody glove at Simpson's home – was guilty of planting evidence in the case. Moreover, they attributed these suspicions to a "plot" on the part of whites to "keep blacks down." Their difficulty with the text, of course, is a testament to how well newsworkers framed the *Primetime* narrative to convey Simpson's guilt. Consequently, these informants were openly critical of the text, opting to amplify understated points and challenge the ones emphasized by newsworkers.

In contrast, most informants in the white group did not have to engage in such labor. For them, the text was a clear window onto the 911 incident and the unfolding trial. When David and Elaine challenged the emerging group consensus, they were promptly sanctioned by other members for questioning what appeared to be incontrovertible case "facts." These "facts," of course, clearly indicated that Simpson was guilty of murder and that Fuhrman was innocent of planting the glove. The framing that shaped the *Primetime* narrative was so consistent with these informants' initial perspectives on the case that it was largely invisible to them.

Conclusions

At the height of the prosecution's presentation of its case-in-chief, informant views in the two study groups echoed the "black-white divide" so prevalent in mainstream news media accounts (e.g., see table 1, chapter 1). Indeed, whether the issue was the prosecution and defense cases, science and DNA, domestic violence, wealth and celebrity, race, conspiracy, or the *Primetime* text itself, informant stances could be organized along a single dividing line: white investment in official institutions and accounts (e.g., criminal justice system, media), black suspicion of them.

Interestingly, given the Domestic Violence and Celebrity Defendant projects (see chapter 2), neither socioeconomic status nor gender seemed to greatly pattern informant stances on the case "facts." Nonetheless, one of the black women informants validated popular accounts of race and gender interactions (cf. Schiller and Willwerth 1996) with her intense animosity toward Nicole Brown-Simpson – a white woman who had won the affection of a black man (Simpson) from a black woman (Simpson's first wife). But when facilitators prompted informants to discuss "the most important news in the [*Primetime*] video," their interpretations of the 911 domestic violence incident were cleanly split along racial lines:[22] male *and* female informants in the white group said that "O. J. had a disease of jealousy" and that "Nicole thought she was gonna be killed by this guy"; meanwhile, for both males *and* females in the black group, the most important news was that Brown-Simpson acknowledged to police officers that Simpson "didn't hit her in four years," suggesting to them that the prosecution's claim of escalating violence was a ruse. In this sense, the power of the *Primetime* text to establish the most important case "facts" was a direct function of what informants came to the screenings prepared to see. And two months into the trial this seeing most clearly diverged along racial lines.

But how would informant views change (if at all) over the next four months of the trial, as prosecutors rested their case and defense attorneys endeavored to lay theirs out? How would the introduction of new "evidence," the emergence of important case developments, and the circulation of related news narratives impact informant understandings of the case "facts?" We explore these questions in the next chapter.

In the four months separating the first and second interviews (March 30–August 1, 1995), much had happened in the Simpson case. Prosecutors had presented the final twenty witnesses of their case-in-chief and Simpson's defense team had presented thirty-three of the fifty-three witnesses it would eventually call (Schmalleger 1996). During this period, a multitude of LAPD, California Department of Justice, and FBI agents and criminalists would testify that physical evidence – blood DNA, human hairs, and shoe prints – conclusively tied Simpson to the murder scene, and the victims to blood found in his Bronco and on items at his Rockingham home. Defense attorneys, of course, had endeavored to discredit and/or impeach these witnesses, their efforts reaching a crescendo, perhaps, with defense attorney Barry Scheck's much-heralded cross-examination of LAPD criminalist Dennis Fung (April 3, 5, 11–14, and 17–18, 1995).

Finally, in what many observers up to that point had described as the nadir of the prosecution's case, prosecutor Christopher Darden asked Simpson to try on the bloody gloves in court. Simpson stood before the jury, wrestled with pulling the leather gloves over the latex ones protecting his hands, and finally announced that the gloves did not fit (June 15–16, 1995). Although prosecutors would suggest that Simpson was acting – and later offer testimony indicating the gloves had shrunk and that the latex gloves further altered the fit – many trial observers felt the impression had already been made: the gloves did not fit.

The defense would begin its case-in-chief by presenting a brisk parade of witnesses – members of Simpson's family, golfing companions, fellow airplane passengers, and so on – who challenged the prosecution's time-line or testified that Simpson's demeanor the night in question was inconsistent with that of someone who had just committed two grisly murders. Robert Heidstra, for example, would testify that while walking his dogs on the night of the murders he heard two men arguing and the gate of Brown-Simpson's condominium clang shut much later than the prosecution's time-line would allow, about 10:40 pm

(July 11–12, 1995). Prosecutors, however, would push Heidstra to admit he had seen a white sports utility vehicle – one that, to the defense's chagrin, "could have been a Bronco" – leaving the area that night, albeit headed in a direction away from Rockingham. Mark Patridge, who sat next to Simpson on the American Airlines flight the celebrity took to Chicago, would testify that he noticed no cuts on Simpson's hands (July 13, 1995) – a critical observation given the blood trail prosecutors argued tied Simpson to the Bundy murder scene (i.e., Simpson would claim he cut or reopened a wound on his hand in Chicago after hearing the news of his ex-wife's death; a physical examination of Simpson shortly after his return from Chicago found no other cuts on his body). Dr. Robert Huizenga, called by the defense to confirm that Simpson suffered from rheumatoid arthritis, at first suggested that Simpson was physically incapable of overpowering two younger victims. Simpson, he quipped, had "the body of Tarzan" but "walked like Tarzan's grandfather" (July 14, 17–18, 1995). But prosecutor Brian Kelberg would have fun with this comparison. Before the jury, he would screen an exercise videotape in which Simpson is seen participating in high-impact aerobics while making jokes about punching his wife. Huizenga would finally concede that Simpson was physically capable of the murders (July 19, 1995).

In the weeks immediately preceding the second interview, defense attorneys presented several witnesses in an effort to support the theory that police had conspired to frame Simpson. Forensic toxicologist Frederic Rieders, for example, would testify that the chemical preservative EDTA was indeed present in some of the blood found on items of prosecution evidence, suggesting that the blood had been planted from reference vials (July 24, 1995). The following morning, FBI agent Roger Martz would concede that his test findings were consistent with the presence of EDTA in the blood, but later in the afternoon deny that the amounts were significant enough to confirm the claim that the blood was planted (July 25, 1995).

On the Thursday preceding the Tuesday interviews (July 27, 1995), a front-page story from the *Los Angeles Sentinel* had questioned whether the cameras-in-the-courtroom controversy surrounding the Simpson case would spill over into another high-profile murder case involving an African American celebrity, rapper Snoop Doggy Dogg. The headline read:

Coverage controversy: O. J. Issues Plague Snoop Doggy Dog Murder Trial

In the same issue of the paper, a weekly opinion column called "The People's Pulse" had asked four African-American children whether they thought Simpson was guilty or innocent. All of the children were in agreement: Simpson had been wrongfully accused. Six-year-old Joshua Randle, for example, responded that "O. J. didn't do it and it's not fair." Similarly, ten-year-old Corintha Flood added, "He didn't do it. They should take him off trial and leave him alone." Accordingly, an ABC/Washington Post poll conducted a week earlier (July 20, 1995) had suggested that black and white ways of seeing the case continued to exist: 78 percent of white respondents thought Simpson was probably guilty, compared to only 28 percent of their black counterparts.

The morning of the second interviews, a front-page headline in the *Los Angeles Times* summarized the previous day's trial testimony:

Ito's Rulings Set Back Simpson Defense Team: Courts: Reporter refuses to testify about socks story, citing protection of shield law. Judge won't help get tapes containing alleged racist remarks by Fuhrman.

The two "set back(s)" suffered by Simpson's defense went to the heart of its conspiracy theory. First, a KNBC newsworker had refused to reveal her source for an early news narrative announcing that Nicole Brown-Simpson's DNA had been found on the socks recovered from Simpson's bedroom. Because the narrative had been constructed and circulated *prior* to the actual testing cited, defense attorneys argued that the accuracy of the source's information was an indication of his/her knowledge that reference sample blood had been or would be planted on the socks. Second, although defense attorneys had been hoping to introduce the infamous Fuhrman tapes as evidence of the detective's racial animus, the attorneys were hampered by a North Carolina judge who ruled against forcing Laura Hart McKinny, the screenwriter who interviewed Fuhrman, to make the tapes available for the California trial.

In court that day, defense attorneys re-enacted the grand jury testimony of Thano Peratis, the LAPD nurse who had withdrawn a sample of blood from Simpson's arm the day after the murders. Defense attorneys would use LAPD evidence records and Peratis's earlier testimony that he had withdrawn 8 milliliters of blood to argue that some of Simpson's reference sample was missing (i.e., police records accounted for only 6.5 milliliters). The implication: the "missing" blood had been planted in an LAPD conspiracy to frame Simpson. Indeed, the KTLA-TV text informants would view during the second interviews had first aired earlier that afternoon and would focus on the "missing-blood" issue – but not until *after* the replaying of excerpts from the morning in which Marcia Clark and Johnnie Cochran argue about the admissibility of photos showing Simpson wearing gloves similar to the blood-stained ones allegedly found at the Bundy murder scene and his Rockingham home.

The KTLA text

The media text screened for study informants was extracted from KTLA-TV's continuing live coverage of the Simpson trial (see chapter 4). The twenty-two-minute segment first aired earlier during the day of the group interviews, August 1, 1995, from about 1:00 pm until 1:22 pm. As KTLA newsworkers and legal analyst Al DeBlanc awaited the resumption of court proceedings, they filled time with discussion and light banter about a number of recent trial developments and ongoing issues, breaking twice for rather lengthy commercial interludes. A verbatim transcript of the text is presented in Appendix 6.

The text begins by juxtaposing sound bites from lead prosecutor Marcia Clark and lead defense attorney Johnnie Cochran concerning photographs that had recently surfaced. The photographs depicted Simpson wearing gloves resembling the bloody ones reportedly collected from the Bundy Drive crime scene and Simpson's Rockingham home. While Clark argues that the photographs would be used to rebut the defense's "conspiracy theme," Cochran responds that prosecutors will never be able to prove Simpson wore the actual gloves apparently used by the killer(s).

Following this introduction, KTLA anchor Marta Waller summarizes the "latest developments" in the case: the director of the LAPD crime lab denied during cross-examination that she had leaked results of DNA tests to the media; a defense expert, Herbert MacDonnell testified following this, but Waller does not reveal what he said. Marta then tosses to KTLA reporter Ron Olsen, who updates the audience on a number of issues: court is expected to resume in about thirty minutes; proceedings may focus on a videotaped interview with Thano Peratis, the male LAPD nurse who withdrew Simpson's blood reference sample; and Judge Ito may rule soon on whether KNBC reporter Tracie Savage can invoke the state's "shield law" (Savage, you will recall, had refused to reveal her source for an early story about blood on socks reportedly recovered from Simpson's room containing Nicole Brown-Simpson's DNA).

Waller next introduces DeBlanc and asks him to comment on several case-related issues, including some of those raised by Olsen. She first asks the legal analyst to comment on the issue of the videotaped Peratis interview, on her observation that "There isn't anything that can be done except play this for the jury." Peratis had been ill, yet his testimony concerning the amount of blood he withdrew from Simpson was critical to the defense's conspiracy theory. DeBlanc agrees with Waller's observation, but notes that attorneys may argue over "interpretation," "what they see" in the videotape. She then asks DeBlanc to compare the videotaped interview of Peratis to the one earlier conducted with defense witness Rosa Lopez, the maid who testified that Simpson's white Bronco was parked on Rockingham around the time the prosecution claimed Simpson was using the vehicle to drive to and from the murder scene. DeBlanc points out that because the Lopez interview was a "conditional examination," defense attorneys might elect never to play it before the jury. Indeed, given that a "problem" was created for the defense by prosecutor Christopher Darden's scathing cross-examination of Lopez, this might just be their decision. Waller thus wonders aloud whether the defense could convince Lopez – who left the United States for her native El Salvador after testifying – to return and testify in person, "or that they want to get her back." DeBlanc responds that Lopez would probably be "unwilling to come back" in any event. Testifying, Waller concludes, has "been grueling for every witness – even those who have had really no, no stake in this."

After a lengthy commercial break (i.e., eight thirty-second commercials), Waller again tosses to Olsen, who reviews speculations permeating the Simpson newsworker corps about how lead prosecutor Clark might prove that the gloves Simpson is seen wearing in the photo are the murder gloves. He mentions the stitching, pointing out that Ito recently acknowledged receiving two reports from the FBI. Could one of these be an analysis of the stitching's distinctive characteristics? Waller poses the question to DeBlanc. DeBlanc confirms the possibility that prosecutors may be able to definitively match the gloves in the photo to the murder gloves. First, he points out, the gloves are handmade and may contain "irregularities." Moreover, he notes that experts can "print" leather gloves much like they do fingers because animal skins also have a discernable pattern.

With the possibility confirmed that prosecutors may be able to link the photographs to the gloves in evidence, Waller again turns to Olsen and poses him a question that "I've gotten from many, many viewers" (see chapter 4 for a discussion of this practice). The question concerned whether the inside of the bloody gloves had been tested, presumably for DNA and trace evidence. Olsen says he has not heard of any such tests, with the exception of those conducted by prosecution witness Richard Rubin to prove that the Bundy and Rockingham gloves were mates. DeBlanc then interjects to note that the glove photographs had only become necessary because of prosecutor Darden's failed courtroom glove demonstration, which suggested that the gloves did not fit Simpson. A lengthy exchange ensues regarding the possibility that Nicole Brown-Simpson may have bought more than one pair of the leather gloves, and that maybe she gave someone else a similar pair as a gift.

DeBlanc acknowledges these possibilities but maintains that "If O.J.'s wearing the gloves [in the photographs], then these are the gloves that she gave him." This point prompts Olsen to ask a hypothetical question: What if an FBI analysis of the gloves in the photographs positively link them to the bloody gloves? "[H]ow would Cochran defend against that?" "Well, the same old way he's defended all the other expert evidence," DeBlanc replies. "Ah, you get an, you get your own expert."

The text concludes with Olsen, DeBlanc and Waller considering whether or not Judge Ito would allow prosecutors to reopen their case-in-chief so they can introduce new evidence against Simpson. Despite the burden of proof faced by the prosecution, DeBlanc suggests, the trial has been so lengthy that the judge may not allow prosecutors to reopen their case. The new "evidence," consequently, "might not get in."

In short, despite consideration of a few peripheral issues, the focus of the text was clearly on what appeared to be new prosecution evidence further incriminating Simpson: the glove photographs. The Simpson newsworker corps, which generally embraced dominant narratives about Simpson's guilt (see chapter 3), was abuzz with these revelations. Accordingly, KTLA newsworkers and legal analyst Al DeBlanc filled air time by speculating on how prosecutors might be able to prove the gloves Simpson wore in the photographs were actually the murder gloves. With DeBlanc's blessing of matching techniques, *potential* prosecution "evidence" was effectively transformed into *actual* prosecution "evidence," prompting KTLA newsworkers to then speculate as to whether this new "evidence" would ultimately be admitted by Judge Ito. In the end, this speculation worked to support a key tenet of the Celebrity Defendant project: if Simpson's high-paid attorneys cannot persuade the judge to keep the evidence out, the implied narrative read, they will probably resort to hiring expert witnesses to challenge the new "evidence," to confuse jurors as to the "truth." Meanwhile, this discussion effectively upstaged other developments of the day, such as defense witness Herbert MacDonnell's testimony suggesting that blood on the socks reportedly recovered from Simpson's bedroom may have been planted.

Simpson reads news narratives

Following his acquittal in the criminal trial, Simpson embarked on what might best be described as a personal crusade against mainstream news media. His actions included unannounced calls to several television and radio programs whose hosts would presumably allow him to air his grievances. Eventually, this activity evolved into full-scale, pre-planned television interviews. Most of his complaints focussed on newsworkers' selection of newsworthy topics and their framing of the resulting case-related news narratives. For example, in a May 1996 interview on Granada television, Simpson questioned whether newsworkers covering the case had actually watched the same trial testimony he saw:

> What I have found since I have been out and I have watched television, and of course I watched a lot of it from my cell, at the end of the day – the wrap-up at the end of the day and quite often when I would go to what they call the lawyer's room, the Attorney room, at the end of the day after the news was off, I would look at whoever was visiting me and we would say "Were they in the same courtroom that we were in today?" because the reports were so, I felt, inaccurate, skewed always and generally to the negative.

Ways of seeing, it seems, are everything. For those who embraced dominant O. J. narratives, so-called "negative" news coverage essentially presented the relevant case "facts." However, for those compelled by less "plausible" O. J. narratives, these "facts" – as Simpson claims – were something different altogether. Mainstream news coverage was a distortion.

So what about study informants? How would black and white group members receive and negotiate KTLA's representations of the most recent case developments? Did the four months between the first and second interviews in any way dislodge the groups from their respective stances on the case "facts?"

Group affirmations – revisited

Between the first and second interviews, as often occurs in longitudinal designs, attrition struck both groups. The white group was reduced from ten to eight members: Jim, a forty-six-year-old Hilton employee, and Paul, a twenty-seven-year-old college student, were both absent. The black group was reduced in size from ten to seven: Barbara, fifty-seven, Denise, a forty-four-year-old administrative assistant, and Skip, a fifty-five-year-old representative for a state employment program, were not present (see table 2, chapter 7 for informant interrelationships).

Despite four months of new "evidence" (i.e., the testimony of fifty-three additional witnesses), the start of the defense's case-in-chief, and a proliferation of news narratives about the case, views about two key issues in the case changed very little in the two groups (see table 4). That is, informants in the white group continued to agree that Simpson was probably guilty of murder and that Fuhrman was most likely innocent of planting evidence against him. The latest scale scores for the group on these items were 2.7 and 8.2, respectively (1 = "guilty," 10 = "innocent"). In contrast, informants in the black group continued to

Table 4. *Perceptions of Simpson's innocence or guilt, and Fuhrman's innocence or guilt in framing Simpson, March 30, 1995 and August 1, 1995, by group.*[a]

Group	March 30	August 1
	Simpson's innocence/guilt	
Black	9.1	8.9
White	3.2	2.7
	Fuhrman's innocence/guilt	
Black	3.3	2.3
White	8.9	8.2

[a] Scales from 1 to 10, 1 = "guilty," 10 = "innocent."
Source: Post-discussion questionnaires, March 30, 1995 and August 1, 1995.

agree that Simpson was probably innocent of the murder charges and that Fuhrman was most likely guilty of planting evidence against him. The latest scale scores for this group on the items were 8.9 and 2.3, respectively.

Appendix 4 summarizes the emergence of discussion themes in the two groups. Talk in the white group moved from the high probability that the gloves Simpson is seen wearing in a photo will be identified, to members' perception that blacks are biased in favor of Simpson, to members' virtual certainty that Simpson is guilty. In the black group, talk moved from questioning the possibility that the gloves might be identified, to the high likelihood that a conspiracy against Simpson exists, to the pro-white bias of the legal system. Below I revisit seven themes that emerged from group discussions during the first interviews in order to explore, in detail, the process by which informants (re)negotiated, (re)articulated, and (re)affirmed these understandings of the case. These themes include informant perspectives on the prosecution and defense cases, DNA and science, domestic violence, wealth and celebrity, race, conspiracy, and the KTLA text. I conclude the chapter with a discussion of the relationships between raced ways of seeing, informant experiences, and ideological investments.

Prosecution and defense cases

Informants in the white group quickly took stock of what they viewed as the salient "evidence" in the case and rather confidently (re)affirmed their earlier belief that Simpson was guilty of the murders. Indeed, since the first interviews, informants seemed to have become even more secure in this belief. In the following exchange, Mary cogently expresses the sentiments of most group members. She suggests that due to Simpson's accomplishments (and the "nice guy" image discussed in chapter 2), the group had been "open-minded before" about his possible guilt, that they had wanted to give him "the benefit of the doubt." Unfortunately, she seems to conclude, "you really knew down in your heart that he really was" guilty:

TOM: Does anybody think that he . . . based on the evidence presented by the prosecution, think he is guilty, based on that alone, where they maybe thought he was innocent before; or is our opinions all the same.

MARY: No, we were opened-minded before, but I feel that there is an overwhelming . . .

BOB: Yeah, my first reaction was . . . oh no, that can't be . . . of guilt.

MARY: You want to give him the benefit of the doubt. I mean . . . he's O.J., he has really had every benefit as far as a newscaster, even though he marbled his words . . . and no one could understand what he was talking about, but regardless . . .

DONNA: He talks like . . . He talks like . . . what's his name?

MARY: . . . with marbles in his mouth.

DONNA: Reverend . . .

(loud talking)

DONNA: . . . Jesse Jackson.

BOB: No. Actually . . .

TOM: Well you would say . . .

(loud talking)

BILL: But he's got a million-dollar smile.

MARY: But . . . yeah.

TOM: But go ahead, I want to hear . . .

MARY: So he's had every benefit and everyone has not placed him on a pedestal, but had some respect for him getting to where he got . . . uh . . . in his career and hard times in his family, so you wanted to give him the benefit of the doubt, so you're not going to say he's 100 percent guilty, although you really knew down in your heart that he really was.

Indeed, developments of the preceding four months had so compellingly validated the prevailing group common sense that even David and Elaine – who both repeatedly transgressed this common sense during the first interview – resigned themselves to the realization that Simpson is "probably" guilty. David attributed his change of heart to two factors: the blood that prosecutors claimed tied Simpson to the crime scenes and his disappointment with the defense's performance. Thus far, as he put it, the defense had done a "shitty job." Bob reminded him, however, that the defense's job would have been much easier if Simpson "were only innocent":

DAVID: I'd say he is probably guilty.
(loud talking)
ELAINE: Probably. But you can't . . .
DAVID: I would say . . . I would say if there weren't the blood at the scene, it would be pretty . . . there's a reasonable doubt.
VICKY: See that's the thing . . . it's the blood.
(loud talking)
DAVID: Because there is . . . you wouldn't have anything to . . . and also, I just don't think, I think the defense is doing a shitty job. I don't think that they've done a very good job at all.
VICKY: Cause I kind of . . .
(Inaudible)
VICKY: I could have saved him.
BOB: I think Cochran was saying to O. J., it would be a lot easier to defend you O. J. if you were only innocent.

In the black group, however, views solidified quite differently. Despite a palpable malaise which seemed to hang over the group as the second interview began, informants ultimately managed to (re)affirm their earlier beliefs that Simpson had been framed. But first they had to neutralize troubling developments like the claim made earlier that day by prosecutor Marcia Clark – that she could "prove" the bloody gloves belonged to Simpson. The KTLA text informants had just viewed analyzed this troubling development at length. Moreover, informants had to overcome their disappointment with the defense's performance thus far. As James put it, "some of this stuff is backfiring." Indeed, Cheryl noted that Simpson's attorneys needed to "be better prepared":

DARYL: I feel he is being framed.
CHERYL: You didn't feel that four months ago?
DARYL: Not really, I was kind of unbalanced.
JAMES: Well you didn't hear all the evidence then. Now . . .
DARYL: Now you're hearing . . .
JAMES: . . . that the prosecution has finished their statements and interviewed all their witnesses, now it's the defense's turn to try to bring some credibility to O. J. and some of this stuff is backfiring.
ELIZABETH: Most of it.
DARYL: That's one thing, yeah.
JAMES: That's the bad part now.
DARYL: Seems like everything the prosecution . . .
CHERYL: You know what I wonder sometime . . . it seems like the defense would know this. As many witnesses as they have put on, it seems like they ought to know by now – this is what's going to happen . . .
DARYL: So they need to go . . .
CHERYL: . . . and they should be better prepared . . .
ELIZABETH: Right. Right.
CHERYL: . . . be better prepared.

The following exchange clearly illustrates the process by which black informants finally succeeded in converting their disappointments about the defense's performance into a renewed faith in the defense's conspiracy theory. That is, in a classic demonstration of informational influence theory (cf. Myers and Lamm 1975), informants embrace a forgotten argument (i.e., the defense need only establish reasonable doubt) that quickly works to reinforce the group's original position:

WILMA: Well you guys feel like the defense . . . you said you feel like the defense is going downhill.
CHERYL: Uh huh.
DARYL: Cause everything they bring out, they shoot it out.
JAMAL: Almost every last one of the witnesses has almost backfired on them.
JAMES: Hey . . . it goes all the way. It turns around . . . they got it turned around.
JAMAL: But I heard DeBlanc [KTLA legal analyst] say today that . . . what's her name, Marta [Waller, KTLA anchor] say that their case seems to be over pretty quick, and he says that they . . . the defense presented at least half of their case during cross.
DARYL: Rebuttal.
JAMAL: So they don't have to . . . and, and you've got to think about what is . . . what is their job? Their job is to . . .
CHERYL: Reasonable doubt.
JAMAL: . . . put a reasonable doubt in the . . . and they feel like they have done that.
CHERYL: And they have done that . . . they have done that.
WILMA: You're right. It is reasonable doubt.
JAMAL: It's according to the jury though now. That's . . .
DARYL: Yeah. They tell the jury, if you have a slight . . . of reasonable doubt.
CHERYL: Right. I think that they have done that. I think there's too many things that are not explained.

In short, four months, fifty-three witnesses, and countless news narratives later, the two groups found themselves (re)negotiating positions about the case strikingly similar to those they had held before. In the white group, the prevailing common sense had even worked to bring the transgressors more in line. Much of this activity – as we also noted during the first interviews – was predicated on the groups' orientations toward science and DNA.

Science and DNA

By the time informants convened for the second interviews the prosecution had begun and concluded its presentation of DNA evidence. Informants had thus been exposed to astronomical figures about the likelihood that blood on the socks reportedly recovered from Simpson's bedroom "matched" Brown-Simpson's. Indeed, one prosecution witness testified that the odds were only about one in 9.7 billion that the blood could have come from anyone other than Simpson's ex-wife. To be sure, this seemed to be particularly damning given that the Earth's population was only about 5 billion. Given the faith informants in the white group expressed in the reliability of science and DNA technology during the first interviews, it is perhaps not surprising that by the second interviews most informants in the group found the new evidence against Simpson to be "profound," and themselves to be a "little more convinced that he is guilty" than before:

BOB: I think I am little more convinced that he is guilty than I was before, because the defense has not come up with anything that resembles a defense.
VICKY: Right.
TOM: And also, since then we've seen the DNA evidence . . .
DONNA: Which is pretty profound too.
TOM: . . . which is pretty profound . . . True.
DONNA: Yeah.

At the same time, white informants deflected any possible chinks in the DNA armor by questioning the legitimacy of defense DNA experts. These experts, you will recall, attempted to sow doubt in the DNA results by suggesting that the LAPD evidence processing lab – through which all samples ultimately passed – was a "cesspool of contamination" and that certain samples appeared to have been tampered with. Informants in the white group generally considered these "experts" to be "sleazy":

DONNA: I mean there's so much blood that even if it were contaminated, if it was three weeks old, three months old, DNA proved it was his.
BOB: No.
DONNA: Alright.
MARY: I mean good DNA experts, not these fleecy . . . not these sleazy . . . Not these . . .
VICKY: Flea-bag DNA experts.
MARY: Right, I just can't believe some of the witnesses on the defense.
VICKY: I thought he was guilty and then I thought . . . well?
BOB: She's [prosecutor Marcia Clark] got him [Simpson] . . . really no room for doubt.

Meanwhile, informants in the black group overcame the prosecution's "mountain" of DNA evidence by employing a strategy similar to the one they used during the first interviews. That is, informants acknowledged the results of tests indicating that crime-scene blood belonged to Simpson, but questioned the prosecution's theory of *how* the blood had gotten there. Here, they clearly embraced "implausible" O. J. narratives about conspiracy (see chapter 1), seizing on the "missing blood" controversy discussed in the KTLA text they had just screened:

CHERYL: What he said was the [blood] vial will hold 10 cc's [sic]. That's how tall the vial is, but he [LAPD nurse Thano Peratis] drew eight.

JAMAL: And how much is missing?

CHERYL: I'm not really sure how much is missing.

STEVE: It's some missing, but we don't know how much.

CHERYL: I don't know . . . I forgot how much is missing.

JAMAL: Because that was the whole purpose of his testimony, right?

DARYL: They've been saying that since this trial started, that blood was missing.

JAMAL: Uh huh.

JAMAL: Right.

But, as in the first interviews, black informants had to work hard (cf. Condit 1994) to negotiate their own preferred meanings from the KTLA text. Returning to the issue of the "missing blood," informants neutralized KTLA legal analyst Al DeBlanc's innocent explanation – that blood may be lost by repeatedly removing the rubber caps to the vials – by arguing that "people that work with blood" are more careful. The following exchange illustrates the prevailing group logic:

CHERYL: But it was something he said that made . . . but oh . . . because [KTLA legal analyst Al] DeBlanc said every time you pull the rubber . . . the rubber out of the blood, you lose some. Now you know people that work with blood . . . Know how to handle it.

(loud talking)

CHERYL: . . . in this day and time . . . do not lose blood when they pull it out . . . when they pull it out . . . when they pull that stopper out. I . . . you know, that's just ridiculous to say. Even if you've got on gloves you're going to be more careful, with blood.

WILMA: I think these people . . . if they're so . . . it's a lot of ridiculous things they're saying, to me, really, to be professional people that suppose to know about all of this stuff . . . a lot of it seems to be so . . .

CHERYL: That's why they're not going to be . . .

(loud talking)

CHERYL: I don't see how they're going to be able to prove that he [Simpson] did it [committed the murders].

In the second interviews, then, both groups were able to use the same scientific "evidence" to (re)affirm their original predispositions about the case "facts." And the resulting stances, of course, were essentially at odds. Similar processes, as we shall see in the next section, came into play surrounding the issue of domestic violence.

Domestic violence

By the second interviews, much of the focus of the trial – as critics would lament – had moved away from the victims. The prosecution had started its case with a focus on domestic violence, but in the period separating the two interviews, had moved on to DNA, hair, and fiber evidence. Moreover, the beginnings of the defense case-in-chief had steered clear of domestic violence, instead focusing on challenging prosecution time-line and demeanor evidence and establishing the defense's conspiracy theory. Nonetheless, informants in the white group managed to resurrect the issue of domestic violence during the second interviews. Indeed, the dominant narrative about an enraged, abusive Simpson continued to be central to their understanding of the case. The following exchange illustrates how informants in this group (re)affirmed Simpson's "motive." Although Elaine would finally concede that Simpson was "probably" guilty, she nonetheless uses her own marital experiences to question the "motive." Her husband, Bill, minimizes her point by turning it into a joke:

DONNA: He [Simpson] was enraged that day [the day of the murders].
MARY: Yes he was enraged . . .
TOM: He was enraged by something.
MARY: . . . He did not go to the party [the dinner at Mezzaluna celebrating his daughter's dance recital].[1] He was . . .
(loud talking)
MARY: . . . excluded and embarrassed . . .
DONNA: He was not invited to the dinner.
MARY: That's right. He was embarrassed.
TOM: Yeah, something occurred though.
ELAINE: Good God, every time that Bill didn't go somewhere with me . . . what, another . . .
VICKY: Yeah, but you guys haven't had . . .
ELAINE: Did you have a knife in . . .
VICKY: . . . that kind of relationship.
ELAINE: . . . your pocket. You did!
MARY: Yeah, but he hasn't beat you up Elaine, and everything.
ELAINE: How do you know?
MARY: Well, I'm . . .
(laughter)
BILL: God knows she deserved it, God only knows.
(laughter)

David, who had by now conceded along with Elaine that Simpson was "probably" guilty, joined his fellow ex-transgressor and continued to question specific aspects of the prosecution's theory of the crime. Specifically, he challenged the notion that Simpson had "planned" the murders. Other members of the white group translated this argument into the notion that Simpson's murder of his ex-wife was a "crime of passion." The knife only came into play, Vicky suggests, because Goldman walked in on the Simpsons' altercation, already in progress:

DAVID: I don't think he planned it.
TOM: You think it was a crime of passion, that's what you're saying.

VICKY: I think so too.

ELAINE: But, now . . . even with a crime of passion, if . . . why would he . . . to go to that length . . . I just don't believe . . . he would knock her around, he probably would have beat her up to death and . . .

VICKY: He did not expect . . .

ELAINE: . . . but not with a knife.

VICKY: . . . he did not expect Ron Goldman to be there.

In contrast, the black group had virtually dropped any discussion of domestic violence by the second interview. Perhaps this was a reflection of the diminished profile the issue had exhibited in the months between the interviews. Or maybe it was related to the group's earlier rejection of the prosecution theory that Simpson's history of domestic violence signified a credible "motive." In any event, the following exchange constitutes the group's sole consideration of domestic violence during the interview. In it, informants criticize the dismissal of black juror Jeanette Harris – who by then many assumed to be pro-Simpson – for omitting on the jury screening questionnaire an instance of "domestic violence" involving her and her husband. Black informants side with the juror and accept her interpretation that the incident did not involve "abuse." From their perspective, the prosecution just "kind of blew it out of proportion" in order to facilitate the removal of a pro-Simpson juror:

STEVE: Wait, hold on now. They dismissed the black one [juror Jeanette Harris] because she lied, because she had – she had problems already.[2]

CHERYL: Well she said it wasn't abuse. She had put a restraining order against her husband, but she said it wasn't abuse.

WILMA: They [prosecutors] kind of blew it out of proportion.

CHERYL: They did, they interpreted that the way they wanted to.

JAMAL: Yeah, because she said she didn't interpret it as . . . in her mind, when she answered that question, she said no, I have never . . .

CHERYL: She said he didn't hit her at all, but he did push her . . . so to them that was abuse.

ELIZABETH: That was abuse?

CHERYL: . . . and here everybody knows that when somebody pushes you it's not . . . I mean it's not the thing to do, but it's not the kind of abuse that you usually talk about.

In short, the two groups again exhibited rather divergent orientations toward the issue of domestic violence. While informants in the white group (re)affirmed domestic violence as *the* foundation for their narrative explaining Simpson's guilt, informants in the black group had rejected it as a credible motive and virtually excised it from their discussion. Thus, despite (or maybe because of) the activities of Domestic Violence project proponents, study informants seemed rather entrenched in their thinking about the case. Similar findings emerged when the groups revisited the issues of wealth and celebrity.

Wealth and celebrity

Following discussion, facilitators administered a scale to informants in both groups designed to gauge how informants felt about Simpson *prior* to hearing about the murders (1 = "liked him very much," 10 = "did not like him at all"). Interestingly, informants in both groups reported having somewhat ambivalent feelings about the defendant prior to the murders. The mean score for the white group was 4.6; for the black group it was 4.1.

Simpson's wealth and celebrity, it seems, provides us with a compelling explanation for the paradox of how groups so divergent in their understandings of the case could profess to have felt so similarly about the defendant prior to the murders. Perhaps the pre-murders Simpson was a genuine American "hero" to white informants. Given his rise from San Francisco's projects, his celebration of hegemonic masculinity on the playing field, and his affirmation of core "American values" in the face of radical threats during the protests of the 1960s (see chapter 2), white informants may have been hard pressed *not* to initially "give him the benefit of the doubt" on the question of guilt. But as discussion in this group illustrated throughout both interviews, most members had always known "deep down in [their] heart[s]" that he was guilty. Perhaps the ambivalence indicated by the group mean on the scale is a post-hoc product of both Simpson's former appeal as a "hero" and the concomitant betrayal informants felt when they finally realized that the (black) pretender had murdered his (white) ex-wife and her (white) male friend. Thus all of the advantages arising from Simpson's former successes are now tainted, soiled, suspect. Members of his "Dream Team" who are not "involved" in the murders themselves, as well as defense witnesses, are all "on the take":

TOM: I think Kardashian's [Simpson attorney] involved too.[3]
DONNA: They let him off.
MARY: Oh, Kardashian is in up to his neck.
TOM: And I think it's a shame that he can't get him on the witness stand and find out what he knows.
MARY: He's protected.
TOM: Well, I think he probably . . . he probably became part of the defense team just so he could avoid . . .
(loud talking)
TOM: The only reason they're paying him to be on the defense team . . .
BOB: That's right.
DONNA: So they can tell . . .
TOM: So he wouldn't have to testify, privileged.
MARY: The whole defense team has been on the take. Haven't they? Every . . .
(loud talking)

MARY: Everyone of the . . . Obviously.
(laughter)
MARY: Everyone of the witnesses and everything. I mean, is that justice or what?

In the black group, Simpson's wealth and celebrity conjured up different meanings, contributing, perhaps, to the similar degree of ambivalence informants professed to feel about the defendant. You will recall from the first interview that informants in this group seemed to resent Simpson's wealth and celebrity because he was seen as a wealthy black athlete who – like so many others – had sold out his black brethren and chosen, "once he made it," to immerse himself in the "white world." His white ex-wife and the other white women he exclusively dated, of course, represented the ultimate symbols of this choice. At the same time, however, Simpson was still "physically" black. As such, informants seemed to derive a sense of racial pride from his many athletic and financial accomplishments. They could thus justify adding him to the list of "prominent black men" who were being targeted by the conspiratorial "plan" (see chapter 7). The following exchange illustrates how black informants – unlike their white counterparts – continued to co-mingle race and wealth, how they continued to see the former trumping the latter in matters of law:

DARYL: But when you become a police officer you take an oath to protect and
    to serve.
ELIZABETH: Protect them. They protect alright.
DARYL: That's the way I look at it.
STEVE: They protecting . . .
ELIZABETH: They protect they own, cause . . .
JAMES: I think the law is . . . is governed to protect a certain amount of people,
    not everybody.
DARYL: Yeah, rich white folk.

In the end, key tenets of the Celebrity Defendant project seemed to resonate with informants in the white group due to intense, yet conflicting feelings they had for the defendant. Informants in the black group also had strong views about Simpson that ultimately resulted in overall ambivalent feelings. In both groups, it seems, these apparent contradictions hinged on informants' invocation – either explicitly or implicitly – of race.

Race

Following discussion in both groups, facilitators again administered a scale (1 = "very important," 10 = "not at all important") to measure how significant a role informants thought race would play in the trial's

Table 5. *Perceptions of the role race will play in the outcome of the trial, March 30, 1995 and August 1, 1995, by group.*[a]

Group	March 30	August 1
Black	3.8	1.8
White	7.5	3.8

[a] Scales from 1 to 10, 1 = "very important," 10 = "not at all important."
Source: Post-discussion questionnaires, March 30, 1995 and August 1, 1995.

outcome. The mean for the white group was 3.8, suggesting that informants felt race would be somewhat important. Black informants were more vehement: the group mean was 1.8.

As table 5 reveals, informants in both groups had changed their minds between the first and second interviews about the significance of race. While black informants became more convinced of its importance, white informants moved from thinking that it would not be terribly important to occupying the exact same location on the scale that the black group had occupied during the first interview: a group mean of 3.8.

In the white group, it seems, this change of heart about race was not unrelated to informants' new predictions/fears that Simpson might be acquitted. How could someone who "you really know down in your heart" is guilty literally get away with murder? Simpson's millions, of course, provided informants with an immediate explanation. But another troubling answer for informants lurked just beneath the surface, perhaps prompted by recent revelations about the Fuhrman tapes. The following exchange illustrates how race rears its ugly head just as informants work to (re)affirm their certainty about Simpson's guilt:

BOB: Anyway, I . . . let's take a vote. How say you?
MARY: A vote for what?
BOB: Guilty or innocent. Right now, if you were a juror, what would you say?
MARY: And guilty . . . if it was guilty, uh what . . .
BOB: It's his turn.
MARY: Guilty?
BOB: Guilty. And what would you say?
MARY: In prison or a death sentence?
BOB: No, no . . . guilty or not guilty?
VICKY: They're not going for that.
MARY: Guilty.
TOM: Guilty.
ELAINE: Undecided.
DAVID: Innocent of course.
BOB: What?

DAVID: I'd say I lean toward guilt.
DONNA: Guilty.
VICKY: Guilty. But, we're all white . . .
MARY: We're all white . . .
VICKY: I don't think that has anything to do with it.

In a later exchange, Tom and Bob[4] more explicitly invoke an important tenet of the Black "Other" project (see chapter 2), the idea that
the black jurors may not be rational/intelligent enough to see through
the smoke screen of race and find Simpson guilty. Meanwhile, other
informants in the group hope against hope that this fear is unjustified:

VICKY: I don't think the jury is going to let him off. I really don't.
TOM: I think the jury is biased though.
VICKY: Oh, I don't know . . . I don't think they'll let him walk.
TOM: Towards O. J.
VICKY: Oh, I don't think so.
BOB: There will be one black person, no matter what, will say he is innocent.
TOM: Yeah.
BOB: There will be one white person, no matter how guilty . . . I mean, how
    innocent he is will say he is guilty. Betcha.
VICKY: No. I don't know. I don't think I . . . I don't think so.
DONNA: I just hope . . . I always keep hope.

Informants in the black group also invoked race and notions about
the jury in order to negotiate their feelings about the case's likely outcome. In this group, however, it was a key tenet of the "Just-Us"
system project that informants seemed to embrace. That is, intertextual
memories of the Rodney King beating trial[5] reminded them of their
disappointment with the trial's outcome and prompted them to (re)affirm
their belief that they would *not* be disappointed by the outcome of the
Simpson trial. Their prediction? A hung jury – at worst. Why? Because
blacks *know* that racist LAPD officers like Fuhrman are not above
planting evidence against black defendants. And, as Jamal put it, "we
ain't got no all-white jury here:"

JAMAL: Okay, so do you think that because of that, at this point in time right
    now, that if they went in that they would have to what? They'd [the jury]
    be hung or –
JAMES: Probably be a hung jury.
ELIZABETH: Really?
JAMAL: Because I remember, I know in the Rodney King thing . . .
DARYL: Cause they [police/prosecution] messed up on the gloves, the sock . . .
ELIZABETH: Don't say it too soon.
JAMAL: . . . people thought those policemen [in the King beating trial] were
    guilty and they thought they was going to come back with a guilty plea. I
    know, everybody thought that.
DARYL: What, on the Rodney King thing?

JAMAL: Uh huh.

DARYL: Yeah and them police just got a smack on the hands.

JAMAL: When they didn't come back . . .

ELIZABETH: Yeah, they're hung, yeah.

JAMAL: . . . and I don't think they [the jury in the case] did nothing wrong, I just don't think that uh, whoever . . . what was that guy's name, the prosecutor, he just . . . he just didn't do his job good enough. I don't remember his name. A skinny black dude.[6]

JAMES: I forgot his name.

CHERYL: That all-white jury wasn't about to do nothing to them cops.

JAMAL: Well we ain't got no all-white jury here.

Black informants ultimately seemed to understand the racial tensions surrounding the case in terms not all that distinct from classic, Marxist analyses of race. In the following exchange, informants imply that it is in the interest of "white" elites (i.e., "this country") to keep blacks and whites "paranoid about one other," and that these elites routinely promote controversies like the ones surrounding the trial in order to divert attention away from other nefarious plans that ultimately work to further disadvantage blacks:

JAMAL: Well, I don't know. I always think that when there's stuff like this going down they ["white" elites] want everybody to look to the right . . .

ELIZABETH: Uh huh, so they . . .

JAMAL: . . . I'm looking to the left cause something's happening to the left.

ELIZABETH: Uh huh.

CHERYL: Well, affirmative action for one thing.

JAMAL: All kinds of things.

CHERYL: No, they are . . . they're dealing with a lot of things that deal with black people right now and black . . . everybody is looking at O.J. Right, everybody's into O.J., you ain't into your own thing. So they . . . they . . . slide stuff on you and you don't even know it and the next thing you know, it's like you're through with O.J. and you've got some other problem that's going on.

WILMA: I agree.

CHERYL: Plus, I think this country really wants blacks and whites to be separate anyway, and against each other . . . and to be paranoid about one another.

In short, while race continued to be a pressing concern for informants in the black group throughout the second interview, they were no longer alone in their overt discussion of this issue. Trial developments in the four months between the interviews had also placed race squarely on the agenda of the white group. But while white informants generally invoked assumptions embedded in the Black "Other" project in order to explain their newfound fears about an acquittal, black informants continued to embrace key tenets of the "Just-Us" system project, again ultimately predicating their faith in the defense's case on a belief in conspiracy.

Conspiracy

In the first interview, you will recall, most white informants outright rejected the notion of a police conspiracy against Simpson as "ludicrous." During the second interview – which occurred after defense attorneys had raised the specter of "missing blood," after defense witnesses had testified about inconsistencies in blood stain patterns, and after audiotapes had surfaced that might impeach the testimony of the detective who claimed to have found the Rockingham glove – the group was prompted by one of its members to revisit the issue. David, formerly a group transgressor who now felt that Simpson was "probably" guilty, reintroduced the argument that LAPD officers may have actually framed a guilty man (i.e., a version of the "overzealousness" narratives reviewed in chapter 1). David's ultimate faith in the scientific and DNA evidence against Simpson, it seems, had combined with the "shitty job" he thought the defense was doing (e.g., no "Perry Mason moments") to establish Simpson's guilt. But the distrust David harbored for the LAPD during the first interview had not diminished. Indeed, the testimony of recent defense witnesses and the Fuhrman tapes bombshell had only fanned the flames of his distrust. In the following exchange, David lays out his conspiracy theory for others in the group to consider:

DAVID: Well, he [Simpson] could have done it and they tried to frame him. You know.
BILL: Say what?
DAVID: Maybe he did do it and they put the [Rockingham] glove there.
VICKY: Yeah?
DONNA: Yeah, that's a possibility.
(loud talking)
DAVID: The bloody socks [found in Simpson's bedroom] never added up. I mean . . . did you ever see the picture. They're [the socks] right in the middle of the room on that rug . . . I mean . . . and O. J.'s going to leave [to go to Chicago]?

However, Bill finally employs an interesting inversion of David's logic in order to discount his conspiracy theory. While David's theory was based on the low probability that a calculating *murderer* would leave incriminating evidence like bloody socks in such a conspicuous location, Bill's theory relied upon the low probability that *conspirators* would plant evidence in such an obvious place. David's theory was thus effectively neutralized (i.e., recall table 4) as other informants agreed with Bill that "you've got to look at it both ways:"

BILL: If it was a conspiracy, wouldn't the cops say, "Won't it look dumb if we leave them right in the middle of the room."
MARY: "We should put them in the laundry."

BILL: I mean . . . "Let's put them in the laundry and say we found them in the laundry . . ."

VICKY: Or just shoved under the bed.

BILL: "Who's going to believe that we found them right in the middle of the room?"

DONNA: Or in the closet stuffed in the . . .

BILL: But you've got to look at it both ways. I mean . . .

DONNA: Yeah.

VICKY: That's true.

BILL: It doesn't make sense.

Meanwhile, informants in the black group continued to embrace their conspiracy theory of the case, invoking the "Just-Us" system project to support it. Appendix 4 reveals that conspiracy-related themes dominated the group's discussion agenda, appearing no less than thirteen times.[7] Indeed, informants again talked at length about a "plan" they felt white power-brokers had instituted to "bring down" prominent black men. Intertextual memories of incidents involving singer Michael Jackson, boxer Mike Tyson, Supreme Court Justice Clarence Thomas, and basketball superstar Michael Jordan were invoked to (re)affirm group belief in the "plan." The following exchange briefly captures the tenor of informants' ongoing reflections:

CHERYL: Well, I don't know, to me . . . all . . . politically, all the black politicians they done brought down. That little Tucker guy, he's getting ready to go to prison.[8]

STEVE: He sure is getting ready to go to prison.

CHERYL: Ron . . . Ron over the Democratic Party, they got him.

JAMES: Ron Brown . . . They got him.[9]

CHERYL: They got the . . .

(loud talking)

CHERYL: . . . and the man with the chickens. They got him. He's out of his job. They bringing them all down, all of them, and not one by one, in groups.

JAMAL: So, so, so, do you think there's anything to . . . 'cause I can remember where . . . I was . . .

CHERYL: Willie Brown.

JAMAL: . . . at the Sports Arena, Farrakhan[10] was saying, they got a plan for ya'll.

ELIZABETH: That's right . . . Didn't he say it.

JAMAL: . . . and if you don't get ready, they going to implement their plan.

CHERYL: It's implemented.

JAMAL: And it seems like something is going down.

JAMES: It's in effect.

DARYL: Yeah.

Despite this acceptance of conspiracy theory, Jamal – who frequently played devil's advocate during the first interview – questions the "rogue cop" theory of the case, the notion that a single officer like Fuhrman could have engineered the conspiracy against Simpson. But his mother, Cheryl, reminds him that other officers could unwittingly (or perhaps intentionally) "do stuff" that make it unlikely a rogue cop's activities would be uncovered:

JAMAL: But you see this is what I have a hard time believing is that . . . like they said the "rogue cop." One policeman could not set up this conspiracy.
DARYL: Why not?
CHERYL: Yeah, he [Fuhrman] could have.
STEVE: If he was the first one there.
JAMAL: No. I don't. I don't. There's too much . . .
DARYL: Was he the one that went over the [Rockingham] wall?
STEVE: Yeah, he was the first one there.
JAMAL: It's too many people involved.
STEVE: Unless he had a . . .
CHERYL: Do you know what can happen, Jamal. One person . . . any one of us could decide to do a conspiracy and the rest of us could come behind that first person and do stuff . . .
DARYL: And clean it up.
CHERYL: . . . not knowing that it's a conspiracy.

As in the first interviews, the two groups again (re)negotiated divergent perspectives regarding the issue of conspiracy, its relevance to understanding the Simpson case. While white informants briefly entertained and then discounted the possibility that conspiracy might be relevant, black informants devoted much of their discussion to (re)affirming their belief in its widespread reality. This divergence, of course, again shaped group orientations toward mainstream news narratives about the case.

The KTLA text

Following discussion, facilitators again administered a media fairness scale (1 = "fair," 10 = "unfair") to informants in both groups. Findings indicated that white informants were somewhat ambivalent concerning the media's fairness (mean = 4.2), while their black counterparts felt that coverage was more "unfair" than not (mean = 7.2). As table 6 reveals, these perceptions were virtually unchanged from the first interviews (March 30, 1995). Black informants clearly continued to distrust the mainstream media, considering them, in fact, to be an integral part of "the [conspiratorial] plan" that occupied so much of the group's discussion agenda. In contrast, the ambivalent feelings white informants had for the media seemed to be the product of two countervailing forces: first, the high degree to which dominant media portrayals of the case were congruent with the informants' understandings of case "facts";

Table 6. *Perceptions of the fairness of trial news coverage, March 30, 1995 and August 1, 1995, by group.*[a]

Group	March 30	August 1
Black	7.4	7.2
White	4.8	4.2

[a] Scales from 1 to 10, 1 = "fair," 10 = "unfair."
Source: Post-discussion questionnaires, March 30, 1995 and August 1, 1995.

and second, the relatively low degree of faith US residents tend to have in the people running the media (Hunt 1997). During the first interviews, you will recall, divergent orientations toward mainstream news media seemed to influence how the groups negotiated the *Primetime* text. A similar process unfolded during the second interviews, when the groups worked to make sense of the KTLA text.

Congruent with the dominant frame of the KTLA text, white informants understood "the most important news" in the video to be leather gloves Simpson is seen wearing in a photo. Prosecutor Marcia Clark had argued earlier in the day that she could "prove" the gloves in question and those reportedly found at the crime scene are the same. The "newsworthiness" of this revelation, of course, was linked to both the certainty with which informants maintained Simpson's guilt and the fears they expressed about his possible acquittal. The following exchange illustrates the importance informants accorded the stitching:

BOB: Oh, the gloves . . . the stitching on the gloves.
TOM: The glove identification.
BOB: The glove identification there. If they can pin that on . . .
VICKY: I'm curious, did they show the nurse thing?
BOB: What nurse thing?
TOM: I don't know. No, we didn't see the nurse thing.
BILL: Was it on . . . was it on this afternoon though . . . I think?
TOM: Yeah, but it didn't . . . we didn't see it tonight.
VICKY: Yeah.
BOB: Sure.
TOM: Next. The stitching on the glove.
BOB: Putting the gloves on.
DAVID: The pictures of him wearing the glove.
VICKY: Yeah.
DONNA: Uh huh.

While two black informants also briefly considered the glove during their group's discussion of the "the most important news," other informants focused on two items buried more deeply within the KTLA text: passing references to a "leak" in the LAPD and to FBI involvement in the case. Not surprisingly, the "newsworthiness" of these latter items was linked to the group's certainty that a conspiracy existed to frame Simpson. Reports suggesting that police were behind incriminating news leaks and that the "FBI works in cahoots with the prosecution" only strengthened group belief in "the plan":

DARYL: The leak in the police department.
(loud talking)
WILMA: That was important.
ELIZABETH: Well the glove was important too.
DARYL: Or the glove.
ELIZABETH: The stitching of the glove.
(loud talking)
WILMA: Yeah.
DARYL: Who was the leak.
JAMAL: And what I realized too is that the FBI works in cahoots with the prosecution.
CHERYL: That's right.
DARYL: And the police.
JAMAL: Free of charge I would imagine [FBI services].

Meanwhile, as in the first interview, white agreement with the text's dominant frame resulted in a "referential" reading of it (cf. Liebes and Katz 1993). Moreover, facilitator questioning suggested that this agreement may have also spilled over into informant appraisals of KTLA reporters. Although Vicky could not label these reporters as "non-biased," informants generally agreed that their commentary was "presented very well." Indeed, three informants admitted to frequently watching the KTLA newsworkers over the course of the trial:

DONNA: The commentary was presented very well.
DAVID: . . . of O. J. wearing the gloves.
DONNA: I felt it was non-biased and it was factual, presented very well.
VICKY: I don't know if they're non-biased.
BOB: They're ones I generally watch and I think they're good.
VICKY: I usually watch them, but I don't know if they're non-biased.
BOB: They're a good objective team.
DONNA: I watch them every night.

The black group also continued the reading practices it exhibited during the first interview. That is, in contrast to their white counterparts, black informants made sense of the KTLA text "metalinguistically" (cf. Liebes and Katz 1993). These informants worked hard to subvert the text's dominant frame (cf. Condit 1994), frequently returning throughout the discussion to techniques they felt KTLA newsworkers employed to legitimize the prosecution's case against Simpson. In fact, KTLA legal analyst Al DeBlanc became a magnet of group ire in this regard. A black defense attorney and former LAPD officer (see chapter 4), DeBlanc was described by informants as a (race) "traitor" who "got bought":

CHERYL: Can you see this . . . I can't stand this DeBlanc, is that his name? I
    can't stand . . .
JAMES: He hates Johnnie Cochran.
(loud talking)
CHERYL: But you know what? When he first started . . . When he first started
    he was on the side of the defense.
STEVE: I know.
(loud talking)
STEVE: Traitor, traitor.
CHERYL: But he changed. I can't stand him.
STEVE: He got bought.

In short, group orientations toward the KTLA text – as they had been toward the *Primetime* text in the first interviews – were a product of informants' initial perspectives on the case "facts." That is, the KTLA text did very little to change any minds. For white informants, the "most important news" in the text renewed hope that an obviously guilty Simpson would indeed be proven guilty and convicted. As this reading was largely congruent with the text's dominant frame, these informants did not have to "work very hard" to negotiate it (cf. Condit 1994). Moreover, they had mostly positive things to say about KTLA newsworkers.

For black informants, however, the "most important news" simply helped them (re)affirm what they already "knew": conspiracies are real, and Simpson seems to be the target of one. Although these meanings were by no means prominent in the text as part of its dominant frame, informants' "hard work" brought the meanings to the surface nonetheless (cf. Condit 1994).

After the verdicts

Given the stability in informant understandings about the case across the four-month period separating the first two interviews (March 30 to August 1, 1995), one might expect to find that there was also little change after the verdicts were announced (October 3, 1995). Indeed, telephone interviews I conducted with selected informants just hours after the reading of the verdicts seem to confirm these expectations. Two of the three white informants I reached continued to hold steadfast to their belief in Simpson's guilt, while both black informants continued to embrace their belief in conspiracy, viewing the verdicts as a validation of their earlier affirmations about police and prosecutors.

Among white informants, for example, Bill said he simply felt "disappointed" at the verdicts. On a scale from 1 to 10 (1 = "wrong," 10 = "right"), he gave the verdicts a 3. Bill, you will recall, was an outspoken critic of the conspiracy theory that was briefly considered in the white group. Accordingly, he continued to feel that Simpson probably committed the murders and that Fuhrman was probably innocent of planting evidence. Indeed, on two final scales measuring Simpson's and Fuhrman's respective guilt (1 = "guilty," 10 = "innocent"), he gave Simpson a 3 and Fuhrman a 7. Meanwhile, another white informant, Tom, said he felt "stunned . . . sick about it." Tom totally rejected the verdicts, giving them a 1 on the scale (1 = "wrong," 10 = "right"). He also totally rejected the idea that Simpson might be innocent, giving Simpson a 1 on the final guilt scale (1 = "guilty," 10 = "innocent"). Moreover, he gave Fuhrman a 7.5 on the scale (1 = "guilty," 10 = "innocent"), indicating that he felt the former LAPD detective was probably innocent of planting evidence. The third white informant I contacted, however, said that when she heard the verdicts she felt "it was just." Elaine, you will recall, had transgressed the group's common sense throughout the interviews, but conceded during the second interview that Simpson was "probably" guilty. Over the two month period separating the second interview and the verdicts, she had again reversed field, placing herself back at odds with her husband, Bill. That is, Elaine gave the verdicts a 9 (1 = "wrong," 10 = "right"), Simpson and Fuhrman a 9 and a 6, respectively, on the final guilt scale (1 = "guilty," 10 = "innocent").

Among black informants, I reached Cheryl and James. Cheryl noted that the verdicts made her "feel good," like "good had triumphed in the case." Cheryl, you will recall, was an outspoken member of the group who argued for the feasibility of the "rogue cop" theory. She totally embraced the verdicts by giving them a 10 on the scale (1 = "wrong," 10 = "right"). Accordingly, she completely affirmed Simpson's innocence and Fuhrman's guilt by giving them a 10 and a 1, respectively, on the guilt scale (1 = "guilty," 10 = "innocent"). Finally, James said the verdicts "cleared some doubt about what the jurors would do." After the verdicts were read, he added, "I went, 'I'm glad it's over.'" James also embraced the verdicts, giving them a 9 on the scale (1 = "wrong," 10 = "right"). He also totally affirmed Simpson's innocence and Fuhrman's guilt by giving them a 10 and a 1, respectively, on the guilt scales (1 = "guilty," 10 = "innocent").

Conclusions

While at first glance the findings of part III seem to suggest that neither gender nor socioeconomic status were major factors in informants' understandings of the Simpson case, we cannot discount the possibility that the findings may have been to *some degree* an artifact of the research design. Additional groups also separated by gender and class would have strengthened the analysis in this regard but could not be obtained given study constraints. Future studies of this type, of course, would greatly benefit from such design enhancements.

With this said, what can we safely conclude from the findings of this chapter and the last?

In the simplest terms, informants' readings of the Simpson case stand as stunning testaments to the notion of polysemy (cf. Fiske 1987). Despite the ideological work of Celebrity Defendant, Domestic Violence, Black "Other," and "Just-Us" system project proponents, despite the possible mainstreaming effects of the dominant O. J. narratives constructed and circulated by "legitimate" media like ABC News (i.e., the *Primetime* text) or KTLA (cf. Gerbner et al. 1986), informants managed to (re)negotiate and (re)affirm rather divergent understandings of the relevant case "facts." And these divergent understandings were deeply rooted in the politics of race.

Although informants' views on Simpson's innocence or guilt generally mirrored the "black-white" divide found in opinion polls, I do not claim that the knowledge informing their views was representative of the *range* of "black" or "white" thinking. Study groups were selected to focus closely on the meaning-negotiation *process*. As such, the two groups were clearly not representative of the black and white populations in the United States. Indeed, many white poll respondents may have rationalized their beliefs in Simpson's guilt differently than informants in the white study group; similarly, many black poll respondents may have talked differently than black informants about their belief in the celebrity's innocence. Moreover, as the polls revealed no monolithic white or black view (e.g., I explore in the next chapter the relatively small percentages of whites who believed Simpson innocent and blacks who believed him guilty), there was also not total agreement *within* the study groups initially. Recall that two informants in the white group consistently challenged the dominant view, speculating that Simpson may have been framed. David, in particular, offered knowledge about the LAPD that was disputed by other members of the white group. Similarly, in the black group, Jamal emphasized that he did not know whether Simpson was innocent or guilty, arguing that black trial observers were as guilty as their white counterparts of judging the case before hearing all of the "evidence."

Nonetheless, a clear dividing line distinguished the two groups. This dividing line cut across different stores of experience, knowledge, and interests and mirrored a major cleavage in US race relations. It defined two competing social realities that are *patterned* by what I call raced ways of seeing (cf. Hunt 1997). Informants on either side of the line were provided with a general orientation toward the recognition and treatment of "evidence," and by later interviews, transgressors were pulled into their respective group mainstreams. While these group positions did not necessarily represent all voices on either side of the line, they clearly reflected concerns connected with very different locations in US social structures.

In many respects, these different structural locations represent different cultural contexts. And culture, of course, has everything to do with values, norms, and the resulting ways of seeing. If we understand race *as representation* – and if we recognize that representations function similarly to Harold Garfinkel's (1967) conceptualization of norms (cf. Hunt 1997) – then the congruence between the so-called black-white differences in the polls (i.e., normative cues) and informant explanations begins to make sense. That is, with race as with norms, there exists an interdependence between individual thought and action at the micro level and *structures* of thought and action at the macro level: race is *used* by actors as frames of reference to interpret others' action (e.g., prejudice, discrimination, raced solidarity) and to share a common view of "empirical circumstances" (e.g., raced inequality/oppression or the lack thereof) (Heritage 1984, p. 131). As bases for common-sense knowledge about these circumstances, race exerts a moral force on actors, demanding that they account for their transgressions of raced expectations (e.g., those regarding interraced dating/marriage, affirmative action, conspiracy, and so on). Due to its constant use over time, race has been naturalized in US society as an important frame for understanding, despite some actors' periodic reservations about it or claims that they ignore it.

Black informants, for example, clearly understood themselves as raced subjects, liberally employing pronouns of racial solidarity during group discussion to describe themselves and their oppressed status in US society. In contrast, white informants rarely spoke of themselves as raced subjects during the interviews. Instead, they talked about other groups in raced terms (particularly blacks), positioning themselves by default as members of some normative group outside race. In the few instances where "white" was explicitly spoken, informants distanced themselves from the object, describing it as "*the* white people" (Emphasis added). This observation is consistent with other empirical studies noting the tendency of white actors to distance themselves from the issue of race in America (e.g., Hunt 1997). For these actors, recognition of race is often a "damned if you do, damned if you don't" proposition. It either dredges up a shameful past and a nagging guilt, or it represents challenges to group position in contemporary society. Often it does both. For these reasons, white informants tended to account for "negative" developments/possibilities in the Simpson case by *implicitly* invoking race-as-representation, while their black counterparts did so much more *explicitly*. This interpretive activity ultimately worked in both groups to (re)negotiate, (re)affirm, and (re)produce competing understandings of social reality.

But what exactly is the nature of these competing understandings? Why did (do) the narratives in circulation about the Simpson case "facts" *mean* so much in this contest? In other words, what was (is) at stake in this struggle to define reality? We turn to these questions in the final chapter.

Part IV

Conclusions

9   O.J. and reality

> What we refer to as "reality" is really a maplike mental image, the end
> product of a process that begins with light refraction in the environ-
> ment and ends in the intricate and complex dynamics of the mind.
>
> (Seward Barry 1997, p. 15)

The "reality" we see is rich with narrative possibilities. For example, I
find it strangely apropos that Simpson's slow-speed waltz with the law,
which was greeted by cheering crowds along the Interstate 405, featured the distraught celebrity stretched out in the back of a *white* Ford
Bronco, while his somber return to taunts and jeers outside a Santa
Monica courthouse, to judgment day, found him sitting in the front of
a *black* Chevrolet Suburban. Black. White. My mind – because it is
shaped by particular concerns and kinds of knowledge – could use
these contrasting images to construct an O.J. narrative that is quite
different from yours.

This realization, of course, is the point. For I have argued throughout
this book that the Simpson case involved much more than just the
murder of two individuals, a police investigation, and the subsequent
legal proceedings. Guilty *or* innocent, Orenthal James Simpson became
the focal point of a first-order *media event*, a societal-wide celebration
and contestation of dominant knowledge about reality. In chapter 1,
you will recall, I proposed a theoretical model that outlined the process
by which the case inflamed public passions and became known as the
"Trial of the Century." This process was largely shaped by six inter-
related factors: political projects, O.J. narratives, intertextual memory,
individual decoding, social network discussions, and negotiated decoding:

Political projects. I employed the concept of "political projects" to refer
to the pre-existing discourses invoked and circulated by proponents
who used the Simpson case as a platform to further their collective
interests. I identified four such projects. First, the Celebrity Defendant
project worked to expose what happens when criminal defendants have
"too many" resources (e.g., Simpson's legal representation). Thus proponents rallied for changes to the criminal justice system (e.g., the

institution of non-unanimous verdicts, professional juries, pay disclosure for expert witnesses, etc.), changes that would hopefully increase the conviction rate of "obviously guilty" defendants like Simpson. Secondly, the Domestic Violence project worked to increase the visibility of domestic violence as a first-order social problem. This project was energized, to be sure, by the widespread belief that Simpson was a batterer whose attempts to control his ex-wife had escalated to murder. Thirdly, the Black "Other" project sought to validate age-old stereotypes of the hypersexual, savage black male (e.g., the enraged Simpson) and the ignorance and tribalism of blacks in general (e.g., the black jury, black celebration of the not-guilty verdicts). Finally, the "Just-Us" system project worked to draw attention to a racist criminal justice system that disproportionately incarcerates people of color, particularly black males (e.g., Simpson, the "prominent" black man). Proponents of each of these projects worked to construct and circulate narrative accounts of the case congruent with their project's goals. But as the "racial divide" in public perceptions of the case suggests (see chapter 1), the racial projects ultimately trumped the other two.

O. J. narratives. These narrative accounts began circulating throughout society shortly after the murders, and continued to do so throughout both legal proceedings, and beyond. They were composed of structured texts that combined salient elements emerging from the Simpson case with convention and formulae in order to tell stories of motive, action, and causality. These stories worked to personify the social issues embedded in political projects by casting case principals as heroes, villains, and fools. For example, narratives supported by proponents of the "Just-Us" system project cast Simpson as a "hero," while those supported by proponents of the Domestic Violence project cast him as "villain"; the converse was true for prosecutors Marcia Clark and Christopher Darden. But mainstream definitions of "plausibility" shaped in large measure *how* the various O. J. narratives were circulated. Indeed, I identified a narrative continuum that grouped accounts of the case into five generic categories, from the most to the least "plausible:" "incompetence" (i.e., a guilty Simpson was acquitted due to police, prosecution, and judicial blunders), "overzealousness" (i.e., a guilty Simpson was acquitted because police were caught tampering with evidence), "mystery" (i.e., it is unclear whether Simpson is innocent or guilty), "rush to judgment" (i.e., Simpson is innocent, but police and prosecutors interpreted evidence so that it conformed with a prior theory of guilt), and "conspiracy" (i.e., an innocent Simpson was framed by police and/or a third party). The dominant, or most "plausible" O. J. narrative – the one privileged by mainstream newsworkers (chapter 3) and media like KTLA-TV or the *Los Angeles Times* (chapters 4 and 5) – cast Simpson as a powerful, obsessed, and *black* wife-abuser who committed the final act of control by savagely murdering his innocent, beautiful, and *white* ex-wife. This plot, of course, resonated nicely with key tenets of the Celebrity Defendant, Domestic Violence and Black "Other" projects. Indeed, complications in the open and shut case against the celebrity defendant could only be attributed to police and prosecution "overzealousness," and/or the "incompetence" of police, prosecutors, the judge, and the predominantly black jury. This "incompetence" and/or "overzealousness," the narrative concluded, provided defense attorneys with the opportunity to successfully play the "race card." As Peter Collier and David Horowitz (1997) put it in their book, *The Race Card: White Guilt, Black Resentment, and the Assault on Truth and Justice*, "It is not hard to imagine what race cards were played when eleven jurors of color in the deliberation room finally confronted a sixty-one-year-old white woman who was a potential holdout" (p. 7). In contrast, "implausible" O. J. narratives – narratives that worked to support Simpson's innocence – enjoyed a much smaller circulation, primarily by alternative media like the *Los Angeles Sentinel* (chapter 6). Intertextual memory in the end, played a central role in both the construction and reception of all O. J. narratives.

Intertextual memories. These texts, narratives, and images stored in memory acted as a prism that refracts the content of O. J. narratives in ways that resonate with the "real" and mediated experiences of individuals. In US society, our experiences are largely a function of our positioning within the racial, gender, and economic orders. This positioning greatly shapes not only our interests, but also the discourses (i.e., packaged in narratives, texts, and images) to which we have likely been exposed and to which we will probably be receptive. In the black study group, for example, memories of the "fall" of other prominent black men validated the Simpson conspiracy theories mainstream newsworkers found so "implausible." Meanwhile, informants in the white study group invoked memories of other famous murder cases to (re)affirm their belief in the legitimacy of police investigations. Intertextual memories, to be sure, also shape the thinking of newsworkers and other gatekeepers who have a tremendous amount of power in establishing mainstream definitions of "plausibility," who are ultimately able to anoint certain O. J. narratives as worthy of widespread circulation throughout society.

Individual decoding, social network discussions, and negotiated decoding. But as recent scholarship in media studies informs us, message sent is not necessarily message received (Hall 1973; Fiske 1987, 1989a; Hunt

1997). In chapters 7 and 8, you will recall, we found that race seemed to pattern the O. J. narratives preferred by study informants. On the one hand, we found that black informants generally embraced key tenets of the "Just-Us" system project, which led them to (re)affirm their belief in what mainstream media depicted as "implausible" O. J. narratives. On the other hand, we found that most white informants invoked knowledge embedded in the Celebrity Defendant, Domestic Violence, and Black "Other" projects in order to (re)affirm their belief in O. J. narratives that the mainstream media treated as more "plausible."

A central theme of this book has been the mediating role raced ways of seeing play in the process by which we all construct and participate in social realities. The Simpson case, of course, symbolized a clash between two particularly salient realities: one "white" and one "black."

In "white reality," America's legacy of white supremacy is largely a thing of the past. Although isolated acts of discrimination may persist at the individual level, we have achieved a "colorblind" society in Post-Civil Rights America, one in which our laws and central institutions (e.g., the criminal justice system) are essentially race neutral. Race conscious social policies like affirmative action are thus anachronistic; they unfairly discriminate against whites (whites males, in particular) and enable/excuse the subpar performance of blacks and other groups who feel entitled to preferences. Today, black cries of white racism are more often than not just empty attempts to exploit any lingering white guilt, to close black ranks and exert power over whites, to play the "race card."

White study informants, you will recall, rarely spoke of themselves as white, opting instead to *implicitly* invoke race in their accounts of the Simpson case. Many scholars have noted that in the United States only whites have both the motivation *and* luxury to avoid overt racial identification when discussing issues of race, inequality, and justice (Waters 1990; Delgado and Stefancic 1997; Hunt 1997). Within this social reality, there exists little evidence powerful enough to shake one's faith in official, "colorblind" evidence. Perhaps there exist a few bad racist apples like Fuhrman "but there is so much [counter-evidence] there." Indeed, scientific "evidence" (e.g., DNA evidence) is embraced as infallible, objective, the foundation for a system of belief superior to other ways of seeing (Ladner 1973; White 1984). Against this backdrop, "black" charges of systematic racial bias appear as hyperbole, paranoia, "playing the race card" (cf. D'Souza 1995). Accordingly, what white study informants generally "know" about US society and its progress over the years suggests that the criminal justice system (like other key political, cultural, and economic institutions) is essentially, as it should be, "colorblind." "Racism" is thus (re)cast as the *recognition* of race rather than the *exercise* of power, and "black people are more racist than the white people."[1] Indeed, when this common-sense view was challenged by David and Elaine, other white informants swiftly moved to punish the transgressors, to blunt their attacks and to restore order.

In "black reality," however, white supremacy continues to be *the* defining characteristic of US society. That is, we have *not* achieved a "colorblind" society in Post-Civil Rights America, and this "fact" is particularly evident in the anti-black bias that pervades key societal institutions. Thus race-conscious social policies like affirmative action are not only expedient, they are also fair: to embrace "colorblind" rules at this late stage of the game is to ignore the head start whites have enjoyed in America and to contribute to the reproduction of racial disparities. For black accusations of white racism are still firmly rooted in actual personal *and* institutional practices that diminish the life chances of blacks and other people of color. These practices are the real cause of the ongoing racial tensions and divisions that plague US society.

This knowledge, of course, prompted black informants to see the criminal "Just-Us" system as a critical component of the machinery of black oppression. Thus, "evidence" contrary to the prosecution's case breathed life into rumors and theories consistent with what these informants "know" about US society (cf. Turner 1993; Fiske 1994). In other words, there seemed to be very little faith in the justice system among black informants, faith that might otherwise have inoculated them against this counter "evidence." Thus charges that the Simpson defense was just "playing the race card" were not in the least persuasive to these informants; group common sense suggested that the entire deck was raced. In the final analysis, these findings echo classic accounts of "black culture" that emphasize the suspicion with which black actors greet social structures and official knowledge (Gwaltney 1980; White 1984). Group knowledge of past "conspiracies" perpetrated against black people in this country only added fuel to the fire of "conspiracy" in this case (e.g., O'Reilly 1989).

Given the social nature of the meaning-negotiation process and the common-sense appeal of raced ways of seeing, it is no wonder that US race relations have produced the tensions evident in recent years. Debates over affirmative action and "illegal" immigration – like those over Simpson's innocence or guilt – represent a struggle to privilege these competing views of social reality. And much is at stake. At this moment in history, the "colorblind" version of social reality is hegemonic (Crenshaw et al. 1995; Steinberg 1995; Delgado and Stefancic 1997). Consequently, its assumptions of equal opportunity, its definition of "evidence," and its interpretation of the law saturate elite discourses and mass media.[2] Recent successes at dismantling longstanding affirmative action programs (i.e., "reverse discrimination") and revoking the rights of "illegal" immigrants (i.e., "minority" immigrants) stand as testaments to the recent dominance of this view of reality.[3] Thus, black informants yearned for Simpson to be exonerated so that his case might expose an unjust criminal justice system, thereby (re)affirming the reality of racism in "colorblind" times. Meanwhile, white informants needed Simpson to be proven guilty in order to (re)affirm their beliefs in a "colorblind" criminal justice system, one that just happens to disproportionately incarcerate (deserving)[4] black males.

But what about trial observers who transgressed the boundaries of these realities? What about postmodern understandings of the fractured and multiple nature of subjectivity, of the realization that monolithic racial perspectives do not exist? What can exceptions to the "racial rule" in the Simpson case possibly tell us about the nature of the rule itself?

Transgressing raced realities

Nearly four months after his acquittal in the criminal trial,[5] Simpson intensified futile efforts to rehabilitate his public image by granting his first live television interview to Black Entertainment Television (BET). The irony, of course, was that the public image of Simpson destroyed by the case had been largely a race-neutral one (see chapter 2). Now Simpson was reduced to pleading his case on a cable television outlet explicitly founded to serve the black community. Earlier, Simpson's representatives had aborted negotiations with mainstream media due to disputes over interview formats and protests by outraged Domestic Violence project proponents. This had been a fortunate turn of events for BET as its ratings for *O. J. Simpson: Beyond the Verdict, The Interview* soared to unprecedented levels (Lipsitz 1997).

Although mainstream observers had questions about the journalistic integrity of BET's upcoming hour-long Simpson interview, BET news anchor Ed Gordon managed to elicit some rather interesting responses from the former defendant, particularly regarding his views on race in America. For example, Simpson discounted the racial divide in public opinion about the case we have examined in this book and maintained that whites and blacks alike have treated him with respect since his acquittal:

I don't believe the polls for one. Judging by the people that I've been exposed to, both white and black Americans, since the polls, the negative part of the polls as far as I'm concerned as white America, I can tell ya that everywhere I've gone I've been treated with respect.

Indeed, reversing the mantra of "Just-Us" system project proponents, Simpson invoked intertextual memories of this "great country's" history and institutions to (re)affirm his belief that he had the *right* to regain his former image:

Well, this country has been a great country for 200 years. Cause we have laws in this country and like 'em or not, people have abided by those laws. There have been decisions made, Mike Tyson, a decision I didn't necessarily agree with, but he was convicted, he served his time, and many people in America say he's a rapist. I was accused of a crime. I feel vindicated in a court of law. I shouldn't be called anything but O. J. Simpson at this time.

Following the interview, BET hosted a call-in program in which viewers were encouraged to express their opinions about Simpson's performance. Not surprisingly, race was a major agenda item. For example, how should blacks make sense of Simpson's "involvement with the African American community?" Michael Dyson, a black cultural scholar and panelist, summed up Simpson's reflections on this issue by suggesting that the black football legend was hopelessly out of touch with reality:

Well, I think his worship of the white world remains undisturbed. His faith in white people remains unabated. I think O. J. Simpson is in colossal denial about how white people view him and about his own relationships with an America that has turned its back on him. The black people who love and support him, O. J. has left. The very white people that he loves, have spurned him. He is in a twilight zone of racial consciousness.

The "racial consciousness" to which Dyson alludes, of course, was a direct reflection of "black reality," and Simpson was clearly a major transgressor.

Just as Jamal often questioned the prevailing common sense (re)-affirmed by black informants, just as David and Elaine periodically challenged that (re)affirmed by white informants, and just as Simpson seemed to deny the "black reality" (re)affirmed by Dyson,[6] a relatively small percentage of trial observers from across the nation transgressed the racial patterns captured by opinion polls. Indeed, if we revisit the national survey I discussed in the Introduction and examine the 11.2 percent of whites who responded that Simpson is "probably not guilty" and the 18 percent of blacks who responded in the opposite manner, then we might learn a little more about the roles played by other factors early in the case.

Figures 14 through 20 compare the background characteristics of black and white "transgressors" and "teamplayers," as well as their views on several case-related issues. I define black "transgressors," of course, as

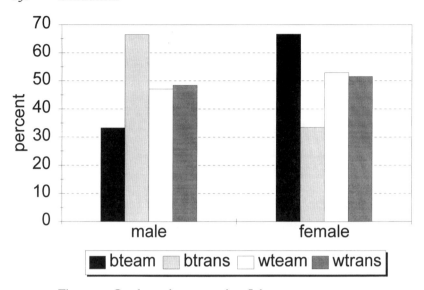

Figure 14. Gender and transgression, July 11–12, 1994.

black respondents who said Simpson is "probably guilty," while black "teamplayers" are defined as those who said he is "probably not guilty." Conversely, I define white "transgressors" as white respondents who said Simpson is "probably not guilty," while white "teamplayers" are defined as those who said he is "probably guilty." Several interesting patterns are suggested by these figures. (I employ logistic regression to more systematically test the effects of race, gender, family income, education, perceptions of the criminal justice system, and interviewer race on respondent views about Simpson's innocence or guilt.[7] See Appendix 7 for results.)

First, consistent with other accounts of the interaction between race and gender in the case,[8] figure 14 reveals that black men were much more likely to be black "transgressors" than were black women. That is, black men accounted for nearly 67 percent of black "transgressors," while black women accounted for the identical percentage of black "teamplayers." Among whites, however, gender appeared to have little impact on "transgressor" status. That is, roughly equal percentages of men and women composed the white "teamplayer" and "transgressor" categories.

Second, figure 15 suggests that higher family income was moderately associated with "transgressor" status for blacks and "teamplayer" status for whites. That is, 20 percent of all black "transgressors" came from

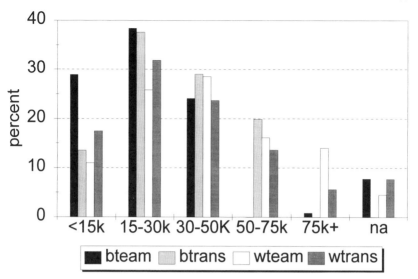

Figure 15. Family income and transgression, July 11–12, 1994.

families with incomes between $50,000 and $75,000, while none of the black "teamplayers" did so. At the other income extreme, black "teamplayers" were twice as likely as black "transgressors" (29 percent versus 14 percent) to be poor (i.e., family incomes less than $15,000). Overshadowing these differences, perhaps, the largest percentage of black "transgressors" *and* "teamplayers" (i.e., more than 35 percent for each group) fell in the same income category: families earning between $15,000 to $30,000 per year. For whites, the pattern was similar, but less pronounced at the income extremes. That is, although white "teamplayers" were more than twice as likely as white "transgressors" (14 percent versus 6 percent) to occupy the highest family income category (i.e., $75,000+), white "transgressors" were only moderately more likely than white "teamplayers" (18 percent versus 11 percent) to be poor (i.e., family incomes less than $15,000).

Thirdly, figure 16 suggests that higher levels of educational attainment were also associated with "transgressor" status for blacks and "teamplayer" status for whites. While black "transgressors" were four times as likely as black "teamplayers" to have obtained at least a college degree (16 percent versus 4 percent), black "teamplayers" were six times as likely as black "transgressors" to have dropped out of high school (12 percent versus 2 percent). Again, however, these extremes are largely overshadowed by the vast majority of black "teamplayers"

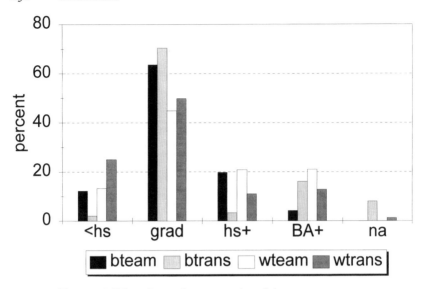

Figure 16. Education and transgression, July 11–12, 1994.

and "transgressors" who fall into a single education category: high school graduates (64 percent and 71 percent, respectively). For whites, the pattern is similar, but respondents are more evenly distributed across the education categories. White "teamplayers" were moderately more likely than white "transgressors" to have obtained at least a college degree (21 percent versus 17 percent), while white "transgressors" were about twice as likely as white "teamplayers" to have dropped out of high school (25 percent versus 13 percent). As was the case with black respondents, the largest percentage of white "transgressors" and "teamplayers" fell into the high school graduate category (50 percent and 45 percent, respectively).

Fourthly, figure 17 suggests that the relationship between age and "transgressor" status was weak at best. For blacks, about 85 percent of "transgressors" and 80 percent of "teamplayers" were nearly equally distributed across the 18–29 and 30–44 age categories. For whites, the most pronounced difference occurs in the youngest age category (18–29), where we find nearly 38 percent of the "transgressors" compared to only 25 percent of the "teamplayers."

Fifthly, figure 18 reveals no clear relationship between political party affiliation and "transgressor" status. The one exception: no black "transgressors" identified themselves as Republican, compared to 9 percent of black "teamplayers" who did so.

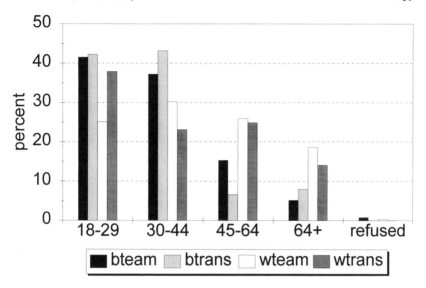

Figure 17. Age and transgression, July 11–12, 1994.

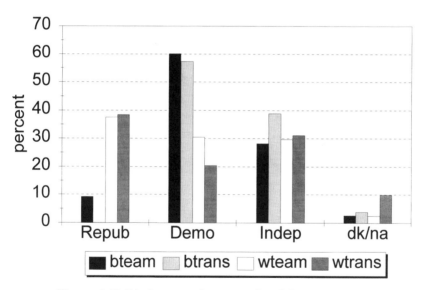

Figure 18. Political party and transgression, July 11–12, 1994.

Sixthly, figure 19 suggests that claiming to follow the trial closely was moderately associated with "transgressor" status for both blacks and whites. That is, a slightly higher percentage of black "transgressors" than "teamplayers" reported following the trial closely (64 percent versus

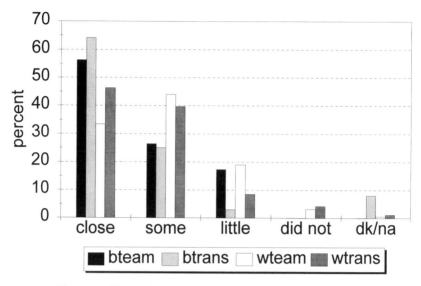

Figure 19. News viewing and transgression, July 11–12, 1994.

56 percent), while a higher percentage of white "transgressors" than "teamplayers" also said they followed the trial closely (46 percent versus 33 percent). In other words, claiming to follow the case closely was associated for blacks with saying that Simpson was probably guilty, but for whites that he was probably innocent. This rather interesting finding, however, is offset somewhat by the small magnitude of the within-race differences (i.e., "teamplayer" versus "transgressor") compared to the between-race differences (i.e., blacks versus whites). Perhaps, the greater tendency among blacks to say they followed the case closely reflects the depth of black investment in the "Just-Us" system project.

Finally, figure 20 suggests that saying the criminal justice system is biased against blacks was associated with "teamplayer" status for blacks and "transgressor" status for whites. That is, black "teamplayers" were more likely than black "transgressors" to say that the system was biased against blacks (73 percent versus 58 percent), while white "transgressors" were more likely than white "teamplayers" to say the same (29 percent versus 16 percent). As in figure 19, the within-group differences in this case ("transgressor" versus "teamplayer") were overwhelmed by between-group differences (blacks versus whites). The greater tendency for black respondents to say the criminal justice system is biased against them, of course, clearly reflects strong black support for the "Just-Us" system project.

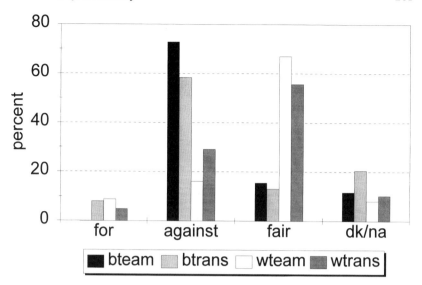

Figure 20. Views on criminal justice system and transgression, July 11–12, 1994.

What are we to make of all this? Simply put, the "racial rule" is not absolute. Indeed, exceptions to the rule suggest that social locations other than race contributed to our interpretations of the Simpson case. In some instances – such as income and education[9] – this contribution seemed to be rather significant (see Appendix 7). In other cases – such as age and political party affiliation – it did not. But we should not understand these contributions as a *direct* function of social location. As Morley (1980, 1992) notes, our interpretations are less a result of social location *itself* than of the discourses and/or institutions to which we have access *because* of social location. This observation is as true for race as it is for class or gender. It is no accident that blacks with relatively high amounts of socio-economic status and whites with relatively low amounts seemed to gravitate toward O. J. narratives different from those the majority of their racial brethren embraced. Because of the racial hierarchy in the United States, "transgression" for blacks and "transgression" for whites meant two radically different things.

At the same time, however, we have to place survey data of the type we have been examining in perspective. That is, our answering of survey questions – like our discussions with important others – is a form of ritual, a performance of expected societal roles that we are "caught up bodily in" (Geertz 1983, p. 30). Survey researchers have long been aware of what are known as "response effects" (cf. Bradburn 1983), the

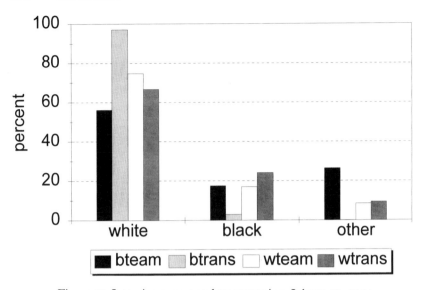

Figure 21. Interviewer race and transgression, July 11–12, 1994.

tendency of survey respondents to offer interviewers answers that they expect to be received as socially acceptable. People generally want to make good impressions. Indeed, this is why many research designs call for matching respondents and interviewers in terms of salient background characteristics – for example, in terms of race (as I did in chapters 7 and 8). But what about studies that involve relatively impersonal telephone interviews of the type examined above? Does the race of the interviewer matter?

In one study of attitudes on racial policy, for example, Kinder and Sanders (1996) found that interviewer race had a profound impact on black and white responses. That is, blacks who talked with black interviewers were much more likely than those who spoke with white interviewers to offer "liberal" responses (i.e., those supporting the redistribution of power and resources along racial lines). The converse was true for whites. The scholars thus concluded: "The racial divide in opinion widens when whites talk with whites and blacks talk with blacks, itself a sign of the difference race makes to our social and political lives" (p. 33).

Courtroom skirmishes aside,[10] figure 21 suggests that the race of the interviewer also had a profound effect on the survey findings we have been examining. That is, nearly 100 percent of black "transgressors" spoke to white interviewers, compared to only about 56 percent of black "teamplayers." If the race of the interviewer had no effect on "transgressor" status, we would expect the percentage distributions of "transgressors" and "teamplayers" across interviewer race categories to be similar. In other words, the percentage of black "transgressors" and "teamplayers" interviewed by whites should have been roughly equal. As this was obviously not the case, we are faced with the possibility that a substantial portion of black "transgressors" actually held views more in line with black "teamplayers." Of course, the converse might also be true: the 18 percent of black "teamplayers" who were confronted with black interviewers may have felt obligated to follow the racial "rule" and affirm Simpson's innocence. In either case, the finding underscores what I have described as the *ritualistic* nature of racial maneuvering in the Simpson case.

Race, ritual, and faith

Race, as we have previously noted, is not a genetic category. It is a social construction rooted in politics – in the gaining, losing, and using of power. In this sense, race functions as representation, a common-sense framework for explaining and justifying social inequality. Throughout its history, US society has been profoundly color conscious because of this basic relationship. We *use* race-as-representation – even when we have doubts about its validity – to make sense of our own locations in social structure and those of other-raced groups. We also use this representation to give our actions and the actions of others a meaningful context. Moreover, because representations are like norms, and because people *use* norms to choose between alternative courses of action (Garfinkel 1967), race-as-representation often determines the positions we feel compelled to take (or challenge) concerning important social issues. This racial maneuvering ultimately exhibits the characteristics of ritual, of performance, of the "practical accomplishment" of "doing-being" one's race (Garfinkel 1967).

Beginning not long after the murders, for example, a lengthy succession of opinion polls like the one discussed above provided trial observers with normative cues about the proper enactment of their raced subject-ivities vis-a-vis the Simpson case, particularly "doing-being white" and "doing-being black." The narrative elements contained by the case (e.g., Simpson's "blackness" and his ex-wife's "whiteness," their sexual relationship, and the brutality of the murders) (re)activated for trial observers narratives about race that have been circulating in America for centuries. All that remained was for trial observers to position themselves relative to these narratives (e.g., narratives contained within the Black "Other" project versus those contained within the "Just-Us" system project). This racial maneuvering was particularly conspicuous in the days immediately following the criminal trial verdicts. As Gates (1995) put it,

So it makes sense that in the aftermath of the Simpson trial the focus of attention has been swiftly displaced from the verdict to the reaction to the verdict, and then to the reaction to the reaction to the verdict, and, finally, to the reaction to the reaction to the reaction to the verdict – which is to say, black indignation at white anger at black jubilation at Simpson's acquittal. It's a spiral made possible by the relay circuit of race. Only in America. (p. 55)

The norm-like quality of race-as-representation, to be sure, provided the grounding for this "relay circuit of race." That is, it supplied the rules for the racial performances of trial observers, ritualistic maneuvers that ultimately work to celebrate and (re)affirm our raced subjectivities.

Rituals, at base, are about faith – about renewing our beliefs in a particular worldview. We generally celebrate the worldview that best fits with the "evidence" (i.e., what we "know") *and* with ideas we find comforting. This latter point is particularly important. Humans strive to bring order to a world that might otherwise appear chaotic, to find meaning in the vicissitudes of existence (Durkheim 1965). In the Simpson case, for example, the Black "Other" and "Just-Us" system projects were both central to the racial maneuvering of trial observers precisely because the projects have much to say about our varying levels of satisfaction with the current racial order and our respective places in it. When members of the dominant group in society racially define a group of others as the "bottom" of society (Baldwin 1961), as a group whose members are also physically distinguishable from themselves, they are provided with the comfort of "knowing" that they are among the elect, regardless of their individual life circumstances (cf. Harris 1995). Similarly, when members of a subordinate group understand themselves as the victims of racial oppression, as unfairly disadvantaged by a long history of dominant group power and privilege, they are provided with the comfort of being able to account for the hardships that disproportionately befall members of their group. For members of *both* groups, faith in what they "know" about the racial order is critical.

Take the concept of "racism," for example. Critical Race Theorists vigorously argue for the "fact" of *structural* "racism," for its *centrality* in US law, politics, and society. But they also illustrate how the mainstream common sense about "racism" has been rearticulated in contemporary times in accordance with a "perpetrator perspective," one that conceptualizes "racism" as a "deviation by a conscious wrongdoer from otherwise neutral, rational, and just ways of distributing jobs, power, prestige, and wealth" (Crenshaw et al. 1995, p. xv). Combined with the basic difficulties inherent in "proving" disparate treatment and disparate impact at the structural level (cf. Myers 1993), this development has worked to reinforce faith in the "reality" of a "colorblind" *system* – even (or especially) among those who purport to be proponents of racial "justice."[11]

Indeed, in a much-celebrated review of legal debates surrounding the Simpson case, Rosen (1996) dismisses Critical Race Theory as a paradigm based on "racialism" and "essentialism" – the antithesis of the "colorblind" society paradigm in which he places so much faith. For Rosen, defense attorney Johnnie Cochran's closing argument to the Simpson jury was the crowning achievement of "applied Critical Race Theory:" a shameless invocation of conspiracy theories and other "counternarratives" that are "widely accepted in the black community, even though they are *factually untrue*" (p. 27; emphasis added). The implication? *Structural* "racism" is a "fiction."

"Facts" and "fictions."

As I have argued throughout this book, "knowledge" about the racial order worked to pattern public stances on the Simpson case along racial lines. These stances, which at times approached fanaticism, were not unlike the beliefs people have in religious concepts. For example, the concept of God posits an unseen, supernatural intelligence whose reality is beyond validation with scientific evidence. Yet most of us – 96 percent of the US population, according to a recent opinion poll (Shermer 1996, p. 275) – "know" that God is real. In the final analysis, it seems, what we define as "evidence" in the Simpson case is *also* necessarily rooted in the faith we have in some self-contained system of knowing – be it day-to-day experience, science, or divine revelation. Let me explain.

When one peels the case against Simpson down to its core, we are left with three basic elements: State institutions, the evidence they amassed, and the media representations of this evidence to which most trial observers had access. Only observers who have a requisite amount of faith in *each* of these elements would admit to being *certain* of Simpson's guilt. Most white informants in this study possessed such faith. Transgressors aside, they accepted the LAPD, the District Attorney's office, and Superior Court as colorblind institutions capable of *and* committed to ferreting out "truth." Consequently, they found compelling the evidence collected, processed, and evaluated by these institutions. Mainstream media representations of the case were similarly embraced as the real thing, as a clear window onto a "mountain of evidence" against the black football legend.

Of course, for those who are skeptical of *any* of the three elements, the entire case against Simpson begins to unravel. Such was the case for black informants in this study. Indeed, they expressed doubts about *all three* elements. Echoing key tenets of the "Just-Us" system project, these informants questioned whether the LAPD, District Attorney's office, and Superior Court were actually colorblind institutions committed to justice in this or other cases involving black defendants. Consequently, they viewed the prosecution's "mountain of evidence" with much suspicion, frequently dismissing as "biased" the mainstream media representations that validated this evidence.

So whose worldview was more "rational" – the one (re)affirmed by black informants who challenged the case against Simpson, or the one embraced by their white counterparts who had so much faith in the case? Conventional wisdom provides us with an immediate answer: as the doubts of black informants were ultimately rooted in a belief in "conspiracy," their understanding of the case was less "plausible" on its face.

Conspiracy, (im)plausibilty, and interests

How do you *prove* "conspiracy?" The Tuskegee Syphilis Experiment and the case against US tobacco companies notwithstanding,[12] the answer depends on (1) how one defines "conspiracy" and (2) what one accepts as compelling "evidence." These two conditions, of course, are integrally connected. The *Webster's New Universal Unabridged Dictionary*[13] defines "conspiracy" as follows:

1. the act of conspiring. 2. an evil, unlawful, treacherous, or surreptitious plan formulated in secret by two or more persons; plot. 3. a combination of persons for a secret, unlawful, or evil purpose: *He joined the conspiracy to overthrow the government.* 4. *Law.* an agreement by two or more persons to commit a crime, fraud, or other wrongful act. 5. any concurrence in action; combination in bringing about a given result. (Emphasis original)

According to this rather straightforward definition, defense allegations of unlawful police practices in the Simpson case (e.g., the planting of blood evidence, rearrangement of evidence at the crime scenes, the deliberate corruption of blood vials, etc.), if true, would constitute "conspiracy" if *two* or more persons were involved in the acts *or* knew of them. But throughout the Simpson case, dominant news narratives rearticulated "conspiracy" to *connote* something altogether different: a grandiose plot necessarily *involving* dozens of LAPD officers. And this plot could not possibly be true because, as prosecutors labored to demonstrate, most of the officers who participated in the investigation hardly knew each other prior to that fateful night in June of 1994. How could they thus trust one another sufficiently to conspire in such a dangerous plot?

In an influential essay, Hofstadter (1965) provides scholarly precedent for the casual dismissal of "grandiose" conspiracy claims. He links belief in conspiracy to what he calls the "paranoid style," a political mind-set characteristic of those who feel persecuted in society. He thus characterizes "conspiracy" as fantasy, as a large-scale, nefarious plot existing primarily in the paranoid imagination: "In the paranoid style, as I conceive it, the feeling of persecution is central, and it is indeed systematized in grandiose theories of conspiracy" (p. 4). Hofstadter suggests that members of "minority groups" – the black informants in this study, for example – are often proponents of the "paranoid style." Like other proponents of the style, these critics of society tend to view the news media as conspiratorial agents in an all-encompassing drama. Indeed, as Hofstadter puts it, "History *is* conspiracy" for them (p. 29). And because they perceive historical developments as the direct result of sinister schemes, they feel compelled to respond to these developments with an "all-out crusade": they consider "the usual methods of political give-and-take" to be insufficient (p. 29). The battle, after all, is between absolute good and evil. In the end, it is this fervor and fanaticism – even more than the actual facticity of the claims – that distinguishes the "paranoid style" from others for Hofstadter.

At the same time, while proponents of the "paranoid style" often build their political platforms on a foundation of defensible propositions, Hofstadter argues that at some point they always make a "curious leap in imagination" (p. 37) in order to reach their "fantastic conclusions." This tendency, he suggests, is clearly reflected in "paranoid" literature:

One of the impressive things about paranoid literature is precisely the elaborate concern with demonstration it almost invariably shows. One should not be misled by the fantastic conclusions that are so characteristic of this political style into imagining that it is not, so to speak, argued out along factual lines. The very fantastic character of its conclusions leads to heroic strivings for "evidence" to prove that the unbelievable is the only thing that can be believed. (pp. 35–36)

In other words, "factual" evidence is neither compelling nor "proof" where the "unbelievable" is concerned.

Shermer (1997) expands on this understanding of "evidence" and "conspiracy" in his book, *Why People Believe Weird Things: Pseudoscience, Superstition, and Other Confusions of Our Time.* A self-proclaimed skeptic, Shermer cites Hume's maxim to support his position that "weird" claims such as those of conspiracy theorists require much stronger evidence than that we might demand for more mundane claims: "The plain consequence is (and it is a general maxim worthy of our attention), 'That no testimony is sufficient to establish a miracle, unless the testimony be of such a kind, that its falsehood would be more miraculous than the fact which it endeavors to establish'" (p. 45). For Shermer, claims only attain the status of "fact" when they are "confirmed to such an extent that it would be reasonable to offer temporary agreement" (p. 16). This burden, of course, can only be met through application of the scientific method, a progressive system of knowing that aims for objectivity, avoids mysticism, and ultimately leads us toward rationality. For Shermer, evidence based on people and their perceptions is never as compelling as physical evidence, which can be evaluated by more reliable, scientific instruments. Although Shermer admits that no "Archimedean point" exists from which to view reality and thus evaluate scientific representations of it (p. 41), he nonetheless defends the requirement that evidence which does not conform to these dominant representations face a stiffer validation test: "[I]t is not enough to have evidence. You must convince others of the validity of your evidence. And when you are an *outsider* this is the price you pay, regardless of whether you are right or wrong" (p. 51; emphasis added). Of course, people who offer evidence of conspiracy *are* "outsiders" as far as dominant representations of reality are concerned. And paraphrasing Hume's maxim, *no* evidence of conspiracy is compelling for Shermer unless the falsehood of the evidence appears to be more unlikely than the unbelievable conspiracy claim it purports to support.

This perspective on "conspiracy" and "evidence" clearly defines the "most-plausible" narratives on reality, such as the "incompetence" narratives offered to explain Simpson's acquittal in the criminal trial (see chapter 1). In *Dreams of Millennium: Report from a Culture on the Brink*, for example, Kingwell (1996) effectively dismisses the reality of "genuine" conspiracies. Indeed, no evidence could ever be compelling enough to constitute "proof":

There is an important difference, a difference well worth preserving, between an analysis that suggests common elite interests, or the internal logic of complex systems, on the one hand, and a genuine conspiracy theory on the other. One is susceptible to proof and the other is not; it is the difference between science fact and science fiction. (pp. 266–267)

Where Hofstadter explains notions of conspiracy in terms of a "paranoid style," Kingwell likens their construction and circulation to religion, a "collective madness" that is "impressively creative in its own self-defense" (p. 273). Moreover, he roots this condition in millennial anxieties, in ever more pressing questions of meaning, and in our yearning for answers no matter how "crazy":

When displaced by a world of apparent meaninglessness, it is natural to crave explanations, however unlikely, for events that defy normal categories of understanding. In the hothouse atmosphere of the late twentieth century, a crazy explanation begins to seem to many people better than no explanation at all. (p. 265)

This conventional wisdom, to be sure, is routinely (re)circulated in mainstream media. For example, note how an article from *Time* magazine on the alleged Roswell UFO incident casually assigns "the racist-police conspiracy to frame O. J. Simpson" to the realm of "pretty sensational stuff" or "ingenious tales":

Like the black helicopters of the new world order *or the racist-police conspiracy to frame O. J. Simpson*, the Incident [Roswell], as it is known, is either *pretty sensational* stuff or yet another of the *ingenious tales* those of us who mistrust mainstream institutions tell ourselves to help make sense of a scary, sometimes depressing world. (Emphasis added)[14]

The problem with the conventional wisdom regarding conspiracy, to use a statistical analogy, is that the value of alpha is set impossibly small in the "reality test." That is, conspiracy debunkers like Hofstadter, Shermer, and Kingwell are so convinced of conspiracy's "unreality" that they are more than happy to disregard the possibility of Type II error – of *not* rejecting the null hypothesis (i.e., no conspiracy exists) when it is actually false. This is indeed problematic when the costs associated with Type II error are so high. For in the Simpson case, this cost would include defending state institutions that trammeled upon the constitutional rights of an affluent citizen, institutions that could do so with even less impunity were poorer citizens involved. As we saw in chapter 2, the US criminal justice system has been quite prolific in its ability to incarcerate large portions of the civilian population, especially people of color. Denying the possibility of Type II error, in effect, increases the societal threat.

In their rush to debunk the "weird" conspiracy theories of "outsiders," it seems, Hofstadter, Shermer, and Kingwell ultimately fail to explore a critical question: Why are the beliefs of "insiders" *not* considered "weird?" Michael Moore (1997), for example, uses satire to underscore what he perceives as a misplaced faith in police accounts of the Bundy murders:

I have felt, long before O. J., that anything the L.A. Police Department says must, at first, not be believed. For any of us to believe another individual, we have to trust them. Have the L.A. police earned your trust? Because they have violated that trust, I am forced to presume they are lying whenever they speak, and only when they can prove that they are not lying can I believe their version of anything. (p. 210)

Nonetheless, newsworkers who constructed and circulated dominant narratives about Simpson's guilt openly embraced the police "version" of the murders. They also worked to neutralize several pieces of defense "evidence" in order to define the racist-police conspiracy narrative as "implausible." That is, despite "evidence" that a police officer lied about not harboring racist beliefs, that his superior also lied about his decision to enter Simpson's Rockingham home without a search warrant, and that blood evidence collected at the crime scenes contained traces of a preservative placed in reference samples, newsworkers continued to favor dominant O.J. narratives. It was as if nothing short of an outright police confession or exposure by a fellow officer would establish the "plausibility" of the conspiracy narrative for these case observers. Given the nature of the criminal justice system, however, either development would be highly unlikely. Law enforcement organizations like the LAPD monopolize access to crime scene information (Hall et al. 1978), which allows them to coordinate official accounts and subsequent officer testimony. In the Simpson case, for example, LAPD officers effectively kept the coroner away from the Bundy crime scene for about nine hours after the bodies were discovered.[15] Moreover, the LAPD is a highly insular organization. Its informal rules and procedures work to constrain officer behavior in ways that protect the "plausibility" of police accounts.[16] For example, in a widely publicized report issued in the aftermath of the Rodney King beating (see Hunt 1997), the Christopher Commission described the inner workings of the organization's "code of silence":

> The code of silence influences the behavior of many LAPD officers in a variety of ways, but it consists of one simple rule: an officer does not provide adverse information against a fellow officer . . . Officers who do give evidence against their fellow officers are often ostracized and harassed, and in some instances themselves become the target of complaints.[17]

Indeed, had King's brutal beating not been videotaped by an onlooker, the report noted, it is doubtful the Commission would have been formed to look into the beating. Twenty-one police officers witnessed the incident and King's brother filed a formal complaint, but police reports were "falsified" to characterize the beating as a necessary use of force. When the officers who knew better did not come forward to contest the reports, we were then presented with what amounts to a "conspiracy of silence."[18] The usual outcome? Without the videotape, accounts of the incident that challenged the official police account (e.g., King's brother's) would have been casually dismissed as "not 'independent'":

> Our Commission owes its existence to the George Holliday videotape of the Rodney King incident. Whether there even would have been a Los Angeles Police Department investigation without the video is doubtful, since the efforts of King's brother, Paul, to file a complaint were frustrated, and the report

of the involved officers was falsified. Even if there had been an investigation, our case-by-case review of the handling of over 700 complaints indicates that without the Holliday videotape the complaint might have been adjudged to be "not sustained," because the officers' version conflicted with the account by King and his two passengers, who typically would have been viewed as not "independent."[19]

What Commissioners could not know when they wrote the report in 1991, however, was that a jury would view the same videotape in 1992 and embrace police accounts that the use of force was justified: King was in control of the situation (Fiske 1994). To what can we attribute the a priori "plausibility" routinely accorded police accounts?

The answer, of course, is that many people – particularly members of dominant social groups – are invested in official accounts of reality. In the United States, police officers, "the thin blue line," simultaneously serve as representatives and protectors of the social order. Contemporary police accounts, in unison with other official accounts, publicly portray this order as a pluralistic, "colorblind" one in which those at the top legitimately attained their privileged positions through hard work and personal merit, qualities that those at the bottom obviously lack (cf. Crenshaw et al. 1995). This official view of reality is comforting for members of dominant social groups who feel the need to protect their privileged position against the incursions of threatening "Others" (e.g., proponents of the Black "Other" project). Consequently, the standard of proof used to evaluate "evidence" that challenges the official view is set so high that it is extremely unlikely the view could ever be presented in the mainstream as anything but taken-for-granted and common sense. To put it another way, the reality game is rigged to ensure the reproduction of official accounts like those of the police. In the Simpson case, you will recall, mainstream media like KTLA-TV (chapter 4) and the *Los Angeles Times* (chapter 5) regularly discounted testimony and reports that might otherwise have supported the conspiracy claims of Simpson's defense. Unlike pro-prosecution testimony and reports, this information was rarely accorded the status of "evidence." The result? The mainstream news media's defining mantra in the case: "Simpson's defense has offered no evidence to support its conspiracy claims." Meanwhile, in the aftermath of a case featuring startling revelations about Mark Fuhrman's racial animus, mainstream news media could still cast the ex-LAPD detective as a credible hero who fell victim to the "race card."[20]

To conclude that conspiracy was involved in the Simpson case, of course, does not preclude the logical possibility that the defendant may have indeed committed the crimes (i.e., the "overzealousness" narratives from chapter 1). But the question we must ask ourselves is this: What, in the overall scheme of things, is the bigger issue: a wealthy double murderer who goes free, or officers of the state who commit unlawful acts in order to facilitate the conviction of an "obviously guilty" defendant?

O. J., seeing, and reality

Newsworkers. Project proponents. And study informants. Observers of the Simpson case exhibited considerable creativity in their ability to assemble the narrative elements invoked by the case into coherent narratives. Whether they were narratives of "incompetence," "overzealousness," "mystery," "rush to judgment" or "conspiracy," these gestalt-like constructions were a direct function of the various ways of seeing people employed to make sense of the case. Indeed, ways of seeing were more determining of the unified images study informants had of the case than any single case "fact." As Seward Barry (1997, p. 65) puts it, "what we see is at least partially what we expect to see and is as much the product of inner-derived meaning as it is a reflection of what's out 'out there.' "

But "inner-derived" meanings do not simply fall from the sky. They are patterned by social experiences, by our locations in social structure, by our interests. Throughout this book, I have focussed primarily on how the "inner-derived" meanings associated with raced ways of seeing shaped our understandings of the Simpson case. These meanings are a critical component of what might be called "organic ideology" (cf. Gramsci 1971; Hall 1986), the practical, everyday consciousness that shapes our responses to the hegemonic order. Hegemonic social orders like the United States continually fashion unstable equilibria out of the complementary forces of coercion (i.e., the threat of force) and consent (i.e., widespread, ideological support for the order). The Simpson case, as media event, played an important role in this process. It served as a high-profile, society-wide ritual through which some of our most basic values (e.g., "truth"), norms (e.g., the scientific method), and social institutions (e.g., the criminal justice system) were celebrated and (re)-affirmed. But as the hegemonic order regularly produces inequality, the organic consciousness of disadvantaged group members often prompts them to challenge the status quo. Media events, in this sense, also signal a legitimation crisis in which opponents of the status quo struggle to circulate counter-hegemonic affirmations of "fact" and opinion.

In the Simpson media event, the ritualistic struggle between hegemonic and counter-hegemonic forces was uncharacteristically overt. The criminal trial acquittals by a predominantly black jury marked a short-term, in-your-face victory for counter-hegemonic forces. Mainstream news media flashed images of those critical of the criminal justice system as they celebrated in the streets. For them, "black reality" had finally been validated. Juxtaposed to these images were the faces of those who embraced dominant O. J. narratives, faces that expressed varying degrees of outrage and/or despair. But less than seventeen months later, a "festive" crowd gathered outside a Santa Monica courthouse for another verdict. This time, a predominantly white civil trial jury found Simpson liable for the murders. "White reality" was validated and equilibrium was restored – for the moment. For this latter O. J. ritual necessarily revealed the precariousness of "colorblind" reality. As Moore and Myerhoff (1977) remind us:

Since ritual is a good form for conveying a message as if it were unquestionable, it often is used to communicate those very things which are most in doubt. Thus where there is conflict, or danger, or political opposition, where there is made-upness and cultural invention, ritual may carry the opposite message in form as well as content. (p. 24)

In the months following the civil trial verdicts, the trinity of case landmarks was transformed one by one. First, it was the Bundy crime scene. The sidewalk that was once covered with the blood of two murder victims and the metal gate police officers found ajar are now gone, both replaced by a new facade that makes the infamous residence barely recognizable. Mezzaluna was next. The chic eatery that employed Ronald Goldman and served Nicole Brown-Simpson's final meal no longer operates in Brentwood. Although the building remains, menus and other identifying mementos were auctioned off to case-obsessed collectors. Finally, more than two years after the murders, television news cameras were present as Simpson's Rockingham home was sold at auction. The $33.5 million civil judgment against Simpson and other financial difficulties had finally resulted in foreclosure on the property. A few months later, the cameras were also present as Simpson moved out of the home he had occupied for two decades.

Much had happened. Bloody murders. A criminal trial acquittal. A huge civil trial liability award. Despite all of the transformations, despite the momentary restoration of equilibrium, the infamous landmarks continued to attract a few curious on-lookers, fingers pointing, cameras clicking, exchanging what they "know" about the case. So it was not surprising when in early 1998 – approaching four years after the murders – the nation was momentarily transfixed by speculation surrounding an exclusive *Esquire* interview with Simpson. "Let's say I committed this crime," Simpson tantalizingly remarked, "Even if I did do this, it would have been because I loved her very much, right?"[21]

In the end, of course, only Simpson – and possibly some other killer(s) – could have *absolute* knowledge of his innocence or guilt. But this is *not* the knowledge that mattered in the ritual I have called the Simpson media event. What was at stake, what continues to matter, is how we differentiate "fact" from "fiction" and (re)affirm what we believe about "reality."

Appendix 1
Page-one narratives, *Los Angeles Times*, January 25–October 4, 1995

January 25, 1995
* Prosecutors Tell Tale of "Other" Simpson: Trial: Revealing a bloody trail of evidence, they say he killed out of desire to control his ex-wife. Judge Ito threatens to cut off TV coverage after a juror is shown. (Newton/Ford) (A1)
* Halt in Trial Hurts Defense, Experts Say (Weinstein) (Legal Analysis) (A1)

February 4, 1995
* Victim's Tearful Sister Alleges Simpson Abuse: Trial: Denise Brown describes two incidents. DNA expert denies prosecution tampered with evidence. (A1) (Newton/Ford)

February 7, 1995
* Victim's Sister Ends Emotional Testimony: Trial: Denise Brown says Simpson called pregnant wife a "fat pig." She admits having had drinking problem. (A1) (Ford/Newton)

February 16, 1995
* Simpson Defense Dealt Setbacks on Two Fronts: Courts: DNA tests tentatively link blood on ex-wife's gate to defendant. Key defense witness disappears (A1) (Ford/Newton)
* Not Everything Is Trying for Simpson Jury (A1) (Jeff Brazil/Tina Daunt)

February 25, 1995
* Key Simpson Defense Witness Contradicts Self (A1) (Newton/Ford)
* Clash Drags Both Sides to Risky Terrain (A1) (Rutten/Weinstein) (news analysis)

February 28, 1995
* Housekeeper Tells of Seeing Simpson's Car: Trial: Rosa Lopez testifies on tape without jury present after prosecutors complain. Defense reveals statement it took from her in July. (A1) (Ford/Newton)

March 11, 1995
* Fuhrman Tells of His Actions at Scene of Slayings (A1) (Newton/Ford)

March 15, 1995
* Bailey Suggests Two Scenarios for Planting a Glove: Simpson case: Attorney hints Fuhrman arranged to have others preoccupied so he could tamper with evidence. New allegations of racist remarks raised. (A1) (Ford/Weinstein/Newton)
* Jurors Look to Mannerisms for Clues to Truth (Elaine Woo) (A1)

March 22, 1995
* Vannatter Offers Explanations for Glove Questions (A1) (Newton/Weinstein)

April 1, 1995
* Neighbor Says He Did Not See Simpson Bronco (A1) (Ford/Newton)

April 8, 1995
* Ito Rejects Bid to Reopen Issue of DNA Credibility (Ford/Newton) (A1)

April 15, 1995
* Fiery Debate Over Blank Form Stalls Simpson Trial: Courts: "This has got to end sometime," impatient Judge Ito says of 90-minute fight over two staple holes (Ford/Newton) (A1)

April 18, 1995
* Prosecutors Play Video to Counter Defense Charge (A1) (Newton/Ford)

April 26, 1995
* Criminalist Quizzed Before a Sterner Ito (A1) (Ford/Newton)

May 3, 1995
* LAPD Chemist Testifies on Blood Test Results: Simpson case: He says defendant is among 0.5% of people whose blood matches one drop. Ex-juror ailing. (Newton/Ford) (A1)

May 12, 1995
* Jury Told of Huge Odds Pointing to Simpson: Trial: Panel hears statistics about DNA matches. Defense questions methods used to derive the numbers. (A1) (Ford/Newton)

May 16, 1995
* Tug-of-War on DNA Continues at Simpson Trial (A1) (Ford/Newton)

May 27, 1995
* Ito Rejects Introduction of Simpson's Statement: Trial: Ousted juror denies she was planning to write a book. Meanwhile, another panelist is under investigation (A1) (Rutten/Weinstein/Ford).

June 3, 1995
* Chief Coroner Concedes Errors in Simpson Case (A1) (Newton/Weinstein)
* Dove Books Publisher Is in the Show-Biz Moment: Celebrities: Founder capitalizes on books on Simpson, Menendez cases. Some question the caliber of the material (A1) (Lawrence Christon)

June 6, 1995
* Ito Ousts 2 More Simpson Jurors; 2 Alternates Left: Trial: A woman accused of passing a note and a man she said intimidated her are dismissed. An emergency appeal by the defense to keep the male panelist is denied (A1) (Weinstein/Rutten/Newton)

June 17, 1995
* Simpson Prosecutors Focus on Shrinkage of Gloves: Courts: Witness says moisture would cause the problem. Clark, Dershowitz clash over dwindling jury (Simon/Rutten/John L. Mitchell) (A1)

June 21, 1995
* Strongest DNA Statistic Yet Offered in Simpson Trial: Courts: Expert says just one person in 57 billion could have left two bloodstains. Prosecution to shorten its case. (A1) (Ford/Newton)

June 29, 1995
* Surprise Hair, Fiber Photos Anger Simpson Attorneys: Trial: Defense accuses prosecutors of violating discovery rules. Judge abruptly recesses proceedings. (A1) (Simon/Weinstein)

July 6, 1995
* Prosecutors Say Hair, Fibers Link Simpson to Scene (Newton/Simon) (A1)

July 13, 1995
* Defense Witness Testimony Called Into Question (Weinstein/Newton) (A1)

July 18, 1995
* Simpson Had Strength to Kill, Doctor Testifies: Trial: Physician also describes defendant's ailments and says he appeared under great stress after the slayings (A1) (Rutten/Newton)

July 26, 1995
* Stains Not From Preserved Blood, Simpson Jury Told (Newton/Rutten) (A1)

August 3, 1995
* Contamination Chronic at LAPD Lab, Expert Testifies: Simpson Trial: Defense witness says problem is serious, but doesn't cite specific tainted evidence in this case (A1) (Weinstein/Newton)

August 9, 1995
* Special Prosecutor Sought to Probe Fuhrman Remarks: Simpson Trial: Defense wants to pursue perjury issue. Legal experts, detective's lawyer predict motion to fail. (A1) (Ford/Newton)

August 16, 1995
* With Trial at Risk, Ito Sends Issue of Tapes to Another Court: Simpson Trial: Prosecution wants judge removed from case, saying Fuhrman's alleged comments about Ito's wife create conflict of interest. Defense objects vehemently (A1) (Newton/Simon)
* LAPD Panel Probes Taped Allegations (A1) (Jean Merl/Newton)
* Shift to New Judge Still Leaves a Host of Questions: Jurisprudence: If Ito recuses himself from case, a mistrial is feared. But experts doubt he can be forced off (A1) (Rutten/Weinstein)

August 22, 1995
* Ito Delays Ruling on Admitting Fuhrman Tapes (A1) (Rutten/Newton)

August 30, 1995
* Fuhrman Tapes Aired: a Recital of Racism, Wrath: Simpson Trial: Judge Ito defers decision on allowing jury to hear statements. Sound of former LAPD detective's words reverberates far beyond courtroom (Newton/Ford/Weinstein) (A1)
* Officers Insist Tapes Don't Reflect LAPD (A1) (Simon/Abrahamson/Wilgoren)

September 6, 1995
* Witnesses Tell Jury of Fuhrman's Racial Epithets: Simpson trial: Ex-detective disparaged interracial couples and bragged about making up charges, two women say. Session ends with playing of writer's tapes (A1) (Newton/Boyarsky)

September 16, 1995
* FBI Agent Says Simpson Defense Expert Lee Erred (A1) (Weinstein/Rutten)

September 21, 1995
* Ito Shows Exasperation as Testimony Winds Down: Simpson case: Jurors snicker at tiff over a syringe. LAPD commander testifies; he could be final witness (A1) (Newton/Ford)

September 27, 1995
* Wealth of Evidence All Points to Simpson, Clark Tells Jury: Trial: The prosecution begins closing arguments by disavowing Mark Fuhrman. Darden accuses defense attorneys of deception and their client of murder (A1) (Newton/ Weinstein)
* Panic Grips World Press as Ito Pulls Plug on Coverage (A1) (unidentified)

October 4, 1995
* Simpson Not Guilty, Drama Ends 474 Days After Arrest: Verdicts: The ex-football star expresses gratitude and returns to his Brentwood estate where friends and family celebrate. Relatives of the victims react with pain and grim silence to the jurors' decision. (A1) (Newton)
* A Corner is Turned in the Lives of 3 Families: Relatives: Some emerge exultant. Others wonder how they will go on (A1) (unidentified)
* Reaction: High-voltage joy, angry denouncement (A1) (John L. Mitchell/Jeff Leeds)
* Case Had Many Holes, Juror Says: Panel: Group agreed with forensic expert Lee that there was "something wrong" with prosecution's evidence, he reports. Opportunities for contamination are cited. (A1) (Edward J. Boyer/Elaine Woo)
* Half of Americans Disagree With Verdict: Times Poll: Many cite race as key factor in trial (A1) (Cathleen Decker/Sheryl Stolberg)
* The Spin: This Case Isn't Open and Shut (A1) (Boyarsky)
* Simpson is Free, but Can He Regain His Life and Image? Aftermath: He faces civil suits and possible custody battle. But his far greater fame may carry a high price (A1) (Alan Abrahamson/Tony Perry)
* Miscalculations, Bad Luck Hurt Prosecution (A1) (Weinstein/Maura Dolan/ Rutten) (news analysis)

Appendix 2
Page-one O. J. narratives, *Los Angeles Sentinel*, January 25–October 5

January 25, 1995
* None

February 2, 1995
* Gloves are Off as Trial Begins (Schatzman)(A1)

February 9, 1995
* Two "Drunks" Join O. J.'s Cast of "Addicts, Liars": Ex-Police Officer Ron Shipp and Denise Brown Join Madcap Cast of Characters (A1) (Schatzman)

February 16, 1995
* Police Security at Scene of Double Murder Termed "Lax" by Physician: Prominent Cardiologist Dr. James A. Mays reveals he was allowed by police to roam murder scene the day after the incident, "and I touched stuff" (A1) (Schatzman)

February 23, 1995
* Reporter Records First Impressions at Simpson Trial (A1) (Parker)

March 2, 1995
* O. J. Simpson: Trial Creates Instant Stars, Sideshows (A1) (Parker)

March 9, 1995
* Johnnie Cochran, Mrs. Lopez Get Roughouse Treatment (A1) (Schatzman)

March 16, 1995
* Many Believe: City is Ripe for Theory That White Cop Framed Simpson (A1) (Julia Prodis, syndicated/wire service)

March 23, 1995
* The Return of Robert Shapiro: Vannatter, Police Get Grilled (A1) (Schatzman)

March 30, 1995
* It's True, But: Often, White Men Can't Think, Either (Schatzman) (A1)

April 6, 1995
* O. J. Simpson vs. the People Turning into a "Blood" Sport (A1) (Schatzman)

April 13, 1995
None

April 20, 1995
* CORE May Seek Justice Dept. Probe If Simpson Cleared (A1) (Schatzman)

April 27, 1995
* Police Chief Willie Williams Defends His, LAPD's Reputation (A1) (Dungee, sports editor)
* Johnnie Cochran Says Celebrity-Studded Group to Seek Release of "Geronimo" Pratt (A1) (Parker)

May 4, 1995
* Simpson Case Black Jurors: And Now There Are Only Seven: Although the defense appears to have suffered a loss of a potentially sympathetic black juror, with four of the five remaining alternates being African American, and the lone Latina left is married to a black man, the advantage still seems to lean toward Simpson. (A1) (Schatzman)

May 11, 1995
* Racist Ito Drawings Enrage Asian Group (A1) (unidentified)
* Prosecutor Honored (A1) (unidentified)

May 18, 1995
None

May 25, 1995
None

June 1, 1995
* New Juror: "Don't Know About O.J." (A1) (unidentified)

June 8, 1995
* Journalists Meet Lawyers (A1) (unidentified)
* Journalists Flex Media Muscles (A1) (Brown)

June 15, 1995
* Despite Dr. Golden's Trashing, Photos of His Work Displayed (A1) (Schatzman)
* Judge Dismisses Most of Lawsuit (A1) (unidentified)

June 22, 1995
* None

June 29, 1995
* None

July 6, 1995
* O.J. Case: Often, Whites and Blacks View Things Differently (A1)(Schatzman)

July 13, 1995
* None

July 20, 1995
* O.J. vs. the People: Defense and the People Win Some, Lose Some (A1)(Schatzman)

July 27, 1995
* Coverage Controversy: O.J. Issues Plague Snoop Doggy Dog Murder Trial (A1) (Bolden)

August 3, 1995
* None

August 10, 1995
* None

August 17, 1995
* Avoids Appearance of Conflict: Judge Ito Bows Out on Fuhrman Tapes as Defense Gains Momentum (A1) (unidentified)

August 24, 1995
* Fuhrman Tapes: Explosive Revelations For O. J. Defense And For Community (A1) (unidentified)
* Fuhrman No Longer Subsidized (A1) (unidentified)
* Deja Vu, "All Over Again': Cochran Ex-wife Joins Crowd Publishes "Tell-All" Book (A1) (unidentified)

August 31, 1995
* Fuhrman Tapes Validate Citizen Complaints (A1) (unidentified)

September 7, 1995
* Massive Response to Ito's Two Excerpts Ruling (A1) (unidentified)

September 14, 1995
* Refuses to Rest: Defense Awaits Writ From Appeals Court (A1) (Parker)

September 21, 1995
* The Simpson Trial: The Jury's Lament: Whose Testimony Most Believable? (A1) (Schatzman)

September 28, 1995
* O. J. Simpson Trial: Beyond a Reasonable Doubt – You Be the Judge (A1) (unidentified)

October 5, 1995
* Strong Emotions Permeate Crowds Waiting to Hear Simpson Verdict (A1) (Parker)
* Residents Respond To Jury's Decision (A1) (Muwwakkil)

Appendix 3
Emerging discussion themes, by group, March 30, 1995

White group

Prompt: Think back to the videotape that we've just viewed. How would you explain what we just saw? Why? Relax. Take your time, you have up to an hour to discuss this amongst yourselves. I'll be around if you need me for anything.

* Domestic violence
* Even if Fuhrman is a racist it doesn't mean he planted evidence in this case
* O.J. probably killed Nicole
* Witnesses interviewed by LAPD
* The Rockingham glove
* How O.J. probably entered Rockingham after murders
* Blood trail
* The Rockingham glove
* Thumps on the air conditioner behind Kato's room
* The limousine driver
* O.J.'s time-line
* O.J.'s alibi
* Figure seen by limousine driver entering Rockingham
* Other possible suspects
* One informant doubts prosecution theory
* Notion of police frame is "ludicrous"
* Police search of Rockingham
* O.J.'s demeanor at dance recital
* Cuts on O.J.'s hands
* Nicole and Goldman had an affair
* O.J.'s jealousy shows in screening video
* O.J. probably killed Nicole out of jealousy
* Order of killings
* O.J.'s jealousy
* O.J.'s motive
* If O.J. was jealous, why didn't he murder Nicole the night he saw her having sex on sofa?
* He wasn't enraged that night
* Jealousy theory inconsistent
* Theory about O.J.'s clothing, gloves and knife

* Drug theory
* O.J.'s jealousy
* Edwin Moses framed
* LAPD's corrupt tactics
* LAPD favors wealthy like O.J.
* O.J.'s investigators
* O.J.'s motive
* LAPD frame theory is improbable
* Rodney King
* Dangers faced by police
* Educational statistics on LAPD officers
* Opening statements
* "Dream Team" witnesses are suspect
* O.J.'s body
* How did blood get in Bronco?
* Kato's testimony
* O.J. trained as killer
* Money and legal defense
* Defense gaffes
* Lie detector tests
* Defense gaffes
* The black bag suspected to hold O.J.'s bloody clothes, knife
* F. Lee Bailey's tactics
* Johnnie Cochran's tactics
* Will O.J. testify?
* Perry Mason
* The black bag suspected to hold O.J.'s bloody clothes, knife
* O.J. complained of being hot in the limousine
* Police officers
* Racism
* Racism and education
* Humans are naturally biased
* Fuhrman and racism
* Defense should not have played "race card"
* Police frame theory
* Screening video shows that LAPD does a "good job"
* LAPD investigation
* One of informants has friend residing in O.J.'s neighborhood
* The akita and the killer
* Cochran's theory
* The struggle
* O.J.'s body
* Goldman's size
* The struggle
* The killing order
* The black bag suspected of carrying O.J.'s bloody clothes, knife
* One informant's theory of how O.J. committed crimes
* The melting ice cream

* Nicole killing scenario
* Location of Nicole's body at murder scene
* Location of Goldman's body at murder scene
* The shovel found in the Bronco
* The prosecution's surprise witness
* Circumstantial evidence
* Abundance of evidence
* LAPD search of Rockingham
* O.J.'s carelessness
* Killing scenario
* Rage killings and professional hits
* Possibility that LAPD may have framed guilty man
* Drug theory
* Mike Tyson and O.J. are easy targets for frame
* Possibility that evidence may have been planted
* Blood preservative not in O.J. blood collected from car and socks

Prompt: Okay, for the last ten minutes I've got a couple of questions here . . .
     What do you feel is the most important news reported in the video?

* Domestic violence
* Nicole's fear
* Police did a "good job"
* O.J.'s jealousy and temper
* No prisoner admits guilt

Prompt: What was good about the video? What was bad about the video?

* Screening video was "very informative"
* Screening video was "totally slanted"
* Screening video was "PR for the LAPD"
* There are "good" and "bad" police
* Motivations for crime
* Screening video was "about just television ratings"
* The secretly recorded tape of the incident
* Poor view of lawyers
* Lawyers attempt to win at all costs
* Television coverage increases stakes of contest
* Changes are needed in justice system
* Money corrupts trial process

Prompt: What do you think about the people shown in the video and how do
     you feel about the news reporters and commentators in the video?

* Nightly newscast reporters "stink"
* Coverage doesn't accurately reflect trial
* Secretly recorded tape doesn't prove O.J. killed Nicole
* Media coverage gives public access to the courtroom
* Money increases the amount of justice that can be bought
* Media is doing "good" job of covering courtroom
* O.J.'s demeanor in court

* Media should pay for space in courthouse
* Taxpayers have to pay high costs of trial
* Ratings
* Attorney's "played for the media"
* Barring cameras from courtroom would facilitate justice
* Attorney posturing
* O. J. case atypical
* O. J.'s money has shaped the case
* What would you do if you were wrongfully accused of murder?

(end: 1:00:00)

Black group

Prompt: Now, think back to the videotape that you just viewed. How would you explain what you just saw and why? Relax. Take your time. You have up to one hour to discuss this amongst yourselves. I'll be around if you need me for anything. The floor is yours. It's all up to you to talk.

* O. J. "not that enraged"
* Nicole was no "perfect angel"
* Nicole and O. J.'s relationship
* Why did Nicole stay with O. J.?
* When she left, why did she move so close?
* Nicole had financial motives
* O. J. had a sickness (jealousy/declining fame)
* But O. J. had not hit Nicole in four years
* Media portrayal of relationship
* Domestic abuse suffered by one of the informants
* O. J. and Nicole had passionate relationship
* O. J. and Nicole were both jealous
* If O. J. were a killer, earlier incidents should have triggered him
* Prosecution theory of trigger is suspect
* Prosecution theory of crime doesn't "make sense"
* The mind of a killer may be unknowable
* If O. J. were killer, movies and books could have helped him plan crime better
* O. J. may know who set him up, but his kids may be in danger if he talks
* Prosecution theory flawed
* The akita would not have barked at O. J.
* Drugs, mafia, Faye Resnick connection
* Recent Miami killings may be related
* Prosecution not considering other suspects/rush to judgment
* Political pressure on district attorney to win case
* Crimes could not have been committed by one person
* O. J. had no scratches
* Nicole had skin and blood under her nails
* Leaks about results of blood test on socks before they had actually been tested
* The collection of O. J.'s blood sample
* No blood trail by Rockingham glove

* How did Bundy glove come off?
* O.J. had no scratches or cuts
* Leather clings, killer would know if s/he lost it
* Why would O.J. take bloody glove to Rockingham?
* The Bundy hat
* Why would O.J. leave kids upstairs with candles burning in house?
* Too many loose ends
* Conspiracy to bring down prominent black men
* New prosecution witness
* Rosa Lopez
* LAPD is racist
* LAPD detectives lied
* Prosecution witnesses were coached
* White people
* Kato acted nervous and drugged on stand
* Kato knows more than he is saying
* Drug connections to murders
* Kato's living arrangements with Nicole
* Bumps on air conditioner behind Kato's room
* Kato angered Marcia Clark
* Limousine driver
* Four men seen in alley near Nicole's condo
* Brentwood residents are "hysterical" about crime
* Why wouldn't neighbors check on source of barking earlier?
* The first officer on the scene
* Screening video didn't flow, edited
* Screening video showed only the "worst"
* The kicked-in door
* O.J. passing blame on to others
* Why did Nicole stay around to call 911?
* Nicole wasn't really afraid of O.J.
* How Nicole should have handled the incident
* O.J.'s car in the middle of Bundy
* Prosecution witness "playing role"
* Media biased against O.J.
* Everybody hates O.J.
* Brentwood does not hate O.J.
* Brentwood hates Nicole
* Nicole was having fun in Brentwood
* Case is a set-up for a race war
* O.J.'s legal fees
* Sydney and Justin
* The Browns as guardians
* The Browns are racists
* Thomas Jefferson was racist
* Nicole probably kept kids from O.J.'s mother
* Sydney and Justin will be integrated into "white society"
* Too many shows on television with "mixed" kids

* Race and case
* Informants' dislike for Nicole
* O. J. lived in a "white world"
* Wealthy sports stars chose white women over black ones
* Informant's hatred for "white people"
* Whites all feel O. J. is guilty
* Blacks all feel he was set-up
* In the US defendants are innocent until proven guilty
* LAPD knew a lot about Nicole's and O. J.'s relationship
* Informant's employment in Brentwood

Prompt: Let me ask you a question, what do you think was the most important news recorded in that video we just saw?

* O. J. hadn't hit Nicole in four years
* Officer secretly taped incident
* Legality of taping
* Police can do "whatever they want to do"
* Secret tape made to "nail" O. J.
* Police frames
* O. J. and Nicole loved to "play games" with each other

Prompt: What do you think was good about the video and what was bad about it?

* Female officer pushing Nicole to leave O. J.
* Why didn't officers arrest O. J.?
* Female officer exaggerated about what she told Nicole
* Screening video was "one-sided"

Prompt: And how did you feel about the people in the video? In particular, I guess, the major characters who were talking in the video . . . but also Marcia Clark, Johnnie Cochran, Robert Shapiro, Darden? How do . . .

* Clark is opportunist
* All attorneys are using case to advance their careers
* Clark hates men
* Clark was abused by a husband
* Clark's custody battle
* Clark's relationship with her husband
* Clark lied about child-care arrangement in order to stall for more time to impeach Rosa Lopez
* Ito gave Clark "a lot of freedom"
* Ito's wife was abused
* Trial is a "circus"
* Men hitting women
* Cochran is "smooth," the lead trial attorney
* Shapiro's expertise is plea bargaining
* Other defense attorneys
* Darden is an "Uncle Tom"
* Informant and O. J. share same astrological sign

Prompt: How did you fell about the reporters . . . the commentators that were
in the video you saw? Diane Sawyer and some of the other people?

* Sawyer biased against O. J.
* Barbara Walters is "nosy"
* Other reporters

(end: 1:00:00)

Source: Verbatim transcripts

Appendix 4
Emerging discussion themes, by group, August 1, 1995

White group

Prompt: Now think back to the videotape that we've just viewed. How would you explain what we just saw, and why. Relax and take your time. You have up to one hour to discuss this amongst yourselves. I'll be around if you need me for anything.

* Stitching of gloves O. J. seen wearing in game photo
* Jury bias, incompetence
* Glove evidence
* Al Cowlings
* Bronco chase shows consciousness of guilt
* Defense team is "on the take"
* Justice and system
* Must be "very sleazy" to be acquitted
* O. J.'s money will probably lead to an acquittal
* Blacks on jury biased toward O. J.
* Opinion polls
* Jury too committed to their duty to let a guilty defendant go free
* There isn't enough evidence for the jury to convict
* Susan Smith case
* Criminal defendants have too many rights
* Number of prisons built in last twelve years
* Susan Smith wrongly accused a black man
* Race and opinion polls
* Bloody socks are suspect
* Conspiracy is improbable
* Strange to find bloody socks in the middle of the room
* Prosecution did a good job of cross-examining defense witnesses
* Theory for pattern of blood drops at Rockingham
* Blood trail
* Cuts on O. J.'s finger
* Kato Kaelin
* Al Cowlings
* Mafia
* Theory that O. J. watched the murders occur
* Chicago glass cuts were intentional to cover cuts obtained during murder

* Admissibility of lie detectors
* O. J.'s blood was everywhere
* Defense experts are not credible
* Defense case is not convincing thus far
* O. J. will be released by Thanksgiving
* Evidence of his guilt is "overwhelming"
* Wouldn't it have been easier for O. J. to shoot the victims if it was planned?
* Case is "mysterious"
* O. J. was enraged during the murders
* Crimes of passion
* Why would O. J. commit crimes in expense Bruno Magli shoes?
* Recital videotape
* If he was so jealous, why didn't O. J. kill Nicole after the oral sex episode?
* Defense is doing a "shitty" job
* Defense witnesses are being paid to lie
* Knifing of victims was professional
* O. J. was a knife collector, trained by frog-men to use them
* Killer knew the layout of Bundy and the dog
* Were the murders premeditated?
* Various theories of how the killings occurred
* Drug theory
* Theory that O. J. witnessed murders
* O. J.'s behavior on the evening of the murders
* Criminal behavior in other cases
* Movie about two boys suspected of murdering their parents
* Kardashian and O. J.'s luggage
* Group votes on whether O. J. did it

Prompt: I have some questions to ask you guys before you wrap this up and for you to just briefly discuss each one. What do you feel was the most important news reported in the video?

* Identification of stitching on gloves O. J. wears in game photo

Prompt: Okay, what was good about the video?

* The commentary was presented well, "objective"

Prompt: What was bad about the video?

* Too many commercials
* Speculation about Rosa Lopez
* Media try to fill air time

Prompt: How do you feel about the people shown in the video?

* Waller and DeBlanc did "good" job
* Media selectively reports information about case

Prompt: How'd you feel about the news reporters and commentators in the video?

* We already discussed how we felt

Prompt: How would you say your feelings about this case have changed since we met last time, and why?

* More convinced of O. J.'s guilt
* Defense failures, prosecutions successes

(end: 1:00:00)

Black group

Prompt: Okay, now think back to the video tape we just viewed. How would you explain what we just saw, and why? Relax, take your time. You have up to one hour to discuss this amongst yourselves. I'll be around if you need to ask for anything. So the floor is yours to discuss between yourselves.

* Stitching of gloves O. J. seen wearing in game photo
* Abundance of gloves similar to killer's gloves
* Possibility of printing gloves for identification
* Gloves handmade
* Nicole's purchasing of gloves
* Clark's claim that she can prove the bloody gloves belong to O. J.
* Gloves didn't fit in courtroom demonstration
* Case should have ended when gloves didn't fit
* Defense "going downhill"
* Leather gloves can't shrink
* Bloody socks planted by police
* Nurse who drew O. J.'s blood sample
* Missing blood from sample vial
* "Can't stand" DeBlanc
* Prosecution can't prove O. J. committed murders
* Bloody socks are suspicious
* Why/how did O. J., if he were murderer, get rid of everything but socks?
* O. J. is neat
* Police planted evidence in O. J.'s room
* Suspenders laying on O. J.'s bed
* Case against O. J. is a racist "set up"
* Conspiracy
* Theory of Fuhrman as "rogue cop"
* One informant walks through LAPD planting theory
* Blood in Rockingham foyer and driveway doesn't fit with planting theory
* Why wasn't blood in the Bronco seen earlier?
* Why target O. J. for a set up? He is not that powerful.
* Drug theory
* Ito biased against O. J.
* North Carolina judge's ruling about the Fuhrman tapes
* O. J. case is a diversion from other important issues affecting blacks in America
* O. J. is probably being framed
* Conspiracy
* Other prominent conspiracies

* AIDS and conspiracy
* "The plan" to "bring down" blacks
* Informant experiences with police
* Ito's decision regarding the admissibility of evidence
* The law as a tool of the oppressor
* Ito is biased in favor of the prosecution
* Defense is "going downhill"
* Defense has raised reasonable doubt
* The case will probably result in a hung jury
* Prosecutors in the Rodney King case
* Race and the jury
* Dismissal of jurors
* Juror domestic violence
* Defense witness performance
* Darden is a race traitor
* The salaries of deputy district attorneys
* Darden and Clark
* Most informants agree that O.J. didn't do it
* O.J. knows who committed murders
* Drug/mafia theory
* O.J.'s children
* Kato has benefitted from case
* Informants will be glad when trial is over
* Conspiracy
* Police protect "they own"
* Law protects rich whites
* Blacks are targeted by the system and need to unite

Prompt: Let me ask you this, what do you think was the most important news
        reported in the video we saw earlier? The most important news?

* Leaks in the police department
* The stitching on the gloves O.J. wore in the game photo
* News that the FBI assisted prosecution in the case

Prompt: What would you say was good about the video? What was good about
        it?

* Nothing was good about the screening video
* The screening video was biased and "one-sided"

Prompt: So, what would you say was bad about the video, I mean – along the
        same line. Did you see anything in particular that you can point to
        that was bad about the video?

* The screening video was "one-sided"
* Reporters were biased

Prompt: Okay. Now, how would you say your feelings about this case have
        changed since the last time we met? We met about four months ago.

* Some informants more convinced that O. J. is being framed
* Some of defense efforts are "backfiring"
* Attorneys in case are good at confusing witnesses
* Disputed witness testimony
* The recognizability of black speech patterns

(end: 1:00:00)

Source: Verbatim transcripts

Appendix 5
Transcript of *Primetime* text

INTRO:

ANNCR: March 29, 1995.

SAWYER: Tonight, a *Primetime* exclusive. A tape of Nicole Brown and O.J. Simpson recorded at her home on the night she made that 911 call. For the first time, O.J. Simpson and Nicole in their own voices telling what happened.

NICOLE: He gets a very animalistic look . . . all his veins pop out, his eyes are black . . . it's just black, cold . . . And when I see him it just scares me.

SAWYER: Two of the police who were there that night tell the story – a minute by minute account that sheds new light on the troubled relationship the state says led to murder.

WOMAN: And I told her, just by looking at him, that she needs to get away from him, that he was going to end up killing her one of these days.

STORY 2: Female inmates stripped and humiliated by all-male emergency response team.

STORY 3: The woman who risked her life to save Ann Frank.

ANNCR: From ABC News, with anchors Dianne Sawyer in New York, Sam Donaldson in Washington, Chief Correspondent Chris Wallace, Judd Rose, Sylvia Chase, John Kionous and Renee Poussaint, this is *Primetime*.

SAWYER: Good evening. Tonight we present a tape never heard before. It's an extraordinary document, one that will take you inside Nicole Brown's home and inside her domestic dispute with O.J. Simpson on the night she called for help. In the aftermath of the troubled night the estranged couple each tells a separate story as a frightened woman lets down her guard to the policeman who answered her call.

(music)

OPERATOR: 911 emergency.

NICOLE: Can you send someone over here now, to 325 Gretna Green – he's back.

SAWYER: We have heard it over and over.

NICOLE: He's O.J. Simpson, I think you know his record.

SAWYER: As we now know, it was 10:05 pm, October 25, 1993 when police arrived. One of the first, officer Robert Lerner.

DARDEN: Could you describe for us the, ah, Nicole Brown's demeanor.

LERNER: Well, she was, ah, she was visibly shaken. She was upset. Ah, she was concerned. And, ah, she was scared.

294

SAWYER: But as Lerner mentioned in court, there was another officer there that night.

LERNER: There was a sergeant named Craig Lally, yes.

LALLY: I double parked my police car and . . .

SAWYER: This is that sergeant, Craig Lally, who has not spoken publicly until now. Earlier this week we took him back to 325 Gretna Green, back to the guest house where Kato Kaelin lived and O.J. Simpson was standing, being questioned by police – the place where, as sergeant Lally joined his colleagues, he decided to do something more.

LALLY: Ah, basically what happened was when I, ah, came to this location I activated my tape recorder and Mr. Simpson was standing here with officers, ah, Spencer Marx and, ah, Rob Lerner. And I believe Kato Kaelin was, ah, in this area. I don't know if he was seated on the couch or bed. And then we had –

SAWYER: And you start your tape recorder?

LALLY: Right. Right when we walked in here. Then we had a –

SAWYER: Sergeant Lally had a tape recorder hidden in his pocket. The taping was legal and he says not too uncommon for police, though he says his fellow officers didn't know.

COCHRAN: And while you were there, did you see him with a tape recorder, taping statements from Nicole Brown Simpson and O.J. Simpson regarding the events that had taken place that evening?

OFFICER: No.

SAWYER: And again, to make clear, they had no idea you were taping.

LALLY: No, nobody knew.

SAWYER: And sergeant Lally tells us this is why he has decided to play the tape now. It proves that police officers did their job professionally, though he says the Dream Team doesn't want people to believe it.

LALLY: . . . because we're all a bunch of liars anyway, from what all the defense team says. And, ah, nobody'd believe me. Nobody would believe us . . . but it's on tape. You can't argue with the tape.

SAWYER: With this, the tape begins, starting as sergeant Lally walks up to O.J. Simpson.

LALLY: Sergeant Lally. How are you? What's going on tonight?

SIMPSON: Just having a little fight with my, ah, argument with, ah, my ex-wife and current girlfriend.

LALLY: What happened tonight, what, what started the fight?

SIMPSON: A ex-boyfriend of hers.

LALLY: Uh huh.

SIMPSON: And, ah . . . neither one of us been drinking or anything –

LALLY: Uh huh.

SIMPSON: We started an argument and she just flies off, then I fly off . . .

LALLY: Uh huh.

SIMPSON: We got into an argument.

SAWYER: Simpson had apparently flown into a rage after finding a photograph of Keith Zlomsowitch, a restaurant manager Nicole had briefly dated.

SIMPSON: This guy said all of this horrible stuff about me . . . this guy had said all of this horrible stuff about me.

SAWYER: Simpson said he and Nicole had a deal, to clean out all of those pictures of others they used to date.

SIMPSON: She said, "Why you ...." I said, "I ain't trying to control you! You wanted us to get back together! I'm just saying, this is . . . I just got . . . I don't want this guy in our life!"

SAWYER: Were you unnerved that it was O. J. Simpson?

LALLY: No, not at all. No, ah, I knew about his prior, ah, incident, ah, when he, ah, beat up his wife and, ah –

SAWYER: So you're saying this wasn't a complete shock to you . . . it wasn't as if you –

LALLY: As a matter of fact, after finding out it was O. J. Simpson you gotta think, well god, you better make the right call on this one (chuckle), whatever it is.

SAWYER: Do it right.

LALLY: Yeah, better do it right.

SAWYER: So, Lally left Kato Kaelin's bungalow.

LALLY: I exited and, ah, went back into the house to talk to the, ah, Nicole.

SAWYER: Who was there in the kitchen.

LALLY: Right, who was seated in the kitchen with Cheryl Kent and Tom O'Grady.

SAWYER: This is that officer, Cheryl Kent, who had arrived before Lally and says she stayed with Nicole Brown as the other officers calmed Simpson down.

KENT: Well, I thought that I should have a talk with Nicole because . . . just the look in his face, I knew she was in danger. And I tried to, um, talk her into arresting him that night. But she wanted to think about it. She didn't want to really deal with it I don't think. I think she was too afraid it would get worse if she sent him to jail.

SAWYER: In a tired voice, Nicole Brown, wearing a tee-shirt, gym shorts and barefoot, told police how she dealt with Simpson and how she felt about it.

NICOLE: (garbled) for the sake of my children . . . and because I've always loved him . . . I'm not really sure why.

OFFICER: Are you afraid – You're not scared – physical. Are you?

NICOLE: Yes.

SAWYER: She said the argument had escalated after angry calls from Simpson about that photo of a former boyfriend, which she said she'd forgotten to throw out.

NICOLE: I said I'm sorry if I've missed something, that I did my best and I think we should talk about it tomorrow – was just going to turn into a big argument.

KENT: She took the phone off the hook. (pause) That just made him mad. He came storming down in his car. Parked it in the middle of the street and proceeded to pound on the front door and then go around to the back door. And that's when he kicked the back door in.

OFFICER: You did a hell of a job on that door, I got to tell ya.

SIMPSON: That door was already broke, you know. The bottom part was already broke.

OFFICER: Have you got any objection to paying for the repair.

SIMPSON: I don't object to paying, but I can't believe that she can't tell them that this door was already broke! And the door – my kids broke the door!

SAWYER: The split is still there.

OFFICER: Yeah, the split, the whole thing's still split. Apparently this is the same door.

SAWYER: So when they're talking about the bottom part being broken already, they're really talking about this sill?

OFFICER: That's what the kids broke. Yeah.

SAWYER: Just this part.

OFFICER: That's what Nicole told me. Yeah, just that little bottom part. And, ah, but this thing was split all the way up this side.

SAWYER: Because the door was locked –

OFFICER: Right. And what he did was, when he, when he kicked it in the bolt was, ah, I believe, ah, well . . . the thing was, I obviously saw it was broken.

SAWYER: But the door was standing, but just splintered in here.

OFFICER: Right, exactly. He blamed the kids for breaking the door. That thing was split all the way up the top. And, ah, I think he had a problem with, ah, admitting mistakes.

SAWYER: Back in the kitchen, Nicole Brown said Simpson had been frightening.

NICOLE: I mean, I don't know, but I get scared when he gets like that.

OFFICER: He didn't harm you physically.

NICOLE: No, he didn't.

SAWYER: She said she hadn't seen that old boyfriend in a year. But the problem was, she said, Simpson wouldn't accept reality.

NICOLE: Sometimes we have good communications, but we didn't for fifteen years – it always was like this. And lately we've been able to talk and try to get past some of this stuff and be a little bit more grown up about it . . . and then, for a few weeks he gets like this – he gets pretty irate. And he can't drop – I mean we've talked about these things. He can't seem to let 'em go.

SAWYER: Officer Lerner then gives her some advice.

LERNER: Would you consider going with him to counseling?

NICOLE: I don't know if it's worth it at this –

LERNER: It's not – a sure thing he's going to hit you again. But you can judge kind of your future on incidents on what's happened in the past, that's true. You know, if he's hit you once, there's nothing really from stopping him from hitting you again. There is a – violence syndrome which does happen where it just escalates. It goes around in circles, you know. And after the incident, the guy's just got a lot of remorse, you know, and begs – and then after a while just takes advantage – it's a circle. All of this can be explained by a counselor.

SAWYER: Officer Kent says earlier she had been far more direct.

KENT: Well, I told, um, Nicole about these domestic violence situations – that they usually escalate to where somebody really gets hurt or even killed. And I told her just by looking at him that she really needs to get away from him because he was going to end up killing her one of these days.

SAWYER: Again, officer Lerner.

LERNER: You know, we can't tell you what to do –

NICOLE: I'm not saying that I'll make it – or I can't. I just got frightened tonight when he –

SAWYER: Is it important for the defense, though, sections of this tape. For instance, when she says, he hadn't hit her that night, right?

OFFICER: That's correct, he didn't.

SAWYER: What did you as a veteran of a number of these calls over the years think is the most important thing on that tape?

OFFICER: First of all, if you listen to the tape, um, ah, she, Nicole Brown describes this, ah, other side of Mr. Simpson – this rage that he gets into on occasion.

NICOLE: He gets a very animalistic look in him. All his veins pop out, his eyes are black, just black, cold, like an animal. I mean, very, very weird. And at the end it just scared me.

OFFICER: At some point, ah, she said, "Well, I, I'm not afraid of him hitting me again because he hasn't hit me in the last four years. Ah, he had to do a lot of community service.

NICOLE: . . . he had to do a lot of community service and stuff like that for it. I just always believed that if it happened one more time that – I don't totally think I believe it would happen, but I was just scared. I think if it happened once more it would be the last time.

OFFICER: I thought that was very prophetic when she said that to me.

SAWYER: And so, sergeant Craig Lally returned outside to O. J. Simpson, who was speaking with officer Lerner.

LERNER: There has been no physical blows thrown, which is good.

SIMPSON: It wasn't even close to that!

SAWYER: But again, Simpson said, it had been her fault.

SIMPSON: Like I said, "I'm back here at your insistence! You're the one that – ! You're the one that – !

OFFICER: A woman who's scared of a man – that's a big thing in their mind, 'cause women value their face, their nails – they know you can inflict some damage – It's not whether you won or not.

SIMPSON: – before we split that she beat on me so many times that all I did was cover my groins and my face and let her beat on me –

OFFICER: . . . but if you're a woman, she'll always be scared of – whether you were or not is irrelevant!

SAWYER: At this point, O. J. Simpson agreed to pay for the door and was escorted away from the premises.

SAWYER: Was it unusual that you didn't book him, for this kind of incident?

OFFICER: Naw, basically on this incident, all you had was a trespass and a vandalism. And, umm, in order to arrest him for that, you have to have a citizen's arrest . . . make the arrest and she chose not to do that. All she wanted was the door fixed.

KENT: One thing that Nicole did discuss with me is that he was having some personal problems then . . . some of his businesses were going bad and he wasn't the big football star . . . he wasn't getting a lot of attention like he used to and all of that, um, was really affecting his ego at the time. And so, she didn't want to push it and make it worse for him. And that's why she didn't really want to arrest him that night.

NICOLE: (inaudible)

OFFICER: Well, let's put it this way, I've been doing this for thirteen years and you're not the first one to go through this and you're not the last, and, ah, just luckily it hasn't come to blows or anything, so –

SAWYER: Lally continues.

LALLY: Yeah, I've already warned him, so, – If I have to come back he's going to go to jail. I think he knows that.

NICOLE: It's funny, you know (pause) You know, you get into these hot fights . . . why don't we say, just talk about it tomorrow and – sleep on it. I've done that for the last (sighs) several fights.

LALLY: Ummhmm.

NICOLE: It just doesn't work.

LALLY: Umhmm. Sometimes you guys just got to draw the line and say, "Hey, this ain't never gonna work." Call and put an end to it. But the problem is, I know, when you get kids involved in this it makes it a lot tougher. Usually, without kids, it's real easy to break off.

NICOLE: Right, I'm sure.

LALLY: Because, you can say, "Hey, I don't want to see you anymore, good-bye, hey, I'm gone. Then when you got kids involved it's real tough. I know it.

SAWYER: Sergeant Lally gave Nicole Brown his last advice.

LALLY: Sometimes you got to draw the sand in the line, ah, the line in the sand and just say, "Hey, I can't do it." Because, ah –

NICOLE: I do say it often. I say it to myself often.

LALLY: Ummhmm.

NICOLE: It doesn't work. It's just – It's beyond arguing. It's just, it's just so dirty.

LALLY: Well see, now, now, that's the point. It's always going to be like that.

NICOLE: I know.

SAWYER: She seemed so tired, so deeply weary.

LALLY: Well, you know what's really so strange about this whole thing? You know, the stuff that she was telling me, it wasn't to get him in trouble. For whatever reason, some point in time, she decided to let it out and, ah, we were there.

SAWYER: Finally, it was time for sergeant Lally to go. His last memory was of Nicole Brown in her kitchen, apologizing for the trouble she had caused the police.

SAWYER: Both sides in the Simpson murder case have copies of this tape. But so far neither side has said whether it intends to use it at the trial. Sergeant Lally and officer Kent are not on the witness list. In court today, we got a glimpse of tomorrow.

DARDEN: Ah, we hope to present, ah, more evidence tomorrow relevant to what happened to the bag in which the bloody clothes were carried in. And tonight I hope to present discovery to the defense on that issue as soon as it comes into our possession. At any event, we shouldn't be trying to trick witnesses.

ITO: Alright, I noted the objection. I sustained the objection. Unless I hear a better foundation, ah, I've indicated . . .

COCHRAN: You ruled, and as usual they're trying to give a sound bite for what might be, what he hopes is going to happen. Their whole case is based upon hopes and dreams. And they're, and they're evaporating.

DARDEN: Nobody calls us the Dream Team, Mr. Cochran.

SAWYER: He did get his sound bite, I guess. Also, tomorrow, Robert Kardashian is expected to take the stand. He is part of the defense team and a long-time friend of O. J. Simpson. And on Friday, Barbara Walters will have an interview with Brian "Kato" Kaelin on *20/20*.

(music)

ANNCR: Still to come, the story of Ann Frank, the final chapter in an unfinished diary. And, shocking scenes from behind the walls of a women's prison . . . Primetime. Brought to you by the all-new Ford Windstar.

(commercials)

Appendix 6
Transcript of KTLA text

August 1, 1995

MUSIC (Simpson trial theme)

CLARK: There are many reasons why those glove photographs will come in in rebuttal. We believe, ah, regardless of whether or not they come in during the defense case. This was simply one chance to put them in during the defense case. There may be others. But if they are not, on rebuttal, to refute the conspiracy theme, and to refute the planting theme, that the defense has throughout carried in this case, I –

ITO: So I take it the bottom line is, Miss Clark, you stand by your statements on the record from yesterday.

CLARK: Yes, your honor.

MUSIC (rises)

COCHRAN: We vigorously dispute that. They will never be able to prove that these gloves, that our client wore those gloves. And you'll see.

MUSIC (rises, then fades out).

WALLER: Good afternoon, I'm Marta Waller along with KTLA legal analyst Al DeBlanc. You're watching channel 5's continuing coverage of the O.J. Simpson murder trial. Court is expected to begin shortly. Here now, the latest developments. The director of the LAPD crime lab took the witness stand this morning. The jury was not present. Peter Nufeld questioned Michelle Kestler about reported leaks of DNA tests to the news media. Kestler denied that she or anyone working for her leaked DNA results. Following Kestler on the stand, the jury came back into the court and heard from blood expert Herbert McDonnell. (pause). And let's check in right now with Ron Olson. He's downtown at the courthouse. Good afternoon, Ron.

OLSEN: Good afternoon, Marta. Well, we just found out that, ah, court will be going back on the record in about, ah, about thirty minutes, about 1:30. What we're going to be hearing this afternoon, we think, will be a videotape of male nurse, Thano Peratis – the nurse that drew the blood from O.J. Simpson's arm. Of course, the defense charging that there is blood missing. They want the jury to see that videotape. Also, author Joe Bosco – he is being called to the stand because of an article in *Penthouse* magazine. I have a copy of it, ah, and the defense wants to know who Joe Bosco's source was or continues to be. Here is what Joe Bosco wrote in

Penthouse over the summer – over last summer, that is: "Within two hours of Judge Ito admonishing the police for reckless disregard of the truth, the LAPD's worst moment to that date, a certain police officer, whose leaks had hitherto been mostly accurate and offered with corroboration, started calling journalists with the story that blood on the socks found in O. J. Simpson's bedroom was a DNA match for Nicole's. This time, however, the officer offered no corroboration and became angry and defensive when asked. A number of journalists turned him down. Apparently KNBC did not. And the rest is ugly history for both the press and the LAPD." That's what Joe Bosco wrote in Penthouse magazine. The defense wants to call Bosco to the stand and say, "Who is that officer you referred to in the *Penthouse* article?" Of course Tracy Savage, already on the stand, has invoked the state's shield law, refusing to reveal her source. And we could have, we might have, a written ruling on what Judge Ito's going to do about Tracy Savage. Ah, possibly by the end of the day today, ah, maybe, maybe not. We'll have to wait and see on that one, but we can expect Joe Bosco, ah, coming into the courtroom with his attorneys this afternoon. That's what we have for you at this point Marta. Back to you.

WALLER: Okay now, Ron, that was originally scheduled to take place at the conclusion of the court day. And I know this is a slightly earlier day because of a juror appointment, but, ah, this is still scheduled for after whatever testimony takes place.

OLSEN: Yeah, yeah –

WALLER: – Thano Peratis' videotape that the jury is going to hear.

OLSEN: Correct. And they're saying now, they were saying that, ah, Judge Ito said he was going to wrap up the court's day at four o'clock. That's been, ah, pushed back, ah, pushed up, rather, to three forty-five. So, ah, I think they are clearly running out of things with which to fill the court's day, ah, we're getting to the end of the witness list for the defense and, ah, I think they're running out of things to do at this point. And we're going to see the Peratis tape and then, so far as I know, after that it's going to be Joe Bosco, ah, and possibly we may revisit the Tracy Savage situation depending upon, you know – Judge Ito said earlier that, ah, this was a very serious matter and that he wanted to give it some serious consideration. Ah, that's why he didn't deal with it . . . yesterday. He wanted to think about it. I don't know if he's had enough time to think about it or not. We'll have to wait and see.

WALLER: Okay, thanks a lot, Ron. We'll check back with you in just a little while. We're going to take a short time out and we'll be back in just a moment.

COMMERCIALS

WALLER: Hi, I'm Marta Waller, joined this evening by KTLA legal analyst and defense attorney Al DeBlanc. One of the things that, ah, Ron was telling us is that Thano Peratis, who – that there's videotape testimony or preliminary hearing testimony and I believe grand jury testimony as well. There isn't anything that can be done except play this for the jury.

DEBLANC: Right.

WALLER: They can't argue about it.

DEBLANC: Well all they can do is argue about what they see. I mean, it's a matter of interpretation and what's depicted in the video. And to the extent that it comes in by grand jury that's one sided – that's prosecution examination of the witness only. Defense lawyers are not in the grand jury proceedings. But certainly the issue, the focal point that the defense is after for this jury is that, ah, there's blood missing and that turns on, ah, how exact was Mr. Peratis when he withdrew the blood. I mean, how good was his measurement. How accurate was he. And then there's the subsequent question of whether or not as some have testified – when you pop the cap you lose blood every time you deal with it. It is something though that, ah, that the defense has consistently argued and that is that there is some blood missing. And certainly to have blood planted they have to get it somewhere. And the suggestion is that they got it from the vial, the vial that Mr. Peratis, ah, with the blood drawn from O. J. Simpson.

WALLER: It's going to be very brief, it's, ah, ten minutes, I think – maximum.

DEBLANC: Yes, and again this is something again that they can argue – to the jury. And ah, and ah, you have to watch out with a jury when you have too many areas that have some, some substance in the criticism by the defense. Ah, that can pose, ah, that can pose a problem because some people will put up with two or three items. But there is a cumulative impact with too many questions unanswered. So the defense, the defense at this point is, I think, looking for that. We know there is a difference based on what we've heard, ah, in the blood, from the blood in the vial and the amount of blood that subsequently was accounted for . There is a missing portion. Whether or not you believe testimony about it depends.

WALLER: Okay now, let's go, let's just sort of take ourselves into the courtroom and there's, there's the testimony of Thano Peratis being presented. What can the attorneys argue? Now can the prosecution then say to the jury. I mean, can they address the jury? Can the defense attorneys, ah, then address the jury about the contents?

DEBLANC: No, it's simply played.

WALLER: It's just played.

DEBLANC: Right.

WALLER: And that's it.

DEBLANC: Right. Comment on it and what it means, ah, ah, its materiality and relevance in the case. Ah, the, the weakness that it has – or whoever wants to argue that – is something that is done in closing argument.

WALLER: So that's it.

DEBLANC: That's it.

WALLER: They'll just look at it. Then it, that'll, that'll be the same thing if the defense suddenly decided they wanted to use the Rosa Lopez tape. Would then –

DEBLANC: Rosa Lopez –

WALLER: Would that be the same thing?

DEBLANC: No. Rosa Lopez is a little different. That's a conditional examination, which means they have to show due diligence in trying to keep up with her before they could introduce it as prior testimony recorded. Those fancy legal terms mean they have to keep track of their witness.

WALLER: So let's say they couldn't find her and they had to use the tape – that's all there was. They couldn't find. They had to use the tape. Then it would be the same. They would just say, "Here it is."

DEBLANC: Right. You get to see it. But it is a little different because there is a lot of examination – that was a conditional exam. There was direct examination and cross examination of Rosa Lopez. I forgot how many days she was on the witness stand.

WALLER: Long time.

DEBLANC: It was some period of time.

WALLER: Long, long time.

DEBLANC: We would have to sit –

WALLER: And watch it again –

DEBLANC: And watch the movies with the jury – that's right –

WALLER: And watch it again. And I would imagine that you lose a little bit of the impact of testimony if it's not a real person – sitting, I mean, let me rephrase that. That was not particularly a good way of phrasing it. You're watching a videotape. You're not watching the actual person on the witness stand.

DEBLANC: It does not have the, it doesn't have the same impact for the jury. And certainly the jury would, would, would wonder why this witness isn't testifying in front of them. And why, and if there's any, and if the witness becomes aware that this person left the country, ah, they're going to want to know why this person left the country. How come this person couldn't be made available live. And I think that might have some impact on the credibility of Rosa Lopez.

WALLER: Which might be why we're not going to see her videotape testimony or any other testimony at least right now.

DEBLANC: Right. Well, there's also the problem, ah, that was created for the defense by Chris Darden's examination of Rosa Lopez. He was very effective in examining her and, ah, to some extent created major problem, ah, for the defense. In addition, the defense is gonna, would be faced with, with, ah, the inconsistency between Rosa Lopez and the neighbor of, of O. J. Simpson who came by and basically refuted what she had to say about the Bronco.

WALLER: What are the realistic chances that they defense could get her back, or that they want to get her back?

DEBLANC: Well, ah . . . she seemed to be strong-willed when she left. I think they'd have a real hard time getting her back. Ah, she'd probably, she's comfortable where she is. As I recall, the lady, when she testified, ah, she didn't, she appeared to not really want to be involved in it. And she was adamant about leaving. And, ah, I suspect that, ah, that ah, unless there's some change in circumstance, that, ah, she would be unwilling to come back and they would be unable to bring her back.

WALLER: Not a totally, not a totally unreasonable response to not want to be a witness in this trial.

DEBLANC: For her, I mean, we could see it then when she testified in the conditional examination – that she did not want to do it.

WALLER: It's been grueling for every witness – even those who have had really no, no stake in this. We're going to take another short time out. We're be back in just a moment.

COMMERCIALS
(DeVry Institute)
(Western Dental Plan)
(Combat Superbait Insecticide)
(Norm's Restaurants)
(Foothill Nissan)
(Liquid Plumber)
(The Injury Helpline)
(AT & T)

WALLER: And let's check in again with Ron Olsen down at the courthouse. Hi, Ron.

OLSEN: Hello, Marta. Well, ah, everybody down here is kind of putting two and two together on what Marcia Clark's evidence – she says she has evidence, she says she can prove that the, ah, gloves O.J. Simpson is seen wearing – while, ah, working as a sportscaster, and there's a shot right there. Now, Marcia Clark says she can prove the glove you see on his hand here is one of the gloves that showed up either at Bundy or Rockingham. She says the gloves O.J. was wearing as a sportscaster and the bloody gloves are the same and she can prove it. Now, as to what her proof might be. A couple of, ah, hints this morning when Marcia Clark, ah, had an exchange in the courtroom with Johnnie Cochran. And, ah, Judge Ito said, "Well, Ms. Clark, you said earlier that it would be about the stitching." And so we, ah, we've got that much – that apparently it's going to deal with the stitching on the gloves. Judge Ito also mentioned that he had just received reports from the FBI. Now, ah, the two and two that everybody here is putting together is this – that the reports from the FBI are probably an analysis of the gloves, of the photos. And there, ah, there you have it, Marta.

WALLER: Pretty interesting. Ah, you know, Ron, I was just sitting here while you were saying that now and I was kind of looking back and forth. I wonder, it has to, it almost has to go beyond the stitching. They're, she's almost going to have to show some little characteristic or flaw or something because we know there was more than one pair of gloves made with that stitching.

OLSEN: Yeah, we were talking about that. A couple of us. And these, ah, these, ah, these gloves, ah, apparently, I think I recall that they're hand sewn. They're handmade gloves and we were wondering if the, ah, if the way the gloves are stitched, if they're aren't certain possible irregularities in the stitching and that a photographic analysis turned up those irregularities. And if the irregularities on the murder gloves are the same as – well, you can see where that's going. If, if, if, if, if, if it's a match, it's a match.

WALLER: Let's have Al address this one.

OLSEN: Yeah.

DEBLANC: Well, Marta, they're leather gloves. In addition, in addition to the stitching, by being, by virtue of the fact that they're leather, they're one time part of the skin of an animal. So they have pores. And they probably have marks and certain features that make them, that, that make these gloves similar or dissimilar. And it's just like fingerprints. A fingerprint expert will come in and testify that there are ten points of dissimilarity or similarity and, ah, make a match in terms of what's the probability of a repeat of that. So, they can blow up the gloves sufficient where they can actually see the pores, the marks, the lines, the scratches that are unique to these gloves, and then find the sufficient number to say there couldn't possibly be a repeat – that this is in fact the exact same glove, then, yes, they could do it. And a matter of fact, they could print gloves because it has a fabric pattern. It has a skin pattern. If you, if you can get it fine enough, if you have a good enough exemplar and you, you have an item of evidence you print, and you can match them up. Yes.

WALLER: You know – Ron, are you still there?

OLSEN: Yes, I am.

WALLER: One of the observations, that I've, that I've gotten from many, many viewers – and I don't know if you've discussed this down there or not – were about the inside of the gloves. Was there ever any kind of testing done on the inside of the gloves. Have you heard anything about that?

OLSEN: No, not, not, not, not with regard to testing, ah, we saw, we saw the glove expert, whose name escapes me right now. We saw the glove expert, ah, ah, prove, prove that the gloves were mated, ah, based on the numbers inside the gloves. But that's, that's about, ah, no I haven't heard anything about testing done on anything inside the gloves.

DEBLANC: And then, you know, the whole issue – the, the question of testing to determine whether or not this gloves matches in the photo the one they found at the crime scene is because the prosecution is uncomfortable about whether or not that glove fit. Because that's the kind of thing they're trying to assert – that's one thing. And certainly if it is a distinctive match, ah, then there's a much bigger problem for O.J. Simpson, because then they would have to have some kind of, the defense would have to have a theory that someone stole or used his gloves.

WALLER: Took them.

DEBLANC: Right, or that they, that he gave them to them. Because there is a question that, well, maybe Nicole gave someone else a pair of gloves.

WALLER: And that has been brought up.

DEBLANC: Right.

WALLER: That's a point that many people have brought up.

DEBLANC: Well –

WALLER: Perhaps, she brought more than one pair, for more than one person.

DEBLANC: Right, right. Well, if O.J.'s wearing the gloves, then these are gloves that she gave him.

OLSEN: Al, what, if, ah, hypothetically if this is what they have, and it appears to be so, ah, there was a LA Times report, ah, I read this morning, ah, which indicated that, ah, the prosecution, ah, was going to try and bring their glove expert back if there's any way they could work that up. And then Marcia Clark said this morning that, ah, this is going to come back. If nothing else, it's going to come back on rebuttal. Ah, what would Johnnie

Cochran's, ah, how would he defend this? I mean, if, if they have analyzed, if the FBI has an analysis of the photographs and they say the gloves Simpson had on (snicker) at the, at the, at the football game are the same gloves that were found at the, ah, Bundy and Rockingham scenes, um . . . And again, we don't know this to be the case, but it, there is some evidence pointing that way now. What, how would Cochran defend against that?

DEBLANC: Well, the same old way he's defended all the other expert evidence. Ah, you get an, you get your own expert. If you have evidence that, ah, the other side is, ah, using someone who has unique experience and knowledge and you get your own person. You'd, you'd have an expert say, "Well, that person's wrong." That the points of similarity or dissimilarity or the matches in the, in the skin that they, they have testified to aren't really there. I mean, you've seen it in this case . . . how, no matter how strong, ah, an expert is, ah, on his or her opinion, there's an expert for the other side to come along and say, "Well, there's a problem with it." So, again, it's the battle of the experts. But then Johnnie would also, ah, ah, ah, well, Marcia Clark would have to get over the hurdle of the judge allowing her to, ah, bring this in. I'm not sure that it is within the scope of rebuttal. If it isn't, he would have to allow her to reopen to a limited, limited extent her, ah, case in chief. And, ah –

OLSEN: Well, the LA Times articles, ah, said that sources close to the prosecution told the LA Times that, ah, they were thinking about asking the judge, ah, for a reopener, Al.

DEBLANC: Okay, well, ah, ah, a lot of judges will allow the prosecution to do that because they have the burden of proof. Ah, and, but some may not. And Judge Ito's pretty strict. He's more of a strict judge then many of the other's I've seen and he's (snicker) likely to not allow it, ah, to open up because it could, could substantially increase the trial time again. It's already been covered quite a bit. So –

OLSEN: It might not get in.

DEBLANC: It might not get in.

OLSEN: Okay, well, ah, we continue waiting here for the, ah, court to go back in session. It should happen very shortly, Marta. We're looking for videotape of male nurse Thano Peratis and, of course, the issue of the shield law and author Joe Bosco. All coming up this afternoon. Back to you.

WALLER: Okay, thank you, Ron. We'll check back with you again in just a little bit. We're going to take a short time out and we'll be right back.

Appendix 7
Logistic regression of perceptions about Simpson's innocence or guilt on race, gender, education, family income, interviewer race, and perceptions of criminal justice system bias

(N = 485; chi2(14) = 72.30**)

Guilt	Odds ratio	Robust standard error	Z
Race			
Black	.21**	.08	−4.16
Other	.60	.25	−1.21
Gender			
Women	1.15	.28	0.59
Education			
High school dropout	.30*	.15	−2.47
High school graduate	.50*	.17	−2.04
Some college	.52	.18	−2.04
Family income			
< $15k	.30*	.16	−2.23
$15k to $30k	.42	.22	−1.69
$30k+ to $50k	.41	.21	−1.77
$50k+ to $75k	.72	.42	−0.56
Interviewer race			
Black	.60	.17	−1.82
Other	.76	.29	−0.74
Justice system			
Biased against blacks	.34**	.09	−4.08
Biased in favor of blacks	1.21	.64	0.35

* significant beyond .05 level
** significant beyond .01 level

Notes

INTRODUCTION

1. *Los Angeles Times*, December 3, 1996, p. A1.
2. Says Quine (1992, p. 102): "What the empirical under-determination of global science shows is that there are various defensible ways of conceiving the world."
3. Judge Lance Ito's instructions to the criminal trial jury, September 22, 1995.
4. CBS/*New York Times* Poll, July 11–12, 1994. Population: Adults 18 and over in the United States with telephones. N = 1306, margin of error +/– 5 percentage points.
5. The survey item was worded as follows: "From what you've heard so far, do you think O.J. Simpson is probably guilty of the crimes he has been charged with, is probably not guilty, or don't know enough about it yet to say?"
6. The survey item was worded as follows: "How much sympathy do you have for O.J. Simpson because of everything that has happened – a great deal, some, not much or none at all?"
7. The survey item was worded as follows: "In general, do you think the criminal justice system in the United States is biased in favor of blacks, or is it biased against blacks, or does it generally give blacks fair treatment?"
8. Note, however, that "other-raced" groups were slightly more likely than whites to believe the system was biased *in favor of* blacks.
9. That is, an implicit agreement was struck between white elites and white workers guaranteeing that, no matter how bad circumstances became, the latter would not fall below the level of nonwhite workers. For elites, this agreement meant increased economic stability and labor force control; for white workers, it amounted to psychic compensation.
10. Throughout this book I use racial labels like "black" and "white" to refer to subjects who have been *raced* in particular ways by social representations, not to subjects who are of some objectively definable "race."
11. Following Geertz (1983, p. 30), I understand "ritual" as the enactment of status quo images of reality that social actors are "caught up bodily in"; these performances shape experiences and generally work to reproduce the status quo. But in some instances, as Moore and Myerhoff (1977) note, rituals may also provide openings for counter-hegemonic change. In chapter 1, I discuss in detail the role ritual played in the Simpson case.

12. This is what Omi and Winant (1994) refer to as the "doublebind" of race. That is, in order to fight racism through social policy, we must first notice and risk reifying race.

1. O.J. AND RITUAL

1. *Los Angeles Sentinel*, October 5, 1995, p. A6.
2. Op-editorial by author Neal Gabler, *Los Angeles Times*, October 8, 1995, p. M1.
3. *Los Angeles Times*, September 19, 1996, p. B1.
4. See *Washington Post*, February 6, 1997, p. A1. WGN-TV in Chicago, for example, garnered the highest audience share in the city by preempting the President's address while other stations aired it.
5. The jury was composed of nine whites, one Asian, one Latina, and a male who described himself as half-Asian and half-black.
6. The standard of proof in the civil trial was much lower than that required in the criminal trial. In the civil trial, only a "preponderance of the evidence" was required to prove "liability." In the criminal trial, guilt "beyond a reasonable doubt" was the legal standard.
7. Personal observations, criminal courts building, Los Angeles, October 3, 1995.
8. *Time*, February 17, 1997, p. 36.
9. Herrnstein and Murray's (1994) bestseller, *The Bell Curve*, used IQ and other standardized test scores to argue that blacks are innately less intelligent than whites and thus not worthy of social programs designed to ameliorate racial inequality.
10. *Los Angeles Sentinel*, February 27, 1997, p. A3.
11. *Los Angeles Times*, February 5, 1997, p. B8.
12. *Los Angeles Times*, January, 25, 1995, p. A13.
13. Wallace (1994) reviews several conspiracy theories that have flourished over the years due to seeming contradictions in the evidence that eventually convicted Hauptmann. One such theory, for example, suggests that the infant was never kidnapped, that Hauptmann was framed in order to cover up for a death caused either accidentally or intentionally by a Lindberg household staffer or family member.
14. *New York Times* Index, 1932–1936.
15. For example, an analysis of the *New York Times* Index reveals that the newspaper devoted considerable space to the case between 1954 and 1956, and again in 1966.
16. *Los Angeles Times*, August 10, 1969, p. A1.
17. For example, see *Los Angeles Times*, August 10, 1969 through August 17, 1969.
18. The US Supreme Court had ruled in 1981 that cameras in the courtroom did not preclude the possibility of a fair trial, ending a forty-year absence of cameras (Kane 1994).
19. For example, in his bestseller, *Murder in Brentwood* (1997), Mark Fuhrman was critical of his colleagues' interrogation of Simpson: "They should have interrogated Simpson until they got a confession, conflicting statements, or

at least one clear time-line for his movements on the night of the murder. They got none of these, precisely because they rushed through the interview. Both detectives clearly appeared uncomfortable interrogating the popular celebrity" (pp. 61–2). Marcia Clark (1997) was more blunt in her trial memoir, *Without a Doubt*: "That interview was one of the worst bits of police work I'd ever seen – but I kept my thoughts to myself. I couldn't afford to alienate my chief investigators" (p. 74). However, in *Evidence Dismissed: The Inside Story of the Police Investigation of O. J. Simpson* (1997), detectives Vannatter and Lange defend their interrogation of Simpson. They blame Fuhrman for striking a "major blow" against the prosecution's efforts: "After actually hearing all of the [Fuhrman] tapes now, Lange and Vannatter know for sure that Fuhrman is a confirmed racist who has lied in court, impeached a portion of his testimony, and struck a major blow against the prosecution's case" (p. 277).

20. In *A Problem of Evidence: How the Prosecution Freed O. J. Simpson* (1996), for example, Joseph Bosco argues that the prosecution's rigid adherence to a single-murderer theory of the case ultimately worked to set Simpson free: "If you [to police/prosecutors] want justice, and you believe O.J. Simpson got away with murder, then investigate and prosecute whoever helped him. If you know this case, you know that, realistically, *if* O.J. Simpson is the killer he had help. Period. Somebody, somewhere knows about missing bloody clothes and a murder weapon. Somebody is a loathsome human being. Somebody *else* is guilty of some kind of murder" (p. 262; emphasis original).

21. This is what prosecutor Christopher Darden had to say about the jury in his trial memoir, *In Contempt*: "I'd known from the beginning, from the moment I walked into that courtroom a year earlier and saw that jury. I could see in their eyes the need to settle some score. And I was the only prosecutor who knew what the score was" (p. 3).

22. Dunne presents his analysis of the case, including these words about the jury, through a fictionalized character named Gus Bailey.

23. In his trial memoir, *The Search For Justice*, Simpson defense attorney Robert L. Shapiro (1996) implies that Fuhrman may have indeed planted the Rockingham glove: "The sudden prominence of Mark Fuhrman in the preliminary hearing rang all of Bill Pavelic's alarm bells. Prior to that, we barely had been aware of Fuhrman's involvement in the case, alone that he was a key – if not *the* key – police detective in the investigation, at least in the all-important first hours . . . Furthermore, nowhere was it stated, in *any* LAPD report, that Fuhrman was the one who discovered the glove at each scene" (p. 93; emphasis original). But because Shapiro does not explicitly state that he believes Simpson is innocent – indeed, he seems to dismiss the not-guilty verdicts as only a "legal victory" at one point in the book (p. 346) – his accusations of police misconduct resonate nicely with overzealousness narratives.

24. Freed and Briggs (1996), for example, speculate that the murders may have been related to drug activity centered around Mezzaluna restaurant, Goldman's employer and the site of Brown-Simpson's final meal. The authors note that two other young men with ties to restaurant employees

had been murdered within a year of the Bundy Drive murders. Brett Cantor was slashed to death about a year before the Bundy murders, while Michael Nigg was gunned down in Hollywood about a year after the Bundy murders. The authors also claim that two other unnamed young men with ties to the restaurant network were missing at the time of their writing.

25. After reviewing the autopsy reports, Henry S. Johnson, a black physician based in Los Angeles, concluded that at least two killers were involved, that the mortal wounds were inflicted by a left-handed killer (Simpson is right-handed), and that at least two different weapons were used to cause the stab wounds. Johnson speculates that the medical examiner who performed the autopsies, Irwin Golden, was not called by prosecutors during the criminal trial because he would/could not shade his testimony to conform with the prosecution theory of one killer. Johnson filed a lawsuit against Los Angeles's coroner and district attorney, claiming malfeasance and collusion to convict Simpson. The suit was eventually thrown out by a judge.

26. In *American Tragedy: The Uncensored Story of the Simpson Defense* (1996), Lawrence Schiller and James Willwerth also construct what is essentially a mystery narrative. Toward the end of the book, they note that Bob Kardashian – their primary source and Simpson's long-time friend and supporter throughout the trial – had begun to have doubts about his friend's innocence. Moreover, the trial and not-guilty verdicts had failed to resolve these lingering questions: "Bob [Kardashian] started out believing in O.J.'s innocence. But over the months, he has begun to doubt – quietly at first, then more insistently. In public he has never wavered. He has kept his private thoughts private. Now the jury has spoken, and, as Kardashian has feared for a long time, it has settled nothing" (p. 682).

27. In *Reasonable Doubts: The O.J. Simpson Case and the Criminal Justice System* (1996), Simpson defense attorney Alan Dershowitz makes similar points. For him, a rush to judgment was signified early on in the case by the lies police offered about their investigation: "In the Simpson case itself the first document presented to a court included deliberate police perjury. Detective Philip Vannatter, in seeking a search warrant, swore that O.J. Simpson's trip to Chicago was unplanned, even though he knew it had been planned long in advance of the murders. Judge Ito generously described this statement as 'at least reckless' in its disregard for the truth" (p. 58).

28. In January of 1996, Simpson established a toll-free line, 1–800-OJTELLS, to market the $19.95 video.

29. Indeed, in a February 5, 1996 telephone call to CNN's *Burden of Proof*, Simpson himself identified this as strong support for the conspiracy narrative: "I can't understand how a trained criminalist looking for blood could climb in that Bronco, and the majority of the area where I'm told is supposed to be Nicole and Ron Goldman's blood on that console, for two months, couldn't find it there. When people climbed in that Bronco, looking for blood, didn't see it, but two months later, they find all of these blood smears, these other blood smears that is essentially Ron Goldman's and Nicole's."

30. For example, a front-page story from the *Los Angeles Times* on April 16, 1997 featured the following headline: "Faulty Testimony, Practices Found in FBI Lab Probe: Investigation: Inaccuracies by expert witnesses, shoddy analysis are cited in sweeping examination of failures at once-vaunted facility. Agency accepts blame, vows reform."

31. For proponents of conspiracy narratives, it probably mattered little that Fuhrman had also asserted this privilege when asked other, more trivial questions. If Fuhrman had answered *any* of the questions he could have been legally compelled to answer *all* of them – even those that were potentially incriminating.

32. In his BET interview, Simpson, too, claimed that the conspiracy was the work of a relatively small number of LAPD insiders: "You got a small group of people at LAPD that I blame. Now I've had police officers since I've been out, one on a motorcycle, drive up, give me a thumbs up, did his thing and mouth to me 'you got screwed.' I had two police officers outside of my house tell me I got screwed. So it is not everybody with LAPD."

33. According to Worth and Jaspers (1996), the acronym "CAUSE" refers to "Christian Aryan Underground Special Enforcers" (p. 10).

34. *Los Angeles Times*, October 9, 1995, p. S3.

35. *Los Angeles Times*, October 9, 1995, p. S4.

36. *Variety*, February 27, 1995, p. 53.

37. *Los Angeles Times*, February 11, 1995, p. A16.

38. Steve Marinucci, San Jose *Mercury News*, April 24, 1995.

39. Although the top-rated Simpson book in 1995 was O.J. Simpson's jailhouse monograph, *I Want to Tell You* ("rush to judgment"), four of the remaining six bestsellers embraced the dominant narrative of Simpson's guilt: Faye Resnick's *Nicole Brown Simpson: The Private Diary of a Life Interrupted* (3); Sheila Weller's *Raging Heart* (4); Marc Eliot's *Kato Kaelin: The Whole Truth* (5); and Michael Knox's *The Private Diary of an O.J. Juror* (6). (Source: USA Today, http://www.usatoday.com/life/enter/books/lebl84.htm).

    Following the criminal trial verdicts, this pattern held. While trial-related books by Christopher Darden, Marcia Clark, and Mark Fuhrman all reached the top position on the best-seller list, Johnnie Cochran's *Journey to Justice* failed to even make the list. Other defense attorneys fared somewhat better: Alan Dershowitz's and Robert Shapiro's books would reach the fifth and twelfth positions, respectively (Source: BookWire Top 15 lists).

40. *Los Angeles Times*, October 5, 1995, p. A7.

41. Nonetheless, the authors do note that media events sometimes work to institute change. But this is presented as a rare occurrence, and thus the major thrust of the study describes media events as broadcasts that "*integrate* societies in a collective heartbeat and evoke a *renewal of loyalty* to the society and its legitimate authority" (p. 9; emphasis original).

42. Dayan and Katz do not seem to accord much counter-hegemonic potential to media events because, as they put it, "Social movements take place outside the home, not inside" (p. 59).

43. Turner conceptualizes society as "a dialectical process with successive phases of structure and communitas" (p. 203). Communitas, he argues, "is of the now; structure is rooted in the past and extends into the future through

language, law, and custom" (p. 113). Because all humans need to participate in both modalities, "persons starved of one in their functional day-to-day activities seek it in ritual liminality" (p. 203).

44. The *Los Angeles Times*, for example, ran a daily scorecard throughout the trial called "The Legal Pad" in which prominent legal experts assessed prosecution and defense performance for the day (see *Los Angeles Times*, January 25, 1995, p. A12).

45. By "text," I mean a bounded set of written words, images and/or audio composed by someone to be communicated to someone else. The meanings people derive from texts correspond to the discourses that are (re)activated in the media-audience encounter. These discourses are in turn composed of various narratives and representations that work to validate or naturalize underlying ideologies. For a more detailed discussion of how I conceptualize these relationships, see Hunt (1997).

46. This model ultimately echoes Neuman et al.'s (1992) conclusion that the media, government and public actively engage in a circular process of reality construction.

2. O.J. AND POLITICS

1. By "discourse," I mean systems of representations that work to communicate arguments or explanations for a given social phenomenon or issue. Discourses are inherently ideological in that they privilege certain understandings of the world over others. See also Hunt (1997).

2. Mills (1956), pp. 71–72.

3. Baker (1978), p. 15.

4. Newhouse (1985, p. 237).

5. Given that Simpson played an LAPD officer in this latter film, it is rather ironic that a linchpin of his defense was the claim that he had been framed by LAPD Detective Fuhrman.

6. "Is O.J. Really Broke?" *Time*, February 3, 1997, p. 44.

7. *Moneyline*, CNN, June 28, 1994.

8. Based on a 1992 study of defendants in the nation's seventy-five largest counties. Source: Department of Justice, Bureau of Justice Statistics, NCJ-159809.

9. "Rich Justice, Poor Justice," *Time*, June 19, 1995.

10. Source: Department of Justice, Bureau of Justice Statistics, NCJ-148826.

11. July 11–12, 1994. "Before all this happened, did you personally think of O.J. Simpson as a role model, or didn't you?" Yes, role model; No, did not; DK/NA. 51.3 percent answered "No."

12. Early news narratives, however, examined whether a celebrity such as Simpson could receive a "fair trial," especially given all of the incriminating media leaks that would likely taint any jury pool. Below, I discuss how these narratives soon gave way to those focussed on Simpson's unfair advantages.

13. *Los Angeles Times*, June 19, 1994, p. A1.

14. June 18, 1994. See also, CBS *Evening News*, June 19, 1994.

15. June 18, 1994.

16. CNN *Breaking News*, June 18, 1994.
17. For example, see ABC *World News Sunday*, June 26, 1994; CNN *Newshour*, June 27, 1994.
18. For example, see NBC *Nightly News*, June 26, 1994.
19. *Capital Gang Saturday*, CNN, July 9, 1994. See also, *CBS Evening News*, July 6, 1994.
20. For example, see CNN *Overnight*, July 21, 1994; CNN *Newsday*, July 21, 1994; ABC *World News Tonight*, July 21, 1994.
21. For example, see CNN *Prime News*, July 21, 1994.
22. August, 2, 1994.
23. August 14, 1994.
24. *60 Minutes*, CBS, September 25, 1994.
25. Rooney made his reward offer on *60 Minutes*, October 15, 1995.
26. NBC, September 27, 1994.
27. Although whites were well-represented among the 900 prospective jurors initially selected for screening (i.e., 37.9 percent white, 28.1 percent black, 17 percent Latino), blacks dominated the jury originally empaneled (i.e., eight of the twelve members). See Schmalleger (1996).
28. For example, see CNN's *The World Today*, November 4, 1994.
29. NBC *Nightly News*, October 2, 1994.
30. January 26, 1995.
31. Editorial by John H. Langbein, *Newsweek*, April 17, 1995, pp. 32–3.
32. When this editorial appeared in *Newsweek*, LAPD criminalist Dennis Fung was on the stand undergoing a blistering cross-examination by defense attorney Barry Scheck about evidence collection procedures. The prosecution would not begin the formal presentation of DNA evidence until about three weeks later (May 8, 1995), when Robin Cotton, director of the lab that processed key samples, began to explain DNA science to the jury.
33. Off Color Press, New York, 1995.
34. *Los Angeles Times*, May 9, 1997, p. B1.
35. Ann G. Sjoerdsma, Norfolk *Virginian-Pilot*, June 26, 1994.
36. As Stets (1988) notes, it was not until the 1970s that "domestic violence reached public awareness as a serious social problem that needed to be stopped" (p. 2). And this awareness was forged largely through a coordinated feminist movement to place the issue on the public agenda (Martin 1985).
37. Source: Family Violence Prevention Fund, http://www.ipg.apc.org/fund/the_facts/stats.html.
38. US Department of Justice, Bureau of Justice Statistics, reports that in 1995 husbands or boyfriends killed 26 percent of the female homicide victims where the victim-offender relationship was known.
39. For example, Messner and Sabo (1992) describe how the press worked to "rehabilitate" the image of boxer Sugar Ray Leonard after he was charged with abusing his wife. The violent incident was recoded in neutral (private) terms as "domestic discord," and Leonard's admitted acts were referred to as his wife's "claims" rather than as facts (p. 61).
40. Lystad (1986) provides an extensive overview of the multitude of approaches that might be grouped into these categories.

41. For example, the discussion of "minimization and denial" provided by Sonkin et al. (1985, p. 42) resonates with this theory.

42. The first prosecution witness was Sharon Gilbert, LAPD 911 dispatcher (January 31, 1995).

43. For example, see CNN's *The World Today*, June 21, 1994.

44. Not long after the incident, for example, Simpson was hired as a football analyst by NBC. At a news conference to announce his hiring, Simpson downplayed the incident: "It was really a bum rap. We had a fight, that's all" (*Los Angeles Times*, June 17, 1994, p. A24).

45. *Newsweek*, June 27, 1994, p. 20.

46. The US Department of Justice, Bureau of Justice Statistics, reports that women in the lowest income groups are four times as likely to be physically abused by intimates (NCJ-162602, December 1996).

47. As Messner (1992) puts it: "In promoting dominance and submission, in equating force and aggression with physical strength, modern sport naturalized the equation of maleness and power, thus legitimating a challenged and faltering system of masculine domination" (p. 15).

48. The US Department of Justice, Bureau of Justice Statistics (NCJ-162602).

49. *Los Angeles Times*, June 15, 1994, p. A1.

50. *Los Angeles Times*, June 16, 1994, p. A1 and p. A13.

51. This coverage was the result of journalistic routines that accord breaking news of that magnitude precedence over practically all else (see chapter 3).

52. June 19, 1994.

53. *Los Angeles Times*, June 21, 1994, p. A19.

54. For example, see CNN *Daybreak*, August 18, 1994.

55. *Los Angeles Times*, August 2, 1994, p. B1.

56. For example, see CNN *Newsday*, November 21, 1994.

57. *Los Angeles Times*, January 19, 1995, p. A1.

58. *Larry King Live*, May 4, 1995. Despite Rivers' claim, only white women appeared on the show.

59. *Good Morning America*, ABC, January 30, 1995.

60. *Los Angeles Times*, October 4, 1995, p. A18.

61. CNN *Prime News*, October 6, 1995.

62. Comedian Dan Wedeking's Brenda Moran–Larry King Interview from "The Unofficial O. J. Simpson Boycott Page" on the internet.

63. As Berger (1993) notes: "We gain a sense of superiority when the ignorance of others is revealed" through humor.

64. Jordan describes English society at the time as one "in a state of rapid flux, undergoing important changes in religious values, and comprised of men who were energetically on the make and acutely and often uncomfortably self-conscious of being so" (p. 43).

65. Allen (1994) critiques Jordan's "search among arcana of genetic evolution to better understand 'white men's attitudes'" as "an exercise in irrelevancy" (p. 22). Instead, he argues, racism was "introduced as a deliberate ruling-class policy" to divide and conquer the masses (p. 23). While I ultimately concur with Allen regarding the economic interests undergirding the institutionalization of racism, I nonetheless feel that the general thrust of Jordan's psychological argument is instructive for understanding contemporary issues of race and identity.

66. As bell hooks (1990) notes, "Images of black men as rapists, as dangerous menaces to society, have been sensational cultural currency for some time. The obsessive media focus on these representations is political. The role it plays in the maintenance of racist domination is to convince the public that black men are a dangerous threat who must be controlled by any means necessary, including annihilation" (p. 61).

67. Kimmel (1994) cogently articulates an important psychological process connected to the "othering" of nonwhite males: "These very groups that have historically been cast as less than manly were also, often simultaneously, cast as hypermasculine, as sexually aggressive, violent rapacious beasts, against whom 'civilized' men must take a decisive stand and thereby rescue civilization . . . These groups became the 'others,' the screens against which traditional conceptions of manhood were developed" (p. 135).

68. The book cites racial differences in IQ scores and standardized test scores to justify recommendations for eliminating government programs designed to address racial inequality. Blacks are ill-equipped to compete on an equal footing with whites, the scholars conclude, and it would thus be inefficient for society to continue subsidizing them.

69. For example, in what may be the earliest explicit invocation of race in the case, Dennis Schatzman of the *Los Angeles Sentinel* on June 16 filed a narrative regarding the racial implications of LAPD officers deciding to handcuff Simpson upon his return from Chicago (see below). *Time*'s infamous darkening of Simpson's mugshot (see below) appeared on the cover of the June 27 edition and immediately sparked a controversy. The *Los Angeles Times* reported poll results on June 28 that suggested blacks were twice as likely as whites to feel sympathy for Simpson. Reports of a CNN/USA/Gallup poll taken on July 1 noted the racial differences in opinions about the case that would be increasingly scrutinized as the weeks progressed. On July 11, *Larry King Live* presented a program entitled, "Does Race Play a Role in the Simpson Case?" Black professionals discussed the racial implications of the case two days later on CNN's *Sonya Live*.

70. *World News Sunday*, ABC, July 17, 1994.

71. For example, see *The O. J. Simpson Trial and Analysis*, CNN, March 13, 1995, and CNN *Morning News* for the same date.

72. For example, see *Morning Edition*, NPR, July 1, 1994.

73. For example, see ABC's *Nightline*, March 10, 1995.

74. April 15, 1995.

75. KTLA, October 3, 1995.

76. Bugliosi (1996), p. 19.

77. That is, Toobin does not attempt here to explain the obvious grammatical or spelling errors. Nor does he highlight these errors. He simply includes a rather neutral caption below the reprint: "Letter from O.J. Simpson to Nicole Brown Simpson, following his plea of no contest to domestic violence charges in 1989."

78. As Fanon (1967) puts it: "The white man is convinced that the Negro is a beast; if it is not the length of his penis, then it is the sexual potency that impresses him. Face to face with this man who is 'different from himself,' he needs to defend himself. In other words, to personify the Other" (p. 170).

79. *Star*, June 27, 1995, p. 37.

80. *Time*, June 27, 1994.

81. *Los Angeles Times*, June 14, 1994, p. A1.

82. Similarly, the day after the criminal trial verdicts were announced, a flyer headed "ATTENTION WHITE PEOPLE" circulated around the campus of the University of Southern California, Simpson's alma mater. The first paragraph read as follows: "Be afraid, be very afraid. Yesterday's verdict in the O.J. Simpson trial gave the right to all niggers in America and around the world to kill white people and get away with it. The Brentwood Butcher took the lives of two innocent people (two white people), yet that nigger and his coon lawyers were able to convince 12 jurors (9 of whom were slack-jawed jigaboos) that Mark Fuhrman planted all of the evidence against O.J. Just like Damien 'Football' Williams [one of the black males accused of attacking white trucker Reginald Denny during the 1992 Los Angeles uprisings], O.J. Simpson's crime was overlooked because of the dirty color of his skin."

83. June 5, 1997, http://www.whitepower.com/simpson/.

84. Berry (1994), pp. 240–41.

85. The national poll of 1306 respondents was conducted on July 11 and 12, 1994.

86. That is, either in prison, on parole, or on probation.

87. *The American Almanac 1994–1995: Statistical Abstract of the United States*, Table #315, "Persons Arrested, by Charge and Race: 1992, US Bureau of the Census.

88. US Department of Justice, Bureau of Justice Statistics, "Criminal Offenders Statistics." www.ojp.usdoj.gov/bjs, updated April 28, 1997.

89. Ibid.

90. "War on Crack Targets Minorities Over Whites," *Los Angeles Times*, May 21, 1995, p. A1.

91. You will recall, for example, that Simpson was not arrested following the 1989 911 incident.

92. In an early editorial about the case, for example, even the *Los Angeles Sentinel* (see chapter 6) commended the LAPD for going "out of its way to be very, very fair to Simpson" (June 23, 1995).

93. For example, see NPR's *Morning Edition* for July 1, 1994. The commentator discusses the common perception that Simpson had forgotten his "roots" and lost his "blackness."

94. For example, on February 10, 1992, former heavy weight boxing champion Mike Tyson was sentenced to six years in prison for raping a Miss Black America contestant who visited him in his hotel room. A few years earlier, the flamboyant black mayor of Washington, D.C., Marion Barry, had been convicted of smoking crack cocaine after a highly publicized sting operation.

95. On January 3, 1979, Eula Love was shot eight times by LAPD officers in an incident surrounding an unpaid utility bill. Officers said they shot Love after she threw a knife at them.

96. "We may be finding," said Daryl Gates by way of explaining the high percentage of black choke-hold deaths, "that in some blacks when [the

choke hold] is applied, the veins or arteries do not open up as fast as they do in *normal* people" (Domanick 1994, p. 299; emphasis added).

97. Toward the end of the 1980s, for example, former Los Angeles Lakers basketball star Jamal Wilkes was pulled over and handcuffed by LAPD officers because his license was "about to expire" (Domanick 1994, p. 356).

98. Jeffrey Dahmer was the white serial killer who preyed on and cannibalized male victims over a ten-year period in the Milwaukee area. Many of the victims were black. Dahmer was beaten to death in prison in 1994.

99. *New Yorker*, July 17, 1995.

100. July 20, 1994.

101. For example, see *CNN & Company*, July 14, 1994.

102. See Dershowitz (1996) for a discussion of the "testilying" controversy.

103. See for example, CNN *Morning News*, October 28, 1994.

104. For example, see CNN *Morning News*, April 14, 1995. In a story entitled, "Prosecution Left to Resurrect Fung as Credible Witness," the news program noted that Scheck had made headway into supporting the defense's conspiracy charges.

105. *Los Angeles Times*, August 30, 1995, p. A14.

106. The two excerpts were relatively innocuous: (1) "We have no niggers where I grew up." (2) "Why do they live in that area? Answer: That's where niggers live."

107. For example, see CNN's *World News*, September 6, 1995.

108. Ibid.

109. For example, the services of Donald Vinson, the jury consultant whose advice Marcia Clark rejected, were provided free of charge.

110. Admittedly, my notion of Celebrity Defendant project conflates a number of different interests – some "conservative," others more "progressive" – under a single ideological grouping. But my point in this conceptualization is that regardless of the *origins* of the individual project proponents, ideologically, they end up in the same place: bemoaning the relative impotence of prosecutorial efforts to secure convictions.

111. The magazine's cover teased an inside story about "O. J. Simpson & Unequal Justice," which began by asking the following rhetorical question: "Did we need O. J. to remind us that money makes all the difference – in the trial and in the verdict (p. 40)?" The article then proceeded to point out several differences between "rich justice" and "poor justice," financial inequalities that were underscored by the Simpson case. *Time*, June 19, 1995.

112. Bolick (1997), for example, advocates shifting the focus on civil rights from "criminal" (i.e., as opposed to "defendant") to victim.

113. In a October 1997 cover story, *Emerge* magazine notes that the US prison industry annually generates from $30 billion to $40 billion and is growing. A large chunk of this growth can be attributed to the 130 percent increase between 1985 and 1995 in the incarceration of black males (p. 38).

114. For example, see CNN *World News*, October 3, 1995.

115. From CNN *World News*, October 3, 1995; cited in Crenshaw (1997), pp. 143–4.

116. Said NOW president Patricia Ireland: "These statements have blotted NOW's otherwise impressive record of committed activism in the fight for racial justice and equality. It pains me that these unfortunate and unwise comments have tainted NOW's reputation and our relationships with people of color and our social justice allies." From *Reuters*, October 6, 1995; cited in Crenshaw (1997), p. 144.

3. PRESS RITES AND O. J. WRONGS

1. Jessica Seigel, *Buzz*, December/January 1997, p. 57.
2. Source: Associated Press.
3. *Los Angeles Times*, October 9, 1995, p. S3.
4. *Los Angeles Times*, October 9, 1995, p. S6.
5. *Los Angeles Times*, October 9, 1995, p. S12.
6. *Los Angeles Times*, October 9, 1995, p. S2.
7. Source: Associated Press.
8. "The Verdict," Tom Elias, pp. 26–27, in Elias and Schatzman (1996).
9. The notion of "Fourth Estate," of course, refers to the role of journalism as essentially the fourth branch of government responsible for checking the power of the other three (Executive, Legislative, Judicial) in the name of the people.
10. See McManus (1994) for a discussion of the importance of "journalistic objectivity" to newsworkers' conceptions of the work they do.
11. Code of Ethics, Society of Professional Journalists; as listed on web page, September, 1997. www.spj.org/ethics/ethics.htm
12. Code of Ethics, National Press Photographers Association; as listed on web page, September 1997. http://sunsite.unc.edu/nppa/nppa_app.html.
13. Code of Ethics adopted by the Radio-Television News Directors Association on August 31, 1987, still in effect in September 1997.
14. "Story conferences" are meetings newsworkers hold to choose from the supply of potential news items those that will compose the day's news agenda.
15. For example, see "Transcript/Video Index: The O. J. Simpson Index, Journal Graphics, June 13, 1994–April 26, 1996.
16. Personal interview with Emmanuel Parker, *Los Angeles Sentinel*, September 11, 1997. See also, *Los Angeles Times*, October 9, 199, p. S6 and S8.
17. *Los Angeles Times*, October 9, 1995, p. S10.
18. Indeed, the ABC, CBS and NBC evening news broadcasts devoted more time to the case over the forty weeks preceding the verdicts than they did to Bosnia and the Oklahoma City bombing combined (*Los Angeles Times*, October 9, 1995, p. S4).
19. Indeed, newsworkers often apply a "dialectical" model of reporting controversial issues (Epstein 1973). According to this model, the ideal of "balanced" news coverage often prompts newsworkers to present two sides of a controversial issue and suggest, in simple fashion, that the "truth" lies somewhere in between (pp. 66–67). In addition to the legacy of Federal Communication Commission policy concerning "fairness" in broadcast news coverage (Kellner 1990), television news – especially local operations – are likely to

adopt this dialectical approach for purely economic reasons: because offended viewers are free to switch channels, it may appear safer (in terms of audience share) for news operations to avoid extreme positions on any issue (McManus 1990, p. 680).

20. For similar statistics, see also "Implementation of Racial and Ethnic Diversity in the American Press: Objectives, Obstacles, and Incentives," The Joan Shorenshein Center, Harvard University, John F. Kennedy School of Government, 1996. This study concludes that the underrepresentation of people of color in the newsroom may in part be the direct result of the profession's continued affirmation of the objectivity ideal. That is, the rationale for increasing the number of "minority" newsworkers – the incorporation of their group experiences into the framing of mainstream news narratives – is fundamentally at odds with the core value celebrated by journalism's strategic ritual.

21. These newsworkers included Dennis Praeger, a KABC talk-show host; Michael Jackson, a KABC talk-show host; Jeffrey Toobin, writer for the *New Yorker* magazine; Fred Graham; David Margolick, writer for the *New York Times*; Steve Dunleavy, *New York Daily News*. Richard Reeve, author and columnist; Jim Moret, correspondent for CNN; Richard Wald, Sr. V. P. of ABC News; Howard Rosenberg, media critic for *Los Angeles Times*; and Craig Hume, news director of KTLA television.

22. These newsworkers included Michael Datcher, *Los Angeles Sentinel*; Kenneth Thomas, *Los Angeles Sentinel*; and Karen Grigsby Bates, free-lance journalist.

23. *Los Angeles Times*, October 9, 1995, p. S8.

24. Personal interview with Ron Brewington, October 1, 1997.

25. Personal interview with Haywood Galbreath, October 10, 1997.

26. This pool, like the television pool camera operated by CourtTV, would be the sole source of trial proceeding photographs. Members of participating news organizations would rotate as designated photographer, sharing the resulting prints with one another throughout the trial.

27. Telephone interview with Tom Elias, December 21, 1996.

28. *Los Angeles Times*, October 9, 1995, p. S8.

29. Telephone interview with Tom Elias, December 21, 1996.

30. Personal interview with Dennis Schatzman, January 14, 1997.

31. *Los Angeles Times*, October 9, 1995, p. S10.

32. *Los Angeles Times*, October 9, 1995, p. S8.

33. Telephone interview with an unnamed white newspaper reporter, January 15, 1997.

34. *Buzz*, December/January 1997, p. 58.

35. ABC *Viewpoint: The Media and the Trial*, October 5, 1995.

36. *Buzz*, December/January 1997, p. 58.

37. Ibid.

38. Jeffrey Toobin, ABC *Viewpoint: The Media and the Trial*, October 5, 1995.

39. *Los Angeles Times*, October 9, 1995, p. S8.

40. Jeffrey Toobin, *ABC Viewpoint: The Media and the Trial*, October 5, 1995.

41. *Los Angeles Times*, October 9, 1995, S8.

42. Personal interview with Emmanuel Parker, September 11, 1997. See also, *Los Angeles Times*, October 9, 1995, p. S6.

43. In chapter 7, I discuss several social-psychological processes by which prevailing attitudes are reinforced in small-group settings. From my interviews with members of the Simpson newsworker corps, it appears that these processes may have been operable in segments of the corps.
44. *Los Angeles Times*, October 9, 1995, p. S8.
45. The one exception was an in-depth feature by David Shaw on media coverage of the case. See *Los Angeles Times*, October 9, 1995, p. S9.
46. *Washington Post* editorial cited in *Los Angeles Times*, October 9, 1995, p. S4.
47. As David Shaw noted: "Most reporters are thinking about beating their competitors, not about selling newspapers or safeguarding a defendant's right to a fair trial or helping either his lawyers or the police." *Los Angeles Times*, October 9, 1995, p. S7.
48. ABC *Viewpoint: The Media and the Trial*, October 5, 1995.
49. Ibid.
50. *Los Angeles Times*, October 9, 1995, p. S4.
51. *Star*, June 27, 1995, p. 1.
52. *National Enquirer*, October 17, 1995, p. 1.
53. Telephone interview with an unnamed black reporter for a major Los Angeles television station., February 18, 1997.
54. ABC *Viewpoint: The Media and the Trial*, October 5, 1995.
55. Ibid.
56. The session was held on Sunday, April 20, 1997 at 11:00 am.
57. *Los Angeles Times*, October 9, 1995, p. S6.

4. O. J. AND KTLA-TV

1. As we shall see below, however, the legal analyst(s) introduced by Waller each day rotated over the course of the trial.
2. ABC *Viewpoint: The Media and the Trial*, October 5, 1995.
3. KTLA 50th Anniversary television special, May 15, 1997.
4. Ibid.
5. Source: *Working Press of the Nation, 1996*, Chicago: The National Research Bureau. Figures based on Los Angeles Designated Market Area (DMA), which includes the cities of Los Angeles, Anaheim, Barstow, Corona, Huntington Beach, Ontario, Riverside, San Bernardino, Santa Ana, and Ventura.
6. Source: County of Los Angeles Statistical Data, http//www.co.la.ca.us/statistics.html. Figures based on the population of the city of Los Angeles.
7. See http://www.triune.com/list.html. Other tribune television stations include: WPIX (New York), WGN (Chicago), WPHL (Philadelphia), WLVI (Boston), WGNX (Atlanta), KWGN (Denver), WGNO (New Orleans), KHTV (Houston), KSWB (San Diego). Newspapers include: the *Chicago Tribune, Sun Sentinel, Orlando Sentinel,* and *Daily Press*.
8. Quote from Stan Chamber's book, *Stan Chambers: News at 10.* Cited in "LA's Treasure: Stan Chambers," http://www.citivu.com/ktla/stan-c.html.
9. KTLA anchor Marta Waller, KTLA 50th Anniversary special, May 15, 1997.
10. Given the tremendous racial diversity of Los Angeles's population (i.e., 41 percent Latino, 37 percent white, 12 percent Asian, and 10 percent black),

this dominance by whites of the local mainstream news media underscores the continuing significance of a US racial order that places whites on top.

11. *Los Angeles Times*, May 7, 1997, p. F4.
12. ABC *Viewpoint: The Media and the Trial*, October 5, 1995.
13. *Los Angeles Times*, August 14, 1996, p. D2.
14. *Los Angeles Times*, June 30, 1994, p. A18.
15. *Los Angeles Times*, October 9, 1995, p. S11.
16. *Buzz*, October 1997, p. 87.
17. That is, viewers are not privy to the activities of other newsworkers in the KTLA production facilities who choose the camera angles, compose graphics, and provide Waller with stage direction.
18. Newsworkers from CourtTV controlled the pool television camera. CourtTV is a 24-hour, seven-day-a-week cable station devoted to reporting on the US legal system. In this capacity, the station routinely broadcasts live trial proceedings. CourtTV began operations in 1991, and is owned by Liberty Media, NBC, and Time Warner.
19. KTLA live coverage, March 21, 1995.
20. KTLA live coverage, July 12, 1995.
21. KTLA live coverage, July 17, 1995.
22. KTLA live coverage, July 25, 1995.
23. KTLA live coverage, September 15, 1995.
24. KTLA live coverage, March 10, 1995.
25. van Dijk (1993, p. 259) identifies "denial" as a routine "semantic move" of media discourse.
26. KTLA live coverage, March 21, 1995.
27. KTLA *Noon News*, September 20, 1995.
28. KTLA live coverage, March 14, 1995.
29. KTLA live coverage, March 31, 1995.
30. KTLA live coverage, June 20, 1995.
31. KTLA live coverage, July 5, 1995.
32. KTLA live coverage, August 15, 1995.
33. KTLA live coverage, September 6, 1995.
34. Although Arenella does not expand on this comment, his use of "this jury" might be construed as a reference to race – to the observation that not only is Simpson a celebrity, but he is also a *black* celebrity who is being tried before a predominantly *black* jury.
35. KTLA live coverage, July 5, 1995.
36. KTLA live coverage, August 21, 1995.
37. KTLA live coverage, October 3, 1995.
38. Ibid.
39. KTLA live coverage, May 11, 1995.
40. Ibid.
41. Ibid.
42. KTLA live coverage, September 20, 1995.
43. KTLA live coverage, October 3, 1995.
44. KTLA live coverage, May 11, 1995.
45. KTLA live coverage, June 20, 1995.
46. Ibid.

47. KTLA live coverage, July 25, 1995.
48. Ibid.
49. Ibid.
50. KTLA live coverage, June 5, 1995.
51. Ibid.
52. KTLA live coverage, September 6, 1995.
53. KTLA live coverage, October 3, 1995.
54. See Knox (1995).
55. KTLA live coverage, October 3, 1995.

5. O.J. AND THE *LOS ANGELES TIMES*

1. In 1995, the Times Mirror Co. posted revenues of $2.3 billion and ranked as the twelfth largest media company in the nation, directly behind the New York Times Co. (*Advertising Age*, August 19, 1996, p. S2).
2. In 1996, only *The Wall Street Journal* (1.8 million), *USA Today* (1.6 million), and *The New York Times* (1.1 million) had larger circulations (*Advertising Age*, November 11, 1996, p. 55).
3. *Los Angeles Times*, October 9, 1995, p. S10.
4. Source: *Los Angeles Times Index*, 1994 and 1995.
5. *Los Angeles Times*, October 9, 1995, p. S10. The article also notes that the *New York Times*, in contrast to the *Los Angeles Times*, published only fifty-two news narratives about the case during the period – the least of any major newspaper in the nation. From opening statements through the verdicts, the *Los Angeles Times* published a front-page narrative about the case every morning after a court session, with the exception of five days (p. S5).
6. *Los Angeles Times*, April 3, 1996, p. A3.
7. Geis (1990), p. 14.
8. Source: Los Angeles Public Library, History Department.
9. Source: County of Los Angeles Statistical Data, http://www.co.la.ca.us/statistics.html.
10. By 1887, the newspaper's nameplate would change to reflect the name so familiar to Los Angelenos today.
11. For example, Otis was a major participant in the formation of the anti-union Merchants and Manufacturers Association and the Chamber of Commerce (Berges 1984; Geis 1990).
12. Source: Los Angeles Public Library, History Department.
13. Indeed, a black woman, Janet Clayton, had been editor of the newspaper's editorial pages when she was named vice president of the newspaper in 1997 (*Jet*, February 17, 1997). Similarly, another black woman, Bonnie Guiton Hill, was named chief executive officer of the Times Mirror Foundation and vice president of the Times Mirror Company later that year (*Jet*, April 28, 1997).
14. Personal interviews conducted with unnamed newsworkers for "Fact-Finding Hearings on Racial and Ethnic Tensions in American Communities: Poverty, Inequality and Discrimination," Los Angeles, CA, June 17, 1993, United States Commission on Civil Rights.

15. *LA Weekly*, October 17, 1997, p. 24.
16. *Los Angeles Times*, October 9, 1995, p. S7.
17. Ibid.
18. Personal interview with unnamed newsworker, October 28, 1997.
19. *Los Angeles Times*, October 10, 1997.
20. CNN *Newshour*, June 16, 1994.
21. *Los Angeles Times*, October 9, 1995, p. S7.
22. Personal interview with unnamed newsworker, October 28, 1997.
23. Personal interviews: Dennis Schatzman, January 14, 1997; Haywood Galbreath, October 6, 1997.
24. Personal interview with unnamed *Los Angeles Times* newsworker, July 7, 1997.
25. Personal interview with unnamed newsworker, October 28, 1997.
26. This figure is somewhat inflated when we consider that the newspaper published 32 of the 193 narratives the morning following the verdicts.
27. *Los Angeles Times*, August 30, 1995, p. B8.
28. *Los Angeles Times*, October 4, 1995, p. B8.
29. For example, a letter from a man in Monterey Park published the morning after the verdicts echoed the dominant O.J. narratives: " 'Send a message,' the jurors were told. They sent a message. The message is that you can get away with murder if you are rich and famous. The message is that if you are black, you can always plead racial prejudice. The message is that women are the property of their husbands and ex-husbands, and it is all right for their men to murder them. The message is that justice is a commodity that can be bought, if you have enough money to hire skillful and devious lawyers. The message is that the taxpayers are getting taken for $9 million. Johnnie Cochran, you got your message across."
30. The *Times* evidently receives many letters from readers hoping to air their views on the editorial page. Indeed, the newspaper provides instructions for readers seeking to have their letters reprinted. In these instructions, prospective letter writers are warned that their letters may not be published due to the large number of letters the newspaper normally receives: "Because of the volume of mail received, unpublished letters cannot be acknowledged." It is inconceivable that *Times* newsworkers would not have had ample pro-defense letters to chose from given the controversy surrounding the case.
31. *Los Angeles Times*, May 12, 1995, p. E2.
32. Categories included: LAPD/other law enforcement; prosecution; unnamed sources; state/city/county officials; experts/insiders; legal experts; psychiatrists/psychologists; social workers/counselors; Goldman friends; Goldman family; Nicole friends; Nicole family; Simpson friends; Simpson family; witnesses/observers/fans/anonymous tipsters; defense experts/witnesses; Goldman neighbors; Nicole neighbors; O.J. neighbors; media experts; media workers; documents/tapes (police); others (e.g., funeral ministers, friends of defense attorneys/prosecutors); Goldman; Nicole; Simpson; documents/transcripts (court); documents (other); books/films/music; USC students/professors; USC officials (including football coach); former USC teammates; professional football players/teammates/coaches; Cowlings;

Cowlings friends; Cowlings neighbors; black leaders; feminist leaders; politicians; other media (e.g., newspapers, television, radio); witness attorneys; opinion polls.

33. See discussions in chapters 1 and 2.
34. That is, Detective Mark Fuhrman made disparaging remarks on the tapes about the judge's wife, the highest ranking female officer in the LAPD.
35. *Los Angeles Times*, February 28, 1995, p. A1.
36. *Los Angeles Times*, July 13, 1995, p. A1.
37. *Los Angeles Times*, July 18, 1995, p. A1.
38. *Los Angeles Times*, October 4, 1995, p. A1.

6. O.J.AND THE *LOS ANGELES SENTINEL*

1. Personal interview with Leroy Foster, September 11, 1997. Foster reported that the estimated pass-along readership is 100,000 and that about one quarter of all subscriptions are mailed "all over the world."
2. The NNPA is an organization of 205 black-owned newspapers across the nation (Shipp 1994).
3. Personal interview with Leroy Foster, September 11, 1997.
4. Personal interview with Leroy Foster, Emmanuel Parker, and Marshall Lowe, September 11, 1997.
5. *Los Angeles Times*, July 13, 1995, p. A12.
6. Ibid.
7. ABC *Viewpoint: The Media and the Trial*, October 5, 1995.
8. *Los Angeles Sentinel*, December 11, 1997, p. A1.
9. Personal interview with Marshall Lowe, September 11, 1997.
10. Personal observations, Angelus Funeral Home, Los Angeles, July 25, 1997.
11. Personal interview with Emmanuel Parker, September 11, 1997.
12. As we observed in the Introduction, blacks were about four times as likely as whites to say early in the case that they felt a "great deal" of sympathy for Simpson (39 percent versus 10 percent). Moreover, another 35 percent of black respondents said they felt "some" sympathy for the famous black defendant.
13. Indeed, some of these narratives were superfluously labelled as "news analysis."
14. *Sentinel*, July 6, 1995. Schatzman identifies the quote as one that originated in an 1858 statement.
15. *Sentinel*, March 23, 1995, p. A6.
16. *Sentinel*, July 13, 1995, p. A6.
17. Given the "hate calls" received by the *Sentinel* throughout the criminal trial, it seems highly unlikely that they would not have also received letters critical of their stance on the case.
18. *Sentinel*, July 13, 1995, p. A6.
19. Categories included: LAPD/other law enforcement; prosecution; unnamed sources; state/city/county officials; experts/insiders; legal experts; psychiatrists/psychologists; social workers/counselors; Goldman friends; Goldman family; Nicole friends; Nicole family; Simpson friends; Simpson family; witnesses/observers/fans/anonymous tipsters; defense experts/witnesses; Goldman neighbors; Nicole neighbors; O.J. neighbors; media experts; media workers;

documents/tapes (police); others (e.g., funeral ministers, friends of defense attorneys/prosecutors); Goldman; Nicole; Simpson; documents/transcripts (court); documents (other); books/films/music; USC students/professors; USC officials (including football coach); former USC teammates; professional football players/teammates/coaches; Cowlings; Cowlings friends; Cowlings neighbors; black leaders; feminist leaders; politicians; other media (e.g., newspapers, television, radio); witness attorneys; opinion polls.

20. Most, but not all, of these narratives were front-page, "O. J. vs. the People" narratives (see Appendix 2).
21. *Sentinel*, January 25, 1995, p. A4.
22. *Sentinel*, August 31, 1995, p. A1.
23. KTLA legal analyst Al DeBlanc, February 6, 1995.
24. *Los Angeles Times*, February 4, 1995, p. A1.
25. *Sentinel*, February 9, 1995, p. A1.
26. Ibid.
27. *Sentinel*, March 23, 1995, p. A1.
28. *Sentinel*, March 30, 1995, p. A15.
29. *Sentinel*, January 25, 1995, p. A4.
30. Of course, if people were free to roam around the murder scene as Mays claims to have done, this would seem to make it more difficult for police to conspire to plant evidence.
31. *Sentinel*, February 16, 1995, p. A1.
32. *Sentinel*, March 30, 1995, p. A13.
33. *Sentinel*, June 29, 1995, p. A4.
34. *Los Angeles Times*, October 4, 1995, p. A1.
35. *Sentinel*, September 28, 1995, p. A1.
36. The four white police officers acquitted of beating Rodney King were later charged with violating the black motorist's civil rights largely on the basis of a videotape of the incident many saw as incontrovertible proof. For example, see Hazen (1992), Fiske (1994).
37. *Sentinel*, May 4, 1995, p. A1.
38. *Sentinel*, July 6, 1995, p. A1.

7. RACED WAYS OF SEEING O. J.

1. All informants identified themselves as either "white" or "black" on telephone screening surveys.
2. On the screening questionnaire, eight out of ten informants in both groups reported that they felt "very well informed" about the case; the remaining informants described themselves as "extremely well informed."
3. The questions included: What do you feel is the most important news reported in the video? What was good about the video? What was bad about the video? How do you feel about the people shown in the video? How do you feel about the news reporters/commentators in the video?
4. Scale scores for each group were constructed on the basis of the following questions: "On a scale from 1 (guilty) to 10 (innocent), how CERTAIN are you of O. J. Simpson's guilt or innocence in the stabbing deaths of Nicole Brown Simpson and Ronald Goldman?" "On a scale from 1 (guilty) to 10

(innocent), how CERTAIN are you of Mark Fuhrman's guilt or innocence in the 'framing' of O. J. Simpson for the stabbing deaths of Nicole Brown Simpson and Ronald Goldman?"

5. Myers and Lamm (1975) cite two theories that seek to explain this phenomenon: "interpersonal comparison theory" and "informational influence theory." The former suggests that people desire to present themselves favorably relative to others. Thus, when a person finds in group discussion that others share his or her position on an issue, he or she may feel free to become an even stronger advocate of this position. The latter theory suggests that, during group discussions, arguments are generated that tend to support and reinforce the initially dominant point of view. Some of these arguments, the theory continues, may not have been considered before (or may have been forgotten) by certain members of the group, thereby leading to a strengthening of these members' original positions and to a hardening of the initially dominant point of view for the group as a whole.

6. Because the study groups had prior histories in which members frequently discussed the case with one another, I assumed that group influences had already produced a degree of attitude polarization and/or convergence before the interviews. I thus expected any additional polarization or convergence detected in this case study to be relatively small.

7. These items read as follows: "On a scale from 1 (very important) to 10 (not at all important), how *important* a role do you think race will play in the outcome of the Simpson trial?" "On a scale from 1 (fair) to 10 (unfair), how *fair* or *unfair* would you say news coverage of the trial has been thus far?" I was careful not to mention "race" or "media" in the initial (pre-discussion) questionnaires so that these issues, if they were to be discussed, would have to be placed on the agenda by the informants themselves.

8. This item read as follows: "On a scale from 1 (like him very much) to 10 (did not like him at all), how would you say you felt about O. J. Simpson BEFORE you heard about the murders on June 12, 1994? (5 to 6 = no opinion, or did not know who he was)."

9. Program press release, dated 1995–1996.

10. Newsworkers evidently deemed two sound bites from Brown-Simpson and Officer Kent so important that they were used twice in the text: once in the preview portion, and later in the text as the narrative unfolds (see preview text above.)

11. Within the context of the *Primetime* narrative, of course, this statement works to (re)affirm a key tenet of the Black "Other" project. As Dyson (1996) puts it, "The unspoken, perhaps unconscious belief of many whites is that if he's guilty, if this could happen to O. J. – the spotless embodiment of domesticated black masculinity – it could happen to any black man. Translation: no black male can really be trusted? (p. 30)"

12. Heidi Fleiss was the "Hollywood Madam" who was sentenced in 1997 to three years in prison for tax evasion, laundering her prostitution profits, and conspiring to cover up her operation.

13. Telephone interviews with O. J. Simpson, March 11, 1996, July 15, 1996.

14. See chapter 1 for a discussion of the "Bronco chase." See also, Fiske (1994) for an insightful overview of the heavily televised and watched spectacle.

15. Richard Ramirez, known as the "Nightstalker," is the serial killer who terrorized Los Angeles during 1985.

16. Mean scale scores for each group were constructed on the basis of informant responses to the following question: "On a scale from 1 (very important) to 10 (not at all important), how important a role do you think race will play in the outcome of the Simpson trial?"

17. Black informants frequently used pronouns of solidarity (e.g., we, us, our) when referring to "blacks" or "African-Americans." White informants, in contrast, rarely used these pronouns when "whites" was the referent. See Cramer and Schuman (1975) and Hunt (1997) for discussions of pronoun usage and identification.

18. Note the informant's decision not to use a pronoun of solidarity here. Instead, "the white people" is used as if "whites" constitute a group distant from how the speaker understands herself.

19. For a discussion of how these concerns find expression in the black community, see Turner (1993).

20. That is, no references were made in this group to the text as construction *prior* to moderator prompts near the end of the interview to discuss what was "good" or "bad" about the video.

21. That is, informants in this group challenged the text *as construction* several times *prior* to the moderator's first prompt to discuss it as such.

22. I found this particularly interesting given that two female informants – one from each group – revealed during discussion that they had been victims of domestic violence.

8. RACED WAYS OF SEEING O.J. – REVISITED

1. Conflicting evidence was introduced at trial concerning whether or not Simpson was angered because his ex-wife told him he was not invited to the dinner.

2. Juror Jeanette Harris was dismissed by Judge Ito on April 5, 1995.

3. Prosecutors threatened throughout the trial to call Kardashian to the stand to explain what happened to a piece of Simpson's luggage he was seen on videotape to carry away from Rockingham after Simpson's return from Chicago on June 13, 1994. Prosecutors would imply that the murder weapon and bloody clothes were concealed in the luggage and subsequently disposed of by Kardashian.

4. Bob quickly "corrects" this invocation by noting that whites would also find Simpson guilty no matter how innocent he is. But Bob, of course, had already declared Simpson guilty, thus ultimately placing the competing positions on unequal footings.

5. On April 29, 1995, an all-white jury acquitted four white LAPD officers of charges connected to the brutal beating of black motorist Rodney King. The beating had been captured on videotape, but defense attorneys were able to convince jurors that King was in control of the situation. See Fiske (1994), and chapters 1 and 2.

6. Here, informants were referring to Terry White, the young black prosecutor in the trial of the officers accused of excessively beating Rodney King.

White was criticized following the not-guilty verdicts for failing to put King on the stand so that the jury could see the extent of his injuries. White would also play a role in the prosecution of Simpson. He helped organize a mock cross-examination of prosecution witness Mark Fuhrman.

7. For example: "bloody socks planted by police"; "missing blood from sample vial"; "bloody socks are suspicious"; "police planted evidence in O.J.'s room"; "case against O.J. is a racist 'set up'"; "one informant walks through LAPD planting theory"; "O.J. is probably being framed"; "conspiracy"; "other prominent conspiracies"; "AIDS and conspiracy"; "'the plan' to 'bring down' blacks"; "conspiracy"; "blacks are targeted by the system and need to unite."

8. Here, informants were invoking intertextual memories of a black politician from the Los Angeles area who had recently been caught taking bribes in a sting operation.

9. Here, informants were invoking intertextual memories of the powerful, black US Secretary of Commerce, Ronald Brown, who would later die in the crash of a government plane. In the aftermath of Brown's death, conspiracy theorists would speculate that the crash may have been a cleverly-designed cover for what was actually his assassination.

10. Here, informants were invoking intertextual memories of a controversial speech made in Los Angeles by Louis Farrakhan, leader of the black Nation of Islam.

9. O.J. AND REALITY

1. As Mahoney (1997) explains it: "In the logic of white privilege, making whites feel white equals racism" (p. 331).

2. See Omi and Winant (1994) for a cogent discussion of how the notion of "colorblind" society forms the cornerstone of the "neoconservative" political project.

3. After the verdicts, several commentators speculated that the verdicts might result in a backlash against affirmative action by angry whites. California voters indeed passed Proposition 209 in the trial's aftermath, which outlawed the use of "racial preferences" in state employment and college admissions.

4. Indeed, D'Souza (1995, pp. 259–262) implies that any contemporary discrimination by the criminal justice system against black males is "rational" because this group is overrepresented among violent offenders.

5. The BET interview first aired on January 24, 1996.

6. To be fair, Simpson seemed to later have second thoughts about his beliefs in a "colorblind" America. He had this to say in a May 13, 1996 interview on Granada television: "My eyes may have been opened up a little more to how much race was impacting, ah, the perception of this case. I may not have said that right. What I mean to say is, in August, long before there was any evidence presented in this case, when you look at the hearing, the 911 calls, the buying the knife at a knife store, and all of that. None of that came into, really came into the case. You know, but still 70 to 80 percent of white

America had already convicted me. I find that so ironic, so hypocritical for them. That same group of people criticizing this jury. They said, 'They only took two hours, ah, three hours to come to a verdict, that's not enough time.' Yet, before there was a jury, before any evidence was presented in court, 80 percent of – from the polls, I don't always believe the polls – but 80 percent of white America based on the polls already had me guilty."

7. The dependent variable, perceptions of Simpson's innocence or guilt, was dichotomized into two categories: "probably not guilty" = 0, "probably guilty" = 1. All other response categories for the dependent variable were deleted from the analysis, reducing the sample to an N of 485. Dummy variables were created for each category of the independent variables. The omitted groups are identified below. The regression estimates identified three central social locations as having a significant impact on respondents' feelings about Simpson's guilt: race, education, and income. First, race seemed to have the largest impact on the dependent variable, net of other factors. That is, whites (the omitted group) were about 4.8 times as likely as blacks ($1/.21$) to consider Simpson "probably guilty," holding other factors constant; other-raced respondents did *not* differ significantly from whites in their odds of considering Simpson "probably guilty." Second, those with a college degree (the omitted group) were about 3.3 times as likely as those with less than a high school degree ($1/.30$) to consider Simpson "probably guilty," net of other factors; they were about twice as likely as those with a high school degree ($1/.50$) to consider him "probably guilty." Third, those with family incomes over $75,000 (omitted group) were about 3.4 times as likely as those with incomes less than $15,000 to consider Simpson "probably guilty," net of other factors. Other factors explored in Figures 14 through 21 also seemed to impact the dependent variable. For example, respondents who felt that the criminal justice system was neutral or "colorblind" (the omitted group) were about three times as likely as those who felt it is biased against blacks ($1/.34$) to consider Simpson "probably guilty," net of other factors. Although not quite significant at the .05 level, respondents who were interviewed by blacks appeared to be less likely than those interviewed by whites (omitted group), holding other factors constant, to consider Simpson "probably guilty." Indeed, as figure 21 suggests, the effect of interviewer race seemed to interact with respondent race (i.e., interviewer race was particularly salient for blacks). Finally, gender (men were the omitted group) did *not* have a significant effect on respondents' feelings about Simpson's guilt, holding other factors constant. However, as figure 14 suggests, gender *did* appear to interact with race, particularly in the case of blacks.

8. For example, Schiller and Willwerth (1996) offer a detailed account of how defense and prosecution focus groups early on alerted trial principals to complicated race and gender interactions surrounding case issues.

9. Although the logistic regression estimates in Appendix 7 indicate that gender did not significantly affect the odds of considering Simpson "probably guilty," net of other factors, for blacks, as figure 14 suggests, an interesting race and gender interaction was evident.

10. During the criminal trial, you will recall, defense attorney Johnnie Cochran and prosecutor Christopher Darden confronted one another in open court over whether or not a "black" voice could be distinguished from an other-raced one at a distance. The dispute revolved around alleged statements by defense witness Robert Heidstra in which he claimed to have heard a "black" male voice and another non-black male voice arguing at Nicole Brown-Simpson's home at about the time the defense argued the murders must have occurred. Although this time frame was later than that preferred by prosecutors, Darden during cross-examination of Heidstra tried to get the witness to acknowledge that the "black" voice he heard could have been Simpson. Incensed, Cochran declared this insinuation racist, that race cannot be determined from the sound of someone's voice.

11. Many Critical Race Theorists are especially critical of Critical Legal Theorists and liberals who see race as just a manifestation of more fundamental social forces like class.

12. These are two highly documented US conspiracies. In the Tuskegee Syphilis Experiment, 400 poor blacks were unwitting subjects in a 40-year (1932–1972), government-sponsored study to document the effects of untreated syphilis. Many of the subjects died, despite the widespread availability of treatments for syphilis. In the case against US tobacco companies, a Minnesota judge ruled that secret industry documents showed a clear "conspiracy of silence and suppression of scientific research" regarding the negative health effects of smoking. Indeed, the industry's public stance had been to vehemently deny any scientific "proof" associating smoking with a variety of ailments commonly attributed to the habit (e.g., see *Washington Post*, December 18, 1997, p. A14).

13. Published in 1996 by Barnes & Noble Books, by arrangement with Random House Publishing, 2230 pages.

14. *Time*, June 23, 1997, p. 64.

15. That is, LAPD officers first arrived at the Bundy crime scene at about 12:17 am on June 13, 1994. The coroner was not called until about five hours later, at 5:30 am. Officers requested that the coroner not come to the crime scene until further notice. The coroner finally arrived at about 9 am (Freed and Briggs 1996).

16. Not surprisingly, perhaps, an internal LAPD probe would later conclude that Fuhrman lied and/or exaggerated on the McKinny tapes when he boasted of targeting black suspects and other acts of police misconduct (*Los Angeles Times*, October 18, 1997, p. A1.)

17. Christopher (1991), pp. 168–170.

18. The *Webster's New Universal Unabridged Dictionary* (1996) defines "conspiracy of silence" as "a usually secret or unstated agreement to remain silent among those who know something whose disclosure might be damaging, harmful, or against their own best interest or that of their associates."

19. Christopher (1991), p. ii.

20. For example, ABC's *Primetime Live* featured an "exclusive" interview with Mark Fuhrman on February 19, 1997 – two weeks after a civil trial jury found Simpson liable for the Bundy Drive murders. Below I provide anchor Diane Sawyer's wrap-up to the sympathetic interview in its entirety.

SAWYER (voice-over): At the end of the first trial, Mark Fuhrman says he was the only person to be vilified, while he had seen others botch their work and even lie. It's a small footnote to Fuhrman's turbulent history, but this is Laura Hart McKinny, the screenwriter who made those tapes of Fuhrman, the ones in which he says he's inventing racist dialogue. Fuhrman says because McKinny was going to testify under oath, he had to confess to his wife something he'd omitted before, that earlier, before he was married, he had a romance with McKinny.

FUHRMAN: That was difficult because I didn't want to pile anything more on her.

SAWYER (voice-over): The irony is, he confessed it for naught.

DARDEN (from proceedings): Your relationship in 1985 with Mark Fuhrman, was it only professional?

MCKINNY: (from proceedings) It was a pro – sorry. It was a business relationship. He was a technical advisor for the screenplay.

DARDEN: (from proceedings) And that is it?

MCKINNY: (from proceedings) Yes.

FUHRMAN: Funny, isn't it?

SAWYER (voice-over): Because of those tapes, Mark Fuhrman pled no contest to perjury. He says he knows he had to continue to fight to prove he's not what every one *thought*. (Emphasis added)

(on-camera) Do you get the feeling, though, that people are still uneasy about what kind of racist heart might still lie in there?

FUHRMAN: I don't sense it, and by God, I'm looking for it.

SAWYER (voice-over): And the man who once said detective work was his life says today he's reconciled to a future in which he'll never be a cop again.

(on-camera) A footnote now – at the time of the murders, O. J. Simpson was on the board of directors of the company that manufactures Swiss army knives. The company confirmed to us that Simpson has bought Swiss army knives but could not confirm which models, saying only there's no record that he bought a locked blade. You may remember, though, there was a limousine driver who allegedly said that Simpson returned from a meeting of the board four days before the murders with a bag full of knives. And while riding in the back seat, flashed one of them saying, "You could really hurt someone with this. You could even kill someone with this." Simpson, as you know, has always maintained his innocence.

21. *Esquire*, February 1998, p. 58.

References

Abramson, Jeffrey (ed.), 1996. *Postmortem: The O. J. Simpson Case: Justice Confronts Race, Domestic Violence, Lawyers, Money, and the Media*, New York: Basic Books.

Adorno, Theodor, 1991. "The Schema of Mass Culture," in J. M. Bernstein (ed.), *The Culture Industry: Selected Essays on Mass Culture*, London: Routledge.

Alexander, Jeffrey C., 1981. "The Mass Media in Systemic, Historical and Comparative Perspective," in Elihu Katz and Thomas Szesko (eds.), *Mass Media and Social Change*, Beverly Hills: Sage.

Alexander, Nikol G. and Drucilla Cornell, 1997. "Dismissed or Banished? A Testament to the Reasonableness of the Simpson Jury," in T. Morrison and C. Lacour (eds.), *Birth of a Nation'hood: Gaze, Script, and Spectacle in the O. J. Simpson Case*, New York: Pantheon.

Allen, Craig M. and Murray A. Straus, 1980. "Resources, Power, and Husband–Wife Violence," in M. Straus and G. Hotaling (eds.), *The Social Causes of Husband–Wife Violence*, Minneapolis, MN: University of Minnesota Press.

Allen, Theodore W., 1994. *The Invention of the White Race*, vol. 1, *Racial Oppression and Social Control*, London: Verso.

Anderson, C. A., and M. Lepper and L. Ross, 1980. "Perseverance of Social Theories: The Role of Explanation in the Persistence of Discredited Information," *Journal of Personality and Social Psychology* 39, 1037–1049.

Altheide, David L. and Robert P. Snow, 1979. *Media Logic*, Beverly Hills: Sage.

Althusser, Louis, 1971. *Lenin and Philosophy and Other Essays*, New York: Monthly Review Press.

Bagdikian, Ben H., 1992. *The Media Monopoly*, Boston: Beacon Press.

Baker, Jim, 1978. *O. J. Simpson's Most Memorable Games*, New York: G. P. Putnam's Sons.

Baldwin, James, 1961. *Nobody Knows My Name*, New York: Laurel.

Banton, Michael, 1987. *Racial Theories*, Cambridge: Cambridge University Press.

Baudrillard, Jean, 1988. "The Masses: The Implosion of the Social in the Media," in M. Poster (ed.), *Selected Writings by Jean Baudrillard*, Palo Alto: Stanford University Press.

Bell, Derrick, 1992. *Faces at the Bottom of the Well: The Permanence of Racism*, New York: Basic Books.

Berger, Arthur Asa, 1993. *An Anatomy of Humor*, London: Transaction Publishers.

1997. *Narratives in Popular Culture, Media, and Everyday Life*, Thousand Oaks, CA: Sage.

Berger, Peter L. and Thomas Luckmann, 1966. *The Social Construction of Reality: A Treatise in the Sociology of Knowledge*, New York: Anchor.

Berges, Marshall, 1984. *The Life and Times of Los Angeles: A Newspaper, A Family and A City*, New York: Atheneum.

Berry, Mary Frances, 1994. *Black Resistance, White Law: A History of Constitutional Racism in America*, New York: Penguin.

Blumler, Jay and Elihu Katz, 1974. *The Uses of Mass Communication*, Beverly Hills: Sage.

Bobo, Lawrence, James H. Johnson, Melvin L. Oliver, James Sidanius and Camille Zubrinsky, 1992. "Public Opinion Before and After a Spring of Discontent: A Preliminary Report on the 1992 Los Angeles County Social Survey," in *UCLA Center for the Study of Urban Poverty Occasional Working Paper Series*, Los Angeles: UCLA Institute for Social Science Research.

Bolick, Clint, 1997. "Civil Rights and the Criminal Justice System," *Harvard Journal of Law and Public Policy* 20:2, 391–396.

Bosco, Joseph, 1996. *A Problem of Evidence: How the Prosecution Freed O. J. Simpson*, New York: William Morrow and Company.

Bradburn, Norman M., 1983. "Response Effects," in P. Rossi, J. Wright, and A. Anderson (eds.), *Handbook of Survey Research*, San Diego: Academic Press.

Broussard, Albert S., 1993. *Black San Francisco: The Struggle for Racial Equality in the West, 1900–1954*, Lawrence, KS: University Press of Kansas.

Brummet, Barry, 1990. "Mediating the Laws: Popular Trials and the Mass Media," in R. Hariman (ed.), *Popular Trials: Rhetoric, Mass Media, and the Law*, Tuscaloosa, AL: University of Alabama Press.

Brunsdon, Charlotte and David Morley, 1978. *Everyday Television: "Nationwide"*, London: British Film Institute.

Bugliosi, Vincent, 1996. *Outrage: The Five Reasons Why O. J. Simpson Got Away With Murder*, New York: W. W. Norton and Company.

Bulhan, Hussein Abdilahi, 1985. *Frantz Fanon and the Psychology of Oppression*, New York: Plenum.

Campbell, Christopher P., 1995. *Race, Myth and the News*, Thousand Oaks, CA: Sage.

Carey, James W., 1975. "A Cultural Approach to Communication," *Communication*, 2:1–22.

Christopher, Warren, 1991. "Report of the Independent Commission," Los Angeles: Independent Commission on the Los Angeles Police Department.

Clark, Marcia, 1997. *Without A Doubt*, New York: Viking.

Cochran, Johnnie L., 1996. *Journey to Justice*, New York: One World.

Coffey, Shelby III (ed.), 1995. *In Pursuit of Justice: The People vs. Orenthal James Simpson*, Los Angeles: Los Angeles Times.

Collier, Peter and David Horowitz, 1997. *The Race Card: White Guilt, Black Resentment, and the Assault on Truth and Justice*, Rocklin, CA: Prima Publishing.

Condit, Celeste Michelle, 1994. "The Rhetorical Limits of Polysemy," in H. Newcomb (ed.), *Television: The Critical View*, New York: Oxford University Press.

Cooley, Armanda, Carrie Bess and Marsha Rubin-Jackson, 1995. *Madam Fore-man: A Rush to Judgment?* Beverly Hills, CA: Dove Books.

Cose, Ellis (ed.), 1997. *The Darden Dilemma: 12 Black Writers on Justice, Race, and Conflicting Loyalties*, New York: HarperPerennial.

Cramer, M. Richard and Howard Schuman, 1975. "We and They: Pronouns as Measures of Political Identification and Estrangement," *Social Science Research* 4, 231–240.

Crenshaw, Kimberlé Williams, 1997. "Color-blind Dreams and Racial Night-mares: Reconfiguring Racism in the Post-Civil Rights Era," in T. Morrison and C. Lacour (eds.), *Birth of a Nation'hood: Gaze, Script, and Spectacle in the O. J. Simpson Case*, New York: Pantheon.

Crenshaw, Kimberlé, Neil Gotanda, Gary Peller and Kendall Thomas (eds.), 1995. *Critical Race Theory: The Key Writings That Formed the Movement*, New York: The New Press.

Cresswell, John W., 1994. *Research Design: Qualitative and Quantitative Approaches*, Thousand Oaks, CA: Sage.

Darden, Christopher, 1996. *In Contempt*, New York: ReganBooks.

Davis, Mike, 1990. *City of Quartz: Excavating the Future in Los Angeles*, New York: Vintage Books.

Dayan, Daniel and Elihu Katz, 1992. *Media Events: The Live Broadcasting of History*, Cambridge, MA: Harvard University Press.

Delgado, Richard and Jean Stefancic, 1997. *Critical White Studies: Looking Behind the Mirror*, Philadelphia: Temple University Press.

Dershowitz, Alan M., 1996. *Reasonable Doubts: The O. J. Simpson Case and the Criminal Justice System*, New York: Simon and Schuster.

Domanick, Joe, 1994. *To Protect and to Serve: The LAPD's Century of War in the City of Dreams*, New York: Pocket Books.

D'Souza, Dinesh, 1995. *The End of Racism: Principles for a Multiracial Society*, New York: The Free Press.

duCille, Ann, 1996. *Skin Trade*, Cambridge, MA: Harvard University Press.

Dunne, Dominick, 1997. *Another City, Not My Own: A Novel in the Form of a Memoir*, New York, Crown.

Durkheim, Emile, 1964. *The Rules of Sociological Method*, New York: Free Press. 1965. *The Elementary Forms of The Religious Life*, New York: Free Press.

Dyson, Michael Eric, 1996. *Race Rules: Navigating the Color Line*, Reading MA: Addison-Wesley.

Ehrlich, Matthew C., 1997. "The Competitive Ethos in Television Newswork," in D. Berkowitz (ed.), *Social Meanings of News: A Text-Reader*, Thousand Oaks, CA: Sage.

Elias, Tom and Dennis Schatzman, 1996. *The Simpson Trial in Black and White*, Los Angeles: General Publishing Group.

Epstein, Edward Jay, 1973. *News From Nowhere: Television and the News*, New York: Vintage Books.

Erickson, Bonnie H., 1988. "The Relational Basis of Attitudes," in Barry Wellman and S. D. Berkowitz (eds.), *Social Structures: Network Approach*, Cambridge: Cambridge University Press.

Ettema, James Stewart, 1997. "Press Rites and Race Relations: A Study of Mass-Mediated Ritual," in D. Berkowitz (ed.), *Social Meanings of News: A Text-Reader*, Thousand Oaks, CA: Sage.

Fanon, Frantz, 1967. *Black Skin, White Masks*, New York: Grove Press.

Farr, Robert M. and Serge Moscovici, 1984. *Social Representations*, Cambridge: Cambridge University Press.

Farrington, Keith M., 1980. "Stress and Family Violence," in M. Straus and G. Hotaling (eds.), *The Social Causes of Husband-Wife Violence*, Minneapolis, MN: University of Minnesota Press.

Finn, Geraldine, 1996. *Why Althusser Killed His Wife: Essays on Discourse and Violence*, Atlantic Highlands, NJ: Humanities Press.

Fishman, Mark, 1980. *Manufacturing the News*, Austin: University of Texas Press.

Fiske, John, 1987. *Television Culture*, London: Routledge.

   1989. "Moments of Television: Neither the Text Nor the Audience," in E. Seiter, H. Borchers, G. Kreutzner, E. Warth (eds.), *Remote Control: Television, Audiences, and Cultural Power*, London: Routledge.

   1989a. *Understanding Popular Culture*, Boston: Unwin Hyman.

   1994. *Media Matters: Everyday Culture and Political Change*, Minneapolis: University of Minnesota Press.

   1994a. "Ethnosemiotics: Some Personal and Theoretical Reflections," in H. Newcomb (ed.), *Television: The Critical View*, New York: Oxford University Press.

   1996. *Media Matters: Race and Gender in U.S. Politics*, Minneapolis: University of Minnesota Press.

Flynn, Kevin and Gary Gerhardt, 1989. *The Silent Brotherhood: Inside America's Racist Underground*, New York: Free Press.

Frazier, E. Franklin, 1957. *Black Bourgeoisie: The Rise of a New Middle Class in the United States*, New York: Collier.

Freed, Donald and Raymond Briggs, 1996. *Killing Time: The First Full Investigation Into the Unsolved Murders of Nicole Brown Simpson and Ronald Goldman*, New York: Macmillan.

Fuhrman, Mark, 1997. *Murder in Brentwood*, Washington, DC: Regnery Publishing.

Gabriel, Teshome H., 1988. "Thoughts on Nomadic Aesthetics and the Black Independent Cinema: Traces of a Journey," in *Blackframes: Critical Perspectives on Black Independent Cinema*, Cambridge: The MIT Press.

Gans, Herbert, 1979. *Deciding What's News*, New York: Pantheon.

Garfinkel, Harold, 1967. *Studies in Ethnomethodology*, Cambridge: Polity Press.

Gates, Henry Louis Jr., 1995. "Thirteen Ways of Looking at a Black Man," *New Yorker*, October 23, 55–65.

Geertz, Clifford, 1973. *The Interpretation of Cultures*, New York: Basic Books.

   1983. *Local Knowledge: Further Essays in Interpretive Anthropology*, New York: Basic Books.

Geis, Darlene (ed.), 1990. *Front Page: A Collection of Historical Headlines from the Los Angeles Times, 1881–1989*, New York: Harry N. Abrams.

Gerbner, George, Larry Gross, Michael Morgan and Nancy Signorielli, 1986. "Living with Television: The Dynamics of the Cultivation Process," in J. Bryant and D. Zillman (eds.), *Perspectives on Media Effects*, Hillsdale, NJ: Lawrence Erlbaum Associates.

Gibbs, Jewelle Taylor, 1996. *Race and Justice: Rodney King and O. J. Simpson in a Divided House*, San Francisco, CA: Jossey-Bass.

Gitlin, Todd, 1980. *The Whole World is Watching*, Berkeley: University of California Press.

Golding, Peter and Graham Murdock, 1991. "Culture, Communications, and Political Economy, in J. Curran and M. Gurevitch, *Mass Media and Society*, London: Edward Arnold.

Gordon, Lewis R., 1996. "Race & Racism in the Last Quarter of '95: The O. J. and Post-OJ Trial & The Million Man March – A Symposium," *The Black Scholar* 25, 37–59.

Gramsci, Antonio, 1971. "The Intellectuals," in Q. Hoare and G. Nowell Smith (eds.), *Selections From the Prison Note-books of Antonio Gramsci*, New York: International Publishers.

Gray, Herman, 1995. *Watching Race: Television and the Struggle for "Blackness,"* Minneapolis: University of Minnesota Press.

Gwaltney, John Langston, 1980. *Drylongso: A Self-Portrait of Black America*, New York: Random House.

Hacker, Andrew, 1992. *Two Nations: Black and White, Separate, Hostile, and Unequal*, New York: Ballantine Books.

Hall, Stuart, 1973. "Encoding and Decoding in the Television Discourse," Birmingham: Centre for Contemporary Cultural Studies.

1986. "Gramsci's Relevance for the Study of Race and Ethnicity," *Journal of Communication Inquiry* 10:2, 5–27.

1988. "New Ethnicities," in K. Mercer (ed.), *Black Film, British Cinema*, London: Institute of Contemporary Arts.

1990. "The Whites of Their Eyes: Racist Ideologies and the Media," in M. Alvarado and J. O. Thompson (eds.), *The Media Reader*, London: BFI Publishing.

Hall, Stuart, Chas Critcher, Tony Jefferson, John Clarke and Brian Roberts, 1978. *Policing the Crisis: Mugging, the State, and Law and Order*, New York: Holmes and Meier.

Hallin, Daniel C., 1984. "The Media, the War in Vietnam, and Political Support: A Critique of the Thesis of an Oppositional Media," *Journal of Politics* 46:1, 2–24.

Hariman, Robert (ed.), 1990. *Popular Trials: Rhetoric, Mass Media, and the Law*, Tuscaloosa, AL: University of Alabama Press.

Harris, Cheryl I., 1995. "Whiteness As Property," in K. Crenshaw, N. Gotanda, G. Peller and K. Thomas (eds.), *Critical Race Theory: The Key Writings that Formed the Movement*, New York: The New Press.

Harris, Joseph E., 1987. *Africans and Their History*, New York: Penguin.

Hazen, Don (ed.), 1992. *Inside the L. A. Riots: What Really Happened – and Why It Will Happen Again*, Institute for Alternative Journalism.

Heritage, John, 1984. *Garfinkel and Ethnomethodology*, Cambridge: Polity Press.

Herman, Edward S. and Noam Chomsky, 1988. *Manufacturing Consent: The Political Economy of the Mass Media*, New York: Pantheon Books.

Herrnstein, Richard J. and Charles Murray, 1994. *The Bell Curve: Intelligence and Class Structure in American Life*, New York: Free Press.

Hilgartner, Stephen and Charles L. Bosk, 1988. "The Rise and Fall of Social Problems: A Public Arenas Model," *American Journal of Sociology* 94:1, 53–78.

Hofstadter, Richard, 1965. *The Paranoid Style in American Politics and Other Essays*, New York: Alfred A. Knopf.

hooks, bell, 1990. *Yearning: Race, Gender and Cultural Politics*, Boston: South End Press.

Horne, Gerald, 1995. *Fire This Time: The Watts Uprising and the 1960s*, Charlottesville: University of Virginia Press.

Hunt, Darnell M., 1997. *Screening the Los Angeles "Riots:" Race, Seeing, and Resistance, Cambridge*: Cambridge University Press.

  1997a. "(Re)Affirming Race: 'Reality,' Negotiation, and the 'Trial of the Century,'" *The Sociological Quarterly* 38:3, 399–422.

Hutchinson, Earl Ofari, 1996. *Beyond O.J.: Race, Sex, and Class Lessons for America*, Los Angeles: Middle Passage Press.

Iyengar, Shanto and Donald R. Kinder, 1987. *News that Matters*, Chicago: University of Chicago Press.

Johnson, Leola and David Roediger, 1997. "'Hertz, Don't It' Becoming Colorless and Staying Black in the Crossover of O.J. Simpson," in T. Morrison and C. Lacour (eds.), *Birth of a Nation'hood: Gaze, Script, and Spectacle in the O.J. Simpson Case*, New York: Pantheon.

Jordan, Winthrop D., 1968. *White Over Black: American Attitudes Toward the Negro 1550–1812*, Chapel Hill, NC: University of North Carolina Press.

Kane, Peter E., 1992. *Murder, Courts, and the Press: Issues in Free Speech/Fair Trial*, Carbondale, IL: Southern Illinois University Press.

Kellner, Douglas, 1990. *Television and the Crisis of Democracy*, Boulder: Westview Press.

Kimmel, Michael S., 1994. "Masculinity as Homophobia: Fear, Shame, and Silence in the Construction of Gender Identity," in H. Brod and M. Kaufman (eds.), Theorizing Masculinities, Thousand Oaks, CA: Sage.

Kinder, Donald R. and Lynn M. Sanders, 1996. *Divided by Color: Racial Politics and Democratic Ideals*, Chicago: University of Chicago Press.

Kingwell, Mark, 1996. *Dreams of Millennium: Report from a Culture on the Brink*, Boston: Faber and Faber.

Klapper, Joseph, 1960. *The Effects of Mass Communication*, New York: Free Press.

Knox, Michael, 1995. *The Private Diary of an O.J. Juror: Behind the Scenes of the Trial of the Century*, Beverly Hills, CA: Dove.

Kozloff, Sarah Ruth, 1987. "Narrative Theory and Television," in R. Allen (ed.), *Channels of Discourse*, Chapel Hill, NC: University of North Carolina Press.

Krueger, Richard A., 1994. *Focus Groups: A Practical Guide for Applied Research*, Thousand Oaks, CA: Sage.

Laclau, Ernesto and Chantal Mouffe, 1985. *Hegemony and Socialist Strategy: Towards A Radical Democratic Politics*, London: Verso.

Ladner, Joyce A., 1973. *The Death of White Sociology*, New York: Random House.

Lange Tom and Philip Vannatter, 1997. *Evidence Dismissed: The Inside Story of the Police Investigation of O.J. Simpson*, New York: Pocket Books.

Laudan, Larry, 1996. *Beyond Positivism and Relativism: Theory, Method, and Evidence*, Boulder: Colorado: Westview Press.

Lee, Martin A. and Norman Solomon, 1990. *Unreliable Sources: A Guide to Detecting Bias in News Media*, New York: Carol Publishing Group.

Liebes, Tamar and Elihu Katz, 1993. *The Export of Meaning: Cross-Cultural Readings of Dallas*, Cambridge: Polity Press.

Lippman, Walter, 1922. *Public Opinion*, New York: Harcourt, Brace and Company.

Lipsitz, George, 1990. *Time Passages*, Minneapolis: University of Minnesota Press.

1997. "The Greatest Story Ever Sold: Marketing and the O. J. Simpson Trial," in T. Morrison and C. Lacour (eds.), *Birth of a Nation'hood: Gaze, Script, and Spectacle in the O. J. Simpson Case*, New York: Pantheon.

Lystad, Mary (ed.), 1986. *Violence in the Home: Interdisciplinary Perspectives*, New York: Brunner/Mazel.

Lule, Jack, 1995. "The Rape of Mike Tyson: Race, the Press and Symbolic Types," *Critical Studies in Mass Communication* 12:2, 176–95.

Lusane, Clarence, 1997. *Race in the Global Era: African Americans at the Millennium*, Boston, MA: South End Press.

Mahoney, Martha R., 1997. "The Social Construction of Whiteness," in R. Delgado and J. Stefancic (eds.), *Critical White Studies: Looking Behind the Mirror*, Philadelphia: Temple University Press.

Martin, Del, 1985. "Domestic Violence: A Sociological Perspective," in D. Sonkin, D. Martin and L. Walker (eds.), *The Male Batterer: A Treatment Approach*, New York: Springer Publishing.

Marx, Karl, 1972. "The German Ideology," in R. Tucker (ed.), *The Marx and Engels Reader*, New York: W. W. Norton.

Mauer, Marc, 1994. "A Generation Behind Bars: Black Males and the Criminal Justice System," in R. Majors and J. Gordon (eds.), *The American Black Male: His Present Status and His Future*, Chicago: Nelson-Hall.

McCombs, Maxwell and Sheldon Gilbert, 1986. "News Influence On Our Pictures of the World," in Bryant, J. and D. Zillman (eds.), *Perspectives on Media Effects*, Hillsdale, NJ: Lawrence Erlbaum Associates.

McKay, Jim and Philip Smith, 1995. "Exonerating the Hero: Frames and Narratives in Media Coverage of the O. J. Simpson Story," *Media Information Australia* 75, 57–66.

McLuhan, Marshall, 1964. *Understanding Media: The Extensions of Man*, New York: McGraw-Hill.

McManus, John, H. 1994. *Market-Driven Journalism: Let the Citizen Beware?* Thousand Oaks, CA: Sage.

McQuail, Denis, 1987. *Mass Communications Theory: An Introduction*, London: Sage.

Messner, Michael A., 1992. *Power at Play: Sports and the Problem of Masculinity*, Boston: Beacon Press.

Messner, Michael A. and Donald F. Sabo, 1994. *Sex, Violence and Power in Sports: Rethinking Masculinity*, Freedom, CA: The Crossing Press.

Miller, Jerome G., 1996. *Search and Destroy: African-American Males in the Criminal Justice System*, Cambridge: Cambridge University Press.

Mills, C. Wright, 1956. *The Power Elite*, London: Oxford University Press.

Moore, Michael, 1997. *Downsize This!* New York: HarperPerennial.

Moore, Sally F. and Barbara G. Myerhoff (eds.), 1977. *Secular Ritual*, Amsterdam: Van Gorcum.

Morley, David, 1974. "Reconceptualizing the Media Audience: Towards an Ethnography of Audiences," Birmingham: Centre for Contemporary Cultural Studies.

1980. *The "Nationwide" Audience*, London: BFI.

1992. *Television, Audiences and Cultural Studies*, London: Routledge.

1993. "Active Audience Theory: Pendulums and Pitfalls," *Journal of Communication* 43:4, 13–19.

Morrison, Toni and Claudia Brodsky Lacour (eds.), 1997. *Birth of a Nation'hood: Gaze, Script, and Spectacle in the O. J. Simpson Case*, New York: Pantheon.

Moscovici, Serge and Marisa Zavalloni, 1969. "The Group as a Polarizer of Attitudes," *Personality and Social Psychology* 12:2, 125–135.

Myers, David G. and George D. Bishop, 1971. "Enhancement of Dominant Attitudes in Group Discussion," *Journal of Personality and Social Psychology* 20:3, 386–391.

Myers, David G. and Helmut Lamm, 1975. "The Polarizing Effect of Group Discussion," *American Scientist* May-June, 297–303.

Myers, Samuel L. Jr., 1993. "Measuring and Detecting Discrimination in the Post-Civil Rights Era," in J. Stanfield II and R. Dennis (eds.), *Race and Ethnicity in Research Methods*, Newbury Park, CA: Sage.

Neuman, W. Russell, Marion R. Just and Ann N. Crigler, 1992. *Common Knowledge: News and the Construction of Political Meaning*, Chicago: University of Chicago Press.

Newhouse, David, 1985. *After the Glory: Heisman*, St. Louis, MO: The Sporting News Publishing Co.

Omi, Michael and Howard Winant, 1986. *Racial Formation in the United States From the 1960s to the 1980s*, New York: Routledge and Kegan Paul.

1994. *Racial Formation in the United States From the 1960s to the 1990s*, New York: Routledge.

O'Reilly, Kenneth, 1989. *Racial Matters: The FBI's Secret File on Black America, 1960–1972*, New York: Free Press.

Osborne Richard, 1995. "Crime and the Media: From Media Studies to Postmodernism," in D. Kidd-Hewitt and R. Osborne (eds.), *Crime and the Media: The Post-Modern Spectacle*, London: Pluto Press.

Parenti, Michael, 1986. *Inventing Reality: The Politics of the Mass Media*, New York: St. Martin's.

Prager, Jeffrey, 1982. "American Racial Ideology as Collective Representation," *Ethnic and Racial Studies* 5, 99–119.

Quine, W. V., 1992. *Pursuit of Truth*, Cambridge, MA: Harvard University Press.

Richey Mann, Coramae, 1987. "The Reality of a Racist Criminal Justice System," *Criminal Justice Research Bulletin* 3:5.

Rosen, Jeffrey, 1996. "The Bloods and the Crits: O. J. Simpson, Critical Race Theory, the Law, and the Triumph of Color in America," *The New Republic*, 27–42, December 9.

Ross, L. D. and M. R. Lepper, 1980. "The Perseverance of Beliefs: Empirical and Normative Considerations," in R. Shweder (ed.), *New Directions for*

Methodology of Behavioral Science: Fallible Judgment in Behavioral Research, San Francisco: Jossey-Bass.

Ryan, William, 1981. *Equality*, New York: Pantheon.

Sarkar, Sahotra, 1996. *The Emergence of Logical Empiricism: From 1900 to The Vienna Circle*, New York: Garland Publishers.

Schiller, Lawrence and James Willwerth, 1996. *American Tragedy: The Uncensored Story of the Simpson Defense*, New York: Random House.

Schudson, Michael, 1978. *Discovering the News: A Social History of American Newspapers*, New York: Basic Books.

1995. *The Power of News*, Cambridge, MA: Harvard University Press.

Schmalleger, Frank, 1996. *Trial of the Century: People of the State of California vs. Orenthal James Simpson*, Upper Saddle River, NJ: Prentice Hall.

Seward Barry, Ann Marie, 1997. *Visual Intelligence: Perception, Image, and Manipulation in Visual Communication*, Albany, NY: State University of New York Press.

Shapiro, Robert L., 1996. *The Search for Justice: A Defense Attorney's Brief on the O. J. Simpson Case*, New York: Warner Books.

Shermer, Michael, 1997. *Why People Believe Weird Things: Pseudoscience, Superstition, and Other Confusions of Our Time*, New York: W. H. Freeman and Company.

Shipp, E. R., 1994. "O. J. and the Black Media," *Columbia Journalism Review* 33:4, 39–41.

Simpson, O. J., 1995. *I Want to Tell You: My Response to Your Letters, Your Messages, Your Questions*, New York: Little, Brown and Company.

Singular, Stephen, 1995. *Legacy of Deception: An Investigation of Mark Fuhrman and Racism in the L.A.P.D.*, Beverly Hills, CA: Dove.

Sonkin, Daniel J., Del Martin, and Lenore E. A. Walker, 1985. *The Male Batterer: A Treatment Approach*, New York: Springer Publishing.

Spence, Gerry, 1997. *O. J.: The Last Word*, New York: St. Martin's Press.

Steinberg, Stephen, 1995. *Turning Back: The Retreat from Racial Justice in American Thought and Policy*, Boston: Beacon Press.

Stets, Jan E., 1988. *Domestic Violence and Control*, New York: Springer-Verlag.

Tice, Carol, 1992. "Helicopter Journalism," in D. Hazen (ed.), *Inside the L. A. Riots: What Really Happened – and Why It Will Happen Again*, New York: Institute for Alternative Journalism.

Toobin, Jeffrey, 1996. *The Run of His Life: The People v. O. J. Simpson*, New York: Random House.

Trilling, Diana, 1996. "Notes on the Trial of the Century," in J. Abramson (ed.), *Postmortem: Justice Confronts Race, Domestic Violence, Lawyers, Money, and the Media*, New York: Basic Books.

Tuchman, Gaye, 1978. *Making News: A Study in the Construction of Reality*, New York: Free Press.

1987. "Representation and the News Narrative: The Web of Facticity," in D. Lazere (ed.), *American Media and Mass Culture*, Berkeley, CA: University of California Press.

Turner, Patricia A., 1993. *I Heard It Through the Grapevine: Rumor in African-American Culture*, Berkeley: University of California Press.

Turner, Victor, 1969. *The Ritual Process: Structure and Anti-Structure*, Chicago: Aldine.

van Dijk, Teun A., 1993. *Elite Discourse and Racism*, Newbury Park, CA: Sage.

Vogt, W. Paul, 1993. "Durkheim's Sociology of Law," in S. Turner (ed.), *Emile Durkheim: Sociologist and Moralist*, London: Routledge.

Wallace, Carol, 1994. "The Kidnapping of the Lindberg Baby," *Conspiracy Nation* 7:78.

Walker, Lenore E. A., 1986. "Psychological Causes of Family Violence," in M. Lystad (ed.), *Violence in the Home: Interdisciplinary Perspectives*, New York: Brunner/Mazel.

Waters, Mary C., 1990. *Ethnic Options: Choosing Identities in America*, Berkeley: University of California Press.

Weber, Max, 1958. "The Social Psychology of the World Religions," in H. Gerth and C. Mills (eds.), *From Max Weber: Essays in Sociology*, New York: Oxford University Press.

White, Joseph L., 1984. *The Psychology of Blacks: An Afro-American Perspective*, Englewood Cliffs, NJ: Prentice-Hall.

Willard, Richard K., 1997. "What is Wrong with American Juries and How to Fix It," *Harvard Journal of Law and Public Policy* 20:2, 483–488.

Wilson, Clint C. II and Felix Gutierrez, 1995. *Race, Multiculturalism, and the Media: From Mass to Class Communication*, Thousand Oaks, CA: Sage.

Wilson, Theo, 1996. *Headline Justice: Inside the Courtroom – The Country's Most Controversial Trials*, New York: Thunder's Mouth Press.

Worth, Steven and Carl Jaspers, 1996. *Blood Oath: The Conspiracy to Murder Nicole Brown Simpson*, Highland City, FL: Rainbow Books.

Index